First published in the USA in 1981 by
Ticknor & Fields

First published in Great Britain by
George Weidenfeld & Nicolson Limited

LIBRARY OF CONGRESS CATALOGING IN PUBLICATION DATA

Mills, John, 1908-
    Up in the clouds, gentlemen please.

    Filmography: p.
    Includes index.
    1. Mills, John, 1908-   2. Actors—Great Britain—
Biography. I. Title.
PN2598.M545A38   1981   792'028'0924 [B]   80-22002
ISBN 0-89919-024-3

Printed in the United States of America

V   10   9   8   7   6   5   4   3   2   1

JOHN MILLS

Up in the Clouds, Gentlemen Please

NEW HAVEN AND NEW YORK

Ticknor & Fields

1981

Contents

CONTENTS

The most important to employ
Must be the Call Boy.
One of the essentials –
with excellent credentials.
BUT –
He may
Not play
Shove halfpenny
On the way
To the actors' dressing-rooms.
He must knock on the door
Of the actors' dressing-rooms
And go *on* knocking
On the door,
THAT is the law,
Until he receives the answer
That he should,
However rude.
Well now, as an example,
Here then is a little sample:
On the third floor
The Chorus door . . .
Knock Knock!
Alright cock!
All down for 'Up In The Clouds', gentlemen please!

M.H.B.

Prologue

It happened during a matinee at the Apollo Theatre where I was playing in a revival of Sir Terence Rattigan's *Separate Tables*. The first of the two plays is a difficult one, but immensely satisfying to perform. The second is, for any emotional actor, and I hope I come into that category, a cakewalk. The construction is so perfect that the principal character grabs the sympathy of the audience with very little effort and retains it to the final curtain.

The scene I always looked forward to and enjoyed, I might even say wallowed in, was the one in which the bogus major breaks down after confessing to a rather shady past, and decides he must leave the hotel. The writing was of such high quality that I nearly always managed to produce real tears at precisely the right moment, without thinking of Mr Chips, our Yorkshire terrier, being run over in Shaftesbury Avenue, or without the aid of Dr Mackenzie's smelling salts (the actor's friend) cunningly concealed in a large handkerchief with the stopper off.

On this particular afternoon to my delight and satisfaction I felt a large tear trickling slowly down my cheek and, squinting down my nose to make sure that it would splash to the stage at exactly the right moment, thereby reducing my rapt and adoring audience to audible sobs and flutterings of Kleenex, I found myself looking straight at a very large lady in the front row busily knitting an even larger white sweater. I was so astonished that the tears stopped as suddenly as if they had been turned off at the main. I dried stone cold, staring at the large lady who gave me an encouraging smile and went happily on with her knitting.

I remember a party after the theatre where one actor was complaining bitterly about an audience's behaviour and lack of manners. The Master, the late Sir Noël Coward, fixed him with a beady eye and, wagging the famous forefinger, said; 'Listen dear, the theatre is a place of entertainment and people pay to be entertained, and as long as they are paying customers and not complimentaries, they are entitled to (a) yawn, (b) go to sleep, (c) snore, (d) eat pounds of chocolates from crinkly brown wrappers, (e) describe the scene taking place in a loud voice to a deaf aunt with an ear trumpet, or (f) even knit!' I have never forgotten that piece of wisdom, and I finished the performance of *Separate Tables* while the large lady finished her white sweater without even dropping a stitch.

One of the advantages of writing this book is that I shall never know if, after a page or two, you take to your knitting, or turn on the television, or send it to someone you want to bore to death. I naturally hope you will not find it a bore – I hope you will find it fairly amusing. So, with trepidation and dread of the enormous hurdles ahead, I must have courage and ask you to turn to the next page where you will discover that . . .

I

I Make My Entrance

I made my first entrance to a small but appreciative audience during the early hours of 22 February 1908 at Watts Naval Training School for Boys in Norfolk, which makes me at the time of writing the ridiculous age of seventy, and that in itself is perhaps a good reason for attempting to write an autobiography. Having imparted that exciting piece of information, I know that I stand a very good chance of its being deleted from my manuscript by the wonderful character with whom I have had the excitement of living for the past thirty-eight years, thirty-six of which have been spent in holy matrimony. Mary Mills, or Mary Hayley Bell as she is known professionally, has always thought it idiotic of me to divulge my great age; but I, through sheer conceit, rather like to brag about it, and I am proud to announce that on the sixteenth of January of every year (the date of our marriage) I put on the sports jacket in which I courted her during 1939, take her out to a large expensive lunch, and still manage to do the middle button up at the end of it.

The first clear pictures that emerge from the montage of my early child-hood days come from Belton, a small village near Great Yarmouth in Suffolk where my father held the post of headmaster at the local school. We lived in the small school house where conditions were primitive. The water supply came from a pump in the yard which also housed the 'thunder box', as my father termed the loo, a small wooden build-ing containing a large wooden seat in which were three holes of different sizes – large, medium and small. One morning, deciding that I must establish at least to myself that I was growing up fast, I chose to perch myself over the hole reserved for my father. All went well until I reached for the sports page of the *Daily Mail*, cut into quarters and hung by a string from a nail in the wall. My reach was too short; I lost my balance and descended into the abyss. My screams brought Aunty Betty, all of four feet three inches, who took one look at my head below the surface and promptly fainted. Somewhat later, smelling strongly of

3

Wright's Coal Tar soap, I was required by my father to copy out three times:

> I must always pause
> Before I sit
> And choose a size that
> Is meant to fit
> A very small boy.

I considered this to be unjust, and also the rhyme seemed to lack bite, so I inserted an 'h' into the last word of the second line. Shortly afterwards I discovered that a ruler could be put to other uses besides measuring.

My father should, I believe, have been an actor. He was a small 'bantam-cock' of a man with piercing blue eyes and large red moustaches waxed into points at both ends. He used a pomade which was pungent to say the least of it, and I can still smell it as I write.

He was a restless individual, full of new ideas for educating the young and a fiend for physical fitness. He was, I understand, removed from one school for taking PT in the snow-covered playground. One of the parents complained that her offspring had suffered a severely frost-bitten nose from having been made to do press-ups in the snow. He moved with rapidity from post to post – I suppose one could say he was 'nomadic by necessity if not by choice'.

The school house at Belton always seemed full of an army of little cottage loaves – my mother's sisters, Aunty Rosa, Aunty Jim and Aunty Betty. They were all teachers, and during the long holidays would come and 'help Edith out'. Thinking back, I marvel how my mother, whom I adored, ever managed to get through the amount of work she was faced with every day. The teaching profession has always been disgracefully underpaid, and I remember money always being desperately short. Daily help was out of the question. Her day started at 6 a.m. with the kitchen range, which had to be raked out and lighted before the morning cup of tea could be made. It then continued with endless cooking and cleaning, finishing with the cleaning and filling of a dozen paraffin lamps. She spent the evenings knitting socks and sweaters and making most of our clothes.

I look back on the Belton period with little or no affection; I attended the village school, but however hard I tried I never managed to become one of the gang. I suppose being the headmaster's son I was always suspect and in their opinion obviously privileged. Consequently, to prove how tough and independent I was, I tried in any way I could to flout authority and prove that I was one of 'them'. A caning in front of the school would do it.

A splendid plan occurred to me. One morning during an arithmetic class that my father was taking, I put up my hand and asked to be excused. I then crept round to the front of the building, shinned up the drainpipe, crossed the slate roof, reached the bell-tower and with a gigantic effort swung the bell forward, at such close quarters the peal nearly deafened me. But the result was even better than I had anticipated – the whole school, hearing this cacophony, proceeded with their fire-drill instructions, and in a trice the playground was full of boys staring up at the diminutive Hunchback of Notre Dame. My father appeared in cap and gown and shouted in his Henry Irving voice, 'Come down, sir – as speedily but as safely as possible.' I made a rather shaky, unspectacular descent, confident, however, that I would now receive the public punishment I so earnestly desired. This, however, was not to be. My father was a strange, complex character and totally unpredictable.

He ordered the boys back into the classroom and told me to stand in front of the class. Then he said that he had for quite some while been aware that Mills, for some obscure reason known only to himself, had been doing his utmost to become the school nuisance and seemed intent on proceeding with any act or escapade that would lead to chastisement, but – and then followed an interminable pause – he was in for a disappointment. This morning's scaling of the heights showed at least that last term's Boy Scouts' climbing sessions had not been altogether in vain, so in view of this he was going to encourage Mills by ordering him to repeat the hazardous and gallant climb at seven o'clock every morning for the next week. The month was November. I have never, to my knowledge, climbed a building since.

The summer holidays I do remember with some pleasure. I used to set off with my mother, or with one of the little aunts if she was too busy, loaded with a fishing-line and tackle, a box of lug-worms, a bag of hundreds and thousands (very small sugary little sweets in various shapes and sizes), sandwiches, lemonade and a bathing costume, and walk the four and a half miles to Gorleston-on-Sea where I'd spend a blissful day fishing for dabs from the small jetty. Nine miles a day is quite a hike for a small boy of six, but the journey was shortened by an idea of my mother's; we each put one of the hundreds and thousands on our tongue and whoever could make it last the longest was the winner.

I had very few friends. I remember two – the Russell twins, sons of the publican. I thought they were very well off and sophisticated because for their holidays they had been as far as Felixstowe, and one year even Clacton-on-Sea. During one blackberrying session they asked me – I was about seven at the time – if I knew how babies were made. On admitting total ignorance they explained in great detail. I was absolutely horrified and went into a complete state of shock, appalling pictures rushing through my mind. I simply could not believe it. Finally I managed to blurt out, 'But you don't mean the King and Queen do it?'

One of the luckiest things that ever happened to me was to be born with a desperate desire to become an actor. I never remember at any age wanting to be anything else. The only time I was ecstatically happy at Belton was when my sister Annette came to stay with us. I idolized her. There was a gap of eighteen years between us. Looking back, I am sure I must have been a complete accident.

My sister's real name was Mabel. She absolutely loathed it, and when finally after years of training she became a professional dancer, 'Mabel' was sent flying, and she became Annette Mills. Annie – I never think of her as anything else – was one of the loveliest characters I have ever met, and of course at the time the mere thought of actually having a sister in the profession was quite breathtaking.

During her visits she taught me to dance. My speciality was the sailor's hornpipe; I performed this at the annual concert in the village hall, accompanied on the pianoforte by Annie and dressed in a sailor suit made by my mother. It was a replica of the real thing, including the flap front instead of fly-buttons. The routine was perfectly straightforward, so I was somewhat surprised when during the second chorus some tittering broke out which developed into gales of rustic mirth. I finished to thunderous applause, and on taking my bow discovered the cause of my enormous success – my flap had fallen, and I realized with horror that the audience had been treated to the hornpipe in the full meaning of the word. My embarrassment was acute. I have made countless thousands of appearances on the stage since then and I always find myself automatically checking my flies half-a-dozen times before each entrance.

My memories of World War I are rather vague. I remember a Zeppelin coming down in flames off Great Yarmouth; and everyone in floods of tears after a telegram arrived at the school house from the War Office stating that Annie's fiancé was seriously wounded and in hospital in France. I heard much later on that my father and mother had taken her to Paris where he died in her arms. Tragedies at the age I was then never bite very deeply. Perhaps the very young have an inner perception that they themselves will have dramas of their own to face in the future, and without knowing it preserve their emotions. I think this explains why the unhappy events are very cloudy in my mind, but anything enjoyable or amusing is crystal clear.

For instance, the first thing that leaps to my mind looking back on World War I is the Aunty Betty incident. My mother left me in her charge for a week; it may have been when she and my father took Annie to Paris. Aunty Betty was minute, the smallest of the aunts. She wore spectacles with steel frames and very thick lenses. I always felt I was being inspected through a microscope. She was very Victorian and very shy. She bathed me staring straight at the kitchen range. This forced her to use the Braille system which I, being also desperately shy, found highly embarrassing. When she was drying me she breathed hard through her nose on to my back. This became known in the family as 'Aunty Bettying' – a freezing process.

One evening she put me to bed, read me a story, kissed me goodnight, reminded me that there was a receptacle under the bed if I needed it in the night, and left me to my dreams. I woke up while it was still dark, climbed out of bed, reached for the receptacle and let go. I was in a semi-conscious state and dimly sensed that the sound wasn't perhaps quite the same as usual, but dismissed it from my mind and climbed back into bed.

The next morning was Sunday and Aunty Betty, looking very smart and neat, led me by the hand to the eleven o'clock service. It was a very warm summer's day and the little church, usually so cool, seemed to grow hotter and hotter. The vicar droned on and on; his sermon seemed to be endless. I had exhausted my supply of wine-gums and longed for it to finish. Suddenly I looked at Aunty Betty and then at her hat, which was rather like a large heliotrope vase with flowers in it. To my amazement clouds of steam were wafting gently out of it and drifting through the shaft of sunlight coming from the stained-glass window above her head. The curious sound was explained; aghast, I realized that I had peed into Aunty Betty's best Sunday hat. God was definitely on my side that day. The sermon came to a merciful end, the service finished, Aunty Betty's hat dried out, she remained blissfully ignorant, and it has never been mentioned from that day to this.

Soon after this my father informed me that I was to be sent to Balham Grammar School. This was a day school, and I was to stay with my Aunty Rosa who taught at another school in Balham. I was horrified at the thought of having to leave home and my mother, and I couldn't understand why this dreadful thing had to happen to me. Suddenly the life I knew at Belton seemed idyllic compared to the unknown and frightening prospect ahead. Things had settled down at this time and I was much happier. Annie had married a Captain McKlenaghan and produced a daughter, who arrived at the school house at the age of eighteen months and took the place by storm. I thought she was quite beautiful and became her devoted companion and slave. So why was I being sent away? My father explained that he wanted me to receive as good an education as possible; I realize now that there were other factors involved, none of which became clear to me until many years later.

London after the country seemed filthy and noisy and I missed my mother desperately, so I was quite relieved when, for some unaccountable reason, after only a few months, my father decided to send me to the St John Leeman School at Beccles in Suffolk; but when the full extent of the plan was explained to me I was appalled: I was to live with perfect strangers at their house as a paying guest. This was a possibility I had never considered. I had so many aunts that I was certain there must be one living in Beccles.

My mother collected me with my belongings and we travelled by train. We sat side by side. She held my hand very tightly and I noticed a small white handkerchief making frequent appearances from her muff.

Mrs Newton, who was to be my guardian, met us at the station. She and her husband lived in a neat little terraced house in the centre of the town. Mr Newton, we were informed, was a watchmaker. The door opened and Mr Newton appeared. He was smiling broadly and said in a very low, bass voice, 'Welcome, welcome. Tea and muffins are on the table.' I stared, transfixed – Mr Newton was a dwarf! I got through tea in a kind of haze.

Finally my mother said she must leave. That parting was one I shall never forget. I remember thinking, 'Whatever else happens, I mustn't cry.' I had just become an avid reader of *The Gem* magazine. Tom Merry was my hero, and he never cried. I watched her small figure walking away into the distance and, standing on the doorstep of that house in Beccles, such a wave of loneliness swept over me that it was almost unbearable. I tore up to my bedroom, flung myself on the bed and wept. Some time later I poured ice-cold water from the jug into the wash-basin, bathed my eyes, combed my hair, went downstairs and played dominoes with a dwarf. I had grown up.

I was happier at Beccles than I ever dreamed possible. The school was attractive with good playing-fields, and like Tom Merry I was desperately keen on games and consequently rather good at them. I was picked for the second eleven cricket team in my first term. My christening consisted of a full toss in the mouth by a demon fast-bowler from Bungay Grammar School, which broke one of my rather large front teeth. This was later crowned by a local dentist who would have made an excellent plumber – the tooth turned jet-black in about six months. I made the second eleven football team, and obtained a pass in a drawing examination. I have the certificate in front of me as I write:

THIS IS TO CERTIFY that LEWIS ERNEST WATTS MILLS
aged 11
A Pupil at St John Leeman's School
Beccles
Obtained a Pass in Division II at the Drawing Examination
HELD JUNE 1919

This, perhaps, is the moment to explain how I happen to be called John Mills. In the Belton days, during my 'show-off, get tough' period, I decided that Lewis was soppy, even cissie. Ernest didn't conjure up the right image, and Watts was frankly a joke – who wanted to be called after a college? I had to find a name that was short, tough and couldn't be held up to ridicule. I plumped for Jack, and Jack it was until many years later when, at my sister's suggestion, I changed it to John. She said that I looked much more like John which would develop into Johnnie which was preferable to Jackie, and anyway John Mills would in her opinion look much better in lights one day. I think she was right.

The great advantage of Beccles, however, as far as I was concerned, was the fact that the headmaster happened to be a keen theatre-goer and the school Amateur Dramatic Society was good enough to have its productions shown to the public in the town hall, and as many as eight performances were given in aid of local charities. The play chosen for the term was *A Midsummer Night's Dream*, and to my intense delight I landed the part of Puck. (By coincidence this was the first part I played at the Old Vic in Tyrone Guthrie's production in 1938.) During rehearsals I fell madly in love for the first time in my life with the most exquisite creature I had ever seen. She had long blonde hair, blue eyes and a small turned-up nose, and she played Titania. There was, however, one great obstacle to the romance. The Fairy Queen was nearly thirteen and I was only eleven, and what's worse, small for my age.

I hung around after rehearsals, and one afternoon plucked up enough courage to ask if I could walk home with her. To my delight she agreed, and for the next few weeks I walked beside her, while she rode her Raleigh, the Rolls Royce of bicycles. There were two steep hills on the way to her house; she would dismount and I would push the vehicle to the summit, where she would remount and free-wheel down to wait for me at the bottom. No word of my devotion had so far passed my lips, but I thought the time and place should be the dress rehearsal. I rehearsed the speech, re-wrote it several times and finally decided on a simple statement – 'Titania, I love you. Will you marry me and wait nine years for me when I'll be twenty and a famous actor?'

The day of the dress rehearsal arrived; I had a stiff sherbert in the interval to bolster me up, made my way to the prompt corner where we sometimes actually held hands, and stopped dead in my tracks. I simply could not believe my eyes, but there on 'a bank whereon the wild thyme grows' sat Titania, my love, with Oberon, who produced a Cadbury's Walnut Whip from his cod-piece and presented it to the Fairy Queen; she then, to my horror, kissed him – on the lips! I was destroyed, my life was in ruins; all my hopes for the future dashed.

And then a strange thing happened. The curtain rose on the second act, I made my entrance, bouncing off a springboard in the wings and flying on to the stage six feet above the boards, landing in the branch of a tree. I got a huge round of applause, and felt a surge of emotion I had never experienced before. From that moment I was captured: I had started an affair that will last as long as I live. Somehow or other, sooner or later, I knew I would make it. This was my home.

Days drifted happily into weeks, weeks into months ... but not for long. My father, to my amazement and horror, informed me by letter that he had enrolled me as a pupil at Norwich High School for Boys and that I was to commence studies there as a full boarder at the beginning of the winter term, the day after my twelfth birthday.

The school house during this particular holiday was fairly buzzing with little aunts; there were four of them now – Aunty Marie had returned from America, where her husband had died leaving her quite comfortably off, and my mother suggested that she should move in with the family until she found somewhere else to live.

'Lewis seems very bristly today,' exclaimed Aunty Betty. Looking back, I think I can understand my father's feelings at this time. He was literally swamped by females. Besides the four little aunts there was Bud, my niece, and very often my sister. So it was six to one.

In the winter of 1920 I was delivered by my father into the hands of J.G.O. Chapman, headmaster of Norwich High School for Boys. Mr Chapman was an impressive figure, short but powerfully built, with a full set of white whiskers, King George v style, and large, fierce eyebrows that jutted straight out over piercing blue eyes. He walked with a slight limp and always carried a large stout stick with a thick rubber knob on the end. He wagged it in front of my face. 'Do you know what I use this for, Lewis?'

Sick with misgiving and fright I managed to whisper, 'No, Sir.'

'To walk with, of course.' The two headmasters laughed. I managed a sickly smile.

After Beccles, Norwich High School for Boys was to me sheer unadulterated hell. I still don't know how I survived the first eighteen months in that establishment. To make matters worse, my father had decided that village life was not for him. Where would the headmastership of a small village school lead him? London was the place for a progressive man with new ideas. And so the caravan rolled again – this time into a cold, dark basement flat at 10 Linden Gardens, Notting Hill Gate, London w2. Worse still, I discovered that my darling mother was forced to accept a job as cook-housekeeper, as money was desperately short. My father had finally been reduced to taking a job as an assistant master at an LCC school in Brixton, taking a drop in salary.

Number 10 was a large house owned by Madame Edith Baird, who ran it as a dancing academy; and at that time my sister was one of the junior teachers. The situation was apparently more desperate than I had imagined, and Annie had managed to make this arrangement so that at least there was a roof over our heads. I only had to spend one of the school holidays there, thank God, but those few weeks I shall never forget. My mother was wonderful, always happy and cheerful, but I could see how terribly tired she was, and she missed her garden; two sad white tulips covered in soot standing on a basement window-ledge are really no substitute.

I duly returned to Norwich High School, and to my dismay discovered that I had been moved to Number 3 dormitory, which had the reputation of being the hot-bed of bullying in the school. I joined the band of small boys whose lives were made a total misery. The days could be endured, but, after the rounds had been made at night by one of the masters, the torture began.

Number 3 dorm was in charge of the most hated and feared boy in the school; he collected round him a gang of thugs whom the Gestapo would have signed up on sight. I was picked as the prime target, perhaps because I was the smallest. The gang decided I was too pretty, looked like a girl, and christened me 'Madge'. The ceremony took place one evening after lights-out. Four of them dragged me out of bed and tore my pyjamas off; then they filled a jug with cold water, and I was made to stand in the middle of the dormitory holding it above my head. Every time I lowered my arms a fraction I was beaten with hair-brushes and flicked with wet towels which, when they connected with the more vulnerable parts of one's anatomy, caused excruciating pain. After a happy half-hour of this exercise, I was locked in the clothes cupboard, still naked, of course, with an acetylene bicycle lamp which, after about ten minutes of intimidating hissing noises, exploded. The gas nearly choked me. I was dragged out vomiting and revived with ice-cold water. As soon as they decided I had recovered enough to savour the grand finale, a chair was produced, to which I was tied with my arms behind my back and then crowned with a po – half full of pee.

This sort of treatment continued with variations throughout the term. I remember, after one particularly vicious attack, seriously considering suicide. I couldn't quite decide, however, on the method. I thought of (a) jumping off the school roof, (b) hanging myself from a chain in the bog, (c) drowning myself. But I am glad to say I abandoned all three courses; I made up my mind, however, that during the next holidays I would run away. I could see no other way out.

During the last week of that term I had a letter from my mother saying how delighted and happy she was as they were moving from 10 Linden

Gardens, and, with some financial assistance from Aunty Marie, had purchased a house in Felixstowe, on the Suffolk coast. I arrived to find my mother and Aunty Marie installed in a pleasant little semi-detached house in Upper Cliff Road only a few minutes from the sea. It was sheer heaven after Number 10, but all I could think about was how I could escape before the next term began. I haunted the docks wondering if I could stow away in one of the barges or tramp steamers when the fatal moment for my departure arrived.

Then the miracle happened. My sister Annie arrived with her dancing partner, Robert Sielle. They intended spending a week's holiday with us before starting an American tour. Bobby Sielle had been a pilot in the Royal Fying Corps during the war, and flew with the famous Squadron 46. The days slipped happily by with swimming lessons from Bobby, excursions to the Roman ruins, picnics on the beach, watching Bobby and Annie rehearse new numbers for their American tour at the old upright piano – 'Diana', 'Ukelele Lady' – it was the best holiday I could ever remember. Then suddenly, with a sickening jolt, I realized that I only had four more days of freedom left.

I was lying in the long grass on the cliff tops making plans for escape. Whatever happened to me, I knew that I could not and would not go back to yet another term at Norwich. Coming face to face with the problem, however, it suddenly seemed quite hopeless. I would never make it. I would be caught, my father would be furious, and I would finally be returned in disgrace to the penitentiary where the situation would, if anything, be worse than before. At that moment of truth I burst into loud uncontrollable sobs.

'Good Lord, chaps, what on earth's going on?' It was Bobby. 'I've been looking for you all the morning. What the devil's up?'

It all came out with a rush. I had been longing to be able to confide in someone, and once I started I couldn't stop. I told him everything, all the beastly details, and finished by stating categorically that if I had to go back I should probably kill myself. There was a long pause. Bobby produced a cigarette, Abdullah of course; then, after staring at it, returned the weed to the case and snapped it shut.

'Nicotine,' he said. 'Very bad for the wind.' Another pause. 'Well,' he said finally, 'it's a stinker, isn't it, but of course, you've got to go back.'

'I, I can't, Bobby. I can't. I, I'm too scared,' I said.

'Do you know something – every time I had to climb into that bloody aircraft, I was scared too. But I knew I should hate myself if I chickened out.' I stared at him, sniffing hard. 'Listen, I've got an idea,' he said. For the next four days I was introduced to the art of ju-jitsu. Bobby taught me the throws, the holds, the breaks, and allowed himself to be hurled all over the beach. He drilled into me how important it was to use an opponent's weight to my advantage. At the end of the four-day crash course, he announced himself satisfied and said that he felt sure that I should be able to cope. My morale had received such a boost that for the first time I felt a small but steady surge of confidence and I knew that, win or lose, I had to get back into that aircraft.

They all saw me off at the station the next morning. A fluttering of white handkerchiefs and the thumbs-up sign from Bobby.

The school was going through its usual first day of term routine. The locker room was crowded with boys checking the padlocks on their tuck-boxes. Any tuck lying around was immediately 'appropriated'. It was rather like the army in that respect: things weren't stolen, they were 'appropriated'. I pushed my way through to the notice board and there it was, in the list of names, as I had feared it would be, L.E.W. Mills – Dormitory 3.

Some days at school seemed interminable, but this one rushed by, and all too soon I found myself filing into the dormitory with the rest of the occupants, unchanged from last term with the addition of Dilla Dati, a small dark Italian, who later became my greatest friend and ally. The Menace was there with his two henchmen. They ignored me. I thought, 'Perhaps it's over and I shan't have to face the moment I've been dreading all day.' Lights out. Silence – an ominous silence. I lay there in the dark and felt all my determination and new-found confidence ebbing away. I forced myself to think of everything Bobby had taught me: 'The bigger they are, the harder they fall, the bigger they are, the harder ...' The well-known hated voice pierced the silence. 'All right, Madge, let's see how pretty you look after the holidays.' The light was switched on and the Menace sat up in bed. 'Out of bed, Madge, and stand in the middle of the room.'

I obeyed this order and walked across the cold linoleum trying to control the shaking of my knees.

'Oh yes! You look lovely, Madge. Take those pyjamas off.'

I swallowed, crossed myself mentally three times and managed to say in a fairly steady, if slightly brittle voice, 'No, if you want them off, you come and take them off.'

There was an astonished pause. Heads appeared from bedclothes. My tormentor stared at me and smiled, or rather stretched his lips across his teeth. 'Madge, is something the matter with my hearing or did I hear you say "No, if you want them off, you come and take them off"?'

A piece of advice from Bobby flashed through my mind: 'If you can make him really angry and make him lose his temper, you've got a better chance.'

'That's what I said, Rake, and if ... there's ... something the matter with your hearing, why don't you wash your big ears out?'

The atmosphere was electric. Rake stared at me without changing his expression, got slowly out of bed and stood up. 'One more chance, Madge. Get them off or you'll wish you'd never been bloody born.'

This was the moment. My whole future hung in the balance. I don't think I have ever felt so frightened in my life, before or since. He looked enormous, a good twelve inches taller than I was, with long ape-like arms hanging at his sides. 'No,' was all I could manage.

He moved slowly across the dormitory towards me and stopped in front of me. 'Right, Madge. You asked for this.'

With that he reached out to grab my hair with his right hand. As he moved towards me I got a firm hold with two hands on the collar of his pyjama jacket and, using his impetus, I fell backwards, at the same time tucking both feet into the pit of his stomach. As my back hit the floor I pushed with all the strength in my legs. Rake literally took off, flew through the air and landed with a thump on his face several yards from the take-off. Before he had a chance to get up I was on him. He was in a perfect position for the Full Nelson. 'If you can get this hold on him,' Bobby had said, 'he'll never break it.'

I slipped my left arm underneath his left arm, my right arm under his right arm, locked my hands together at the back of his neck. He made a gigantic effort to break the hold and managed to get his face a few inches from the floor. All the horrors and tortures that the brute had put me through flashed through my mind. I put on some pressure and banged his face down onto the floor with all my strength. Hate is a dangerous emotion and one the world could well do without, but at that moment I was full of it; I think I must have gone berserk. I remember bashing his head on the floor again and again and again. There seemed to be a lot of shouting going on round me. Then suddenly there was quiet. The door opened and the housemaster appeared on the threshold.

The Menace didn't look his best. I was shaking like a leaf, but I could see through a reddish mist that he had a bloody nose, two eyes rapidly closing, and a large gap in his front teeth.

After a full and searching enquiry, the Menace was expelled. An entirely new system of dormitory discipline was introduced. Bullying of that vicious description was entirely wiped out of the school, which goes to show what a danger a small, violent minority can be to any community. The ju-jitsu expert received a lecture from the headmaster on control and violence; he was, he stated, quite appalled at the amount of damage I, especially for my size, had managed to inflict on my opponent.

Then I saw another side of a man who, in the next few years, I came to admire greatly. Under the mortar board and gown was a very warm individual with compassion and a sense of humour. His blue eyes twinkled: 'Well, Mills, that is the end of that chapter. I suppose one could say that the school owes you a vote of thanks.'

The result of the preceding drama was, as far as I was concerned, quite wonderful. I became popular, especially with the lower orders. I was naturally good at games, which also helped. I worked my way through from the third eleven soccer team to the first eleven in three years, always playing at outside right with a marvellous little character called Tiddler Leathers at inside right. We knew each other's game so well that we instinctively knew where either of us would be at any given moment.

Once a month the members of the school teams were taken to watch Norwich City, then in the third division, play at their ground called The Nest. Football, in those days, was totally different from the game played today. It was rougher and tougher. Players, especially the full-backs, wore layers of shin-pads that jutted out in a ledge at least an inch wide below the knee. The referee's whistle was seldom heard; shoulder-barging was allowed, and there was no such thing as obstruction. Tackling by the full-backs was deadly, and the men playing in that position were always the biggest and heaviest in the side. Unlike the very fluid and much more exciting game of today, the players stayed in their positions. It was almost unheard of for a full-back to score a goal, unless by a penalty. The three half-backs remained in the centre of the field and the five forwards stayed forward, and if the half-backs didn't feed the forwards the wingers hardly ever got a touch of the ball, and on really cold days almost froze to death.

During my last term at school another boy called Rope and I were given a trial for Norwich City. We played in a match with the reserves at The Nest. I soon realized the enormous gap that existed between the amateur and the professional; after the game I was informed very charmingly by their manager that I was too small and too light, and he suggested that I went home, ate a lot of plum-duff and came back to him in two years' time when I was eighteen. So again, fate took a hand. If I had been offered the job I would have taken it and become, at any rate for a while, a professional footballer, and it might have taken me much longer to reach my first stage door.

The school also boasted a very successful rowing club, and I became an enthusiastic Wet Bob, and coxed the senior maiden four. I also played in the first eleven at cricket. The classroom was a different matter: I was backward and slow, hated being inside and spent most of the time gazing out of the window at the playing-fields. At the end of my third term I established a school record, which I should imagine remains unbroken to this day. Out of a possible 300 marks in the algebra, trigonometry and arithmetic examination, my magnificent total was 8.

I was very definitely on the carpet. My father placed my report carefully on the desk before him, produced a packet of Wills's Gold Flake cigarettes from his Norfolk jacket, lit one, and inhaled deeply. I stared unhappily at my parent.

'Are you enjoying Norwich High School, Lewis?'

'Yes, father, very much indeed. It's the best school I've ever been to.'

'Right,' said my father, 'you shall have one more chance. If your name does not appear in the top six in your class at the end of next term, I shall feel forced to remove you from Norwich.' I broke out into a cold, clammy sweat. 'However, I will do everything in my power to help you. During these holidays you will do four hours' work per day under my supervision in the subjects you are backward in. The rest is up to you. Do I make myself clear?'

'Yes, father. Thank you very much, father.'

I couldn't bear the thought of leaving Norwich and all my friends, so I worked; I flogged my brain until it was dizzy, and crammed trigonometry, algebra and maths into my head. I never really understood any of it, but somehow photographed them in my mind, and the pictures lasted long enough to get me through the examinations, then faded forever.

During the next term I worked feverishly hard and, to my intense relief, ended up sixth in the class. I remained in that fairly select company for the rest of my time at school and I realized then that, had it not been for my father's strength and help, I should have emerged from Mr Chapman's establishment a complete ignoramus.

During my last term at Norwich, my father arranged an interview with one of the partners in a firm of corn-merchants called R. and W. Paul Ltd, whose head office was in Ipswich. He informed me that his financial position was not strong enough to enable him to pay for any further education, and that it was necessary for me to start contributing something, however small, towards the family budget.

This decision was a shattering blow. I was really happy at Norwich and had visions of a further two years of glory as captain of the school, with blues for everything, and loaded with silver cups. Then, after a hero's farewell, I should pack my bags for Cambridge – I preferred it to Oxford, who had lost the boat-race three years running – where I would soon be spotted by a talent scout, giving a breathtaking performance as Hamlet or Charlie's Aunt, the part was unimportant.

All these fantasies ran through my mind as I sat in the train which was carrying me through the flat, East Anglian countryside to apply for a job as junior clerk with, as I was informed by my father, very good prospects indeed, and a handsome pension of as much as £500 per annum at the retiring age of sixty-five.

My mother met me at the station, and we walked through the little county town of Ipswich to the offices of Messrs R. and W. Paul Ltd which were situated on the docks, where the flat, squat barges drifted slowly up the river Yare and unloaded their cargoes of barley, wheat and maize at the warehouses on the quayside. During the walk my mother never stopped talking. She was, she said, praying that I would get the job, because although she knew I rather wanted to stay at school it would be wonderful for her because I should be living at home in Felixstowe and travelling up by train every morning to the office. She was, she said, very lonely. My father only managed occasional weekends from London, and she missed a man in the house.

Immediately, my attitude changed. I couldn't wait to leave school. Cambridge would have been a bore, a waste of time. The only thing that mattered now was to get this job: for I understood at that moment how vitally important it is to be needed.

The office was large, with sixty clerks at work amidst a continuous chatter of typewriters and telephones. I was interviewed by Mr Cyril Paul, the junior partner, a charming man rather like a hearty games-master. I subsequently discovered he held a high position in the Boy Scout movement. He asked me why I was interested in joining a firm of corn-merchants, and I racked my brains for a suitable reply. I couldn't very well say 'For the money, sir.' Then an inspiration hit me: 'Well, sir, I thought it was a good idea. My grandfather was, I believe, the oldest member of the London Corn Exchange.' This was totally untrue, but it went down very well.

'I see,' said Mr Cyril. 'It seems you have made a sensible choice. I wish you luck. With perseverance and hard work you may end up in your grandfather's elevated position. You have the job, Mills. Congratulations.'

Then something happened that nearly deprived the firm of my services, which, looking back, I can see they could have well done without.

One Saturday afternoon, Dilla Dati and I, as the two senior boys, were detailed to take the lower school for a walk through the town, taking in the cathedral where we were to enrich their minds with potted histories of the kings and knights buried in the precincts. Our route took us past the new, impressive Woolworth's stores, which had opened its doors to the public the previous week.

It was Dilla's idea, but I jumped at it. The plan was quite simple. We would let the crocodile wander on ahead, nip into Woolworth's, have a quick look round, buy two ounces of liquorice allsorts, make our way out through the rear exit and pick up the crocodile which would, we thought, still be ambling aimlessly along the main thoroughfare. As we approached the store we slackened our pace, and unnoticed, as we thought, slipped through the main entrance. I was paying for the liquorice allsorts when Dilla, who was standing behind me, grabbed my arm and said: 'Crikey, look!'

I looked, and to my horror saw the junior school pouring into the store. Fifty boys between the ages of eight and twelve can wreak more damage than a cartload of monkeys or a swarm of locusts. Chaos reigned supreme. It took us a long time, with liberal cuffings, to round up the mob. Eventually Dilla led them out into the street and I made an abject apology to the manageress, who looked at me quivering with rage and said: 'You are from Norwich High School, aren't you?'

'Yes, madam,' I said. 'And I . . .' She cut me short.

'I will not waste words with hooligans. I am sure the headmaster will be very proud of the behaviour of his pupils in the city. Kindly leave the store.'

I walked slowly away through the debris and, as I opened the door, looked back over my shoulder. She was making a telephone call. Filled with foreboding I joined the crocodile, which wound its way slowly back up St Giles to the Judgement Seat.

We were given two hours to sweat it out, and sweat it out is exactly what I did. The hour of judgment finally arrived. Dilla and I found ourselves facing the headmaster. The dialogue, or rather monologue, burnt itself into my brain to such an extent that I can quote it, after all these years, almost verbatim. I had never seen the head in all the years I had known him look quite so awe-inspiring.

'I shall dispense with all the usual opening clichés, like, for instance, "Have you any explanation?" or "Have you anything to say that could possibly excuse your disgraceful behaviour?" simply because (a) there cannot be any explanation and (b) there cannot be any excuse.'

During these opening remarks he had moved slowly round us, ending up facing the two miserable objects across his desk. 'It seems that two senior boys, whom I had a certain regard for, have done their best to besmirch the good name of their school. I shall examine carefully what steps I shall take in the matter. Irresponsibility of this magnitude bodes ill for the future, especially yours, Mills. I may decide to write to your future employers informing them of this escapade, and I feel it is not beyond the bounds of possibility that they may decide that there are more worthy and trustworthy applicants than yourself to carry on the proud tradition of their family concern. You will now go to your dormitory and remain there until you report to me here in the morning, at which time I shall inform you of my decisions for both your futures.'

The next fifteen hours seemed like fifteen weeks. After lights-out, Tiddler Leathers produced two soggy doughnuts and half a tin of sardines, but on this particular occasion the two condemned men were only able to toy with the usually most popular 'dish of the day'.

At last the waiting was over. Dilla and I again found ourselves facing the headmaster in his study. I was ready for the worst; I would lose the job that I now so desperately wanted, and the thought of returning home and facing my father was too appalling to contemplate.

'Well,' said Mr Chapman, 'have you two boys spent a happy evening and enjoyed a good night's sleep?'

'No sir. No sir,' we both stuttered.

'Oh really. Was anything preying on your mind? If so, perhaps you would like to unburden yourselves.'

I found my voice, and it all came out in a rush. I made an impassioned plea for both of us, admitting the most heinous crime, pleaded guilty, and with tears in my eyes begged for the mercy of the court.

There was a long pause – then he spoke: 'Well, Mills, that was an admirable performance, and, like all good performances, it contains more than an element of truth. I think it is only fair to let you know my decision without further ado. After careful thought and consideration of your records over the last three years I have decided not to let one stupid escapade ruin your futures, and as far as punishment is concerned, I feel the last fifteen hours has amply filled the bill.'

We left the study; neither of us spoke, the relief was too intense. Crikey, I thought, what a really ripping man Old Cheese is. The bell went and we ran to the classroom.

We beat Bracknell College by six goals to two. I scored a hat trick. My contribution was made easy by Tiddler Leathers, who laid on three perfect passes. I had no one to beat but the goalkeeper.

The term came to an end. I finished up with quite a reasonable record, passing the College of Preceptors Examination with distinction in English. Looking back over my schooldays I think I only really enjoyed the last two years, and I have one deep regret.

My music teacher, a charming but very strict lady called Miss J.P. Walker, could not understand my passion for 'modern' music. It was strictly Chopin, Mozart, Beethoven and Liszt. 'Yes We Have No Bananas' and 'Ukelele Lady' were definitely out, and whenever I was caught indulging in this hideous syncopation at the old upright piano at 7 a.m. in a freezing classroom, Miss Walker awarded me with an hour's extra scales which I detested. This left me with no ambition to continue lessons after leaving school. If I had been encouraged and allowed to have my way I might now play the piano very well indeed.

There are, however, always exceptions that prove the rule – Noël Coward, for instance, only had two music lessons in his life. But then there is one slight difference between us: he was a genius – I am not!

2

The Great Escape

On a cold, raw morning in January I joined a crowd of commuters hurrying to catch the 7.57 a.m. train from Felixstowe to Ipswich. I wore a smart, but rather stiff, dark grey suit, a striped shirt and a collar made of a rubber-like substance which only needed sponging with soap and water every night to preserve its shining, pristine whiteness. I wore black boots with metal tips on the heels and toes, and to crown this picture of sartorial elegance a grey trilby hat with a very large brim. This fashionable piece of headgear did not, I'm afraid, suit me. My small, rather ordinary face was completely overshadowed, and I must have given an impression of a thin walking mushroom.

The carriage was occupied by seven men who, immediately they were seated, produced cigarettes. I watched with fascination and envy as the smoke poured out of their nostrils, and drifted over the morning newspapers. They were confident, calm, relaxed. I, on the other hand, was suffering a bad attack of first-night nerves. The atmosphere in the compartment was thick; my eyes smarted, I felt sick, and it was with relief that I realized the train had stopped at my destination, a small station called The Halt, a mile and a half from Ipswich town. I had decided to book my season ticket to The Halt because it meant a saving of five shillings per month, and as my salary was to start at 15s. 6d. per week, this economy was important to the budget.

A tall, good-looking, dark young man caught up with me. 'I'm Vic Jennings,' he said. 'Are you the new junior clerk just joining the firm?'

I told him that I was, and that I was feeling very nervous.

'Who are you under to start with?'

'Mr Whitman,' I said. 'What's he like?'

'He's all right, he's a bit brusque and sharp, if you know what I mean, but quite popular – runs the football team. You any good at it?'

'Well I'm not too bad,' I said, and couldn't resist bragging about Norwich City. I switched the story slightly in my favour by saying that I had been offered the job at The Nest, but had to turn it down because my father did not want me to be a professional footballer! Vic Jennings was visibly impressed. 'Well, unless you're a complete twit in the office, you'll be all right with Whitman,' he said.

Mr Whitman was small, quick in his movements, with a lightning brain for figures. He was in charge of the department that dealt with invoices and accounts. My first job was to go to the enormous safe and load a large trolley with about thirty huge ledgers, wheel it through the office to his department and stack the ledgers on the desks. I was then told to check yesterday's entries. The first read as follows: '20 quarters of plate maize @ 47/6 per quarter.' There were about fifty pages of them. I had laboriously started multiplying on paper when a hand descended on my shoulder. 'What are you doing, Mills? That will take you a week: it's simple. Twenty times 47s 6d is £47 10s. Just work on that principle and you'll eat that lot in an hour.'

'Thank you very much, sir,' I said. My introduction to the higher realms of mathematical wizardry had begun.

After eighteen months under Mr Whitman's eagle eye, I moved to the shipping department, run by two gentlemen call Mr Ling and Mr Morphey. Mr Ling was meticulous, tidy, concise, quiet and conservative. Mr Morphey was rather like his moustache, all over the place and nearly out of control. During the pollen season he suffered from severe hay fever which produced violent attacks of sneezing followed by torrents of liquid which poured from his nose in endless streams. He placed a large sheet of blotting paper on the floor and then by leaning over his left shoulder allowed the miniature Niagara to fall on the centre of the target. This used to go on all the summer. Mr Ling usually suffered in silence, except for disapproving sniffs which increased in volume during the waterworks display. On one occasion, however, Mr Morphey's aim was slightly off, and a small sheet of spray landed on Mr Ling's highly polished left toe-cap. 'Mills,' said Mr Ling in his quietly controlled voice, 'would you be good enough to provide Mr Morphey with a fresh sheet of blotting paper. He seems to be awash!'

Mr Ling and Mr Morphey were two respected senior clerks who had served the firm faithfully all their lives; both were due to retire in two years' time, and like all the other sixty workers in the office could barely wait for the day of release to arrive. I discovered soon after my arrival in the firm that ninety-nine per cent of the entire staff existed from Monday morning at 8.30 until Saturday at noon, and lived from that moment until 8.30 the following Monday morning. The job was merely a way of earning enough money to allow them to indulge in the things they enjoyed doing over the all-too-short weekends and the two weeks' annual summer holiday.

I've always been keenly conscious of how lucky I am (DV, touch wood, like most actors I am ridiculously superstitious – never walk under ladders, never whistle in a dressing-room, always throw salt over my left shoulder if any spills on the table, etc.) to have been working for the past fifty years in a profession that is still so enthralling and stimulating that retirement is unthinkable. Like the old soldier, I should simply fade away. Sir John Gielgud, not long ago, was questioned by a reporter on the subject of retirement. 'Sir John, you are over seventy, still playing long parts and acting them with your usual brilliance; if, God forbid, at some time in the hopefully long-distant future your memory begins to fail and you find it impossible to remember your lines, I suppose you will be forced reluctantly to retire.'

Sir John regarded the reporter with a slightly incredulous look on his face and replied, 'My dear fellow, there's always the radio!'

The shipping department, after the close confinement and claustrophobia of the inside office, was a blessed relief. My job was to deal with barge skippers, checking their bills of lading, etc.; this gave me the chance of escaping across the road to the docks at least once or twice a day. I was also in charge of Tate and Lyle's sugar, which was stored and delivered from one of our large warehouses. This domain was under the control of an incredible old character who rejoiced rightly in the name of Fiddler. He was a short, square, enormously powerful old man with a full set of white whiskers, stained with nicotine from the cut plug which was permanently wedged in his cheek. Fiddler had been with the firm for forty years, and had one claim to fame. The warehouses were infested with rats; Fiddler hated them, and his method of exterminating them was simple but horrific. He would manœuvre the rodent into a corner – the sacks were piled nine feet high and so there was no escape – grab the rat with his enormous hands, and then calmly and with relish bite its head off. When I was first told this story by my young predecessor in the shipping department I refused to believe it. Two weeks later, however, having been witness to an execution, I knew it to be true.

There were other sides to his character. He was kind, and if he took a fancy to anyone there was nothing he wouldn't do to help. At the end of every quarter, stock-taking took place. The number of bags of Tate and Lyle sugar in the warehouse had to tally with my ledger entry. An inspector came down from the firm to check the quantity in hand.

On one occasion shortly after I'd taken over, Fiddler and I did our preliminary count. To my dismay we discovered that I was well below the water-mark. The bags were stacked in a square about twenty yards long by twenty yards deep; the end row on one side was short by twenty bags. That represented about a year's salary. I visualized an interview with Mr Cyril: no possible excuse, rats could hardly have consumed one ton of sugar in three months. 'Oh Lord, Fiddler, what am I going to say?'

Fiddler shifted the cut plug from one cheek to the other and squirted a stream of nicotine with deadly accuracy into a spittoon ten feet away in the corner of his office. 'Do you know why they call me Fiddler?'

I shook my head.

'You nip back to the office, tell the inspector some funny stories, come back with him for the count in half an hour and you'll find out. If I didn't like you, I wouldn't bloody do it.'

I managed to stall the inspector, and when we returned Fiddler was waiting.

'Good morning, sir. All ready for the stock-taking? I think you'll find it correct.' He led Mohammed to the mountain. The inspector walked slowly round, counting carefully, To my amazement, every row was now complete. I glanced at Fiddler. who rubbed his nose and winked back. The inspector made a rapid calculation and looked at the invoices. '500 bags. Right, that's correct. Any damaged ones, Fiddler?'

'No, sir. Do you want to climb up and have a look?'

'No thank you, Fiddler. I can trust you.'

That pronouncement must have been the mis-statement of the year. He signed beside my entry in the ledger, and was gone.

I looked at the Ancient Mariner, who was smiling. 'Fiddler, where the hell did you get those bags? We've no other stock, and no delivery till next month.'

'Have a look up in the rigging.' He clasped his hands together, I put one foot in them, he bunched his shoulder muscles, heaved and catapulted me to the top of the pile. I crawled towards the middle to find a large, empty space which had been occupied by twenty bags of Tate and Lyle's best. I looked down at my saviour. 'Thanks, Fiddler. You saved my life.' Then a thought struck me. 'But what happens when we're short on deliveries?'

'Don't worry,' said Fiddler, 'bags often get busted in transit. Can't help accidents, can you?'

When the office closed that evening I took Fiddler to the local on the docks, and blew a large percentage of my week's salary on his favourite tipple, Navy Rum chasers: a double rum, washed down with a pint of ale. He insisted I drank drink for drink with him, and so, as I was still a novice in the alcoholic stakes, I chose Tetley's light ale, the least lethal beverage in the hostelry. Even so, after four rounds (beer was beer in those days), I arrived home at Felixstowe after missing four trains, happily plastered, for the first, but certainly not the last time in my life.

The only happening that broke the deadly monotony of the office took place in 1926 in the form of the General Strike. A notice appeared on the board stating that the police needed volunteers to act as special constables, and one of our directors had added a rider to the effect that any of the staff who felt it their duty to answer the call to arms would be granted indefinite leave from the office on full pay. Thirty of us, all the young clerks, reported to Ipswich Police Station on the following morning. We were given a short pep-talk by the sergeant in charge, who advised us to keep calm if and when violence broke out, and to retaliate only when vitally necessary. We were then issued with arm-bands and short wooden truncheons with leather thongs attached. Our job was to endeavour to keep order on the docks where the dockers were gathered in force.

We left the station in the charge of a constable, who marched us through the narrow streets to our destination. On arrival we were halted and lined up into two ranks facing a group of men, about 150 in all, with corduroy trousers, waistcoats and leather belts, any one of whom looked as if he could have eaten us for breakfast. Their instructions were to prevent the grain being unloaded from the barges into the warehouse, and as there were apparently no volunteers for this front-line action, the instructions were being carried out to the letter.

The young heroes, in arm-bands and trilby hats, stood facing the mob, who glared at us. The atmosphere was tense. Some women arrived with flasks and sandwiches which they distributed to their men. One of them, after glancing in our direction, detached herself from the group and advanced towards us like a large, black barge in full sail. She paused at the end of our front line, proceeded slowly along it and came to a stop opposite me. She was huge – built like an all-in wrestler, with a large wart on one side of her nose. After a close inspection, she looked me straight in the eye and said in a loud voice, 'It's dinner-time, love. Why don't you go home and suck your mother's tit?' This sparkling 'one-liner' brought the house down; it really hit the mark. I looked at that time very young, and standing there in those props, very silly. The tension lifted, however; absolutely nothing happened, and after two hours of acute embarrassment we were marched back to the police station.

During this period at Felixstowe I joined two amateur dramatic societies – the Felixstowe Players, and the vicar's Amateur Dramatic Society. Both these groups were extremely enthusiastic, and the standard, particularly of the Felixstowe Players, was high. They were good enough to take the Felixstowe Playhouse, a charming little Georgian theatre, and fill it for the week. Although I was fifty years too young for the part, I enjoyed playing Lobb in J.M. Barrie's *Dear Brutus*.

I was still determined that one day I would succeed in becoming a professional actor; but as the months rolled on I began to feel trapped. The insistent regularity of the daily, unchanging programme seemed to build a wall over which there was little chance of escape. There was also the question of finance: my salary had climbed, during the two years, to the magnificent sum of 27s. 6d. per week which, after putting something in the kitty to help with the housekeeping, left very little in the savings bank to subsidize 'the great escape'.

Then something happened that seemed to snap the trap shut. I think it was the Russian boots that did it, helped, of course, by the lipstick. I've always been very much in favour of make-up, and have never really gone for the 'natural' look for girls – shiny faces, no eye-shading and no lips.

Her name was Marjorie Plant. She was small, with red hair, and beautifully, fatally made up. After two weeks of train journeys from Felixstowe to Ipswich and secret rendezvous in Felixstowe gardens at night I was completely under her spell. One of my biggest problems in life has been the fact that, being an incurable romantic, I have constantly and with great rapidity fallen in love before the hat could reach the floor.

The affair, pathetically innocent as far as any physical relationship was concerned, flourished on every other plane; and before long I found that we were discussing the future. She worked at Fisons, the fertilizer factory (I didn't see the joke at the time) in Ipswich, and during one of our discussions she suggested that perhaps it would be better to set up home in Ipswich rather than Felixstowe, after we were married – it would, she said, 'give us longer in bed in the morning'. This statement left me weak with excitement, and my dreams of the theatre faded into a dim, distant future.

My mother (at the time I couldn't understand why) didn't seem at all keen on the idea of our getting married, and did everything she could to discourage it. Then out of the blue a letter arrived from my sister inviting me to London for a weekend. She was living with Bobby at that time in a flat in Half Moon Street; a return ticket was enclosed in the letter.

At that time the smartest and most elegant club in London was the famous Ciro's. Gentlemen in black ties were admitted rather grudgingly: white ties and tails were the thing. Annie and Bobby had been engaged for the season and were enjoying an enormous success.

The whole operation had been meticulously planned to have the maximum effect. After tea in the flat I was whisked off to Moss Bros and fitted out with a dinner jacket, stiff-fronted shirt, a wing collar and a black tie. Arrayed in all this finery I walked through the doors of Ciro's into a magical world. The evening had a dream-like quality, induced, no doubt, by my first glass of champagne, which I decided was definitely superior to Tetley's light ale.

Annie and Bobby went on at eleven o'clock, and their act was a riot.

They must have danced for a full hour. Exhibition dancing was the rage at that time, but they were unique because they had introduced comedy numbers, which at that time were unheard of. Finally, after several encores, they came back to the table where I was sitting in a state of euphoria, bolt upright in my chair. Any other position was quite impossible because the stiff shirt from Moss Bros reached from my Adam's apple to my crutch. During supper a tall, very good-looking man came up to the table. My sister said, 'Hallo, Jack. This is my brother. I know he'd love to meet you.' And I found myself shaking hands with one of my heroes, Jack Buchanan.

I think we arrived back at Half Moon Street some time during the early hours of the morning. Annie suggested that I should get undressed, get into bed, and then she would come and say goodnight to me. Ten minutes later she found me sitting bolt upright in a chair asleep in the stiff dress shirt.

After breakfast the next morning I was still in a state of starry-eyed daze. Annie said that she would like to have a talk with me. 'I hear that you're thinking of getting married,' she said. 'Is that true?'

'Well,' I replied, 'yes, I suppose it is. I mean, there's nothing definite, but we both thought that if we could afford it we would ... sort of ... set up home in about five years' time.'

Annie looked at me. 'I see,' she said. 'Well, that sounds very ... er, nice. But I thought that you were determined to become an actor. Do you think getting married will really help? I mean, you could go on working with the Amateur Dramatic Society, but that wasn't quite what you were after, was it? And anyway, you're not eighteen yet, and I do think perhaps it's just a little bit too early to be thinking of marriage.' I stared at her; and already I was having serious doubts.

'I've had a talk to Bobby,' said Annie, 'and we are both convinced that you really have some talent, and we feel that you should be brave and take a chance as soon as possible. We both know quite a lot of people in the musical side of the profession, and we'll do all we can to help with introductions. Anyway, think it over, but if I were you, when you get back I should explain the position to your girlfriend, and suggest that perhaps it might not be a good idea to get married to an impecunious young actor who would probably be out of work for forty weeks of the year.'

I received the message loud and clear, and I knew for certain that she was right. I returned to Felixstowe on that Sunday afternoon on a very slow train from Liverpool Street, and during the journey I rehearsed the speech that I'd have to make.

On arriving home I discovered that my father was there on one of his very infrequent visits. He informed me that he had made this trip especially to have a talk with me: 'I understand from your mother that you are considering getting married.'

'Well, I was,' I said. 'But ...'

He interrupted. 'So I think it's the right moment to have a talk to you about the physical side of any possible relationship. For instance, you see that boy and girl across the other side of the pier – well you see, that is what one could call magnetism. In other words, they are, in a way ... er ... attracted to each other, rather like the north and south poles.'

'I see,' I said.

'You see, it really is a question of nature. That's what it is, nature. I mean ... shall we say ... fertilization. Take for instance a ... bee.'

'Where to?' I said.

He didn't see the joke, and pressed on. 'Well, I mean, in an orchard. There's a male tree and a female tree, and mm ... they need bees to fertilize or pollinate,' he said. 'And of course it's the same with that boy and girl on the bench. So you see it's really quite simple. And I'm sure ... very easy to understand. So I don't really think you'll have very much of a problem. Would you like a beer?'

We went to the local pub together, and I could see that he was enormously relieved; he had done his duty as a father. I'm sure he would have been shocked and amazed if he had been at the Russell twins' lecture on sex all those years ago! I had, of course, by this time gathered most of the details, and it did cross my mind that I might stand a better chance of having a first crack at propagating and fertilizing if I could reach the magical world of the theatre rather than waiting for the golden moment in five years' time with Marjorie Plant in a small, semi-detached house in Ipswich.

Very shortly after this – while the memory of Ciro's, Annie and Bobby, Jack Buchanan and the whole glorious, glamorous evening was fresh in my mind – I screwed up my courage and poured out the whole story to Marjorie. Unfortunately, she was looking her prettiest that evening. It was winter-time and she was wearing the famous Russian boots, a long coat with fur trimmings and the inevitable twenties cloche hat, covering up most of her lovely red hair. She was very upset, but she had a marvellous character and really took it quite well. I must say that I painted a very grim picture of my future living conditions in London. I would obviously only be able to afford a bed-sitting-room on the wrong side of the river, and could not possibly ask her to share the disreputable life of an unsuccessful strolling player.

She wished me luck, and said goodbye with tears in her eyes. I am sure at that moment the thought struck both of us that we were bound to meet on the platform at Felixstowe station at 7.57 the following morning, and I decided that, somehow or other, I must avoid this continual torture. I invested some of my small savings on a very old, second-hand Morgan three-wheeler, for which I paid the princely sum of £12 10s., and travelled up by road each morning with my old chum, Vic Jennings.

We discovered that to be sure of reaching the office at 8.30 in the morning it was safer to leave home round about 6 a.m. The journey was only a matter of about twelve miles, but we usually managed to break down at least twice during the trip. Also, starting was a fiendish problem. The beast usually needed cranking for half an hour, and when it finally exploded into life it rocked from side to side like a lifeboat in a rough sea. But it served its purpose by keeping us off the train.

During this period my father had decided to leave home for good. He had been living for some time with a Mr and Mrs Buhler. Mr Buhler was a Swiss gentleman who worked as head waiter in Gennaro's restaurant in Soho, and Mrs Buhler was a large, fat, happy Swiss housewife and an incredibly good pastry-cook. The pastry was, I think, my father's undoing. I personally never really believed that his relationship with the good lady was anything more than platonic, but apparently on one of my mother's rare visits to London she discovered a photograph of Mrs Buhler on my father's bedroom mantelpiece. That, apparently, did the trick. When I heard about this from my mother I was appalled. I couldn't believe that anybody could behave like that to the most wonderful woman in the world. I sat down and wrote a letter to my father, stating, amongst other things, that if ever I set eyes on him again I would horsewhip him.

When, six months later, I decided that I had saved enough money – £25 – to give notice to Messrs R. & W. Paul Ltd, and to take off for the wicked city, I realized that I would need a roof over my head. I had had no communication with my father whatsoever after the break, but I swallowed my pride, took my courage and my pen in my hand and wrote to him, telling him my position and asking if there was a possibility of a room with bed and breakfast in Mr and Mrs Buhler's house at 75 Walcot Square, SE11. I received a letter back by return of post:

My dear Jack,
Thank you for your letter, which I received two days ago. I think, if I may say so, that you have made a most unwise decision. You had a secure job and your future was assured. You might have risen to a position of importance in the firm and retired on a handsome pension at the end of your service. You have, however, decided to take what in my opinion is an almost fatal gamble. But it is your life and not mine, and I can only stand aside and hope for the best.
I have discussed the matter with Mr and Mrs Buhler and they have kindly consented to let you a bedroom in the house. You can have a cooked breakfast with the family, free baths and an occasional free meal thrown in in the evenings, if you're hard pushed, for the sum of 7/6d per week.

Let me know when you are arriving. I look forward to seeing you again.

Your loving father,
Lewis

ᴘs In return for this, may I ask a small favour: would you be good enough to leave the horsewhip in Felixstowe?

My mother's reaction was happily predictable. I had always felt that she was very keen for me to try to become an actor. She adored the theatre and everything to do with it, although the only contact she had with it was when she was, for a time, manager of the box office at the Haymarket Theatre in London. I assured her that I would, at every possible opportunity, spend as much time at home in Felixstowe as my successful long runs would permit. I'm glad to say that I managed to keep my word. I wasn't too worried about her being lonely as I knew that during all the long school holidays the house as usual would be buzzing with the little maiden aunts.

3

Travelling Hopefully

I arrived at 75 Walcot Square to find a reception committee of my father and Mr and Mrs Buhler. The Buhlers were a charming couple and I liked them immediately. We had tea, strong Indian – my father didn't consider a cup worth drinking unless, as he said, he could stand a spoon in it – and a large Swiss layer-cake, one of Mrs Buhler's specialities. I began to see my father's point. He had a *very* sweet tooth.

Walcot Square was situated not far from Lambeth Bridge on what was then known as the 'wrong' side of the river. Number 75 was a small terraced house, and my bedroom was about twelve feet by eight feet, with just enough room to contain a bed, a dressing-table, and a wash-basin and water-jug. I found a letter from my sister waiting for me. She and Bobby had left for a tour of South Africa; she had, however, left me several letters of introduction. One was to the managing director of the Sanitas Company, whom she knew personally. She said that it was important that I got some sort of job to pay the rent while I was struggling to get a start in the theatre.

I went down to the head office of the Sanitas Company in Limehouse, and was offered the job of a travelling salesman at a salary of £3 a week plus ten per cent commission on sales. My territory was to be Streatham, Lambeth, Brixton and as far south as Guildford. Before I left the office I was turned over to the sales manager, who showed me how to demonstrate the deodorants, the soap powders and, finally, the *pièce de résistance*, the Sanitas toilet-paper, which, although more expensive than any other brand, was, he explained, better in every way – particularly as it would pass the 'moisture test'. He demonstrated this, with apparently no embarrassment, with a moist forefinger. I wondered if I would ever be able to get around to that part of the act. He impressed upon me the urgent need to open new accounts; 'Fresh fields to conquer for Sanitas,' he said. 'Make that your watchword.'

I left 75 Walcot Square one morning at nine o'clock with a list of chemists' shops to call on in Brixton. I wore a new navy-blue serge suit from Burton's, which cost me £2 17s. 6d. It looked very smart, but the material was so stiff that it wasn't easy to sit down. I sported a bowler hat, a raincoat and an umbrella, all essential props for the commercial traveller. Clutched in my right hand was the case, which after a very short time seemed to weigh a ton. I found the chemist's shop next to the Bon Marché. I was suddenly overcome with the most ghastly attack of nerves. I must have walked up and down for half an hour before I had the courage to go in. When I eventually crossed the threshold I approached the owner behind the counter and said, 'Good morning.' I produced the Sanitas visiting card, looked at it, licked my dry lips, put it back in my pocket and said, 'Could I have a toothbrush, medium hard please?' 'Certainly, sir.' I bought it and left the shop.

I thought, 'This is no good. Pull yourself together. You've just got to make a start.' I made about twenty calls before lunch, and by one o'clock I hadn't even sold a bar of soap, let alone a roll of toilet-paper.

I found myself at the Elephant and Castle, went into a pub and had half of bitter and a ham sandwich. I was in despair. I thought I was never going to make it. I just wasn't the type. I looked at the list of calls that I'd planned for the afternoon, and found a convent was amongst them. I tottered along at about three o'clock. My right arm by this time was numb. I rang the bell and asked to see the Mother Superior. She was enchanting. It was suddenly like walking into heaven, and I decided that if I had the time I would definitely become a Roman Catholic. We chatted away quite happily, and I did several demonstrations, but avoided the *pièce de résistance*. We had a cup of tea together, and then, to my delight, she gave me an order – quite a large one. I left in a state of euphoria.

I have to face it: I really was a total failure as a commercial traveller, but I managed somehow to survive for about six months. I searched the telephone directory for convents, and they were my saving grace. Every Mother Superior seemed to be nicer than the last: it was always free tea and business later. I also invested in a second-hand two-cylinder GN. These marvellous animals are now extinct; I haven't seen one for years. They were small, open two-seaters and, when they went, they went like bombs. The only drawback was, they didn't go very often.

Dilla by this time had left school and was working at his father's restaurant in Soho. His father was a lovely Italian, quite successful, and owned a super Lancia motorcar. Dilla received many SOS calls from Reigate, Redhill, Dorking and Guildford, saying that the GN had broken down and could he get out with the Lancia and tow me home. Without Dilla's help at this time my exploits on the road would have been an even greater disaster.

Annie left me another letter addressed to a Miss Zelia Raye, a great friend of hers who owned the Zelia Raye School of Dancing, which was opposite the stage door of the London Hippodrome. Zelia Raye was vital, exciting and a wonderful teacher. She had been a great friend of Annie's for years, and asked me what she could do to help. I explained that I was at the moment suffering as a commercial traveller to keep a roof over my head until I could get a job on the stage. I explained that I could dance a little but that I needed to learn tap-dancing, which was a must before one could get a job in the chorus. I suggested that if she would take me on and give me three or four lessons a week, I would repay her by giving her five per cent of my salary when I started in the theatre, for the next ten years. Zelia looked at me, and her eyes twinkled. She said, 'You know, if you're lucky, that could amount to an awful lot of money. Do you think it's wise?'

I said, 'Well, of course I do. I haven't got the cash to pay you, and if you're willing to take a gamble, I'd consider it most generous of you.'

'Right,' said Zelia, 'it's a deal. But we don't need a written contract. Annie's my greatest friend, so let's just shake hands on it.'

I then began the routine which eventually proved to be my undoing, as far as the Sanitas Company was concerned. I discovered that trying to take dancing lessons in the evening was not a success. Usually by the time I crawled into 75 Walcot Square at around 6.30 p.m. I was a physical and mental wreck – frustrated, hot, depressed, with hardly any orders to compensate for the blisters on my heels. One evening, luxuriating in a hot bath, I hit upon a scheme which, for a while at any rate, made the aforementioned routine work like a charm. I used to leave home early every morning, make my first call at around 8.30, and then work solidly until the pubs opened, or, if I was meeting with some small success, which wasn't often, until lunchtime. During the lunch-break I consulted the telephone directory and found the names of shops or schools in the district I was working in. I made out my authentic morning report sheet, which never showed any great successes. I then concocted a list of clients I was supposed to have called on in the afternoon. I was at pains to make this as interesting and as hopeful as possible, because naturally, without making the calls, there couldn't possibly have been any sales. I became quite carried away with these reports and thoroughly enjoyed writing them, and almost believed some of them had actually happened.

The next few months passed very pleasantly. I even managed to get through the mornings without too much torture. I had developed a 'sales patter' and, with the regular customers, when they were short of stocks, managed to obtain an order. But the new accounts eluded me; these were what really counted with the firm and I knew it, but I just wasn't good enough to break through into undiscovered territory.

The weekends were a joy, thanks entirely to the Dati family. They were warm, laughing, loving Italians – Mama and Papa Dati, Dilla, who was doing very well and would soon own a restaurant of his own, and two daughters, Florrie and Gina. Gina was the eldest, and ravishing.

On Sundays Papa Dati closed his restaurant in Soho and we all set off in the Lancia loaded with Valpolicella wine, salami, chicken, Italian cheeses, long crisp loaves, fresh butter and superb salads. There were unforgettable afternoons in bluebell woods in Surrey; a white tablecloth with the magnificent feast spread out on it; ice, wine-buckets and shining glasses. Papa Dati was very particular: 'Even a poor wine', he used to say, 'drunk from a highly polished glass seems to grow in character.'

After an enormous feast Papa went to sleep with a white handkerchief knotted at the four corners over his face, with Mama beside him. The rest of us wandered off and talked of all that we hoped to do in the future. That, I'm afraid, thinking back, is a mis-statement: I talked, they listened. With the almost daily dancing lessons, my desire to get into the theatre had become an obsession. I couldn't think or talk of anything else. I probably bored for Britain, but if I did they were polite enough not to show it. My best and most attentive audience was Gina. Compared to the others she always seemed rather quiet, thoughtful and subdued. After the first two Sunday excursions I was, it goes without saying, completely under her spell. She was small, with long black hair and enormous brown eyes.

One afternoon in the middle of a dissertation on how long it would be sensible for me to remain a star in musical comedy before playing Hamlet and Richard III at the Old Vic, I noticed that not only was her attention wandering but that there appeared to be something resembling a small tear in the corner of one eye. I stopped dead in my tracks. 'Gina,' I said, 'I must be an awful bore, but I can't really be boring you to *tears*, or can I? What is it? What on earth's the matter?'

'Oh, it's nothing,' she said. 'It's stupid really, but you seem to be so young and full of marvellous dreams and plans for the future that I suddenly felt lost, and full of self-pity, but I'll be all right in a moment; just leave me alone to get over it.' She walked away, stood with her back towards me and I noticed a small movement of her shoulders. I walked over to her, turned her round to face me, and saw the tears running down her cheeks. I suddenly felt very old and protective. 'Come along,' I said, 'sit down and tell me all about it. It always helps to spit it out on the wall. I found that out several years ago.'

She looked at me for a long time, and finally said: 'I really don't know quite why I want to tell you about all this. I can't talk to Mama and Papa or my sister or Dilla, but somehow it will be easier to talk to someone outside the family, especially someone like you. You're so very young and eager; you make me laugh; also you're very sweet, and I'm really terribly fond of you – too fond of you, and it's quite ridiculous.'

My heart stopped, turned a fast somersault, and luckily re-started in time for me to gulp: 'What on earth do you mean? What's eight years? Damn it, you're only twenty-seven now.'

'Darling, at your age that's a life-time.' She smiled at me. (Why is English spoken with a slight Italian accent so much more attractive and provocative?)

Then she told me her story. She'd fallen madly in love when she was twenty with, as she thought at the time, the answer to every maiden's prayer. He was older than she was, tall, handsome, successful and he had assured her that they would get married when he was in a position to set her up in the manner that she deserved – an apartment in Albany (which he already occupied), plus a villa in Portofino with a speedboat (both to be acquired). On the firm promise of holy matrimony in the not-too-distant future Gina, after battling with her conscience – she was a devout Roman Catholic – agreed to disobey the edicts of the church and gave in.

On the fateful evening Gina had arranged to meet her lover and bride-groom-to-be at his chambers in Albany at seven o'clock. She arrived very early, hoping to find her betrothed already there. The living-room was empty, so to surprise him she tiptoed to the bedroom door, and opened it. There was her lover in bed and beside him, on her pillow, was a blond head; and when the figure sat bolt upright she found herself staring at a young Adonis of about sixteen summers. Curtain!

It was, of course, for Gina, traumatic. She was in a state of shock for some time, and it not unnaturally put her right off the opposite sex.

After this confidence, we became very close friends. I was sensitive enough not to make any advances, and sensible enough, for a change, not to ask her to marry me. Whenever I was free in the evenings I would take her to a film, in the cheapest seats of course (the front three rows were a shilling), and after Movietone News and two feature films one was half-blind with the most excruciating pains in the neck. When we were a little flush we saw some plays from the gallery, and sometimes even managed the back row of the pit.

One evening after supper at Lyons Corner House in Piccadilly I took her home as usual by bus. Travelling on the top, which in those days was open, was the only way to see London. I still regret the passing of that enthralling and romantic way of transport. We arrived at the family house at the top of Streatham Hill. Gina looked at me and took my hand. 'I've had another lovely evening, darling. You've been so dear to me, I don't want you to go. Come and talk to me for a while.'

I travelled back by the 5 a.m. tram to Walcot Square the next morning in a haze. There was one thing, however, that I was quite clear about, namely, that the King and Queen were absolutely right to do it. After the hat-trick I scored at Bracknell College, I reckoned this to be the most marvellous thing that had ever happened to me in my life. Actually, before the tram eased to a grinding halt at Walcot Square, the hat-trick had dropped away to a rather poor second place.

I have been able to recall on paper that rather intimate chapter of my life because the charming, lovable Dati family regrettably are no longer with us. When I was caught in Eamonn Andrews's trap for *This Is Your Life*, Mary, who knew all about my affection for the family, tried to find Dilla Dati. She thought it would be a wonderful surprise for me to have him on the programme; I hadn't seen him or any of them for over twenty years. Alas, researchers discovered that Dilla had died only the day before she thought of asking him, and sadly he was apparently the last of the clan. I have been able, therefore, to mention a lady's name without, I hope, being accused of bad taste. I am sure if Gina ever hears of this, if anything ever drifts upwards to her seat on an Italian cloud, she will smile, sip her chilled glass of Valpolicella and be happy to know that, with her sense of humour, warmth and understanding, she made my first night an outstanding success.

Returning from the sublime to the ridiculous – while my social life had taken wings, my sales for the Sanitas Company had taken a slow but steady downward trend. The blow came in the form of a letter from the managing director requesting my presence in his office at 9 o'clock on Monday morning. I had a strong premonition that all was not going to be well.

I was shown into an imposing office, and behind an enormous desk sat the boss. He had my record-sheet in front of him. 'Mills, I notice that you have not succeeded in opening one new account, and the record of sales, even to our regular customers, has hit an all-time low for the firm. You have tomorrow, from dawn till dusk, at your disposal, and if by the end of the day you haven't gathered a new customer for our firm I regret that I shall reluctantly have to dispense with your services. We don't want to lose you, but unless you are going to come up with the goods we think you ought to go.'

That evening I spent poring over my notes and maps of the various districts that I visited. I finally plumped for Guildford, where I had had some small success – with the Mother Superior at the convent. But there was a pub there that I had never visited but had always liked the look of, and I thought I'd give that a crack.

Early next morning I loaded up the GN with a bagful of samples, my bowler hat, umbrella and raincoat. Arriving at Guildford I parked the animal outside the pub, hid my bag, bowler hat, umbrella and raincoat in the boot, and at eleven o'clock precisely entered the portals. I was in a fairly desperate frame of mind because I had not been able to accumulate enough money to survive for more than a week or two without a salary. The saloon bar was quiet and cool and smelled of that marvellous mixture of ale and Virginia tobacco and the polish on the bar, behind which stood a man who was obviously the proprietor. He was short, fat, very jolly-looking, with white side-burns which joined up to a magnificent large white moustache. He wore small gold spectacles and an old tweed waistcoat with a large fob watch and chain across his ample midriff. The whole ensemble produced a Dickensian effect. I liked the look of him immediately and felt perhaps I'd made a lucky choice.

For the next half hour I must have been the most entertaining customer he'd served for years. I told jokes, talked about cricket, racing – in fact, I talked about everything except the real purpose of my visit. I paused for breath. Mine host looked at me and said: 'By the way, sir, what do you do?'

I took a deep breath and said, 'Well, as a matter of fact, sir, I'm a commercial traveller.'

'Oh really? What do you sell?'

I took an even deeper breath before I said, 'Well, I represent the Sanitas Company, sir, and sell all their products.'

'Where's your bag then?'

'It's in the car, sir.'

'Well, why don't you go and get it, and let's have a look?'

For the next twenty minutes I did the real 'hard sell'. I started off with the things I dreaded least – the atomizers, and in no time at all the bar smelt like the casualty ward at Charing Cross Hospital. I then went on to the deodorizers for lavatories and kitchens, and finally I reached the *pièce de résistance* – the lavatory paper. I explained that it was slightly more expensive than the other brands but they were very inferior because they were not impregnated with disinfectant: also, because of their texture, they could at times prove to be disastrous. I ended up by demonstrating the moist finger test . . . I was desperate. I looked at my friend the publican, who seemed riveted. I produced my order book and pencil and said, 'Well sir, may I have the pleasure of opening a new account for you with us?'

There was a pregnant pause. He looked at me, and said, 'Young man, I don't remember having had a more enjoyable and interesting half-hour in this bar for many a long day. And you know I'd really like to help you. But you see there are thirty-six pages in the *Daily Mail*!'

I was duly sacked the following Friday.

4

First Call

By this time I had become proficient enough at tap-dancing to attend auditions in an endeavour to get a job in the chorus of a musical comedy. I soon discovered what a rough racket it was that I was trying so hard to join. I always seemed to be either, from the producer's point of view, too young or too short, or too tall, but never right.

Just when I began to feel I should never make it, another lucky coin dropped into my plate: during one of the evening classes Zelia told me that she'd heard through the grape-vine that there was to be an audition at the London Hippodrome for a new musical in about a month's time. One of Zelia's other pupils, whom I had never met, was a girl called Frances Day, and Zelia suggested that it might be a good idea if she worked out a routine that Frances and I could do together. She thought it might catch the eye of the producer who would be expecting the usual solo routine.

I met Frances the following evening. She was what in those days one called 'a knock-out'. She was small with blonde hair and so well-endowed up front that, frankly, to put it in army terms, she sported the largest pair of 'Bristols' it had ever been my pleasure to set eyes upon. (For the uninitiated, Bristols is an abbreviation of Bristol *City* in cockney rhyming slang.)

She was devastatingly attractive, and I discovered later on, when I was in a show with her, that the men in the audience simply couldn't take their eyes off her. She also had terrific character; for instance, when Zelia suggested that Frances and I should work on a routine for this audition for places in the chorus, Frances immediately said that she had no intention of taking a job in the chorus: she intended to audition for the part of the leading lady. She further indicated that in no way would she give an audition on the stage of an empty theatre, and to our amazement, she said that she intended to ring up R.H. Gillespie, who at that time owned the London Hippodrome, and say that she wished to give the audition with her new dancing partner at any variety theatre under Mr Gillespie's control in front of an audience with a full orchestra.

I could see that Zelia, who was used to being startled by members of the profession, was quite flabbergasted by this audacity. You can imagine, therefore, with what astonishment we heard that Frances had succeeded. She informed us that she had arranged with Mr Gillespie that we should appear in the bill at the New Cross Empire and do our act there in a week's time.

'Frances. How the hell did you fix it? I mean, being able to talk to Mr Gillespie is like talking to God.'

She gave me one of her quizzical looks, which were a blend of cunning, subtlety and childlike innocence: 'What's wrong with that? I often talk to Him too, and He has to be much more important than Mr Gillespie.'

I soon realized that I had been lucky enough to join forces with one of the greatest 'fixers' of all time. Anything she really wanted and set her sights on somehow or other just seemed to happen. Not only had Frances arranged the New Cross Empire, but she had also managed to obtain a copy of the main duet from the show before anyone, except the management and the producer, had seen it. 'Thinking Of You' was a charming number written for the leading man and woman. And, as Frances explained, the vital point was that she was fairly certain the parts had not yet been cast. And she added that she had informed the great R.H. (as he was affectionately known in the profession) that although at the moment neither of us was exactly well-known, we were, in her opinion, perfect casting. It seemed, she said, that the author must have had us in mind when he wrote the characters.

We worked like slaves on the routine and finally Zelia and Joan Davis, her assistant, declared themselves satisfied. Frances decided that it was essential for the act to have class, which, in my case, meant top hat, white tie and tails. On Zelia's suggestion I took myself off to Berman's, the famous theatrical costumiers in Green Street. Berman's was a wonderful establishment. It was rather more like a theatrical club than a shop. The walls, like Sardi's in New York, were covered with signed photographs of all the actors and actresses, great and small, that had at one time or another been fitted out by Monty Senior the owner, affectionately known as Pop, who knew just about everyone in the theatre.

The day I walked into Pop's establishment I met Monty Junior, the young son and heir, and we have remained firm friends for fifty years. The firm, now under his control, has grown into an enormous concern and is, I am sure, one of the largest of its kind in the world. But thanks to the character of its owner it has retained its personal touch, and most of the staff have been there as long as I can remember.

I explained to Pop what I wanted and why I wanted it. He thought for a moment, and then said: 'Where are you doing the audition, son?'

'At the New Cross Empire,' I said.

'Really?' said the man who held my fate and my tails in his hands. 'That's quite a date. You ever been on before?'

'No,' I said. 'Not professionally, anyhow.'

'Oh well, you've got to start somewhere, and you may as well jump into the deep end, I suppose.'

I was then fitted out with the props that were intended to give the act class. In the full-length mirror in the fitting-room I saw reflected what I hoped looked like my hero – a young Fred Astaire. Dear God, I thought, if only you would wave your magic wand over me, so that when I go into the routine on the stage of the New Cross Empire R.H. Gillespie will grab his producer's arm and say, 'I'm dreaming, I must be, But that young man is the dead image of Fred Astaire. I mean, look at the movement, the poetry of it. He dances with everything – his hands, arms, look at that graceful, slow turn of the left hand. You see that? It's making you look at his feet.' I came to earth with a bump when I was informed of the price for hiring the outfit for the evening. Pop noticed me blanch slightly.

'OK,' he said. 'Let's cut it in half. But don't forget I'll expect your business in the future.'

'Thank you very much, Mr Berman,' I said. 'I'm very grateful, and I certainly will not forget, I promise you.' I kept that promise, and there is hardly a play or film that I can think of in which I have not been dressed exclusively by Berman's.

The evening of destiny finally arrived. I found myself sitting beside Frances Day in a taxi-cab, facing her enormous bull-dog. Fred, as he was called, was a lugubrious character, who suffered permanently from chronic asthma and hay fever. I suddenly thought of Mr Morphey in the office at Ipswich. We could have used some of his blotting paper; Fred dribbled over everything, including on this occasion my new shoes.

We had taken a taxi from Newport Street, because as usual I lost the argument. I thought, naturally, that we should make the journey by tube; the underground station was within a stone's throw of the New Cross Empire. But Frances was adamant: 'If we can't arrive at the stage door in a chauffeur-driven limousine we at least must arrive in a taxi. Do remember we are not after a job in the chorus.'

The stage door keeper looked us up and down. He was so old I felt he must have been welded into the theatre when it was built. 'Yes, what can I do for you?' he said.

I felt, being the male member of the act, that it was up to me to take over. 'Mills and Day,' I said. 'We have been invited by Mr Gillespie to appear tonight for one special performance.'

'Wrong,' said Frances. 'Day and Mills. Frances Day and John Mills, to be precise. The female star, as you probably know, always comes first.' The stage door keeper's mouth opened and shut without utterance. I am sure he had never encountered anything quite like my partner in the whole of his stage door keeping days.

Dressing-room Number 7 was small and smelly. It was situated next door to the gentlemen's lavatory, which on inspection I discovered could have benefited from several hundredweights of my old firm's deodorants. The process of make-up and changing from street clothes into stage clothes presented quite a problem. Some innate sense of self-preservation had early on, after my first meeting with Frances, dictated that my relationship with this fantastic character would only prove successful if it was kept on a totally platonic level. (But I'm not conceited enough to think I could have got to first base with Frances, even if I'd decided to try.) In retrospect I'm sure that it was a wise decision, but I must admit that I had some fairly desperate moments during rehearsals with those prize-winning Bristols bouncing up and down on my left forearm during the 'pas de quatre'.

Frances, as usual, had everything totally under control. She produced a long, glamorous dressing-gown from her suitcase and slipped out of her clothes underneath it. I, on the other hand, was forced to strip down to my pants, which really didn't do anything for me. They were off-white and rather long, like a pair of football shorts, which in those days reached to the knee. I sported a singlet. (At that time Clark Gable had not yet made *It Happened One Night*. The King, as he was known at the time, appeared in one scene with Claudette Colbert naked from the shorts up. This breakthrough in men's fashions must have cut the sales of men's underclothes by half. Such was Gable's popularity and influence that any man who had any pride at all in his masculinity threw his old-fashioned singlet into the clothes-basket and never wore it again.)

I sat down beside Frances at the make-up bench with a towel on my lap: the football shorts were rather insecure at the front. I then produced two sticks of Leichner greasepaint Numbers 5 and 9, a black liner, a powder-puff and a box of powder from a brown paper bag, and proceeded to make up. After ten minutes of concentrated effort, gazing at me from the dressing-table mirror was a flat pink blancmange that had grown large black eyebrows that would have been the envy of Groucho Marx. The blancmange had no eyes or lips. As I picked up the black liner to try to rectify this, there was a loud knock on the dressing-room door, and a voice shouted: 'Half an hour, please.' That was the first call I ever heard in the theatre. Up to that moment I had been too concerned with my props, make-up, etc., to have time to feel nervous. But that call did it. Real panic set in, and for the next half-hour I lived through a nightmare that no one outside the theatre can ever quite appreciate or understand.

First-night nerves do not diminish; in my opinion, if anything they increase with experience. At the beginning of one's career there is nothing to lose and everything to gain, but if, after a time, success begins to rear its desirable but dangerous head, and one finds oneself in a position of some importance and responsibility, the situation is reversed. There is not a great deal to gain, and everything to lose. Several years ago, first nights became such mental torture for me that I actually turned down two plays I certainly should have done. And it wasn't until I had analysed the problem that I was able to come to terms with it. I asked myself a series of questions: a) Was I afraid of getting the bird? Answer, no. I had experienced it twice already. b) Was I afraid of being pelted with eggs and tomatoes? Answer, no. That had also happened to me on one boat-race night at the Adelphi Theatre. c) Was I afraid of having a heart attack on the stage? Answer, no. Because I shouldn't have known much about it, and also it would have made all the front pages. d) Was I afraid of drying up? Answer, yes. That, to me, was the real terror: to be stranded in the middle of the stage, so far gone that I would be unable to take in the line hissed from the prompt corner.

Having sorted that one out, I managed to get back on the boards again. I convinced myself that, should I dry up and not be able to hear the prompter, it would be perfectly possible to walk calmly off the stage into the prompt corner, find the line in the script, stroll back on and continue the performance.

Several years later, I was playing in a comedy called *Figure of Fun* at the Aldwych Theatre. The play had been running for about four months, a dangerous period, as I discovered. During the first act I had a long speech of about two pages to deliver, while the rest of the cast consumed lunch on the stage. At one performance of this scene I dried stone cold. I didn't even know what theatre I was in, let alone what line came next. I looked towards the prompt corner to find to my horror that there was no one there. The ASM who was supposed to be on the book had obviously nipped out for a quick one. I looked hopefully, with raised eyebrows, at Brenda Bruce, Joyce Heron and Arthur Macrae, but their contribution was to stare back at me, with their mouths full of banana (the substitute for chicken on the stage). They obviously hadn't a clue either as to what came next, lulled into a false sense of security by my droning on with the same old speech which they had listened to for 150 odd performances. I rose to my feet, sauntered off into the wings, found the page in the script and the elusive line, walked back on and continued the scene where I left off. I had some friends in front that afternoon, and neither of them was conscious that anything unusual had occurred.

Back in Number 7 dressing-room, after a fiendish struggle with trembling fingers I managed to encase myself in the stiff white shirt and wing-collar. The white tie, no matter what I did to it, refused to look anything like a bow.

'Let me have it,' said Frances, who had been ready for fifteen minutes. Standing behind me, she took the tie in steady hands and in a matter of seconds it became a bow. 'Get your tail-coat on, and let's get down there. If we hear the audience and get a feel of the stage before we go on it'll help.'

'I'm ready,' I said.

'Good,' said Frances. 'You look terrific in that outfit. It suits you.' She picked up the bull-dog's lead. 'Come along, Fred, let's wow them.'

'What do you mean? Where are you taking him?'

'I'm taking him to the prompt corner,' said my remarkable partner. 'And while we're singing the first chorus he's going to walk on and sit at our feet.'

'But, good God, Frances ...' She cut me short. I gave way. When Frances made up her mind, that was that. We made our way down a dingy staircase and found ourselves facing a heavy red door with TO THE STAGE painted on it in large white letters. I pushed it open and followed Frances through. That is one moment in my life that has stayed as sharply in focus as any other I can remember. My mouth had suddenly gone dry and my knees felt wobbly. I knew I looked like a pink blancmange, and if I didn't grab hold of myself I was going to shake like one. This wasn't the vicar's Amateur Dramatic Society or the Felixstowe Players. This was for real.

The act was arranged so that, on a music cue, I should make my entrance from the prompt corner and Frances would appear from the other side. We would then meet centre stage and sing a verse and chorus of 'Why Is It I Spend The Day Thinking Of You?' holding hands and gazing rapturously into each other's eyes. At the end of the vocal we would then slide into the dance.

I made my way back-stage to the prompt corner. The stage manager said, 'OK, you're next. You follow the Nesbitt brothers. They're on now. You're not billed, you know, but don't worry about that, they're used to anything here!' Max and Harry Nesbitt were a well-known act on the halls at that time. They played ukeleles and told jokes. Something that night upset their audience. I will never know what it was, but I do know that in the middle of their performance one stentorian voice suddenly shouted: 'Get off! Get off!' This triggered a barrage of cat-calls, whistles and jeers. The Nesbitt brothers broke into a new number on their ukeleles, but the sound was completely blotted out by the uproar out front.

I stared, transfixed, from the wings. This was my first experience of hearing anyone get the bird in the theatre, and it was nerve-racking. I thought, 'If they're doing that to a well-known act like the Nesbitts, what the hell will they do to us?' After struggling against overwhelming odds, the Nesbitt brothers gave in. They shook hands with each other, bowed politely to the mob and made a dignified exit. As they passed me in the prompt corner, Max Nesbitt glanced at me, and out of the corner of his mouth said: 'They want blood tonight.'

Before I had time to faint dead away, the stage manager pressed a button on the switchboard and seconds later I heard the orchestra strike up our introduction music, playing it forte to drown the cacophony of noise that was still coming from the front of house. I looked across at Frances standing in the opposite corner, crossed myself (I have performed this ceremony before every entrance since), took a deep breath and walked on to join Frances stage centre. There was a sudden deadly hush. They obviously couldn't believe their eyes. What they saw was a beautiful young blonde holding the hand of a very young man in white tie and tails, sweating profusely, who, with the make-up he had so generously applied, looked just about old enough to be taken for a walk in his pram. We sang the verse and started on the first chorus to a riveted audience who obviously had been stunned into silence. The programmes had not been slipped, so they had no idea of who or what we were, or what the hell we were doing on the stage of the New Cross Empire.

Frances glanced over to her corner, and bang on cue Fred made his entrance, waddled over and sat heavily at her feet. I, as ordered, took no notice. Neither did the audience. And we continued the number. After the next few bars to my horror someone in the audience laughed. This triggered them all off and the whole house fell about in their seats. I thought, 'Oh God, we're getting the bird now. What are they laughing at? The lyrics aren't supposed to be funny. My flies are done up, and Frances's Bristols haven't slipped out of her dress.' Then something made me glance downwards, and there was Fred glaring malevolently at the conductor and peeing on the footlights. When Fred peed, he really peed. He could have competed successfully with any fireman's hosepipe. Frances, with no change of expression, kicked Fred smartly up the arse. The brute looked up, cut off the stream and strode majestically towards his corner. He stopped just short of it, stared at the audience, lifted his hind leg, gave the curtain a final squirt, and made his exit to roars of applause.

We started the dance routine. The laughter by this time was so deafening that not a tap was heard. As far as the audience was concerned, it looked like a soft-shoe shuffle. We finished the routine, bowed and left the stage. The laughter and applause still continued. The stage manager was smiling hugely: 'Go on and take a call. They want to see you again. You've had a success.' He shoved us back on to the stage. But as we stood hand in hand bowing and smiling, I knew exactly who had made the success. It wasn't Frances Day and John Mills – it was Fred.

Frances and I were, after our sensational debut, offered jobs in the chorus in *The Five O'Clock Girl* at the London Hippodrome. Frances, as I thought she would, gracefully turned it down. I, on the other hand, accepted with excitement and alacrity. I could hardly believe my luck. I'd made it. I was in the theatre, an actor, a member of the profession. I shall always recall with gratitude that it was Frances's determination and talent and Fred's perfect sense of comedy timing that helped open the door to the magic world that I had for so many years longed to be part of.

5

In the Steps of Astaire

I had tried to imagine for years what life in the theatre would be like, and never in my wildest dreams was it as exciting and wonderful as it turned out to be. It seemed to have everything I wanted, and nothing that I disliked. I was not shut up like a caged animal in an office for fifty weeks out of the year, and I was not trudging the streets trying to flog toilet paper that nobody seemed the slightest bit interested in.

Zelia, of course, was thrilled and so was my mother. My father, however, was still very sceptical, although I could see that he was surprised that I managed to land a job so quickly. After a discussion with Zelia it was decided that I should try and persuade an agent called Vincent Earne to handle my contract for the London Hippodrome. Zelia said that although I had landed this job on my own it was vitally important for a young actor to be in the hands of an agent.

My salary was the princely sum of £4 per week, out of which I paid ten per cent to Mr Earne, and five per cent to Zelia, as I had promised. This left me with £3 8s. a week and, believe it or not, I found this sum quite possible to survive on. There were ways, I discovered, of supplementing the food supply: Lyons Corner House in Piccadilly was a very satisfactory place. I used to watch carefully until somebody left a table with a roll of bread on it and make a dash for it and instal myself. This extra hunk of starch was a very helpful addition to the meal. I regret to say that on occasions when I was really up against it, if I discovered a few pence left under a plate as a tip, they found their way into my trouser-pocket. In those days one could get a really good blow-out for under a shilling. My usual choice was fish-cakes and fried potatoes, which I'd discovered was the most filling meal of the lot.

I loved every minute of the rehearsals. For the first three weeks we worked in filthy old rehearsal rooms in Poland Street, and then in the last week moved into the theatre. The London Hippodrome in those days was a beautiful theatre, and although it has not been pulled down, as so many have, or turned into a bingo hall, alterations have destroyed some of its charm. The principals in *The Five O'Clock Girl* were George Grossmith, a brilliant comedy actor, Jean Collin, the leading lady, Gina Malo and Hermione Baddeley. There were thirty-two of us in the chorus, sixteen boys and sixteen girls.

In the office or as a commercial traveller I had had no push or drive whatsoever. This, however, was definitely not the case in the theatre. I felt happy and confident and willing to take on anything. The producer was a charming American called Carl Judd, and I persuaded him half-way through rehearsals to let me do an audition for the understudy to the leading man, Ernest Truex. Mr Truex was a very fine American actor who had been brought over from New York for the production. It was his first experience in musical comedy, and I could see that he was having a problem with some of the numbers, particularly 'Thinking Of You', which one had to start by hitting top C. Mr Judd thought I was rather young for the part, but I explained that I was a master of make-up and that, having already enjoyed a remarkable success at the New Cross Empire with 'Thinking Of You' I did feel that, if Mr Truex was ever unfortunately indisposed, I would be able to more than fill the bill. I gave the audition, and was given the understudy. My salary wasn't in-creased, but I couldn't have cared less: it was an enormous step in the right direction.

I shared a dressing-room at the top of the theatre with the rest of the male chorus. There was no tannoy system in those days, and every theatre had a call-boy. On the first night, he called 'the half', 'the quarter', 'five minutes' and, finally, 'Overture and beginners please', whereupon we all clattered down the stairs on to the stage. First nights for members of the chorus involve none of the miseries and panics described in the previous chapter, because there is everything to gain and nothing to lose. If the show flopped the stars and the producer inevitably got the blame, and so my first night in a West End musical comedy was one of pure excitement, thrills and pleasure. When, before the opening of the second act, the call-boy knocked on the dressing-room door and called, 'All down for "Up In The Clouds", gentlemen please' ('Up In The Clouds' was the title of one of the hit tunes in the show) nothing could have more accurately described my feelings at that moment.

The audience was warm and seemed anxious to enjoy the show from the moment the curtain went up; and when it finally fell, after countless curtain calls, we knew that if the notices were not disastrous, we had a hit. This meant that I would be able to eat and pay the rent for a long time ahead. By the time the show opened I had a balance of exactly 2s. 6d. in my Post Office savings account.

The theatre in the 1920s was in many ways vastly different from the theatre of today. The plays that were being written called, with few exceptions, for actors who could speak what was then known as the 'King's English' without even a mild regional accent. I personally worked very hard to lose a slight Suffolk accent. Another young actor of my age strove to iron out a quite pronounced northern accent. Luckily he didn't quite succeed, and the remaining trace helped to produce one of the most beautiful voices of any actor of his generation. Later on I had the enormous pleasure of acting with him in a play and a film. He was a joy to listen to. His name was Robert Donat.

During this period I had another stroke of luck. Annie was back from her South African tour with Bobby and came to see *The Five O'Clock Girl* one Friday night. During supper at the Criterion I suggested that, now the show was launched and we seemed to be in for a run, it would be an opportunity for me to put together a cabaret act – a double act with a male pianist who could also sing – which would include close harmony, mixed up with a few gags and a tap routine or two. Not only would it be great experience, but it would help the bank balance; my wardrobe at the time consisted of two suits which were looking decidedly the worse for wear.

Annie thought for a moment, and then said, 'I know exactly who we've got to get hold of. He would be perfect for the job. He's young, about your age, he's just come down from Cambridge and is dying to get into the theatre in one way or another. He also composes. I've heard some of his numbers and I have a feeling that one day he will write something really good.' That forecast of my sister's came true. The young man's name was George Posford, and not many years later he wrote a successful musical called *Balaleika*, which enjoyed a long run in the West End.

I met the young maestro the following day. George Posford was tall, with sandy hair and marvellous teeth, which I was very conscious of as their owner had a wild sense of humour and laughed a great deal. But the enormous advantage about George from my point of view was the fact that he possessed exactly the sort of accent I needed, and I was sure that after a few months in his company I should be confident enough for parts that were plentiful in those days – for instance, the son of a noble earl, a sub-lieutenant in the Royal Navy, or an old Etonian.

George and I liked each other immediately and we set to at once to put together an act. We listened to all the 'greats' of the time. Bing Crosby had just made what I believe was one of his first records. He sang the solo with the famous Mills Brothers in 'When the sun goes down and the tide goes out, darkies gather round and they all begin to shout, Hey hey Uncle Dud, it's a treat to beat your feet on the Mississippi mud', etc. He also sang 'Dinah', like nobody has ever sung it before or since. Then Al Jolson swept the town with 'Sonny Boy'. We built our act round these hits, interspersed with comedy numbers like 'Back in Nagasaki, where the fellahs chew tobacci and the women wicky-wacky-woo', whatever that meant. I kept the tap-dancing down to a minimum. I hadn't, I considered, quite reached Fred Astaire's standard.

George had worked out some marvellous close harmonies. He was a brilliant pianist and hoped his expertise on the pianoforte would compensate for his voice, which he had decided sounded like a constipated bullfrog (actually, and I'm sure, with his sense of humour, he won't mind me saying this, he was right!). We decided to call the act 'Posford and Mills – Rhythmic Duettists'. George got first billing. We tossed up for it, and I lost.

It was through George that the act was finally launched. He had discovered that a cinema was opening in New Malden and, after entertaining the manager at the local, had persuaded him that if he engaged a sophisticated West End act like Posford and Mills to appear on the stage on the first night before the feature film, his cinema would get away to a flying start. Also, and this was very important, the event would almost certainly be recorded in the national press, because he, George, knew for a fact that there was great interest in our debut. My partner had such authority and 'class' that the manager swallowed this story hook, line and sinker. The truth was, however, that nobody was remotely interested in Posford and Mills at that time except Posford and Mills.

The cinema was a small, unpretentious brick building in the centre of the town. There was nowhere for us to change but the tiny projection room, which was occupied by a rather bored young 'projie' leaning against an enormous projector, surrounded by cans of film. The next twenty minutes were pure Marx Brothers slapstick. While we were struggling into our white ties and tails, George, bending over to do his patent leather shoes up, bumped into the projie, who at that moment was lacing up the first reels of the film. He lost control, the motor spun into reverse and in a few seconds the three of us were deeply entangled in *The Garden of Allah*. By some miracle, by the time we heard the manager call us, we were ready.

George and I marched down the aisle, through the audience, to the strains of 'Pale Hands I Loved Beside The Shalimar' – not exactly the swinging fanfare the Rhythmic Duettists needed for a build-up. There was a small amount of polite applause as we mounted the steps to the stage, which presented an immediate problem as it was only about five feet deep, leaving just enough room for an upright piano; we had carefully worked out our routines with a grand piano, with me occasionally leaning nonchalantly against it.

The act went surprisingly well considering all the problems. I even got through the tap routine without breaking my neck. It was rather like trying to dance on a plank. We had decided to end on a big emotional note, with 'Sonny Boy'. As I sank down on one knee with arms outstretched for the lines 'You're sent from Heaven, and I know your worth, You've made a Heaven for me, right here on earth', with a sound like emery paper being torn in half my trousers split from stem to stern; and as I had 'borrowed' the outfit – it was my costume from *The Five O'Clock Girl*, and it was a strict rule that no stage clothes should leave the theatre – in a split (sorry!) second I realized that my arse was hanging out of my trousers metaphorically as well as physically. George at that moment was fortunately bashing away on the old upright, which prevented the sound of the catastrophe from reaching the stalls.

We finished to enthusiastic applause, which I acknowledged with rather tentative bows, with one hand behind my back trying to prevent my shirt escaping through the gap. We made a fast exit doing the quick-step up the aisle, glued together like Siamese twins, collected our fee (£8) and returned in triumph to Lyons Corner House where we blew £1 on a celebration supper of pints of lager, eggs, sausages, bacon and chips.

We only had one more engagement after this, at a rather sleezy little night-club in Regent Street called Nunky's. We decided to open with a comedy number called 'Ready For The River'. The high-spot, which we hoped would bring the house down and grab our audience early on, was a piece of original 'business' – on the line 'I'm going to drown my troubles and leave just a bubble to indicate what used to be me', the idea was to produce a miniature striped bathing costume, blow my nose on it and return it to my pocket. I performed the gag as rehearsed and brought the house down, but not quite in the way I had anticipated. There was a sudden, high-pitched scream from a corner followed by a dull thud, a crash of glass, then a bottle went whizzing past my nose. This was the signal for a free-for-all. All hell broke loose and in seconds Nunky's was a battleground. George and I, ignoring the old theatrical adage that the curtain must stay up, decided under the circumstances that discretion was definitely the better part of valour, left the stage and made a smart exit through the kitchens. We reckoned there was little chance of being paid, so we helped ourselves to a veal and ham pie and a bottle of wine on the way out. It turned out to be a wise decision. When we went to collect our fee the next morning, Nunky's was firmly closed.

That evening was the swan-song for Posford and Mills, although at the time we didn't know it. Soon after that memorable performance, *The Five O'Clock Girl* closed after a very happy run. Unfortunately it hadn't run long enough to allow me to build up an emergency balance. In fact there was very little left in the kitty. I desperately needed to get into another show, and during the weeks that followed I discovered that the theatre, as well as being a haven of fun and enjoyment, was also the jungle in which only the fittest survived. An actor out of work is like a fish out of water, especially in the early unsuccessful days when he hasn't the means to take a holiday in the south of France or even Southend; when he hasn't the wherewithal to pay the rent or occasionally even to eat enough, and no offers materialize, desperation sets in.

I haunted the West End pubs – the Wellington in St Martin's Lane was a favourite haunt of the young members of the profession; also Billy's Café in the alleyway opposite the stage door of Wyndham's Theatre – to try and find out if there were any auditions going on. Every morning I climbed the stairs of my agent's office at 9.45 precisely and gave my name to the uninterested female secretary with pebble-lens spectacles.

Throughout the morning a series of actors and actresses arrived, gave their names, and after being announced on the buzzer, were admitted to the 'presence'. These were the privileged ones who had actually managed to arrange interviews on the telephone. Some left the inner office after a very short time, trying to look successful; some, after longer sessions, emerged looking positively smug and with a lighthearted 'Goodbye darling' to Pebble-Lenses, breezed down the stairs. I hated them, and hoped they would trip on the worn linoleum and break their conceited necks.

At one o'clock, the buzzer buzzed. It sounded rather like a 'raspberry'. I wondered idly if Mr Earne had a sense of humour. 'Yes, Mr Earne, of course, thank you.' She addressed us: 'Mr Earne is sorry, but he's having lunch now and there's not time to see any more people this morning. But if you like to come back tomorrow he will try to fit you in.'

This routine lasted for over three weeks. Every morning I presented myself, always with the same result. Funds had run out. I was too proud to ask my father for a loan, and for the first time in my life I found out what it was like to be really hungry. Just when I'd reached the point when I thought I should be forced to find some other temporary job in order to survive, something happened. I was sitting in the outer office of Mr Earne's 'Heartbreak House' one morning, and for some reason or other I was the only actor who had turned up. At ten o'clock there were footsteps on the stairs, familiar ones by this time. Mr Earne appeared. 'Good morning, Mr Earne.'

He nodded and reached for the door handle. The moment of truth had arrived, and I said loudly, 'Mr Earne, I have been waiting in your office every morning for four hours for four weeks, and if you cannot find time to see me now I regret that I shall have to ask another agent to represent me. After all, I have been paying you ten per cent of my salary for the past eight months, and I would like to add that *I* found the job – all *you* had to do was to sit on your backside in your office and collect.'

There was a long pause. Mr Earne stared at me. Pebble-Lenses's jaw dropped. She couldn't believe that any young actor would dare to speak to her boss like that. Neither could I. But desperate situations call for desperate measures.

'What's your name?'

'John Mills, Mr Earne, and I've been in the chorus of *The Five O'Clock Girl* for the last eight months, and understudying Ernest Truex. I have also been doing a cabaret act which has, I'm delighted to say, been a huge success, but I'm sure you wouldn't have heard about that.'

'You're right there, young man. I haven't heard about it. Did you pay the commission?' I realized I'd landed myself right in it. 'Come into my office. I want to talk to you.'

I followed him in, shrinking visibly. He settled himself behind his desk. The office was small, with an old upright piano in one corner. The walls were covered with photographs of his clients, with effusive messages on them: 'Love to dear Vincent', 'What would I have done without you?', 'Love, darling. I owe everything to you.' There were some very well-known faces among them. Mr Earne, who had been very concerned with some papers on his desk, looked up at me. 'Would you like to go to India?'

'Yes, Mr Earne, very much,' I said. ('Yes' seemed to be the safest bet on this occasion.)

'Right.' He reached for a card, scribbled something on it and handed it to me.

'Take this to the Prince of Wales Theatre. Be there sharp at eleven o'clock. They're auditioning for a tour of the Far East. You might be lucky. You deserve to be. You've got some bloody nerve, and you need it in this racket.'

Walking through Leicester Square that sunny morning I could hardly believe that at last I had a chance of a job. I looked at the card. On it was written, 'John Mills, audition for *Journey's End*, R.B. Salisbury's Far Eastern tour'. I sat down on one of the seats in the square. The information was too much to take standing. *Journey's End*! I'd seen it three times already from the gallery and not only was it, I thought, the greatest play I'd ever seen, but there was a part in it, Lieutenant Raleigh (played by Maurice Evans, a successful young West End actor), which I would have given my right arm and, if necessary, my right leg to play. Lieutenant Raleigh was twenty years old, keen, eager, ex-public school, and of course spoke the 'King's English'. And so, thanks to George Posford, did I. R.C. Sherriff could have written the part for me. I suddenly felt that fate was smiling on me again. I knew the play, I loved the part, and felt sure that after the audition it had to be mine.

I joined about twenty other young actors in the wings of the Prince of Wales Theatre, and handed my card to the stage manager. The nerves and tension began to build up. Waiting in the wings, listening to other actors audition, is a very refined torture. You listen and think, 'Oh God, he's too good. He's bound to get it.' Luckily for me, in this case no one had so far read Raleigh. One actor before me read Stanhope (the Colin Clive part), another Trotter (George Melville Cooper), and another Hibbert, the coward, played by Robert Speight.

'OK. You're next. Here's the script. On you go, and good luck.'

I took a deep breath, crossed myself, walked on to the stage, and found myself in the set of *Journey's End*. It seemed amazingly real. I knew it well from the gallery, but it was even better at close quarters. A voice boomed out from the darkness of the stalls, 'Name?'

'John Mills, sir.'

'Just a minute.'

I could dimly distinguish four figures huddled in the seats. There was a whispered consultation. 'Right, will you please turn to Scene III and read the part of Hibbert.'

I could hardly believe what I'd heard. I mean, couldn't he see that I was Raleigh? How could I possibly be Hibbert the coward? I stood there in a kind of daze. The ASM was waiting with his script open ready to cue me. I shaded the glare from the footlights with my left forearm. 'Excuse me, sir. Would it be possible to read Raleigh?'

'No,' said the voice. 'It would not. Will you please get on with it, and not waste any more of our valuable time.'

With a sinking heart I found the place and started. It was a difficult scene to play, let alone read. It was the scene where Hibbert breaks down in front of Stanhope, his CO, and has an hysterical outburst. I plunged in, and did the best I could with it. But I knew it wasn't good, and I wasn't at all surprised when the voice cut into the middle of the scene and said, 'All right. Thank you very much. We'll let you know.'

I closed the script, managed to say, 'Thank you sir,' in the direction of the voice, and dribbled slowly off-stage. I had just reached the wings when the voice said, 'Just a minute. Would you mind coming back?'

I stared out into the abyss. 'Yes, sir?'

There was another whispered conversation. Then the voice said, 'Would you please read the part of Lieutenant Raleigh? You can take a few minutes to look at it, if you like.'

The ASM found the scene and gave it to me. It was one of the best scenes in the play. I almost knew it by heart. By this time I was in a state of shock. I could hardly believe what was happening to me. A condemned man had been reprieved. Why? This I was to find out later.

I read the scene. In fact I did more than that. Because I'd seen Maurice Evans play it three times I was able to give something that resembled quite a passable performance. I finished. There was a long pause. 'Thank you very much. Will you please give your agent's name to the stage manager.'

'Er ... yes sir, thank you sir.' I stumbled off the stage. I thought, 'I've got it. They never, ever, ask for your agent's telephone number unless you've got it. I really believe I've got it. I'm going to play Lieutenant Raleigh.'

I know that already in this book I've often mentioned the word 'luck'. On this occasion a thousand-to-one chance not only landed me the part I longed for, but launched me on a voyage during which I was destined to have the greatest good fortune that in my wildest dreams I could never have imagined.

On the same day, at the same time as I was walking across Leicester Square on my way to the audition, a certain gentleman named R.C. Sherriff was walking along Piccadilly taking the air, and no doubt cogitating on the fact that he was responsible for one of the most extraordinary phenomena in world theatre. He must have been remembering with secret pleasure that his play had been hawked round to every reputable management in London, and that every single one of them had turned it down flat. They just didn't regard it as having any chance whatsoever in the commercial theatre. One set, World War I, an all male cast – impossible! Not worth the risk. Sorry.

An unknown (at the time) producer named Maurice Browne liked it, bought it, and against all advice presented it. The reaction was extraordinary. It was the immediate smash hit of the decade. While it was being played at the Prince of Wales Theatre there were already two touring companies out on the road in England. It was also being translated into practically every known language. Not even the actors who were in the play believed in it. The cast of *Journey's End* was offered a small salary plus a percentage of the gross for the West End run. They all turned it down, thinking they might as well collect their full salaries for the few weeks that it might survive in the West End. If they had accepted the gamble they would have all made a small fortune. You can imagine their feelings when night after night they arrived at the Prince of Wales Theatre to find the House Full boards out an hour before the curtain was due to rise.

And my own thousand-to-one chance? R.C. Sherriff is by this time walking past the Prince of Wales Theatre, where his masterpiece is being played. On a sudden whim, he walks through the foyer into the stalls to find an audition in progress, and joins R.B. Salisbury and Grant Anderson. As I heard later, Mr Sherriff whispered to Mr Salisbury, 'What's that boy reading Hibbert for? He looks like the perfect Raleigh to me. If you haven't already cast the part, get him to read it.'

It is strange, almost frightening, to think how my whole life was changed by the author of *Journey's End* deciding to take a stroll in London on that particular morning. I should certainly not have taken the road to the Far East, and this road, I am sure, led me to the West End years ahead of any other route I could possibly have taken.

The next morning I phoned Mr Earne, and to my surprise was put through to him personally. 'Hallo,' he said. 'You must have done quite well yesterday, because Mr Salisbury has phoned to say that he wants you to audition at the Poland Street rehearsal rooms at twelve o'clock this morning.'

'But Mr Earne,' I said, 'I understood that I had the part that I auditioned for – Raleigh in *Journey's End*.'

'Oh yes, they're quite happy about that,' he said, 'but they're also doing a lot of musicals and they want to see what your singing and dancing are like.'

'Oh heavens,' I thought, 'I'm not through yet.' I walked into the Poland Street rehearsal rooms to find a group of about twenty young actors and actresses. There was a pianist at an upright piano, and behind a trestle table sat two men. One was small and genial and the other was a very striking character – swarthy, dark, with large expressive eyes. He called me over to the table: 'I'm James Grant Anderson. And this is Mr R.B. Salisbury, who owns the company. We saw your audition yesterday, and we both agree you're right for Raleigh, but we have to see you sing and dance. Have you got your music?'

I struggled into my tap shoes and handed the music to the pianist. I was extremely nervous. I knew my voice wasn't sounding all that good, and I was fighting a losing battle with the pianist right from the start. He had decided to play the number at the pace of 'The Galloping Major', and beat me to the finish by a good two bars.

There was a long whispered conversation between the two judges. Grant Anderson called me over to the table: 'I'm sorry, but Mr Salisbury doesn't think you sing or dance quite well enough. He hopes to do several musical comedies in this season's repertoire, and he feels that he must engage someone rather stronger in that area. I'm sorry, but don't get depressed, we think you've got some talent.'

The ride home to Walcot Square on the top of the bus did nothing to blow away the total despair. As the bus crossed Lambeth Bridge the Thames seemed very inviting – but not quite inviting enough. This was just a set-back. I had to keep plugging on. This was the jungle and I was in it. I decided that whatever happened I would present myself as usual at Mr Earne's office the following morning.

As I was bolting my breakfast the telephone rang in the hall. Mrs Buhler came into the room. 'It's for you, John,' she said. 'I believe he said his name was Anderson. Grant Anderson.' I walked to the telephone.

'Is that John Mills? I know it's rather early, but if you haven't cut your throat, I've got some good news for you. We saw a lot of other actors yesterday, and we weren't very happy about them, and I persuaded Mr Salisbury that you were so good as Raleigh that we should take you with us. I pointed out to him that *Journey's End* ought to be our most important production, and it was essential that the cast, with the play's reputation, should be as good as we could get it. You'll have to work bloody hard on your singing and dancing, but you're in. So come to the office and sign your contract at twelve o'clock.'

Mr Salisbury had been taking a company out to the Far East for years. It was in reality a concert party consisting of about twelve people, which, for some reason best known to himself, Mr Salisbury called 'The Quaints'. They had become very well known and successful, and R.B., when he decided to move with the times and provide musical comedies and straight plays, including Shakespeare, for the enjoyment and edification of the British sahibs and mem-sahibs, flatly refused to change the name. Customers were therefore faced with the somewhat peculiar posters which announced: THE QUAINTS in JOURNEY'S END.

James Grant Anderson had been engaged to direct the 1929 company and also play some of the leading parts. Jimmy Anderson was a character. I had never met anyone quite like him, and I spent hours listening to his fund of stories about the theatre. Life for Jimmy outside the theatre just didn't exist, and if it did it was far too boring for him even to discuss it for a moment. As a very young actor, he had played small parts and worked ASM with some of the giants of the past – Sir Charles Hawtrey, Sir George Alexander, Mrs Patrick Campbell, Sir Herbert Beerbohm Tree and Sir John Martin-Harvey. During World War I, when I'm sure he picked up most of his vibrant vocabulary, he served in the Black Watch and was badly wounded in the right leg. I didn't discover this until I asked him why he had a slight limp. 'Because I've got a bloody great steel peg in my leg, that's why.' If you asked J.G.A. a question you got a straight answer.

When I presented myself at the office he was in sole charge. 'Good morning, Mr Anderson,' I said. 'I can't tell you how grateful I am.' He cut me short.

'Oh balls to that. I wouldn't have done anything about you if I hadn't thought you'd got something. If you don't have something in this business, the sooner you get your arse out of it the better. Sign here.' He pushed a single sheet of paper across the table. 'I wouldn't bother to read it. That's it, whatever your bloody agent says. And you're lucky to get it. And if he complains tell him to go and get stuffed.'

I had signed my name almost before he'd finished speaking. 'Thank you very much, Mr Anderson,' I said.

'OK. Now I'll tell you what you've let yourself in for,' said my mentor. 'You are under contract to Mr R.B. Salisbury for a period of not less than one year. You are to portray, to the best of your at the moment limited bloody ability, any part the said Mr Salisbury so desires. Your salary will be £7 per week, but, and the next part's bloody important, everything's found. Which means that you will be put up at the best hotels in the Far East and also travel first class on any train journeys. Which also means you won't be squirted with betel-nut juice by the bloody nig-nogs. You start rehearsing at 9.30 tomorrow morning at the Poland Street rehearsal rooms. Any questions?'

'None at all, Mr Anderson,' I said.

'Oh, by the way, have you seen Bobby Howes in *Mr Cinders*?'

'Yes, Mr Anderson. I've seen it several times – from the gallery, of course. It's a wonderful show and I think Mr Howes is terrific.'

'Yes, I think he's pretty good too. Do you think you could play the part?'

'Play the part? Me?' I gasped.

'Yes. I think with a lot of sweat you could tackle it. I told R.B., so he's promised to get hold of the rights if he can.'

Travelling back to Number 75 on the bus that night, I could hardly persuade myself that what had happened was true. Raleigh in *Journey's End* and possibly Mr Cinders. Bobby Howes was one of my heroes. In my opinion he was the best light comedian on the London stage. He was a superb dancer and had a charming, light singing voice. In my cabaret act with George Posford I had copied him flagrantly. Shaftesbury Avenue seemed that evening to be the most exciting avenue in the world. I saw my name up in lights outside all those famous theatres – the Saville, the Shaftesbury, the Lyric, the Globe, Queen's and the Apollo. Every play, of course, had been a smash hit.

At the first rehearsal the next morning I met the rest of the male cast. The ladies had not yet been chosen. They were to join the company later on in the tour. There were eight of us – Geoffrey Salisbury (R.B.'s son), a smaller and rather nicer edition of his father, John Salew, Kenneth Birrell, Bruce Carfax, Ronald Brantford, Edgar Owen, James Grant Anderson and Reggie Wingrove, who was also our advance manager. There was a great air of excitement in the Poland Street rehearsal rooms that morning. I could still hardly believe my luck. A year's solid work ahead, travelling through the Far East (I'd never even crossed the English Channel), and having the chance to gain experience by playing a variety of parts. The plays were not all chosen, but I understood we should be doing at least eight. When I finally heard the complete repertoire I decided that as far as variety was concerned, it couldn't be beaten.

We were informed by the advance manager, Reggie Wingrove, to fit ourselves out with lightweight tropical suits for daily wear. All the props would be provided by the company. We were also advised to purchase solar topees. Jimmy Anderson suggested that to save the actors money he would sell to the company a selection of the required headgear that he had used in one of his productions in rep. The offer was accepted with alacrity. We were all becoming rather concerned about the expense of a lightweight wardrobe. The only topee that fitted me was an enormous white helmet, obviously a relic of the Boer War. It gave me the appearance of a bugler boy in the Bengal Lancers.

The rehearsals came to an end. I thought J.G.A. was a very good director – one of the old 'no nonsense, speak up and get on with it' school. He addressed us thus: 'Get the bloody scripts out of your hand as soon as possible. I've got no intention of sitting on my arse wasting my bloody time while you lot wander around the stage learning your bloody lines. So go home and get them into your bloody heads. Then we'll see how much, if anything, you know about bloody acting. I want you word-perfect by the time we get on the boat. That'll give me three weeks to polish it up, and as I'm used to weekly rep it should be a bloody cake-walk.'

We got the message.

I had three farewell parties – one at Felixstowe with my mother, Annie and Bobby, and three of the little cottage loaves, Aunties Betty, Rosa and Jimmy: one at Number 75 with my father and the Buhler family, and one with the Datis. They were all given to celebrate the hero's departure in search of fame and fortune; also to mark the fact that I had reached my twenty-first birthday. My mother presented me with a travelling clock with 'To J.L.E.W. Mills on his twenty-first birthday, with love from his mother' inscribed on the back. I still have it beside my bed, and it still keeps good time. My father gave me five golden sovereigns in a leather purse, which I regret to say found their way into 'Uncle's' (the pawn shop in Brixton Road) many years ago and were never reclaimed.

I managed to cram in a few more theatres before I left. I saw Frank Lawton's superb performance again as Woodley in *Young Woodley* at the Savoy Theatre. The whole cast was excellent – Jack Hawkins, Frances Doble and Henry Mollison. The play was directed by a man who struck terror into the hearts of young actors – his name was Basil Dean.

On the first night of *Young Woodley*, after the first act, there was apparently a feeling in the audience that they were half-way through what looked like developing into a sensational success. People in the bar were actually talking about the play, and a tremendous performance being given by a young actor called Frank Lawton, and not about the weather or Aunty Mabel's cough. In the interval, while the young and relatively inexperienced cast were doing their best to keep calm and not allow themselves to be carrried away by the enormous amount of applause that hit them when the curtain fell, a demented man, whom they recognized as their director, tore into their dressing-rooms, his hair flying, seeming about to burst:'What the hell do you think you're all playing at? What is this, a performance? It's a disaster! They're all in the bars now getting drunk. And if they've any sense they won't come back. I've got to watch the second act, because I was paid to direct the play, so I'll be out front, and if you don't pull yourselves together and remember you are supposed to be professional actors and therefore getting paid, this will undoubtedly be your opening and closing night at the Savoy Theatre.'

This was a carefully thought-out, well-timed attack. Basil Dean was a very experienced director and he knew there was a chance that the cast, hearing the prolonged applause, would relax slightly, and because of their inexperience lose their 'edge', which was vital for the second act of the play. The attack had the desired effect. For the rest of the evening the young cast gave a performance charged with such electricity that when the final curtain fell they received an ovation. This story was recounted to me by Henry Mollison who, a few years after, became a great friend.

I also found time to go to one of my favourite theatres: the Haymarket (about the only theatre I have never had the pleasure of playing in myself)to see the great Marie Tempest in *The First Mrs Frazer*. There was a beautiful young actress in the cast called Ursula Jeans, with whom (had I known it) I was to act in the not-too-distant future.

The day before my departure I called at my agent's office. I must have risen in the ranks, so to speak, because after giving my name to Pebble-Lenses, who pretended not to know the conceited, cheeky young Thespian, I was ushered in to Mr Earne's office. I noticed a subtle change in his manner. He was charming, and said he hoped that I'd enjoy the tour and gain valuable experience. He understood from the management that I was to have the chance of playing some other very interesting roles as well as Lieutenant Raleigh. He had also heard, he said, that Grant Anderson considered me promising, and he hoped that I would come and see him on my return. He added that if I felt he could be of further use to me I could then re-sign with the agency, as my present contract terminated after twelve months. I realized that if by some outside chance I happened to make it, Mr Earne did not intend to find himself sitting outside the safe watching his young client inside counting the money.

Theatrical agents have been the butt of actors from time immemorial. They get blamed for everything. When actors are out of work, if no offers are forthcoming after a couple of weeks they blame the agent for not being quick enough in suggesting them for the part that so-and-so is playing. They can never believe *they* have been turned down, and if it happens to be true they certainly don't want to hear it. Actors are, by and large, the most insecure people in the world. We have to find someone to blame when things are going badly, otherwise our morale would suffer permanent damage, and who better than our agent? 'I get the job, and all he does is to sit on his arse in the office and sign the contract.' I must have heard that sentence thousands of times. As in every other profession, there are good and bad. Some agents really work for their clients, some don't, and some sit on the fence between the producer and their client and try to play it both ways; this is nearly always fatal for the actor.

I went to say goodbye to Zelia, and make the necessary arrangements to pay her, as we had agreed, five per cent of my salary. I suggested that I should send a postal order home every month during the period of the tour. Zelia looked blank. 'Commission? What commission are you talking about?'

'The five per cent commission I agreed to pay you on any salary I earn in the theatre for the next ten years.'

'I don't remember that,' said Zelia. 'I do remember accepting five per cent of your salary when you were in *The Five O'Clock Girl*, because you said you hadn't the cash to pay for the lessons.'

'That's right,' I said. 'But I can remember the conversation clearly. "In ten years' time," you said, "if you're lucky, that could amount to an awful lot of money. Do you think it's wise?" And I said, "Of course I do."'

Zelia smiled and said, 'Johnny darling, of course I do remember. But I never had any intention of taking another penny from you after *The Five O'Clock Girl* closed. I told you at the time, if you remember, that Annie was my greatest friend. Do you really think I would seriously make a deal like that with her brother? Don't you realize you may, if you're lucky, be earning a great deal of money in a few years' time? Do you think I want a penny of it? What I do want is for you to go out on this tour, which is a great opportunity, work like a slave at your dancing, and if you make a success I should like to feel that perhaps I was responsible for a very small part of it. Believe me, that will be payment enough.'

One never forgets the people who were kind and helpful when one was struggling up the first few rough steps of the ladder. Zelia Raye was one of them. I shall always be in her debt.

6

The Strolling Player

We sailed on the evening tide from Birkenhead in the s.s. *City of Lahore*. The date was 17 August 1929 – a good omen. Seven had always been my lucky number and the start of the great adventure was full of them: the year added up to twenty-one, so it could be reckoned there were four sevens in all.

The *City of Lahore* was a mail boat bound for Calcutta, calling at Naples, Port Said, Colombo and Bombay. She carried very few passengers and on this particular voyage there was only a handful of mahogany-faced tea and rubber planters and their wives. The day before we sailed Mr Salisbury had obtained the rights of *Young Woodley* and the actresses had been engaged. One, a very pretty blonde, Towyna Thomas, arrived at Birkenhead on the arm of Bruce Carfax. The other young actress was not joining the boat until we reached Naples, after having made the journey by train via Paris escorted by R.B. Salisbury and his son Geoffrey. The first officer had informed me over a drink on the first night aboard that the *City of Lahore* was, in his words, 'a fair bastard in a rough sea', and he hoped I was a good sailor. I hoped so too, but as my only previous experience had been in a rowing boat on the Serpentine in Hyde Park, the elements at sea were an unknown quantity – but not for long. The Bay of Biscay has a reputation, and on this occasion it more than lived up to it. After a calm, enjoyable day I had turned in early and was lying in my top bunk, reading, when it hit us. The ship shuddered, then did a quick sideways roll; I was thrown out on to the floor and joined Bruce Carfax and Jimmy Anderson who had reached it at the same speed a split second before me.

The next twenty-four hours were a nightmare. The ship did everything but sink. Several times I prayed she would. She rolled, plunged, twisted, turned; she behaved like a whale with an advanced case of delirium tremens. I don't think there's any feeling quite as awful as real seasickness; I didn't want to be an actor. I didn't want to be anything. I just wanted to die. Eventually, after two days that seemed like two years, we became conscious that the ship was behaving normally, and I staggered up on deck. As we drifted slowly towards the harbour Naples was shrouded in an early-morning mist: it was breathtakingly beautiful. 'See Naples and die.' Leaning over the ship's rail at that moment, for me it was 'See Naples and live'.

We were told the ship would not be sailing until the early tide the following morning, which gave us time to explore our first foreign port. We had a marvellous day. Actors are wonderful company – at least for actors. They have a keen eye for spotting any interesting characters and situations, and nearly always possess a sense of humour and a sense of the ridiculous. Consequently, whenever a few actors are gathered together there is always laughter; and that day we laughed a great deal. We wandered around the town, found an attractive little water-side restaurant, and stuffed ourselves with spaghetti bolognese washed down with gallons of rough red Chianti. Later the same day, most of the male members of the Quaints were sitting outside a café discussing the best way to spend the first evening ashore, when a small dark Italian in a white linen suit approached the table and suggested in quite reasonable English that we might like to see some entertainment.

'What sort of entertainment?' asked Jimmy Anderson.

'Well, you know . . . ladies, pretty ladies . . . bellissime, molto, molto bellissime.' He winked at us.

'Any of you lot ever been to a brothel before?' Jimmy asked. There was an embarrassed pause.

'I thought not. You're too bleedin' young. I think we ought to start your education. Don't worry. You won't have to do anything. We'll just have a drink and a laugh and then get back to the ship. We're rehearsing in the morning and I don't want a bunch of wobbly-kneed twits with hangovers to direct.'

A taxi disgorged us at the door of a large house in a rather smelly narrow street on the other side of the harbour. We were greeted by a large bespectacled Italian lady with her hair swept back into a neat bun on the nape of her neck. She reminded me of my kind Mother Superior at Dorking. She ushered us into a large room with mirrors covering the walls and ceiling. Everything was red plush. A large round divan stood in the centre of the room surrounded by chairs. Our hostess pulled a long red tassel hanging by the door, smiled and left the room. Another glass-panelled door opened and a waitress appeared carrying a tray on which stood two bottles of champagne and glasses. She was like every other waitress I'd ever seen except for the fact that, apart from the small white frilly apron, she was stark naked. I did my best to pass this off as an everyday occurrence.

Through yet another door eight young ladies made their entrance. They were dressed in a wild and weird assortment of underclothes. Without as much as by your leave, they plumped themselves down on our laps and started knocking back our champagne. There was a great deal of giggling and chattering, and I had a feeling that they knew how naïve we were and how awkward we felt. I personally was giving the worst performance of a young sophisticate out on the town that one could possibly imagine.

The large lady who had chosen my lap suddenly jumped to her feet, produced a whistle from her brassiere (or bust-bodice as it was called in those days) and blew a loud shrill blast on it. This was a signal for her cast to fling themselves with abandon into a display of sexual gymnastics which would have won any one of them a gold medal at the Olympics. I was full of admiration. I thought, 'Well, whatever else they do, they must be fit.' Exhausted by their performance the ladies collapsed in small heaps on the round divan. Their leader approached Jimmy Anderson: 'You all like make fooky with ladies?'

'What, and twist a bloody vertebra? No thanks. You tell young ladies very good but they can now fooky off. But listen, have you got "look-through room" here. You know, look through mirror, see show!'

'Si, si, signore. Ancora mille lire. Good show. Very good. You like?'

Our hostess led us up the back stairs, along a landing, opened a door and, putting her fingers to her lips, led us into a small room, dimly lit with what looked like a mirror in the middle of the far wall. When I looked into it I discovered that it wasn't a mirror but a pane of plain glass through which could be seen another small room with a bed and a dressing-table. The ceiling was one large mirror. 'Show start in minute,' said our hostess, and left the room.

Jimmy then explained to his uninitiated cast that the glass on the other side looked like a proper mirror and anyone looking in it would never guess for one moment that it was constructed so that from our side we could see straight through it.

The door of the small room opened. A very pretty young Italian girl walked through it, leading by the hand . . . one of the members of the Quaints! (He, of course, for obvious reasons, must remain anonymous.) We couldn't believe our eyes. By a thousand-to-one chance he had landed up in our establishment. We stared, riveted, then looked at each other. Hysteria started to set in. I crammed my handkerchief into my mouth to try and stifle the laughter. The rest of the act was pure silent comedy of the top class. Our hero was invited by gestures to avail himself of the bathroom. He reappeared to the sound of a running flush and disrobed, folding his clothes and placing them carefully on the chair by the dressing-table. He started to undo the strap of his wristwatch, paused, then did it up again. 'Sensible,' whispered Jimmy. 'Never take anything off but your bloody clothes.' Our friend then walked over to the mirror and, staring me straight in the eye, flexed his biceps, moistened his finger and smoothed his eyebrows, combed his hair, and then took a pace back and smiled in admiration at his reflection.

I can say in all honesty that his performance was terrific. I don't think he ever reached that peak of perfection in any other part that he played during the tour. His audience may have been small, but it was completely satisfied, and no one complained about the rather exorbitant price of the seats. Weak and purple with suppressed laughter, we quietly left the building – the moment the curtain fell our hostess had made it quite clear that we were not to be discovered. She made it a strict rule never to embarrass a client. On the way back to the ship we decided that we too would not embarrass our hero by letting him know of our intrusion into his private evening.

As I walked up the gangway later that evening I noticed two figures standing at the ship's rail: one was a slim young man in a smart white tropical suit, the other was a young woman, small, dark, in a white dress, with a large white Ascot hat perched at a very becoming angle. I walked across the deck to join them. 'Aileen, this is Johnny, Johnny Mills.' She smiled at me with her large brown eyes; the smile was very attractive.

'Johnny, this is Aileen Raymond. I've just brought her out by train from Paris.

'Hallo,' I said. 'Good trip?'

'Yes, marvellous, thanks. But I'm looking forward to the boat, and the rehearsals. You are playing Woodley, aren't you?'

'Yes I am,' I said. 'It's a lovely part. Are you playing Laura?'

'Yes I am.'

'But ... mm ... you're a bit young for it, aren't you? I mean, she's my housemaster's wife.'

'Well a bit, perhaps. But I can always grey up.'

'Yes of course. It's a terrific play isn't it? I'm looking forward to it.'

The smile returned. 'Yes so am I. Very much.'

I did a quick mental 'reccy' of the situation. There was a certain proprietary air about young Geoffrey Salisbury; after all, he was the boss's son and he had been to Paris with her. 'Well,' I said, 'I think I'll hit the bunk. We've had quite a night on the town. See you in the morning. Good night.'

I left them standing at the rail. Neither I nor Geoffrey had the remotest idea that he had just introduced me to my future wife.

The sea was calm, the weather was fair and the *City of Lahore* was behaving like a perfect lady. I began to enjoy the voyage. We slipped into a sort of pattern: rehearsal in the morning, a swim in the small canvas pool on the forward deck, lunch, more rehearsals. At five o'clock each day we were free to do as we liked. We only spent a few hours ashore at Port Said, Colombo and Bombay, and at the end of August a group of sun-tanned, well-travelled, sophisticated actors stepped ashore at Calcutta. We stayed at the Grand Hotel. It was my first experience of real luxury. The hotels in those far-off days, at the height of the Raj, were superb: they were spotlessly clean, the food was excellent and the service had to be experienced to be believed. (When I returned to India many years later, I was shattered by the change.) There was nothing about the hotel that I didn't like: tall white columns, cool marble floors, attractive cane furniture and the long bar above which the wooden fans turned silently like aeroplane propellers.

I shared a bedroom with Bruce Carfax, which was as large as the whole of 75 Walcot Square. There was a bathroom off it on one side, and on the other side were dividing doors which separated us from Aileen Raymond and Towyna Thomas. These doors were locked: this was of no concern to me at the time, but I noticed that Bruce was giving them a rather old-fashioned look.

On 4 September 1929 we opened at the Old Empire Theatre. The house had been sold out for a week. *Journey's End* was the most extraordinary play: it needed no publicity whatsoever. It was being played simultaneously in Paris, Berlin, London, New York, Johannesburg and Sydney. Jimmy Anderson had been working like mad to get the set and the set-dressing perfect, and it really looked as good as the London production. There was no air-conditioning in the theatre and it was cooled, or slightly cooled, by wooden fans suspended by long iron bars from the roof. These had the most appalling effect on the sound; they cut voices in half before they reached the auditorium. At the two dress rehearsals Jimmy, being an old campaigner from the reps, directed us from the back of the pit and sometimes from the back of the circle. Every so often we were brought to an abrupt halt by his stentorian shouts from the darkness, 'Speak up. Can't hear a bloody word.' I've never stopped being grateful for that initiation into the now almost lost art of projection. Jimmy made sure that, whatever happened, they would hear as well as see *Journey's End*. 'It's better to be bad and heard than good and not heard,' he said. And there was a great deal of truth in it.

These days in the theatre I am often absolutely maddened by the actors' lack of projection. I'm sure that nearly all the blame must be attached to that box that stands in the corner of every living-room. The worst offenders are the actors and actresses who have a sudden enormous success in a television series and then decide to do a play in the theatre. They have never had the chance to learn the art of projection, and they are lucky if they are heard further back than the fifth or sixth row of the stalls.

The first night was a triumph for the Quaints, all of whom gave remarkably good performances. I think it might be difficult today to get together a cast who could acquit themselves creditably in modern straight plays, musical comedies (which called for quite expert tap-dancing), and Shakespeare's tragedies all in the same week. Bruce Carfax, who before this had only played in musicals on tour in England (he had a fine tenor voice), gave an excellent performance as Stanhope, the CO. Jimmy Anderson doubled the parts of Hardy and Trotter. (This had never been attempted before, but Jimmy was a master of make-up and quick changes. During his one-man-show he played as many as twenty characters during the evening and made up on the stage for each one in front of the audience.) He gave a splendid performance as Trotter, and stood up well in comparison with that fine actor George Melville Cooper, whose portrayal I had witnessed three times from the gallery in the London production. Ronald Brantford, who was a speciality dancer with Jack Buchanan in *That's A Good Girl* at the London Hippodrome, coped amazingly well with the difficult part of Hibbert. John Salew as Osborne, Kenneth Birrell as Mason the cockney cook, Reggie Wingrove, our advance manager, as the Sergeant Major, and Edgar Owen as the Colonel all gave good performances.

The notice in the paper in Calcutta (everybody read it because it was the only one) was a rave. They couldn't, of course, without looking idiotic, attack the play, but they could have suggested that the Quaints were not perhaps quite up to the standard required for R.C. Sherriff's magnificent piece of work.

I am now going to do something that is really 'not done' in my profession, 'show you one of my notices', but I make this excuse: it was the first notice I had ever received in any paper as a professional actor, and it was quite a long time ago – fifty years to be exact. The critic who wrote about my first performance started me off on my career with a terrific boost. If he had dealt unkindly with me, it might, at that very vulnerable age, have dented my confidence and seriously affected my morale. If, by some miraculous chance, he happens to read this book, I should like him (whoever he is, the notice was unsigned) to know that I am very grateful for the encouragement he gave me at exactly the right moment. I have the cutting in a scrap book in front of me: it is yellow with age and slightly the worse for wear, having survived countless moves.

After praising the play, 'the best straight play I've ever seen', he gave all the cast good notices. I'd got three-quarters of the way down the column and neither my name nor Lieutenant Raleigh's had appeared. I thought, 'Oh lord, I'm not even going to be mentioned.' Then I read:

'Young Raleigh is most ably portrayed by John Mills. His youth, his eagerness, his delight at being in the same company under the command of the hero of his boyhood days, were all so perfectly depicted that our hearts went out to the youngster, and suffered most when he was carried back to the dug-out, dying.'

I have collected a few stinking notices since that time and I am sure those words of praise, written half a century ago, have helped prevent me, in moments of frustration, depression and despair, from throwing in the towel or cutting my throat.

The *Statesman* notice ended with a paragraph that showed our superlative critic in Calcutta also possessed a sense of humour. He wrote: 'The part of the German soldier was taken by Mr R.B. Salisbury's son, Mr Geoffrey Salisbury, who was making his debut at the age of eighteen. He showed poise and determination by taking in his stride something that might have thrown many more experienced actors. On descending the steps of the dug-out he walked out of his German boots (which were obviously intended for a giant). Instead of holding up the action by putting them back on he proceeded down-stage to his position and played the scene without them. The fact that his right toe was plainly visible trying to make its escape through a large hole in one of the grey army socks did nothing to detract from his performance.'

The curtain fell to loud applause. It was only when it was over that I realized quite how stiflingly hot it was. The theatre was like an oven. We were all wearing thick 1914 uniforms, boots, webbing, gas-masks, tin helmets, and we were soaked through with sweat. But the evening had been worth every drop of it. We celebrated at the Grand Hotel until the Indian dawn.

I have never quite believed in love at first sight, but I do believe, and believe very firmly because I experienced it, in 'love at the first rehearsal'. I had been avoiding whenever possible close contact with my co-star in *Young Woodley*, but each time I saw her I found her more attractive and more desirable.

The first rehearsal took place at 10.30 at the Empire Theatre the morning after the first night. I was sitting on a box in the set of *Journey's End*, trying to rise above a rather brittle, electric hang-over, when she walked on to the stage. We both said simultaneously, 'Good morning,' and opened our scripts. A voice boomed out from the darkness of the stalls, 'All right. Now you've condescended to appear, let's get on with the bloody rehearsal. Act One, Scene One. And I hope you've learned most of the bloody words. We open next week.' It was J.G.A. in top gear. Through the whole of the tour I never remember him being late, or tired. His energy was sometimes quite exhausting.

We'd both done our homework and hardly needed the scripts. After Act One, we broke for coffee and then started Act Two. Halfway through this act the author, John van Druten, had written a very touching and tender love scene. Young Woodley, under enormous stress, suddenly breaks down and confesses his love for Laura, his housemaster's wife, and ends up sobbing with his head in her lap. This scene suddenly took wings. We both knew at that moment that the lines we were speaking were true, and there was an unspoken acceptance of the attraction that we had both instinctively felt for the last two or three weeks. J.G.A. seemed to sense something rather special was happening, because when we'd finished the rehearsal, he said: 'Well, not bad, not bad at all. We'll work on Act One tomorrow, but we'll leave Act Two for a bit. If you manage to play the love-scene like that on the first night they're in for a treat. They'll really believe it. So don't bugger it up. The most important thing about acting is *truth*, so don't bleedin' forget it. Let's go and have some char.'

That evening, after *Journey's End*, Bruce, Towyna, Aileen and I had supper together. The Grand Hôtel seemed more luxurious and beautiful than ever. The fans revolved slowly, the turbaned waiters glided to and from the table, their bare brown feet moving silently across the marble floor. The food was superb, the lager was ice-cold, the string quartet played 'Pale Hands I Loved Beside The Shalimar' (shades of the New Malden cinema). What more could four young strolling players ask for?

Later that night Bruce and I were in our room. He was halfway through the last cigarette of the day – the sixtieth to be exact, he was a three-pack man – when I caught him looking thoughtfully at me for a moment. Then, without a word, he left the room. When he came back I was in my pyjamas cleaning my teeth. He closed the door behind him, held up a key, winked, walked over to the dividing doors and unlocked them. Needless to say, they remained that way for the rest of the stay.

Young Woodley opened on 14 September in Calcutta, and the company chalked up another success. The critics were again generous in their praise and we were, as we were to discover, lulled into a false sense of security.

Jimmy cantered easily through the matinees of *Hamlet*. He gave, I thought, an excellent performance, but the Indian students didn't really have time to appreciate it: they were far too busy trying to find where the hell the gloomy Dane had got to in their copies of the play. Jimmy had decided, in view of the fact that we would be playing *Journey's End* that evening, and also because he only had a skeleton cast available, that he must 'cut his coat according to his cloth'. And cut it he did. In fact he ripped it apart at the seams. This not only caused a certain amount of confusion amongst the keen followers of the Bard out front, but also with his loyal cast backstage, who were all doubling at least three or four characters, and the J.G.A. lightning version of the tragedy made some of the quick changes almost impossible. Young Hamlet was therefore slightly surprised to find, when the grave was disclosed, the second grave-digger made up as Osric, with scarlet lips, thick black eyelashes and a large feather-plumed hat perched at a becoming angle on a golden wig. I had, after appearing as the Second Player, torn into Osric's make-up, completely forgetting my scene as the grave-digger, and there was no time even to whip off my hat before being shoved into the grave in time for the cue.

The scene has always contained a few laughs, but at that matinee in Calcutta it was hilarious. The first grave-digger, Edgar Owen, was purple with laughter and could hardly utter a word, but Jimmy was more than equal to the occasion. He asked the questions and supplied the answers. He 'collaborated with the Bard' on several occasions in emergencies, and I could never tell where Shakespeare finished and J.G.A. began: ad-libbing is difficult enough in a modern play but to succeed with it in Shakespeare requires a touch of genius.

We left Calcutta, travelling to Rangoon and then on to Malaya, which I found a wonderful country, and the Malayans charming, gentle people. We played Penang and stayed at an attractive hotel on the sea – the E. and O. Mary and I spent a week in Penang three months ago, coming back from Australia. The town has grown with time, but the E. and O. Hotel has remained obstinately unchanged in the fifty years since my last visit. We had drinks on the terrace beside the ancient black guns pointing out to sea ... half a century – it seemed at that moment to have passed far too quickly. It was difficult to believe I have a son who is now eight years older than I was the last time I sat there sipping gin fizzes, staring out to sea and pondering on what the future had in store for me.

After Penang we played mostly one-night stands at Ipoh, Kuala Lumpur, Serenbam and Malacca. Then on to Singapore, the gateway to the East. It was the one place I had always hoped to visit, and here I was sitting at the famous long bar at Raffles Hotel. It had cost me nothing to get here, the hotel was paid for and I was being paid £7 per week to see the world. The only payment I had to make in return was to act in eight shows a week, which I would have been perfectly happy to do for nothing.

Singapore seemed to be a water-city. Every narrow street led us to the sea. Ships of all sizes and shapes were being fussed around by sampans, their brown sails fluttering like moths' wings in the heat. The Singapore river was alive with the river-people, who never left it from the day they were born till the day they died. I had enjoyed Calcutta but was captivated by Singapore. I liked everything about it – the cosmopolitan, colourful crowds of Malays, Chinese and Indians, an enchanting city. I even liked its own peculiar smell, a mixture of chop suey, curry, dried fish, spices, drains and swamp.

The Victoria Theatre was a relief to play in after some of the others. It was built over water, which had the effect of making the acoustics far better than anything we were used to. Even with the usual wooden fans at work, it was possible to be heard without belting out the lines as if one was playing to a deaf aunt in the back row of the grandstand at Wembley Stadium. We only played for a week in Singapore, as R.B.'s plan was to return in the new year when the company would be at full strength. Les Girls were to join us in Colombo for rehearsals.

In the smaller places where, because of the limited audience available, the Quaints up till now had only been able to play two performances. From now on, however, R.B. decided to play a full week. The repertoire was daring to say the least of it. The bills were to announce:

A Week with The Quaints

Mon 7 p.m.	JOURNEY'S END, the most famous play of the decade
Tues 7 p.m.	FUNNY FACE, a new musical straight from the West End
Wed mat	HAMLET by William Shakespeare
Wed 7 p.m.	SO THIS IS LOVE, a new musical from the Wintergarden Theatre
Thurs mat	WHEN KNIGHTS WERE BOLD, the famous farce
Thurs 7 p.m.	YOUNG WOODLEY, still playing in the West End
Fri 7 p.m.	MR CINDERS, a new musical still playing in London
Sat mat	JULIUS CAESAR, by William Shakespeare
Sat 7 p.m.	JOURNEY'S END

Psychologically it was a sound plan: hit them hard on Monday night with the big one, and knock them out cold with it on the last night.

All through the tour at every place we played in we had been treated royally. People had been kind, enthusiastic, generous, and we were nearly killed by hospitality. The critics had all been fulsome in their praise, the flattery reaching dangerous proportions. There had not been even one slightly bad notice. We were, however, very soon to receive a salutary and possibly necessary lesson.

The management had decided that it would be a splendid idea to delight the audience at the Opera House in Bombay with a special matinee of *Hamlet* on, of all days, Christmas Day. This seemed a strange, if not dangerous choice. The upholders of our far-flung empire celebrated Christmas in a more dedicated and vigorous way than people at home. The Christmas Eve party at the beautiful Taj Mahal Hotel, where we were staying, went on till dawn, when most of the guests laid a foundation for the Christmas Day festivities with an enormous breakfast of kedgeree, kidneys, eggs and bacon and ice-cold lager. Somehow, I could not see many of them making the pilgrimage to the Opera House that afternoon.

I was therefore prepared for a rather meagre gathering; but what I was not prepared for was a broadside from the Bombay critic writing in *The Times of India*. In two full columns he proceeded to tear the cast limb from limb – we were 'amateurs trading illegally as professionals', 'inarticulate beyond belief', we 'managed to make Shakespeare sound like a second-rate musical comedy', and finally he 'hoped that the young cast would spend some time at a drama school before inflicting themselves on the audiences in England'.

We were outraged. The wretched man didn't know a thing about the theatre. What about all the other critics? They couldn't all be wrong. Making up in my dressing-room that evening for *Young Woodley*, doubts began to creep in. Perhaps *The Times of India* was right. It was an important paper. Perhaps their critic was a professional and really knew about the theatre and acting, and the others just keen amateurs, sports writers, switched for our visit from the polo page to the theatre column. I gave a very poor, subdued performance that evening, and it took me a while to regain some sort of assurance and self-confidence.

Several years later I received a lecture from the Master: wise words which I have never forgotten. I was invited, with some of the cast of *Words and Music* (the revue written and directed by our host which had just opened at the Adelphi Theatre), to spend the weekend at Goldenhurst, his farm in Kent. The show had gone tremendously well, and Noël looked set for another success.

The next morning we gathered in the great man's bedroom. The Master was sitting up in bed in white silk pyjamas and a red silk dressing-gown with the inevitable cigarette in a small quill holder, surrounded by all the Sunday papers. 'Well done, darlings, you can all relax. They've been more than kind, so you should be able to pay the rent for quite some time.'

Noël had written some wonderful material. I had good parts in some very witty sketches, and he had also written a number especially for me called 'Something To Do With Spring', a duet I performed with Joyce Barbour. This finished with an intricate tap-routine arranged by a very talented coloured dancer called Buddy Bradley. With this golden opportunity I secretly hoped I might be discovered as 'the best new young leading man in musicals in the last twenty-five years', and I was praying for a marvellous personal press.

We made a dive for the Sunday newspapers. The gentlemen of Fleet Street were unanimous in their praise. The show was a hit. The notices were all good, some raves. 'Coward has done it again', 'Brilliantly witty and enchanting evening'. All the cast came off well. No one could ask for more, except the best young leading man in musicals, who, try as he might, was unable to find a single notice in any of the papers, until he finally reached the last one, which informed the readers that 'last night Mr John Mills made his debut in a musical; Mr Fred Astaire has absolutely nothing to worry about'. I read it three times. It took a while to sink in. What had happened? The number had gone well – as well as anything in the show. Of course I couldn't be compared to my idol; nobody could. The silly sod ought to have known that. But I had slaved for two months on the routine, and I knew I was good. Besides, in the dressing-room after the show, Noël had obviously been delighted and said that he couldn't have asked for the number to have been done better.

'What's the matter with you, dear?' The Master's voice pierced the gloom. I held up the paper.

'Oh, that gentleman. Yes, I thought that would upset you. But it's a good thing it's happened to you now. You have nothing to worry about, because the wonder-boy who wrote that is quite obviously a silly twit who knows nothing about the theatre. You must believe what I told you in the dressing-room, because I am definitely not a silly twit and I *do* know about the theatre.' He paused. 'Now listen ... when you read your first rave notice, that's the time to start worrying.'

'But why?' I said.

'Because, if you believe the good ones, you have to believe the bad ones. I've had some absolute stinkers in my time. If I'd believed them I would never have been able to walk on the stage on the second night. Of course we all like to be praised and we always pray for a good press, because, naturally, we want the show to run. But don't, repeat don't, believe them. They're not consistent anyway. People who take one paper will ring up and congratulate you on a smash hit, and the people who take another will ring up and commiserate with you because you have a disaster on your hands. I have about five people whom I trust and who know, really know, about the theatre. I listen to them, because I am sure they will give me an honest opinion even if it hurts, and sometimes it does. So, Johnny dear, press on regardless. You have a great deal of talent – if you hadn't you wouldn't be in my stunning, brilliant and in every way exquisite production.'

At Colombo we met the rest of the company, who had just arrived from England. The girls – Betty Hare, Susy Stanbridge, Noreen Hamilton (Peter Owen's wife), Dorothy James – and the pianist Ronnie Paget, a small cockney who lived with a State Express cigarette glued to the corner of his bottom lip, which flapped up and down and sprayed everyone within reach with ash as he talked. Betty Hare belonged to the famous Hare family, all marvellous touring pros (Doris, her sister, I later worked with in *Words and Music*). Betty was the sort of person one liked immediately. She had a wonderful sense of humour and was cast opposite me in the Binnie Hale part in *Mr Cinders*. Susy Stanbridge, the soubrette, was small and blonde; Noreen Hamilton, dark, pretty, and soon (although at the time none expected it) to become the *femme fatale*. Dorothy James was the experienced campaigner: an old and trusted member of the Quaints concert party, she had already completed three tours of the Far East. She also played the piano; her repertoire seemed to stop abruptly in the early 1920s. Finally, R.B. himself, who arrived minus most of his breath, because, as I was later informed by Betty Hare, when he was not rehearsing them all in a stiflingly hot saloon he was chasing them round the deck with only occasional pauses for refreshment at the ship's bar.

For the last few weeks Reggie Wingrove, our advance manager, had been conspicuous by his absence for quite long periods. We were not concerned about this, but took it for granted that he was ahead of us, fixing the arrangements for our coming dates. It was during one of the long, hot train journeys in India that the company began to suspect that all was perhaps not quite as it should be. The Quaints found themselves sharing a third-class compartment with 'the natives' and spent a memorable six hours endeavouring to avoid cooking vessels bubbling with curry that, judging by its aroma, would have burned a hole through the wooden seats, squalling children, and squirts of betel-nut juice aimed inaccurately at a spittoon by a very thin, very old Indian gentleman with one large yellow tooth.

After this character-building trek I tackled Geoffrey Salisbury, who by this time had become a firm friend, and who recently, I noticed, had not been his happy, carefree, eighteen-year-old self. I asked him point-blank why the company had been booked to travel third class when our contracts stipulated first-class travel by land and sea. Geoffrey looked thoughtfully at me for a moment, and then said, 'It's Reggie.' He paused. I let him go on. 'You know my father engaged him as an advance manager. Well he's been advancing all right, but not on our next dates, he's been advancing on the bottle. The finance is all over the bloody shop, and I've been going nearly mad trying to scrounge enough money together to pay all your salaries. And the reason we had to travel third class on the train was lack of funds to buy first-class tickets.'

'But where has Reggie been?'

'In a home drying out. I had to fix it. My ruddy old man left me in charge of the company, so it's been up to me, and I can tell you it's been bloody awful.'

He seemed relieved to be able to pour it all out. After all, eighteen is pretty young to be in charge of a company of irresponsible English actors travelling through the Far East. 'You don't know what happened on the boat after we left Naples, do you?'

'Well, I remember Reggie being ill with a temperature, and not being able to leave his cabin for a few days,' I said.

'Temperature, my arse,' said Geoffrey with a wealth of meaning. 'He was so pissed he couldn't walk.'

As far as I can remember Reggie Wingrove only had two more lapses after this. I was glad, because he was a warm, likeable man, and very popular with the company. He was very fond of Aileen, and obviously approved of our relationship, because he often went to the trouble of organizing things so that when we arrived at a new hotel we found to our delight that the accommodation had been arranged so that stealthy journeys along endless dark corridors were happily unnecessary.

If Reggie approved, Jimmy Anderson most certainly did not, and true to form expressed himself volubly. The lecture took place in my dressing-room after the show one evening. 'Is this a serious thing between you and Aileen?'

'Yes,' I said. 'Anything wrong?'

'Everything's bloody wrong. How old are you?'

'Twenty-one,' I said.

'That's what I mean. Now you listen to me: you've got a future in this bloody profession. You could go anywhere. It could easily be to the top. And there's not much room up there. Never has been. And any actor who makes it has got to be totally dedicated, and that means selfish. He should be able to say at a moment's notice, "I'm going on tour to Iceland in *Charley's Aunt* or play Hamlet in the Scunthorpe rep, or stay out of work and wash up at Lyons Corner House", while he's waiting for his big chance. His only responsibility should be to himself. I'm talking particularly about a young actor like yourself who's just starting. You haven't even got a foot in the bleedin' door yet. And anyway it's not fair on the poor ruddy girl. Do you think you've got much chance of being in the same show together again? Of course you bloody haven't. So you'd be separated for months on end. Then supposing one of you makes it, and the other doesn't. How many times do you think people can cope with that situation? I've been in the business quite a few years now and the list of marriages that have lasted is pretty damn short. I can only think of one couple at the moment who look as if they might be in for a long run, the Lunts. But you two are not the bloody Lunts. Think about it.

I did think about it, for about two seconds, then dismissed everything he had said from my mind. None of it made any sense as far as I was concerned. I could see no reason whatsoever why the idyllic state that we were living in at the moment shouldn't continue for ever. Many years later I delivered three lectures on three different occasions to my own children on the problems and dangers of getting married at too early an age in our profession. They all listened politely and took absolutely no notice.

After rehearsing the musicals during the day and playing *Journey's End*, *Young Woodley* and *Hamlet* in the evenings, the, by this time, slightly punch-drunk Quaints took to the road again. We hardly knew what town it was, what day it was or what show we were playing.

We opened with *Mr Cinders*, the first musical that was ready, in Madras. I would give a great deal to have a record on film of that production. It must have been quite hysterical. On the first night I had to make one lightning change in the wings from a dinner jacket to white flannels and a blazer in one and a half minutes flat. During this time the audience were being entertained with a big ensemble number on the downstage side of the front cloth by the full chorus, which consisted of four girls – Susie, Dorothy, Towyna, and Aileen who, although she flung herself into the routine with abandon, never seemed quite able to shed the mantle of the Queen in *Hamlet*. When the number finished, the front cloth was raised to disclose the terrace outside the house, where the family were seated at a table having breakfast. I was supposed to make my entrance through the French windows in my 'Who's for tennis?' outfit, and deliver the line, 'Good morning all. Good morning eggs, good morning bacon.' I heard the number finish, walked across the stage, frantically doing up my fly-buttons, which, because the flannels were new, was proving to be a nail-breaking operation. A sudden burst of laughter stopped me in my tracks – I looked up to discover that I was in full view of the audience; the stage hands had forgotten to put up the flat (the wall of the house) that was intended to mask me from the audience before I reached the French windows. 'Good morning eggs, good morning bacon' – not one of the greatest comedy lines – that evening brought the house down.

By the time we reached Singapore again, our repertoire was complete. It was on this second visit that a miracle took place.

7

Enter the Master

On our arrival in Singapore at the end of March we were greeted by Reggie Wingrove who looked, I was glad to see, in remarkably good shape. 'How are you feeling, Johnnie, fit?'

'Yes, pretty good,' I said. 'A bit tired, though. What are we playing tonight?'

'*Mr Cinders*,' said Reggie, 'and you'd better get yourself to Raffles, have a rest and a shower, because you've got to be on top form this evening – Noël Coward's in front.'

'So is God,' I said.

'I'm not joking. It's on the level. Noël Coward is coming to the show tonight.'

We stared at each other. Singapore, and the great man was here? How could it possibly be true?

It was an extraordinary chain of events that had resulted in Noël's presence at the opening of *Mr Cinders* in Singapore on that evening in March 1930. He had been directing his production of *Bitter Sweet* in New York, which became an overnight success. He decided to take a well-deserved break and travel home via the Far East with a great friend of his, Geoffrey Amhurst, who on arrival at Singapore was rushed straight from the ship into hospital with an acute attack of dysentery; Noël found himself stranded with two weeks to fill in before they could continue their homeward journey. On the afternoon of our arrival he was travelling past the Victoria Theatre in a rickshaw, when he saw to his amazement a bill on the front of the house which read:

TONIGHT AT 7.30

THE QUAINTS

in

HAMLET*

* *Mr Cinders* was, in fact, the play we were performing that night, but the Front of House Manager had forgotten to change the bill from our last visit. The Quaints in a musical would obviously not have seemed so weird to Coward.

This was too good to miss. What exactly did it mean? He paid off the rickshaw coolie, wandered into the box office, woke up the manager, who was enjoying his siesta, and asked him what and who were the Quaints. The manager put him in the picture. The Master, more than ever intrigued, booked a seat for the evening performance.

The Quaints were in a state of unsuppressed excitement. At that time Noël Coward was at the height of his fame. His position in the theatre was unique. His talent seemed limitless. He was a successful writer, composer, director and actor, and, incredible though it seemed, this man of magic was actually coming to see the show tonight. The tension built up during the day, and after tea I couldn't bear the inactivity any longer and took off for the theatre. I found the usual chaos. Jimmy Anderson was lighting the show and trying to drill the stage hands at the same time. There was no room on the stage to run through any of the routines so I returned to my dressing-room and 'opened up the pipes', bawling all the songs at the top of my voice. Whatever else happened, I was determined at least to be heard by the maestro. I put on my tap shoes and walloped through the numbers, which, as the room was about eight feet by four, was a fairly dangerous exercise.

I was fully made up and dressed before the call-boy had even called the half-hour. Then I heard sounds of the company arriving and Ronnie Paget in the orchestra pit running through the score with his musicians, drums, double bass, saxophone and violin. The door opened from time to time, thumbs-up signs and shouts of good luck. The Quaints were marvellous that evening: they all sensed what I was obviously going through, and they were sensitive enough to leave me to sweat it out alone.

All well-constructed plays from Shakespeare onwards have provided the star with an effective entrance, and *Mr Cinders* was no exception. The hero of the evening made a sensational entrance on roller-skates with his arms full of parcels, gliding gracefully round the stage and depositing his gifts at the feet of his beloved. I had up till now performed this not too difficult entrance without mishap. On this night of nights, however, my arrival on the stage was slightly different, but a great deal more spectacular.

I had skated halfway round the set; my speed, through my anxiety to make my first appearance impressive, was faster than usual, when the wheels of one skate caught a knot of wood (the stages in some of the theatres presented quite an obstacle course), I flew up in the air, did one complete somersault and landed heavily on my back with my left arm underneath me. No professional acrobat could have hoped for anything better, and the laugh that followed shook the Victoria Theatre to its foundations. It got me off to a flying start. Anything and everything I did after that, the audience thought was funny. I was so drunk with excitement that I didn't realize anything was wrong until I dashed off into the wings for my first quick change.

Jimmy Anderson was in the prompt corner. 'God Almighty, that was a hell of a fall. Are you all right?'

'Er, yes,' I said. '... a bit dizzy. I thought I'd broken my bloody neck.'

Jimmy was staring at my left hand. 'Your neck's OK. But what about that finger?'

I looked at my hand and suddenly felt sick. My third finger was pointing rather rudely in the wrong direction. I hadn't even felt it – I did then. Jimmy grabbed it, gave it a quick vicious pull and twist at the same time. Luckily at this moment Ronnie Paget and his boys were blowing their brains out in the orchestra pit, so that my shout of 'Oh shit!' at the top of my voice was lost before it reached the front row of the stalls. Jimmy bound a handkerchief tightly round my finger. All this had taken place while I was struggling with a quick change. 'You're OK,' said Jimmy. 'You're going great. Keep it up. They're the best bloody audience we've ever had.' He gave me a shove and on I went.

There are, happily, some rare occasions in the theatre when everything seems to go right and nothing goes wrong. That performance of *Mr Cinders* at the Victoria Theatre, Singapore, was one of them. Betty Hare and I stopped the show with 'Just A One Man Girl'. Betty was wonderful that evening; her timing was immaculate and we found laughs that had been undiscovered for weeks. At the final curtain the show got a reception that we had never experienced during the whole of the tour.

I was sitting in my dressing-room in a slightly dazed state, pouring with sweat, my finger aching like hell, thinking 'Oh well, the show went like a bomb anyway. The best it's ever gone. So he hasn't come round? The curtain's been down ten minutes. So what? It's not the end of the bloody world.' But, of course, it was nearly the end of the bloody world, because I felt that I had been good, and I knew that I'd given the best performance I had managed so far, but it obviously just wasn't good enough, and I had missed the chance of a lifetime. I reached for the remover and started to wipe off what was left of my make-up. There was a sudden knock on the door and Jimmy walked into the room, followed by a slim young man in a well-cut tropical suit. 'This is Johnnie Mills, Mr Coward.'

I stood there gaping at him with one eye full of mascara.

'Where did you learn to fall like that? Were you trained in a circus?'

'No, sir,' I managed to stutter. 'I've never done it before. It was an accident.'

'Well you'd better keep it in. A laugh like that is gold on a first entrance.'

'I don't think it's advisable, Mr Coward. You see he dislocated his finger,' Jimmy said.

'Good God, so that's what the handkerchief was for. I couldn't think what you were doing with it. Does it hurt?'

'Yes, sir,' I said. 'It didn't at the time, but now it's murder.'

'Right,' said the maestro. 'I shall go ahead to the hotel and arrange a suitable pain-killer. I've had a marvellous evening and I've asked Mr Anderson to bring the Quaints to supper. But just to keep you going I would like you to know that you were good, very, very good tonight. You can tell me all about your spectacular career later. So hurry up. Get your make-up off, slip out of your jock-strap and join us at Raffles. There's plenty of room at the bar. It's the longest in the world.'

The door closed behind them. I sat down and stared at myself in the mirror. It was some time before I could move. I needed time for it all to sink in. He *had* come backstage, and he *had* said all those things. I heard him. I wasn't dreaming. It was true. A drink at Raffles bar with Noël Coward and supper with him afterwards. The penny dropped with a thud. I made a dash for the washbasin, caught my braces in the chair and fell flat on my face.

No member of the Quaints will ever forget that evening in Singapore. To start with, we were elevated to an enviable social position – the guests of Noël Coward – that had to be the top of the ladder. At this period of his career it was difficult to pick up any top-drawer magazine like the *Bystander* or the *Tatler* without finding a photograph, an interview or a piece of gossip about our host. And here we were, the Quaints – judging by the laughter coming from our table, members of a select and much sought-after circle.

Many years later Charles Castle made a filmed biography of Noël's life in which most of the actors who had worked with him, including myself, took part. According to Mr Castle, when the last day's filming arrived and they were ready to shoot the final sequence, he asked the Master if he could make a final comment on his life's work. This is what he said, off the cuff, and people who have not had the luck and privilege to see all sides of the great man may find it perhaps not very typical: 'Sum it up? Well, now comes the terrible decision as to whether to be corny or not. The answer is one word – love. To know that you are among people whom you love and who love you. That has made all the successes wonderful, much more wonderful than they'd have been anyway. I don't think there's any more to be said than that. That's it.'

The evening in Singapore took place forty years before he made that statement, but the words were true then. He loved the theatre passionately. He loved people, particularly actors and actresses. In fact, anyone in any branch of his beloved profession was ahead in his affection to start with; and he was always happiest when he was amongst them. They were his people, and that night, with his warmth, humour, wit, encouragement and interest, without any apparent effort whatsoever, he made the Quaints his slaves for life.

The next few weeks in Singapore became an extended Midsummer Night's Dream. Mr Coward was in town and Mr Coward was inundated with invitations to luncheons and dinners in his honour. He accepted the luncheon invitations with one proviso – he would only come if he could bring his friends the Quaints. The dinner invitations he turned down. He was most awfully sorry, but he would be at the Victoria Theatre watching his friends the Quaints in their repertoire. He took us everywhere with him, including a party given in his honour at Government House.

The *Straits Times* of 26 March 1930 carried a sensational headline on its front page. In large black print it proclaimed: 'NOEL COWARD TO ACT HERE. QUAINTS' ACQUISITION. To play Stanhope in JOURNEY'S END.'

Mr Noël Coward, the noted actor, playwright and producer, and withal one of the most brilliant young men of modern times, came to the East, it will be recalled from an interview which he granted the press upon his arrival in Singapore last week, with the idea of enjoying a complete rest on a seven months' tour of the world.

As a start to his self-imposed rest-cure, he wrote what he confessed to be another 'light and superficial play' while in Shanghai, the title of which has not yet been fixed. And now Singapore's little theatrical world will be startled (and Noël Coward's hopes of a rest made less probable) with the announcement that he is to take the part of Captain Stanhope in *Journey's End*, of which R.B. Salisbury's The Quaints are to give three performances beginning next Wednesday. But it is his own fault. The decision was arrived at yesterday, and it was his own ...

I remember asking him if it was true that he hadn't decided on a title for the play he wrote in Shanghai.

'Of course it isn't true, dear. I always like to have a title to write to. But I didn't want our little friend to have it.'

'Can you tell us?' I asked.

'It's very short, and I rather like it,' said the Master. 'It's *Private Lives*.'

The facts of the write-up were true. Bruce Carfax had fallen ill with dysentery, and soon afterwards had to return to England. Edgar Owen was now playing Stanhope, and Noël asked him personally if he would mind standing down for three performances. Edgar was only too happy to oblige and took over the part of the Colonel, which was being played by an actor from the Singapore Amateur Dramatic Society who had stepped in to help us out.

Stanhope is a long and complicated part, full of army jargon and technicalities. I shall never know how he did it, but Noël was word-perfect in three days. He must have had a photographic memory. Apart from the actual lines, he had all the complicated moves and business to remember. As we were playing different shows every evening, he only had time for one run-through with the cast on the afternoon before we opened. I simply couldn't believe how calm and collected he appeared: not only was he word-perfect – I don't remember a single fluff – but he actually had the confidence to alter one or two moves that had already been set in the play.

In the last scene Raleigh dies on the bed in the dug-out. Stanhope leans over him and then walks to the dug-out steps. There is a loud rattle of machine-gun fire. Star shells illuminate the parapet above, as Stanhope walks slowly up the steps to face the barrage. At the dress rehearsal Noël, after he had played the scene, said: 'I've got an idea, Johnnie. If you think it'll work, would you like to try it out tonight?' This was one of his most endearing characteristics. He would frequently ask people in very lowly positions what they thought. It wasn't condescension. He genuinely wanted their reaction. 'Yes, of course, sir. I'm sure the scene could be improved.' I was still very much in awe of him, and had quite a problem preventing myself from jumping up and standing to attention every time he addressed me.

'Right. But before we go any further, although I find it enchanting and flattering to be addressed as sir, we are two actors working together in a play, and having watched you perform on several occasions from the front, I am delighted to have the opportunity of being on the stage with you, and I'm sure unless I pull out all the right stops at the right moment, I shall, at the drop of a tin hat, be acted right off it. And so, Johnnie dear, I think it calls for Christian names from now on.'

I stared at him. 'Well, I, I shall never forget what you've said, sir, but somehow it just doesn't seem right. After all, you are, well, I mean, well ... you're the Master.'

That title stuck. He was known as and called the Master by many people and friends who loved him throughout his career, and one of my claims to fame must be that I was the originator. When finally he was knighted, we sent him a cable which read: 'Darling Master, and about bloody time too stop Up the Quaints stop Love Johnnie and Mary.'

The Master then suggested the following alteration to the direction of the scene. After Raleigh's death, he said he thought it would be more effective if, when Stanhope reached the dug-out steps, he put on his tin hat, then instead of making his exit walked down the stage once more, leaned over Raleigh, looked at him for a moment, and then walked slowly back upstage, and without pausing, continued up the dug-out steps into oblivion. I naturally said I thought it was terrific, it would obviously make the final curtain.

We had always done excellent business with *Journey's End*, but on this unique occasion the House Full boards were outside the theatre when we arrived for a run-through that afternoon. The atmosphere in the theatre that evening was electric, and also cool – in fact, arctic. Air-conditioning had been installed since our previous visit and the system must have been slightly beyond the engineer in charge because our audience in white dinner jackets and backless evening dresses were practically frozen stiff by the end of the first act. We, on the other hand, for the first time, were comfortable in our heavyweight uniforms.

The first act went well. The adrenalin was running and Noël's first-night nerves worked for him and gave his performance all the edge and inner tensions that were an integral part of Captain Stanhope's character. The second act really took off. Noël was giving a magnificent performance. He'd sparked off vibrations like a dynamo, raising the cast to a standard I'm sure we had never attained before. My death scene finally arrived, and after the first few lines of dialogue with Captain Stanhope young Lieutenant Raleigh emitted a heartbreaking (I hoped) cry and died in the Captain's arms.

I lay there on the bed in the dug-out with my eyes closed, holding my breath so that my diaphragm wouldn't pump up and down. I sensed Stanhope rise to his feet, then heard him walk up-stage; there was a pause, the rat-tat-tat of machine guns, the footsteps returned, and I knew that, as rehearsed, he was standing at the bed giving Raleigh a last poignant look before his final exit. I was still holding my breath and had nearly reached bursting-point when suddenly I let out a piercing scream, sat bolt upright and stared at the gallant Captain, who was bare-headed – from quite a considerable height his tin hat had fallen on to the most treasured and delicate part of my anatomy.

Having come back to life in this startling fashion the gallant young lieutenant emitted another rather *sotto voce* second death-cry and collapsed again on the bed. I lay there, waiting for the laugh that I felt must come and ruin everything, but to my relief not a sound came from the audience. They were obviously so caught up with the emotion that was being generated, so held by the play, that nothing, with perhaps the exception of the theatre collapsing on their heads, would have broken the spell.

The curtain fell. The show was a riot, as it thoroughly deserved to be. Geoffrey Amhurst, who had been discharged from hospital without telling Noël, had secretly booked a seat. He said that in his opinion it was one of the best performances of the play he had ever seen, and he had seen three other productions.

The hero of the evening threw a party at Raffles. He was in tremendous form. After the orchestra had finished he took over the piano and sang and played for hours. It was 'request time', and Noël was only too eager to comply. It is quite astonishing to consider how many hits he had already to his credit by the year 1930. We listened enraptured that night in Singapore to 'Parisian Pierrot', which that divine actress Gertrude Lawrence sang in *London Calling* in 1923. Then there was a marvellous number called 'Poor Little Rich Girl' from *On With The Dance*. This had been his first authentic song hit in 1925. It had, he told us, survived a stormy career. The great impresario Charles B. Cochran wanted to throw it out of the revue during the try-out in Manchester. Noël 'fought like a steer for it', and so, luckily, did Alice Delysia, who sang it. The song stayed in and became the hit of the show. Later, Gertie Lawrence had a smash hit with it in the second *Charlot's Review* in New York. He sang the two lovely numbers from *This Year of Grace* which he wrote in 1928: 'A Room With A View' and 'Dance Little Lady'. He finally finished with the unforgettable music from *Bitter Sweet*, which he had just left playing to capacity in New York. We made him play 'I'll See You Again' over and over again. It is a number that begs to be harmonized, and the Quaints that night were in full voice. We nearly stopped the fans. I remember Noël saying to me, 'I think this one might turn out to be a nice little insurance policy for Master. Anyway I think it's delicious. Let's sing it again – in key this time.'

I have heard that number played thousands of times in various places all over the world and always loved it; but I never hear it without remembering that evening of pure magic in Singapore when we sat enthralled at the feet of the composer while he played and sang it to us.

Geoffrey Amhurst had completely recovered by this time, and he and Noël saw all our productions. In fact they did more than that, they appeared in one together. *When Knights Were Bold* had entertained audiences for years; but Noël, who was a man of extremes, hated it. This was unfortunate for Aileen, who was playing the lead; the period clothes suited her; it was 'wimple time', and as she felt she was quite good in the part she naturallly hoped the Master would think so too. Fate on that evening, however, was less than kind – in fact it was brutal. A telegram arrived at the theatre before the show addressed to Geoffrey Salisbury. It read, 'Wishing you a dismal failure, Yours roguishly, Violet Vanburgh.' He didn't need a clairvoyant to inform him who sent it.

During the second act of the play Lady Rowena is discovered walking up and down the battlements of the castle. Clashings of swords and warlike shouts off-stage inform the audience that a fight is in progress below. Lady Rowena – Aileen – strode up to the battlements, leaned over, and declaimed: 'Sir Guy is a hundred feet below fighting for my honour.' At that precise moment two very tall 'ladies of the period' with wimples, made up like dames in a pantomime, appeared from the prompt side and strolled arm-in-arm across the stage on the other side of the battlements. They were only visible from the waist up, and as they paused before their exit one of them was heard to say, 'A hundred feet, dear? A slight exaggeration, wouldn't you say? It can't possibly be more than three.' It was of course the Master with Geoffrey Amhurst in attendance. This little diversion broke up the cast and the audience, but it didn't break up Lady Rowena, who was, and rightly so, absolutely furious, and who after the show had the courage to tell the unpaid extras exactly what she thought of their performance. 'The ladies' apologized profusely and admitted that the fact that they had been silly stage-struck girls for years in no way excused them from ruining a very fine performance.

The night before he left Singapore, the Master told me to get in touch with his secretary, Lorne Lorraine, when I returned to England. He had, he said, been discussing writing some new material for a revue which C.B. Cochran was producing the following year, and he suggested it wasn't beyond the bounds of possibility that if the famous impresario considered I possessed a modicum of talent, there might be a chance of his engaging me. Later that evening, in case of loss, theft, fire or earthquake, I made six copies of the address and telephone number at which I could contact Miss Lorraine. I was taking no chances.

Our next date was Hong Kong, a lovely peaceful place, very different from the bedlam it presents today. We played for one week there. Two things remain in my memory – swimming in Repulse Bay and a certain matinee of *Hamlet*. Jimmy Anderson, in full spate, thundered out the line, 'To a nunnery go', whereupon, as if desperately anxious to obey the command, Ophelia promptly disappeared from view through the trapdoor in the stage. A Chinese stage hand had accidentally leaned against the lever and provided Towyna with the fastest and most spectacular exit she had ever made from the boards.

From Hong Kong we travelled to Shanghai, which still ranks with me as one of the most exciting cities in the world. The buildings were beautiful, the hotels luxurious and I loved the people – charming, friendly and, as there seemed to be seven washing-days in the week, spotlessly clean. It will, however, remain in my memory because of a slight accident that occurred there which could have had a quite serious consequence.

On the Monday night we opened with *Journey's End* and during the first scene I scratched the forefinger of my right hand on a rusty nail protruding from the box in the dug-out. It didn't seem serious enough to bandage so I sucked it for a second or two and got on with the show. Within forty-eight hours the finger became horribly swollen and inflamed and ached like hell. Jimmy took a look at it and said, 'Hospital right away after the show.'

The doctor was a small Japanese gentleman who inspected the finger none too gently, I thought, and then delivered the verdict: serious poisoning which could spread, and I was to stay in hospital while he treated it. The treatment had to be experienced to be believed. The small Japanese gentleman hissed good morning as he entered my room with an English nurse. Placing a tray of horrific-looking instruments beside the bed he took hold of my wrist with his left hand in an iron grip. At the same time he picked up with his right a scalpel with which he slowly made a deep incision by the side of the nail. He then picked up a pair of elongated pliers and with a quick movement picked up my finger and squeezed hard. I screamed and nearly passed out. The English nurse looked out of the window. He then shook some yellow powder into the wound which was now a horrifying suppurating mess.

This treatment continued for two days. The nurse refused to be present during the fourth treatment, as she couldn't stand any more. The patient couldn't either. I passed clean out in the middle of it. When I came to the room was empty. I was in excruciating pain, the finger was several degrees worse and there was a pronounced swelling under my armpit. I lay there as the realization dawned on me that I was in the hands of a sadist. Unless I did something, and did something quickly, I should probably lose not only my finger but my arm, or even my life. A few minutes later I was phoning the hotel. I caught Aileen as she was leaving for the theatre and poured out the whole story. There was a pause. Then her voice came over the phone: 'Now don't worry, I'll be at the hospital as soon as the curtain drops, and I'll bring Jimmy with me. But don't tell anyone. Just get back into bed and ask the nurse to bring you some aspirin for the pain and a sedative to make you sleep. But don't take it, the sedative, I mean. Must rush. See you soon.'

I did as I was ordered, swallowed the aspirin and palmed the sedative. I had no problems keeping awake. The pain by this time was almost unbearable. Just after midnight the door opened slowly and Aileen appeared. She put her finger to her lips, moved silently to the cupboard and bundled my clothes into a small suitcase. Then, after a struggle (by this time I could hardly move my arm) she got me into a dressing-gown. I felt light-headed and strange. I swayed slightly and thought, 'Oh God, I'm going to pass out again.' She looked at me, sat me gently down on the bed and said, 'Hang on darling. Just a few more minutes. We're going to get you out of here. Jimmy is ear-bashing the night nurse, offering her tickets for the matinee, and while he's keeping her occupied in the Matron's office we're going to slip down the fire escape. I've got a taxi waiting at the rear of the hospital. OK? Ready?'

The great escape worked perfectly, and in under half an hour I was back in my bedroom at the Majestic Hotel with an English doctor in

ABOVE LEFT My mother and father before I knew them

ABOVE RIGHT Myself at the age of six months, eagerly searching for the lens

BELOW LEFT Me and my dog Rover

BELOW RIGHT As Puck, when I was at St John Leeman School, Beccles

End-of-term production at Norwich House. I'm centre stage again.
Mr Chapman ('Cheese'), the headmaster, is on the left

BELOW LEFT In Peking, 1928. BELOW RIGHT The Quaints in Quetta, 1928: (*left to right*) Peter Owen, Chubby Salew, Ronald Brantford, Bruce Carfax, James Grant Anderson and me

With Aileen in the Far East. ABOVE RIGHT Rehearsing 'Ready For The River' cabaret disaster, 1929

On the beach with Doris Hare in Noël Coward's *Words and Music*, Adelphi Theatre, 1932

LEFT 'I'm On A Seesaw' with Louise Browne, *Jill Darling*, Saville Theatre, 1934

BELOW LEFT Able Seaman Brown in *Brown on Resolution*, 1934

ABOVE RIGHT With Frances Day in *Floodlight*, Saville Theatre, 1938

RIGHT Me as Marlow in *She Stoops To Conquer* with Ursula Jeans, Old Vic Season 1938–9

LEFT As George in *Of Mice and Men*, Apollo Theatre, 1939

ABOVE The girl I took to The Boy and Donkey in 1939. BELOW LEFT Sapper J. Mills 1400808, Royston, 4 September 1939. BELOW RIGHT With my sister Annette

2nd Lt J. Mills married Mary Hayley Bell (his tennis partner in Tientsin in 1928) on 16 January 1941

attendance. He carefully unwrapped the bandage from my finger. 'Good God Almighty,' he said. I glanced at it and nearly threw up. The stench was indescribable. I was slowly but surely going rotten.

'All right young man, there's only one remedy for that finger: the old-fashioned hot poultice, hotter than you can stand. I'll stay and start you off with the first two, then if you want him to keep that finger' – he looked at Aileen – 'and it's quite possible you do, you must keep that poulticing up every hour all through the night. And I'll be here at eight in the morning, OK?'

Within a week I was back on the stage with a heavily bandaged finger, but fit. And the only memento I have of that drama in Shanghai is a slightly deformed right forefinger which, because it is not quite so elegant as its companions, I take pains to conceal whenever I have to hold a book or any other object in a close-up.

From Shanghai we travelled eight hundred miles up the Yangtse river to Hangkow, and after Hangkow we invaded Tientsin. It was here that the Quaints were invited to tea and tennis by a striking character called Colonel Hayley Bell. The Colonel held a position which suited him perfectly: he was Commissioner of Chinese Maritime Customs. This job had nothing to do with chalking boxes; it entailed his being responsible for keeping down smuggling, gun-running and piracy. Amongst other things under his command was a gun-boat standing by for instant action, of which, to the Colonel's delight, there was plenty.

The house was beautiful. I had never seen such grandeur – white pillars, high ceilings, cool marble floors. The place appeared to be a veritable rabbit warren of servants: the Number One boy in white, the Number Two boy in blue, the nanny amah, the laundry amah, the all-purpose amah, the cook, her two ADCs and four rickshaw coolies. I felt as if I'd wandered into the second act of *The Mikado*. The garden, or rather gardens, were a mass of flowers and flowering creepers. The tennis court was hidden discreetly behind a tall hedge of feathery bamboos.

Colonel Hayley Bell introduced us to his wife and two daughters – one was tall, thin, elegant, her name was Winifred; and the other was quite small, with a slim boyish figure and the most marvellous golden-red hair that framed a beautiful, delicately shaped pale little face from which two enormous green eyes stared at me. I remember thinking, 'You ought to be on a wire, you'd make the most sensational Peter Pan.' The Colonel's voice interrupted this brilliant piece of instant casting. 'And this is my eldest daughter, Mary. This is John Mills. We saw him play Mr Cinders last night.'

'How do you do,' I said.

'How do you do,' she said.

I wish I could report some memorable, unforgettable lines that were spoken at this momentous meeting, but honesty forbids any romantic exaggeration. I do remember, however, having a feeling that I'd met this strange little person somewhere before.

If I am offered wine cup at a party my heart sinks slightly, and I am inclined to enquire in a rather timid voice if there just happens to be a tiny drop of whisky, gin or vodka in the vicinity. Sweet hock, which has had any excitement and stimulation removed by the addition of pints of soda water and handfuls of mushy strawberries, cherries and slices of cooking apples, does absolutely nothing for me. The Colonel's cup, however, belonged to another world. He wouldn't divulge the secret recipe, but the result was nothing short of sensational. It tasted like a drink you would happily serve in the nursery but it had a kick like several army mules, and after quaffing several large glasses of this delicious concoction the Quaints were, as they misguidedly thought, ready for tennis.

I strode on to the court, correctly attired in my Mr Cinders second act outfit, feeling fairly confident. We spun for partners and I found myself lumbered with the golden-haired midget. 'Oh well,' I thought, 'I can carry her. Someone's got to play with her. She can hardly see over the net.'

'I'll serve first,' I said firmly. 'And you stay at the net. Leave the base line to me.' I threw the ball up high with my left hand, looked up, saw six, made a mighty swipe at them, and missed the lot. 'Heavens,' I thought, 'the wine cup or the Colonel's revenge!' I pulled myself together, threw the next ball up and this time I hit it – hard. It landed with a loud thwack on the small bottom of Peter Pan who was, as ordered, standing facing our opponents at the net.

The match proceeded. We beat our opponents by six games to two. During the contest I think I managed to strike the ball about six times, mostly into the net. My partner, however, was quite incredible. She realized during the first game that her partner, the gallant young Thespian, had become another victim of her father's brew, and took the game into her own hands. She left the net and covered the court. She seemed to be everywhere at once. I frequently saw six of her. She moved like lightning, served like a demon and got everything back. She was so wonderful to watch I forgot to feel mortified and just wandered about the court in an alcoholic haze, trying not to get in her way.

Later, over China tea and cucumber sandwiches, I remarked to the Colonel what a splendid tennis-player his daughter was. He looked across the lawn to where she was standing with some of the company. Her head was thrown back and I heard that delicious laugh again. 'Muggins? Yes, she's pretty good, isn't she? As a matter of fact she's good at all games. She's what one might call a natural. There's a very good chance that she will be picked to play lacrosse for England next term.'

'Really,' I said. 'That's terrific!'

'Yes,' said my host, 'but you know she doesn't really care about it. It's not important to her. All she really cares about is the theatre.'

'Do you mean she wants to be an actress?'

The Colonel nodded. 'Yes,' he said. 'She's a very determined young lady. If she sets her heart on something it usually happens.'

I looked across at my tennis partner again. 'Oh Lord,' I thought, 'what chance do you think you've got? Thousands of girls want to become actresses. They only see the glamour of it from the outside and haven't the remotest idea just how rough, tough and sometimes brutal the inside can be.'

'Well, sir, if that's what she really wants, I hope she makes it. It's a marvellous profession, if, of course, you're willing to take the chance of starving to death.'

We said goodbye to the Hayley Bell family with the usual farewell 'hands across the sea' remarks: 'The best afternoon we've had since we left home', 'We really enjoyed ourselves.' As I shook the hand of the aspiring young actress I thanked her for her support on the court and said that I hoped I should have the pleasure of meeting her again in England one day. But as I said it I thought, 'Idiotic, what chance do you think there is? It's a million-to-one shot, especially as she'll never make the theatre.' Time did not take very long to prove me totally wrong on both counts.

We left China with regret and worked our way back to Bombay where, after playing a farewell week of the musical, the ladies of the company were dispatched home by boat. The men were to take *Journey's End* on a quick tour of the hill stations, which the management hoped would ensure the tour's ending up showing a profit. We watched their ship disappear into the distance. Edgar Owen stood beside me on the quay biting hard on his pipe. I wished I could have borrowed it, to save my bottom lip. I suddenly felt rather like the small boy who waved goodbye to his mother in Beccles all those years ago. Home seemed and was miles away.

The heroes of *Journey's End*, deprived of their female companions, wandered back, a forlorn little company, to the Taj Mahal Hotel, and as one man headed straight for the bar. Several burra-pegs later I felt I stood a reasonable chance of surviving the dangers and rigours of the hill stations and returning in triumph to England, home and beauty.

I had not really enjoyed the plains of India, but the hill stations seemed to belong to another and in every way more desirable country. The climate was lovely – gone was the depressing damp heat of the monsoons – and the scenery was breathtaking. We played Lahore, Quetta, Simla, Poona and Rawalpindi. This final leg of the tour, which we were dreading as a possible anti-climax, turned out to be a social riot. Any new faces were always welcome in these remote strongholds of the Empire, but when the faces belonged to actors who had made the trip especially to entertain them their hospitality assumed almost dangerous proportions. An Indian dawn has a delicacy, a refinement of colour unparalleled in any other part of the world. I can claim to be an authority on the subject, as there were parties given for us every night after the show, and I didn't miss one of them for six weeks.

I think perhaps Simla stays in my mind as the most beautiful of all. We lived in a small hotel which commanded a view of the snow-capped Himalayas. The CO of the regiment lent us his polo ponies, and Edgar Owen and I rode out every morning into the mountains, or, to be more exact, he rode and I sat in the saddle hanging on to the pommel while he led my charger with a bridle rein. As my only previous mount had been a beach pony at Gorleston-on-Sea I found the experience nerve-racking but enthralling. My horse, realizing straight away that he had a novice on board, managed with no apparent difficulty to unseat me four times in the first half-hour. But each time I climbed back into the saddle, I felt a greater affinity with the animal beneath me. I was hooked from that morning on.

Our last date on the hill-station circuit was undoubtedly the most unusual and exciting: Landi Khotal, at the top of the famous Khyber Pass. We boarded a train that boasted carriages like cattle-trucks and started on the slow crawl up the pass. After an hour travelling through the barren, rocky landscape, our engine emitted a painful, slightly effeminate wheeze, and promptly stopped in its tracks. An Indian guard told us the repairs would take about an hour; so we unglued ourselves from the wooden seats and climbed down into the shade. After a few minutes I saw a dozen or so small figures approaching from a distance, some on horseback and some on foot. They continued until they were about thirty yards or so from us and then came to a halt. They all carried rifles and were dressed in a superb assortment of 'props'. They looked like a bunch of Mexican extras in an early Hollywood Western.

'Who are they?' I asked the guard who, I noticed, was staring rather anxiously at them, and then switching his look to the horizon on the other side of the train.

'Not very nice, not very happy, sahib, not most friendly persons, you see, brigands you see, and they wait for some other not friendly people to fight at. It is important we repair quickly and continue, you see.' He shifted his gaze to the other side of the tracks. I looked and saw another group, obviously the opposing team, emerge from behind some boulders and converge on us from the opposite side of the train. There was an ominous quiet. The new group came to a halt and stood motionless, gazing across the track at the first arrivals. Hoping to prove that we were merely a band of happy, friendly travellers, I stood up and waved my hat in their direction. There was a sharp crack, a high-pitched whine, and a bullet smacked into the woodwork a few inches above my Simon Artz special solar topee.

'I don't like the look of this at all. Everybody back in the train, quick,' said J.G.A. Before he'd finished speaking all hell broke loose. The Mexican extras were not using blanks and the Quaints cowered, face down, on the floor of the carriage, while bullets flew under the train, through the windows and between the shafts. We were providing excellent cover for both sides. After a few minutes that seemed like an eternity we felt the train get under way and gradually gather speed. Green with fright the gallant Quaints remained prone until the firing receded into the distance.

The ADC was waiting to welcome us at the station: 'Hallo chaps, glad to see you. The CO sends his compliments and is looking forward to seeing you at a party in the mess before the show. Good journey?'

'Terrific,' said Jimmy, 'by far the most interesting one so far on the tour.' On the way to the barracks he told the ADC what had happened. The management had made it a rule that the company should not accept invitations to parties before the performance, but rules are made to be broken and on this occasion it was not only broken but smashed into fragments. Pale and visibly shaken by their ordeal the Quaints knocked back burra-pegs as if the bottles of Scotch in the mess were the only ones left in the world. Before the sun was over the yard-arm the heroes of *Journey's End* were well over the eight.

The performance that evening was, as can be imagined, slightly more exuberant than usual. The drill-hall was packed to the roof. The CO ordered the guard to be changed twelve times in the two hours, so that every soldier on the strength had a chance of seeing at least some of the show. In the de-lousing scene, Jimmy, playing Trotter, after scratching himself under the armpit, had the line, 'Ah, bugs I see.' On this night of nights, he scratched his crutch and came up with, 'Ah, crabs I see.' It stopped the show. A young subaltern fell out of his chair in the front row and the laugh went on for several minutes. After that it was a free-for-all. The party after the show went on till dawn, which was greeted with bacon and eggs and pints of cold lager. They poured us on to the train at eight in the morning. We waved until the crowd of khaki figures disappeared from view. After two hours of jolting about in the cattle-truck the warning signs of a gigantic hangover appeared. I fingered the stubble on my chin and licked my dry lips. Geoffrey Salisbury nudged my arm. 'Feeling a bit rough?'

'Mmm . . .' was all I could manage.

'How about a heart-starter?' He reached under the seat and produced a rucksack which contained some cold bottles of beer. 'The ADC gave me these. He said they were a survival kit for the journey.'

A few minutes later the silent, subdued band of strolling players were back to noisy normal. It was unanimously agreed that Landi Khotal would remain in our memories as one of the high spots of the tour. We gave a final performance of *Journey's End* in Karachi and sailed for home the following day.

8

London Calling

I walked down the gangplank, stepped ashore at Tilbury Docks and experienced for the first time the joy and excitement of returning home. 'An Englishman's home is his castle', but on that crystal-clear early morning 'an Englishman's home was England'. I made a decision I would never leave my country for so long a period again. I never have. During the past fifty years I have spent a great deal of time working abroad, but never for more than eight months at a time. After about six months, however lucrative the job and pleasant the surroundings and friends have been, I have always felt this desperate itch to get back home; with all its problems, strikes, go-slows, inflation, unemployment, crippling taxation, traffic jams and its maddeningly fickle climate, it is the only country in the world I can happily live in.

What you lose on the roundabouts you gain on the swings. The fact that my father had decided to desert the family nest permanently gave me two hero's-return parties – one at 75 Walcot Square and the other with my mother and all the little maiden aunts at Felixstowe. Both camps, to my surprise and embarrassment, were agreed on one issue: they were opposed, and quite vociferously, to the young Far-Eastern romance. I decided to cool things down by moving temporarily to my old friend George Posford's flat in town as a paying guest. The first thing I did after installing myself and my possessions (all of which fitted comfortably into two suitcases) was, with some trepidation, to dial the telephone number that Noël Coward had given me in Singapore. 'I'm awfully sorry to bother you,' I said, 'but Mr Coward very kindly suggested that I should ring him when I got back from the Far East. My name is John Mills.'

'Oh, I know about you. Mr Coward has told me about the marvellous time he had with you all in Singapore. Have you recovered from that slight accident that happened during the first night of *Journey's End*?' She laughed. I laughed too, with relief. He *had* remembered. Even talked about it.

'My name's Lorne Lorraine. I know he would like to talk to you, he's writing . . . but hold on a minute . . .'

It seemed like ten. Then her voice said, 'Mr Coward says he can't break off now, but if you can get to the box office at the Phoenix Theatre tonight without any serious accident you will find a seat waiting for you, and will you please go round and see him after the show, even if you don't approve of his performance.'

Private Lives, 'the little, light and superficial play' that the Master had written in Shanghai before he joined the Quaints in Singapore, had taken London by storm. It opened the Phoenix Theatre in Charing Cross Road; the house was sold out for three months. The avalanche of advance bookings no doubt had something to do with the fact that the author had stated quite firmly, before they opened, that he would only play in it himself for three months.

There have been a few evenings in the theatre which have stood out vividly in my memory: that evening at the Phoenix was one of them. It was pure magic. *Private Lives* was an example of what can happen in the theatre if all the ingredients for success are mixed with experience, love and care. The result was a well-constructed, beautifully written comedy, directed with impeccable taste and brilliantly acted by exactly the right cast: Noël Coward, Gertrude Lawrence, Laurence Olivier and Adrienne Allen. I've seen the play performed many times by excellent actors and actresses since that night, but none of them have quite been able to compete with the original cast. Noël had written the main parts for himself and Gertie Lawrence: the chemistry was perfect.

After the show I suddenly felt nervous. It was a long time since I'd seen the maestro, and Singapore – that was something different. What would the king be like in his own country? I needn't have worried; he welcomed me like an old friend. 'Well, Johnnie, dear, did you enjoy it? And what about my performance? Did you approve of it?'

Something clicked inside my head and I found myself saying, 'Yes, I did. In fact it was so good I really think you ought to take it up professionally.'

He stared at me with a slightly surprised look, and then roared with laughter. I realized I had stumbled on the key; the Master was in such an exalted position at that time that all the younger generation of actors were naturally in awe of him. I decided to be as reverently irreverent as possible, without over-stepping the mark. It worked. I made him laugh. That evening saw the start of a close friendship that would last as long as he lived.

'Well Johnnie, dear, the profession is just the teeniest bit over-crowded, but if you really think my performance deserves some compensation I'll have a word with the management. Any profound thoughts on the rest of the cast?'

One joke's enough, I thought. Don't press your luck. I said I considered that Gertrude Lawrence was the most exciting and glamorous actress I'd ever seen.

'What about Laurence Olivier?' The author was obviously enjoying the learned critic's opinions.

'Well,' I said, 'I couldn't believe that anyone as good-looking as that could be such a rivetingly good actor.'

'I'll tell you something: with my unmatched, priceless perception and without the aid of a crystal ball, in my much-sought-after opinion that young man, unless something goes radically wrong, will, before long, be acknowledged as our greatest actor.'

During the tour with the Quaints I had from time to time sent Vincent Earne, my agent, press-cuttings from the shows I'd appeared in. I very naturally made sure he would only read the good ones; the bad ones were torn up and dismissed from everything except my mind. The carefully culled collection would, I was sure, impress upon Mr Earne that he had under his wing a young actor of enormous potential who, guided by his experienced hand, would provide his office with a handsome income for an indefinite period of time. My confidence was justified. Mr Earne had obviously been impressed, because when I phoned his office and asked the secretary if I could see my agent that afternoon, after only a few minutes' delay she informed me that Mr Earne would be available at three o'clock.

Mr Earne was not only available, but full of charm. He congratulated me on a successful tour and informed me that auditions were being held at the New Theatre in two weeks' time for the annual revival of that most famous of all farces, *Charley's Aunt*. He felt, he said, that after playing three big comedy parts with the Quaints I should ask the management if I could read for the leading role, Lord Fancourt Babberley, the young undergraduate who impersonates Charley's aunt. He pointed out that for years this part had been played by tried comedians who by no stretch of the imagination would pass as undergraduates, and that the management might consider it a new and bold step to engage an actor who would look the right age for a student at the university.

I procured a copy of the play from French's, worked hard on two of the big comedy scenes and by the time the audition arrived I was not only word-perfect but had worked out some original and, I hoped, funny 'business'. It payed off: I was engaged to play Babberley in *Charley's Aunt* at the New Theatre in St Martin's Lane at the handsome salary of £15 per week plus star billing, my name in lights outside the theatre, rehearsals to start in two weeks' time and the show to open on 22 December. I floated home that night on a cloud.

Charley's Aunt, played in the right way and at the right time of year, namely the Christmas holidays, is and always has been a cast-iron cert. It is a well-constructed piece which grandchildren and grandparents can be taken to with no fear of embarrassment. The cast of the 1930 production was a good one – Ernest Holloway, a fine character actor, played Stephen Spettigew; Colonel Sir Francis Chesney was, as the notices proclaimed, 'in the capable hands of Mr Arthur P. Bell, who was renewing his acquaintance with the character'; Donna Lucia D'Alvadorez was played by Elizabeth Vaughan; and Lord Fancourt Babberley's two friends, Jack Chesney and Charles Wickham, were in the hands of Arthur Bradford and Patrick O'Moore. The latter became a very close friend and I am happy to say has remained one over the past half-century. Patrick was a good-looking young Irish actor with a huge sense of humour, which he had great trouble controlling during some of the slightly cornier scenes of the comedy. We laughed uproariously and drank immoderately.

I occupied the star dressing-room at the New Theatre. Compared to some of the hot little hat-boxes that masqueraded as dressing-rooms in some of the West End theatres, my room at the New was like a glamorous suite at the Ritz. I was devoted to it, and spent hours there. I was always the first to arrive at the theatre and the last to leave it. When the firemen appeared to lock the dressing-rooms I usually wandered back on to the empty stage, illuminated only by a pilot light which cast mysterious shadows back to the dock doors. After all the activity and noise of the performance the silence was intense, and it needed little imagination to conjure up the voices of the great actors of the past, the music of the orchestras and the applause echoing round the auditorium.

Not long ago an old friend of mine, Sir Ralph Richardson, was asked the question that columnists have been repeatedly asking across the years: 'Which do you enjoy most – acting in the theatre or the studios?' Sir Ralph paused for quite some time before answering. This pause can be quite disconcerting, because during it he fixes the questioner with a thoughtful, deliberate gaze which is inclined to put a fledgling interviewer right off his stroke.

'Well,' said the great man, 'you see it's like this: when the curtain drops after the play I stroll back to my dressing-room, take off my stage clothes, put on my dressing-gown and remove my make-up. Friends usually appear who have seen the performance and we have a drink or two and chat for a while. They leave, then I dress myself, walk back to the stage, wander about for a while and then leave the theatre. That process I have just described usually takes the best part of an hour. Now, er, when I'm working in the film studios, the moment the first assistant says "It's a wrap, boys", meaning we are finished for the day, as I walk across the set I undo my tie, and by the time I arrive at my dressing-room I am half undressed, in another two minutes I am seated on my motor-cycle leaving for home ... do you think that answers your question, dear boy ?'

I enjoyed every moment of the short Christmas season in *Charley's Aunt*. We played to capacity houses and I went through my baptism of fire with the enthusiastic, noisily uncontrolled audiences of children at the matinees. The critics had been more than kind, and my first batch of West End notices were all I could have asked for. Critics like nothing more than discovering new actors. It is later on in an actor's career that the going can become rough. Performances, however good, tend to be accepted as a matter of course. I spent a memorable evening in Hollywood in 1947 with Spencer Tracy, who, in my opinion, was just about the best screen actor I ever saw. As actors do, we talked until the early hours about the problems of the theatre and acting. The subject of criticism came up, and I remember Spence saying rather ruefully that, for years, critics seemed to have become rather bored with him because the notices invariably read: 'And Mr Spencer Tracy gives another of his solid per-formances.'

Charley's Aunt was due to close at the end of January. There had been no more communication from Miss Lorraine, and I began rather anxi-ously to look round for another job. February is not the happiest or easiest month in the theatre to land one. As I was leaving George Posford's flat one morning the phone rang in the hall. I picked it up and a female voice said, 'Can I speak to John Mills please?'

'You certainly can. This is the great actor in person,' I said facetiously. 'What can I do for you?'

'This is Lorne Lorraine, and if the great actor could spare a moment, Mr Noël Coward would like to have a word with him.'

I nearly dropped the phone. After a few moments a well-known voice said, 'Is that that awful common little actor I played with in *Journey's End* in Singapore? I hear you're marvellous in *Charley's Aunt*, but wild horses couldn't drag me to it. I played Jack in it years ago. It's a dreadful part and I was dreadful in it, and the play, dear, as far as I'm concerned, is a dreadful bore. Have you anything in view when it's finished?'

'No, not a thing,' I said.

'Well, you may have now. I've arranged an audition for you with C.B. Cochran. Can you be at His Majesty's Theatre at eleven in the morning?'

'Absolutely,' I said, excitement rising.

'Right, well take along some music and your tap shoes, a pianist will be there. If Mr Cochran agrees with me that you are not entirely devoid of talent, he may engage you for his new revue. I've written some numbers for it. I've had a word with him, but now it's entirely up to you. Let me know how it goes. Good luck, Johnnie dear.'

I arrived at His Majesty's Theatre the next morning at 10.30. The stage door keeper is a very important person; he practically owns the theatre. He wields a great deal of power from his sentry box, and is treated with great respect by all the casts that pass by his domain. He sees managements come and go, plays that run and plays that flop. There are several of these stalwarts in the West End who have been at the same theatre for over forty years. The guardian of His Majesty's at that time was a small, cockney gentleman with a large 'old Bill' moustache that reached from his nose to his chin, from the middle of which protruded a meerschaum pipe which, judging by its nut-brown colour, must have given its owner many hours of pleasure. I approached him rather tentatively, and asked if it would be possible for me to go on the stage and limber up as I was auditioning at eleven for Mr Cochran.

'Yes, of course, sir. I'll come down and switch the working light on for you.' That 'sir' helped a lot. I was already beginning to feel desperately nervous.

The stage at His Majesty's was empty except for a small upright piano on the prompt side. After some of the theatres I had acted in it seemed like the Royal Albert Hall. I had decided to do the hit number from *Mr Cinders* – 'Just A One Man Girl', an easy song to sing with a lovely melody. I ran through this a couple of times and then went through the two choruses of soft-shoe and tap which I had put together with what I hoped would be a smash finish – a series of bucks and wings performed at double time over the last eight bars. I looked at my watch, realized that it was nearly eleven o'clock, and that no other actors had appeared. At that moment a large gentleman arrived on the stage, introduced himself as the pianist, and suggested I might like to put him in the picture as far as routine was concerned. I hadn't quite finished explaining the various tempos when a voice from the front of the house said, 'Mr Cochran's here now. If you're ready, could you begin please?'

The footlights were switched on. I walked down stage centre, filled my diaphragm, nodded to the pianist and started the vocal. All seemed to be going reasonably well; nerves made one top C slightly vibrato; I left it to take care of itself and pressed on to the end of the chorus. I went into the soft-shoe arrangement, then straight into the tap routine. All was going well. I was relaxed by this time, and the beats were clear and staccato. Then to my consternation the tempo changed to double time, eight bars too soon. I made frantic efforts to keep up with the pianist but he was gaining all the time. In a last desperate attempt to get even with him, during the bucks and wings I caught one foot behind the other, crashed to the stage and missed falling head-first into the orchestra pit by about six inches. I lost the race by two clear bars. As I struggled to my feet I thought to myself, 'You've not only lost the race, you've lost the bloody job. Why on earth when you were given the chance didn't you say you weren't quite ready and would like to run through with the pianist once more?'

In the silence I limped across and leaned on the piano. I had sprained an ankle which was already beginning to throb. A voice came across the footlights: 'Thank you very much.'

I'd heard that sentence too many times before. It was always followed by, 'We'll let you know', which meant you were out.

'Thank you, sir,' I said, and picked up my music.

'If you haven't broken your leg and find it possible to walk could you please come down into the stalls, Mr Cochran would like to talk to you.'

I stared out into the darkness. I could hardly believe what I'd heard. When I reached the stalls a man was waiting beside the pass door. 'I'm Frank Collins, Mr Cochran's manager,' he said quietly. 'I'm going back to the office. Don't look so scared, he won't bite.' He winked at me and disappeared.

Sitting in the front row of the stalls was Charles B. Cochran, the most important and successful impresario of the time. I saw a small man, elegantly dressed in a dark grey, beautifully cut suit, a light fawn double-breasted waistcoat, highly polished shoes and grey spats. A red carnation completed the picture. He had an impressive face, a strong square jaw, bright intelligent eyes, and he wore his hair parted neatly in the middle. On the seat beside him was a brown bowler hat, a pair of gloves and a black cane with a heavy silver knob mounted on the end of it. The great man looked at me and smiled. 'Do you make a habit of nearly killing yourself to get a job?'

'I don't think so, sir,' I stuttered.

'Well, I think you do. Mr Coward described to me your startling entrance in *Mr Cinders* at the Victoria Theatre in Singapore. Now I have another appointment at the Coliseum in a few minutes, so come along with me; we can discuss our business in the car. Can you walk?'

'Yes of course. Thank you sir.' Who needed feet? I floated out of His Majesty's Theatre on air.

When I stepped out of the car at the Coliseum I had been engaged to appear in Cochran's new show *The 1931 Revue* at a salary of £15 per week; rehearsals to start shortly. The show was to open at the Palace Theatre, Manchester, on 18 February, with a West End première at the London Pavilion towards the end of March. I hobbled up St Martin's Lane and stopped outside the New Theatre. If the 1930s go on like this, I thought, they're just going to be too good to be true.

The West End theatres were full of stars – Fay Compton and Frances Lederer in *Autumn Crocus* at the Lyric, that delicious French actress

Yvonne Arnaud in *And So To Bed* at the Globe, Owen Nares and Isobel Jeans in *Counsel's Opinion* at the Strand and John Mills (whom nobody had ever heard of) in *Charley's Aunt* at the New. I looked up at my billing. 'It may be a long time before you're in that position again,' I said to myself. 'That's just a lucky flash in the pan, so don't let it go to your head. You may need a large magnifying glass to find your name on the next bill, but at any rate you'll still be in the West End.'

I walked through the stage door, told my friend Charlie, the stage door keeper, the good news, and asked him to get hold of the theatre doctor – the ankle was swollen and painful by this time I knew that to get through the matinee I would need it strapped up. I made two phone calls – one to Aileen and one to my benefactor.

The cast that Cochran had assembled for his new revue was impressive. Ada May, the leading lady, was a small attractive actress with a wonderful voice; she was one of America's top musical stars. He also brought over from the United States two hilarious slapstick comics, Clark and McCulloch, at that time the most successful double act in American variety. They were not strangers to this country though, since several of their short comedy films had already been seen in our cinemas. The supporting cast included George Melville Cooper, straight from his brilliant performance as Lieutenant Trotter in *Journey's End*: Henry Mollison, the youngest member of the famous Mollison family (Bill Mollison his elder brother was a very successful producer and Clifford was already an established musical comedy star); a young actor, Anthony Pélissier (the son of the famous Harry Pélissier, founder of the Pélissier Follies which were an institution in the London theatre before World War I); Fay Compton; and Bernardi, a superb character with a north-country accent you could cut with a knife and a fantastic tenor voice. Until he changed his name to Bernardi, he informed me, he never got a chance to open his trap.

I found to my delight when the scripts were handed out at the first rehearsal that I had a very interesting selection of parts: an old man of seventy-five, a young 'property boy' in a sketch with the comics, and several trios, including one of Noël's – a very funny number called 'Three Suburban Fathers'. Cochran had at that time a staggering record of success. Everything he touched turned to gold, and, like all his previous casts, we felt confident that we should not have to look for another job for at least nine months. This feeling of security tempted Henry Mollison to have the small house he owned in West Drayton completely redecorated, and George Melville Cooper to buy a large, expensive flat. I wasn't quite so reckless, but I did order a dinner jacket and two suits.

Like most dress rehearsals ours was fairly chaotic, but nobody gave it a thought; the old theatrical adage is 'bad dress rehearsal means good first night'. Mr Cochran was in front, and after the rehearsal Frank Collins came back stage with some personal notes for the cast. Bernardi's is the only one that has stayed in my memory. Bernardi had a number in the show entitled 'City, Why Are You Casting This Spell On Me?' which he sang in a rather strange, futuristic setting with skyscrapers apparently about to topple on his head. The costume designer had decided to dress Bernardi as a harlequin – from the waist down he was encased in red silk tights. Nature had been over-generous with our tenor amidships – his appendage was known by envious male members of the cast as 'the pride of the profession'. Frank Collins said: 'Mr Bernardi, Mr Cochran is delighted with the way you are singing the number, but he does feel that unless you wear a jock strap the audience may not be able to pay full attention to the lyrics.'

'But Mr Collins,' said Bernardi in his full-blooded Lancashire accent, 'I was wearing one. I've got it on now, packed with brown paper!'

Frank Collins's face was a study. His glance dropped a few inches. 'I see, Bernardi,' he said. 'I'll tell Mr Cochran, but he's really quite concerned. He may suggest an operation.'

The opening night at the Palace Theatre, Manchester, was a sensational success. Ada May stopped the show twice with two numbers that Noël had written for her, 'Half-Caste Woman' and 'Any Little Fish'. Clark and McCulloch were a riot. The notice in the *Manchester Evening News* of 19 February, by their critic Roderick Random, said: 'It would be the poorest compliment one could offer him to say that Mr C.B. Cochran, whose revue was produced at the Palace Theatre last night, had "done it again", for he has done nothing of the sort. On the contrary, he has done something entirely new and has done it brilliantly.'

All our hopes were confirmed. We were, without doubt, heading for a triumph in London and at least a year's run. During the four weeks at the Playhouse the show was tightened and polished. The Master appeared several times and announced himself delighted; he also gave an ex-Quaints party at the Midland Hotel.

Overflowing with confidence we opened at the London Pavilion in the middle of March. Any first night in those days was an occasion, but a Cochran first night was rather like a Royal Command Performance: anyone who was anyone just had to be there. The stalls were ablaze with diamonds, tiaras, white ties and tails. Dinner jackets were allowed, but they were in a minority and usually banished to the back rows in front of the pit.

We were kept so busy during the first half, tearing in and out of wigs and struggling with the quick changes, that we didn't really have time to get the feel of the audience. Ada May's first number went well, and so did our comedy trio 'Three Suburban Fathers', but I sensed that Clark and McCulloch didn't seem to be going down quite as well as they had in Manchester.

The sketch that I was looking forward to came halfway through the second half of the show. Clark was playing an actor in a third-rate touring company rehearsing a thriller. I was the property boy who ruined his performance by always appearing with the wrong props. I had, brilliantly, I thought, decided to play this character with a Suffolk accent. The scene had been greatly applauded in Manchester and I was hoping for the same reception in the West End. It seemed that my hopes were going to be justified: all my lines and business were going as well if not better than they had done on the road. When I made my last exit I received to my delight a round of applause. Henry Mollison was standing in the wings. I whispered to him, 'Henry, listen. I've got a round.' He looked at me with a rather strange expression on his face. 'Well listen again,' he said, 'that's not a round, that's the slow hand-clap. They're getting the bird. That's what they're getting, the bloody bird!' It was only too true – the slow, rhythmic clapping went on insistently for about half a minute, and then stopped. Clark and McCulloch finished the sketch in dead silence.

The curtain fell. The full company assembled on stage for the curtain call. What followed was one of the most painful experiences I have ever been through in the theatre. The smartest audience in the world just sat there; hardly any applause filtered across the footlights. Our experienced stage manager had had the sense to announce before the curtain fell that there would be no single calls, so the full company stood shoulder to shoulder and bowed to tiny, frantic bursts of applause from their relations and friends. The rest was silence.

The notices the next morning left us in no doubt: we were obviously not going to enjoy a long run in another Cochran triumph. We did not, however, realize the extent of the disaster until the following afternoon when Mr Cochran addressed the cast in the theatre. The box office bell, he informed us, was depressingly silent, and he felt the wisest thing to do would be to cut the losses and very reluctantly give the cast two weeks' notice. But, he added, his three American stars had behaved magnificently and had generously offered to take no salaries at all for two weeks to give the general public a chance to prove the critics wrong, and to give all of us a chance of at least a respectable run in the West End.

This marvellous gesture by the stars was of no avail. The show was doomed. We limped along, playing to dreadful houses, and after two weeks a notice appeared on the board saying that the management regretted that the show would close on the following Saturday evening.

'Good heavens,' said Henry Mollison, 'what the hell am I going to do?

I've got eight workmen in the bloody house. They've got to be paid. I can't stop them, because they're only half finished. If something doesn't turn up we shall have to move out and leave them the bloody house.'

Something did turn up. In this hectic, precarious, nerve-racking profession things happily have a habit of turning up just at the moment they are urgently needed and least expected. On the Friday night before we closed, Henry arrived at the theatre to announce that he had landed a leading part in a play called *London Wall* written by John van Druten, which was to be directed by a lady called Auriel Lee, considered to be one of the best producers at that time in the theatre.

Henry, on reading the script, had discovered that there was a character in the play called Birkenshaw, a young, grubby, dirty-minded little cockney office-boy. Henry informed me that as he considered I was perfect casting for it, he could almost say 'type'-casting, he had suggested my name to Auriel Lee. I read Birkenshaw the next morning. John van Druten and Miss Lee were in front. I was engaged immediately at a salary of £20 a week – a handsome increase which staved off, temporarily at least, a financial disaster.

The play opened at the Duke of York's Theatre on 1 May with one of my heroes, Frank Lawton, in the leading part. Heather Angel, Marie Ney, Helen Goss, Nadine March, Frank Royde, Katie Johnson and Henry Mollison completed the cast. The first night audience was more than enthusiastic. The notices were excellent. I was exceptionally fortunate – Birkenshaw was a cakewalk, the only really comic character in the play. It paid off: my personal notices were exactly the kind I needed to give my career a boost at precisely the right moment.

Looking through my cutting books I am reminded how much audiences have changed since the 1930s. They were more full-blooded in those days, expressing their dislike or approval loudly and clearly during the performance. The critic in the *Sunday Dispatch* of 3 May wrote, after seeing *London Wall*, 'At the close of one scene the stalls were being polite but the gallery was cheering.' I can't remember that happening in a straight play for years. In the 1930s, if they liked it they cheered, if they didn't like it they booed, blew raspberries, shouted 'Speak up, can't hear you!' and occasionally walked out.

We settled down to an enjoyable run. I could hardly believe that I was actually acting with Frank Lawton. It seemed such a short while ago that I was sitting in the gallery watching him play Young Woodley. He was charming, helpful, modest, and I learned a great deal from watching his performances.

My luck since I returned from the Far East had been phenomenal: three shows in the West End with no nerve-racking out-of-work gaps in between. My career in its fledgling stage seemed to be running smoothly. On the other hand my domestic life wasn't running at all – it was panting along painfully over a frustrating and awkward obstacle race.

In this permissive society anything goes; but in those far-off days living together openly without the blessing of the church or the legal contract signed in the registry office was a ticklish business. It was 'living in sin' with capital letters. Aileen and I were finding it uncomfortable. Because of the open disapproval on both fronts we were forced into a deceitful way of life, full of evasions and pitfalls. The tour had been a different matter: the mere fact that we had been living in hotels for over a year had solved the major problem that confronted us at home.

During the run of *London Wall* we decided that even at the risk of great disapproval we must at least live in the same house, and after searching we found two bed-sitting-rooms – on separate floors of course – at 45 Acacia Road, St John's Wood. The rent of 25s. (in today's unattractive equivalent £1.25) per bed-sit seemed extortionate, but necessary if we were to avoid becoming frustrated nervous wrecks. During this difficult period a cool, warning wind blew occasionally through my thoughts. At the same time that I had received that lecture from Jimmy Anderson in Singapore, Aileen had, she told me, been on the receiving end of a similar one from the Master, who, wagging the famous forefinger, had let her know in his very direct 'no holds barred' way that it would be foolish and imprudent if she allowed us to get married before my career was really established. She assured him that we had no intention of rushing into things and that she was willing, if necessary, to wait for years.

To allay the family's fears we gave a house-warming party at Number 45, hoping to prove that we were being circumspect. Our quarters would be seen to be separate; and we felt that our landlady, a dignified, gentle, well-bred late-Victorian character, might perhaps set the seal of respectability on our arrangements. I had invited a few actor friends, whom I hoped would be on their best behaviour. The party was proceeding sedately; the South African cooking sherry was being sipped from a weird variety of glasses, including tooth mugs. I sensed that the relations were impressed. They were realizing, I hoped, that the theatre, far from being a den of shameful moral and sexual iniquity, was a place where high-minded, sober, God-fearing young actors and actresses spent their time and their talent entertaining, illuminating and educating their grateful public. These hopes were cut short by the late arrival of George Melville Cooper. I had an uneasy feeling that George, knowing that it was to be a sherry party, had fortified himself with several belts of Scotch. 'Sorry I'm late,' said George. 'I got rather held up at the club. Then when I got here I made a mistake and went to your apartment, Johnnie.'

'Oh that's all right, George. Come and meet the relations.'

He smiled hugely. 'It's a great set-up. Is your room like this one?'

'Yes,' I said quickly, hoping to steer the conversation away. 'It's exactly the same.'

'Is it?' said George in a voice that would have penetrated to the back of the gallery. 'I thought it might be, but I couldn't see for cobwebs.'

The deathly hush that followed was broken by a bellowing laugh from Bobby Sielle. It almost, but not quite, saved the day. I noticed to my dismay that the VIPs were not exactly rocking back on their heels with mirth. That party will not remain in my memory in a list of outstanding successes. But our living arrangements were not the only complication in my life with Aileen.

In the 1930s the provincial theatres were flourishing. Almost immediately after any new play opened in the West End, the touring company went out on the road. With the big hits it was not unknown for three companies to be playing the provinces at the same time. There were the number one dates – the best theatres in the largest cities – the number twos and the not-so-popular number threes. The first touring company of *London Wall* took to the road a few weeks after the London opening with Aileen in the cast. She was anxious to work; living in London even in those days was expensive. I had been able to persuade Auriel Lee and John van Druten to see her. She read for them and got the part. This of course entailed our separating again, only a short while after my return to England. Although I didn't realize it at the time this was probably the very thin edge of a wedge that did not manifest itself until several years later.

One morning in August the Master telephoned to ask if I knew how long *London Wall* was going to run. I said I'd no idea – business still seemed to be quite good.

'Who is presenting the play?'

'Frank Gregory. Why? What's it all about?' I said, excitement rising.

'Well,' said the Master, 'I need you for rehearsals in three weeks' time. I've written a marvellous part for you in a modest little piece that Mr Cochran is presenting at Drury Lane in October. Now listen, dear. Ring your Mr Frank Gregory and ask him if he's free for lunch today. I'll meet him at the Ivy at one o'clock. You'd better come along too. An eager spaniel look at the right moment might help, but don't overdo it. And you know nothing. Mum is once again the word.'

The Ivy Restaurant was Mecca as far as the theatre was concerned. Presided over by a little Italian genius called Mario, it became a very select club for all the leading actors and actresses playing in the West End. Mario loved the theatre and anybody and anything to do with it. If he discovered that any member of his clientele was going through a somewhat lean time, they would quite often find that when the bill was presented it had been signed by Mario 'with the compliments of the management'. Mario became and remained a firm friend. (Many years after that famous luncheon he admitted falling madly in love with my eldest daughter Juliet. She was then seven. But Mario decided that age was no barrier and they corresponded regularly, and a highlight of every holiday for Juliet was an invitation from Mario to lunch.)

Noël's regular table was situated in a position which commanded a view of the entrances and exits, always worth watching. My introduction to the Ivy was so important to me that I remember that luncheon in detail. I could see that Mr Gregory, although he took pains to conceal it, was almost as thrilled as I was to be Noël's guest. Before lunch he had asked if I knew the purpose of the meeting: I was, I said, just as curious as he was.

After a brief general skirmish on the state of the West End theatre, Noël congratulated Mr Gregory on *London Wall*. He said he was impressed with the writing, direction and the acting. Then he said, 'Mr Gregory, do you think that Johnnie Mills has a future in the theatre?'

Clever, I thought. How can he say no, with me sitting at the table?

'Yes I do, Mr Coward. He's excellent in the play and I think if he has luck and gets the opportunity, he most certainly will have a future, and a successful one.'

Mr Gregory had led with his chin. From that sentence on he was trapped.

'I couldn't agree with you more,' said the Master. 'Luck is important, and at this moment I can provide the opportunity, but I need your co-operation before it can become a reality. The position is this: I have completed – as you may have heard – a play called *Cavalcade* which is going into Drury Lane in October. There's a part in it, a very important leading part which I need Johnnie to play. I've written it with him in mind because in my opinion there's no young actor at the moment who could play it as well.'

I could see by the expression on Mr Gregory's face that the message was beginning to filter through.

'Now, Frank' – the Christian name was slipped in unobtrusively – 'how much longer in your opinion do you think *London Wall* will run?'

'Well ... the box office looks quite healthy. I'm hoping until the autumn.'

'I see,' said the Master. 'Well, the latest Johnnie could start rehearsals would be mid-September. I would really hate him to lose this opportunity for the sake of a week or two. And from what you've said I think you would too. Frank, will you do me a great personal favour and release him from his contract in the middle of September?'

There was a pause. Frank Gregory was a strong character. He looked serious. 'Well, Mr Coward,' he said at last, 'I appreciate the situation and I would like to help, but I have my own play and the Duke of York's Theatre to consider.'

Noël jumped in quickly. 'But of course, Frank. You're absolutely right. Your first consideration must be to your theatre. But I hoped that, as Johnnie is not playing a leading part, you might be able to replace him for the last weeks without shortening the run. But naturally I understand, it is an enormous responsibility running a theatre.' He paused for a moment, and then asked, 'Have you anything in view when *London Wall* closes?'

'Not actually,' said Mr Gregory. 'I'm reading some new plays, but I'm not very keen on any of them. I may have to fall back on a revival.'

'Mmm ...' said the Master, thoughtfully stirring his coffee. 'I have an idea for a comedy – it will only have a small cast, like *Private Lives*, and it will need an intimate theatre – something the size of the Duke of York's would be perfect. With *Cavalcade* on my hands I haven't had a chance to get a word down on paper, but after the opening, if the idea is not still-born I intend to get on with it.'

The fish was hooked and landed. 'Well, Noël' – the martinis had been dry and strong, it was Christian name time – 'I should appreciate the chance to read it.'

'One good turn deserves another,' said Noël. 'I'm late for an appointment at the Lane. I'm glad to have met you, Frank. Could you let me know about Johnnie in the morning?'

Later that afternoon the suspense was too great. I phoned 17 Gerald Road. 'I'm awfully sorry to bother you, Master, but I'm going mad. Do you think there's a chance of Mr Gregory agreeing?'

'Of course he'll agree, Johnnie dear. It's in the bag: you will play Joey Marryott for me, and I have a hunch we may just be in for quite a nice little success.'

Before the matinee the next day Mr Gregory told me that after a discussion with the author and the director, during which he met with great opposition, he had decided that he couldn't stand in the way of an opportunity of working with Mr Coward at Drury Lane and that he was going to release me from my contract in three weeks.

9

Cavalcade

We started rehearsing *Cavalcade* during the first week of September. The 'modest little piece' contained forty-three speaking parts, two hundred non-speaking parts and twenty-three scenes, which included a railway station plus locomotive (full-scale), a Victorian theatre, the deck of an Atlantic liner, the beach of a popular resort and, thrown in for good measure, Trafalgar Square.

Casting had apparently been a nightmare. The Master would have liked to have given every out-of-work actor and actress a job, but as over 1,200 applied and were auditioned, the odds were three to one against them being engaged. He cast that lovely actress Mary Clare for Jane Marryott and a practically unknown actor, Edward Sinclair, as Robert, her husband. Arthur Macrae, who became a great friend (a very necessary relationship if you are to share a dressing-room for a year, which we did), played Edward the eldest son, and I played Joe, the youngest. The other principal parts were played by Irene Brown, Alison Leggatt, Binnie Barnes, Una O'Connor and Fred Groves. I was delighted to discover that my old friend from the Quaints, Betty Hare, was in it too, and Anthony Pélissier also had a small part. Nothing on the scale of *Cavalcade* had been attempted in the theatre for years, and I doubt very much whether anyone other than Cochran would have had the courage to gamble £30,000, a colossal budget in those times, on the production.

For the first few days Noël rehearsed the principal characters in the large bar, the only possible space. An army of workmen was tearing the stage apart and building two extra hydraulic lifts, making six in all, that could be lowered and raised at acute angles during the show.

I shall never forget the first rehearsal with the full cast on stage: it looked rather like Cup Final day at Wembley. There were 250 extras, and I noticed that they were wearing large numbers on their fronts and backs. Noël was directing from the dress circle. 'Sybil, dear, could you move over stage left and join the little group there?' Sybil stood rooted to the spot, nearly fainting with pride and pleasure. 'Yes, of course, Mr Coward. Thank you.'

A little later on Alfred got the same treatment, then Maud, then Doris. I thought, 'What a marvellous thing to do, and what a memory. They'll never forget it – Noël Coward knowing their Christian names and speaking to them in front of the entire company.' I discovered after the rehearsal that Noël had a list in front of him with all the extras' full names and their numbers beside them. I thought it was one of the most considerate and thoughtful things that I have ever seen a director do in the theatre.

I enjoyed every minute of rehearsals. When I wasn't actually on stage, I spent all my time in the stalls or dress circle watching Noël patiently mould this enormous production into shape. Because of the complicated technical problems which made it impossible to try the show out on the road we had four full dress rehearsals. The scene changes were like army manœuvres – nearly a hundred stage hands had been drilled by the stage manager, Danny O'Neil, a marvellous little character with a quick cockney wit. Nothing seemed to disconcert him. When everyone else was tearing their hair, Danny always appeared to be cool, calm and collected. Noël considered him invaluable and used him on all his productions.

At the final dress rehearsal the hydraulic lift jammed. The engineers and the electricians went to work, but it was over two hours before they rectified the fault and the show could continue. With the six lifts out of position, it was virtually impossible to make a scene-change. During this hiatus Noël was on stage discussing the problem with Gladys Calthrop, a brilliant designer and one of Noël's closest friends, who had designed the production. There was a pregnant pause while the thought flashed through everyone's mind: 'What if the same thing happened on the first night?'

The Master stood there, thoughtfully and carefully picking his nose. Tension built up. Danny, at his usual post at the author's elbow, regarded Noël with interest, and then suddenly said to him, 'Wave when you come to the bridge.'

Everyone roared with laughter. The lifts re-started as if on cue, and the rehearsal continued.

On the first night I walked across the vast stage of Drury Lane Theatre to get to my dressing-room. It looked like Piccadilly Circus at night with road-works in progress. There were several platforms about twenty-five feet high, built on rostrums with danger signs in red electric lights at the top of them, and guide-ropes for the cast to use during the black-out.

One of the most nerve-racking things for an actor to endure is a long wait before he makes his first entrance. This was my lot in *Cavalcade*; Joe Marryott didn't appear until Scene Three in Act Two. Because of the enormous crowd of people and the lightning changes that had to be made, the cast were asked not to wait in the wings until their call came for their entrances. Consequently I spent the first hour after the curtain rose in our dressing-room checking and re-checking my props, my make-up and my changes, during which totally unnecessary procedure I made frequent trips to the lavatory.

Arthur Macrae was luckier. His first scene opened the second act. He came back into the room looking excited, and told me that everything was going splendidly. The first-night audience seemed to be absolutely with the play and so far none of the extras had fallen off the rostrum and broken their necks. I looked at my wrist watch (a 1909 model); there was still fifteen minutes to go. We heard a sudden commotion in the passage. Someone opened our door and shouted, 'The lifts have stuck.' Without speaking we made our way on to the stage where we found all hell had broken loose. Actors were standing in anxious little groups flattened against the wall, while the stage hands attacked the lifts which had jammed right across the stage at all angles. I crept along to the prompt corner and saw to my horror our cool, calm and collected stage manager Danny O'Neil on his knees banging the stage with a hammer and shouting at the top of his voice, 'Jesus, Jesus, Jesus.' I heard the orchestra playing a period waltz, 'Lover Of My Dreams', which Noël had written as a parody of the popular tunes of 1900. They finished it, and then played it again, and again, and again, musically ad-libbing, waiting for the moment when the curtain would eventually rise on the next scene.

I worked my way into a position where I could peep through the curtains in the corner. The author was sitting very straight-backed in a chair in the royal box, in full view of the audience, with a fixed smile on his face and beads of perspiration gathering on his forehead. Still nothing happened. The conductor, wild-eyed and puce in the face by this time, having plugged 'Lover Of My Dreams' to death, switched to a medley of the old war songs. Some of the audience nervously joined in, but soon faded out into an embarrassed silence. The gallery became restless and began the dreaded slow hand-clap. I saw Noël tense as if to rise to his feet. At that moment, four and a half minutes after Danny O'Neil's impassioned appeal to a higher power, the lifts lurched back to life. The curtain rose and *Cavalcade* continued on its nerve-racking and breathtaking way. The whole drama had had such a shattering effect on me that I went through the show in a haze, and remember little of what happened until the curtain fell at the end of it.

What followed was unforgettable. The whole vast audience – stalls, pit, circle, gallery and boxes – rose to their feet as one man and cheered. Ordinary applause was not enough. They went on cheering and refused to stop until Noël, somehow managing to look calm, in spite of the fact that his white starched shirt and collar resembled a limp wet tennis outfit, appeared on stage and addressed the audience: 'I hope this play has made you feel that in spite of the troublous times we are living in it is still a pretty exciting thing to be English.'

Alan Parsons in the *Daily Mail* of 1 November 1931 ended his notice with this sentence: 'Drury Lane has come into its own again. Our national theatre has a theme worthy of itself.' *Cavalcade* ran for 405 performances. It was indeed, as the author had predicted, 'quite a nice little success'.

The production had a very marked effect on the theatre of the time. Managers were deeply and, as it turned out, unnecessarily, concerned by the advent of their monstrous rival, the talking picture. Desperate measures were obviously going to be needed to entice their public to remain loyal to the live theatre. Gargantuan spectacles were obviously the answer, and very soon in *Cavalcade*'s wake we were treated to *The White Horse Inn* at the Coliseum – a noisy extravaganza set in the Tyrol complete with mountains, rain-storms, a steam-boat and a lake, live goats and a pony, who, the night I saw the show, left his visiting card in the centre of the stage just before the Tyrolean dancers made their entrance. Needless to say, at that performance, their number was a riot. Sir Oswald Stoll joined the band-wagon with *Waltzes from Vienna* at the old Alhambra Theatre in Leicester Square. *Late Night Final*, an American spectacle, arrived at the Phoenix Theatre, and a production of *Grand Hotel* was so overloaded with enormous sets that the actors seemed to be swallowed up by the scenery. *Cavalcade* started a trend that was not easy to follow successfully.

The run of *Cavalcade* coincided with two important happenings. When Aileen returned from the tour of *London Wall* we took the plunge and were married secretly at Marylebone Registry Office before a Wednesday matinee in March. Looking back, I realize this was not the cleverest of moves: we missed out on all the wedding presents and didn't even have a toast rack to set up home with. The only person I took into my confidence was my sister Annie who, because she loved me, did her best to look pleased; and as we had no capital to draw on she let us have a room above the flat in Belsize Park where she was living at the time with her husband Bobby Sielle. We had hoped to be able to keep the marriage a secret for another six months, by which time we thought our respective parents might accept the fact that we intended to be together. After a few weeks, which we spent happily basking in the thought that whatever anyone else thought, we were sinners no longer, the bomb dropped. 'The Stroller' (the gossip-columnist in the *Evening News*) informed the public and of course our parents that he had just discovered that there had been a secret *Cavalcade* wedding a month ago. This was definitely not a good start.

The second event, towards the end of the run, came in the form of an offer from Twentieth Century Fox to play Joey Marryott in the film of *Cavalcade* to be made in Hollywood when the production at Drury Lane finished. The salary seemed to me phenomenal, staggering – £100 per week – but, and it was a big but, for the chance and privilege of playing my part in the picture, Fox were insisting that I had to sign a seven-year deal with the studio, a no-option deal with rises in salary each year, culminating in a mind-boggling £500 per week.

The temptation was enormous, and my first inclination was to say 'yes' straight away. The contract meant financial security. That sort of money in those days was a fortune, and of course the income tax was negligible. In my mind's eye I visualized a white clap-board Beverly Hills mansion with a convertible Cadillac standing in the driveway, a modest garden of about an acre with orange and lemon trees, and of course the inevitable large kidney-shaped blue-tiled pool – too much to miss, I thought, quite apart from the bonus of becoming an international film star. Before I actually signed on the dotted line, I decided I should at least go and tell the Master of my decision. He listened attentively to all the details. When I'd finished I asked him if he thought I'd made the right decision. 'Most definitely not,' was the reply.

'But why?' I asked. 'Surely it's the chance of a lifetime.'

'It all depends what you want to make of your life. This is probably the most important decision you will ever have to make as far as your career is concerned, and this is my advice for what it is worth, and of course, being mine, I consider it to be worth a great deal. There are two roads ahead of you – let's take the Hollywood road first. It offers you, as you say, financial security and, as you are a naturally good actor, a successful career as a Hollywood film star with all the trappings. You will have no choice of parts, however. You will play exactly what they choose you to play. They make personalities, not actors. And in my view you will end up as a cross between Jimmy Cagney and Johnnie Garfield, and not as good as either of them, because they're American and you're English. Now, if you have the courage to take the other, probably much tougher road, you will stay in England and learn everything you can about your job, and you will only achieve that by staying in the theatre playing any part you can lay your hands on, looking and listening to people that you admire. If you take that road, with a certain amount of luck you will, in my opinion, more than probably become a great actor. You will also have a background of experience to fall back on, and when you're ninety still be able to earn a living playing character parts, if necessary in a wheelchair. Finally, I think that you're too English, and that you would feel after a while that you had sold your birthright for a mess of pottage.'

I wrestled with the problem until dawn the next morning. I went over the pros and cons so many times that they faded into each other and made no sense. The thing that finally clinched my decision was the theatre. I realized that if I signed the Hollywood deal I should not be able to walk through a stage door for seven years. I turned down the offer, and to this day I have never regretted it for one single moment.

It is strange to think how completely different my life would have been had I taken that road to California, and quite frightening to think that I should have missed spending forty glorious years with the one woman in the world who was so obviously meant for me. And Juliet, Hayley and Jonathan would have been nothing more than whispers in the wind.

The film version of *Cavalcade* was made in Hollywood in 1932 directed by Frank Lloyd. Frank Lawton played my part, with Clive Brook and Diana Wynyard as Robert and Jane Marryott. Fox, having paid a vast sum of money for the film rights, lost interest, considering it to be too English for American consumption, and were astonished when it turned out to be an enormous box-office success.

I realize now that when Noël advised me to turn down the tantalizing Hollywood offer he knew that I was not going to have to endure a period of being out of work when *Cavalcade* finished. If this had happened I should have had serious doubts about the wisdom of the decision. Most actors, after only three or four weeks of idleness, are convinced that they will never work again. You may imagine, therefore, with what relief and excitement I heard two weeks before *Cavalcade* closed in August that I was due to start rehearsals for a new revue called *Words and Music* that Noël had written, and which Cochran was presenting in London in September. My salary was to be increased to £40 per week, but better still I found that I had been entrusted with two of the best numbers in the show – 'Something To Do With Spring' and 'Mad Dogs and Englishmen'. The first number was a duet which contained a complicated tap routine. Joyce Barbour and I were dispatched to Buddy Bradley three weeks before general rehearsals started.

We slaved for eight hours a day. Buddy was tireless and his patience endless. Some of the steps were so complicated that we tied ourselves into knots trying to master them, but it was a rewarding experience. The routine was a classic, and it was so drilled into me that I've never forgotten it, and have used parts of it, camouflaged slightly, in one or two shows since.

The principals in the revue were Ivy St Helier, Joyce Barbour, Romney Brent, an American light comedian, Doris Hare and myself. We opened at the Opera House in Manchester on 5 August 1932 and played there until 7 September. Lynne Fontanne and Alfred Lunt, the most famous couple in the American theatre, and great friends of Noël's, arrived to see the show on the opening night. They were an enchanting couple besotted by the theatre, and never really happy when they were not in it. Stories in the theatre about the Lunts are legion, but my favourite one concerned the Lunts and their Hollywood excursion. For years the big studios had been doing their best to persuade them to make a film, without any success. Finally, after much pressure, they agreed to act together in a film for MGM called *The Guardsman*.

After the second morning's shooting the director asked them if they would like to see the dailies with him. (The dailies, or rushes as they're usually called in England, are the scenes of the previous day's work, cut together roughly, and usually shown at lunchtime for the benefit of the producer-director and the leading actors if they wish to see them.) Lynne Fontanne had no idea what the dailies were; she told the director that she hadn't had time to read the papers. When it was explained to her that they could see the scene they had played yesterday, she said of course they'd be delighted. They'd been acting for twenty years and had never had the chance of watching themselves perform. Alfred Lunt said no; nothing, not even the wildest of horses, could drag him to the viewing. He was at the moment convinced that he was a magnificent actor, and he had no desire to be disillusioned. Half an hour later a distraught Lynne Fontanne appeared in his dressing-room. 'Well, how were we?'

'Oh, my God,' gasped Lynne Fontanne, 'I can't believe it.'

'What's the matter? Were we awful?'

'Oh, not you, darling. You were wonderful. You played the scene beautifully. You were relaxed, charming, and moved so elegantly, and you were distinguished and good-looking, the only tiny thing I noticed was that you didn't seem to have any lips. But Alfred, you should have seen me. I'll never get over it. I'm going to ask them to replace me.'

Alfred Lunt sat staring at his wife as she paced the dressing-room.

'I mean, I look grotesque! My neck was too long. I looked positively gawky, and I seemed to be so hideously uncomfortable when I moved. And, Alfred, I always hoped I had some sort of charm, but I was charmless; and my voice – I've always been rather proud of my voice. It's a croak, Alfred, a croak!' She sank down on to the sofa. 'Oh Lord, Alfred, what am I going to do?'

The great American actor, who had been staring at himself fixedly in the dressing-room mirror, switched his gaze to his wife, and after a slight pause said, 'No lips, eh?'

At this point in my career I was bursting with confidence and felt I could take on anything. Then something happened that shocked me into realizing I had my limitations, and there were things that I couldn't at that age do as well as somebody else.

'Mad Dogs and Englishmen' is perhaps the number from *Words and Music* that has survived and will be remembered when some of the others have been forgotten. After a few performances Noël informed me regretfully that he had made a mistake. 'Mad Dogs and Englishmen' was not the right number for me. It needed, he said, more authority, age and sophistication. He was sorry, but in the right hands he felt the number would become a hit, and he had decided to take it away from me and give it to Romney Brent, who was ten years older than I, and a great deal more experienced. The decision, of course, was absolutely right. I had never really enjoyed the number and always felt that it was not going over as well as it should. None of these feelings, however, helped my embarrassment, which was intense. I felt that I'd lost face with the company.

I crept about with my head under my arm while Romney Brent rehearsed the number. It was a painful situation. He was very conscious of what I was going through, learnt it in two days and took over on the third performance. Watching from the wings I had to admit he was, although nervous, infinitely better than I had been. Looking back I realize that it was fortunate that a setback of that nature happened when it did; I have, I'm sure, always learnt more from my failures than my successes, however painful the process has been.

The final thing that lingers in my memory from Manchester happened on the second night of the show. Reginald Burston, the musical director, had a disagreement with the management and walked out just before the curtain rose on the second night, leaving us without a conductor. Undaunted, the author, always at his best in an emergency, seized the baton, jumped down into the orchestra pit, tapped the music-stand twice and commenced the overture. He had never conducted a show before. All went well until it came to my duet with Joyce Barbour halfway through the second half. Our slightly over-confident conductor took the number at such a clip that during the tap routine, vainly trying to catch up – we were at least a bar behind – we collided with each other and only by a superhuman effort managed to avoid falling head-first into the bass drum in the orchestra pit. By this stage the maestro with the baton seemed to be in a trance, and powerless to ease off the tempo. He recalls the occasion in his introduction to the second volume of *Play Parade*:

When I read *Words and Music*, I remember the terrible night when I had to conduct the orchestra unexpectedly, never having done so before; the breathless agony on the faces of Joyce Barbour and John Mills when I took the tempo of 'What Shall We Do With Spring' so fast they couldn't fit their very complicated dance to it and finally staggered off the stage cursing and exhausted.

Words and Music opened at the Adelphi Theatre, London, on 16 September 1932. The notices were nearly unanimous in their praise, but, as I have mentioned earlier, my name was conspicuous by its absence. I had not, at least in the opinion of the critics, taken London by storm. This time, however, the public did not apparently agree with the notices. The business dropped away alarmingly after four months, and the show closed after 164 performances.

Although the run was short, I remember it as one of the most exciting periods of my life. Weekends at Goldenhurst, Noël's lovely farmhouse in Kent, with other friends from the cast; the thrill of meeting the Lunts, the Oliviers, Douglas Fairbanks Senior (one of my heroes – I'd seen *The Thief of Baghdad, Robin Hood* and *The Black Pirate* at least six times each – on the screen he always appeared to be well over six feet, and I was astonished to find that he was shorter than I was), Mary Pickford, Harold Lloyd and a host of other magical names from the then-mysterious silver screen.

The day that the dreaded notice stating that the run was to be terminated in two weeks' time was posted on the notice board I received a call from the casting director at Gaumont British Studios offering me the part of Midshipman Golightly in a film called *The Midshipmaid* starring Jessie Matthews. They needed a young actor who could sing and dance – and, of course, speak the 'King's English'. Again, Lady Luck was smiling; I began to believe she would never stop.

10

On Camera

I had no great desire to become a film actor. I was besotted by the theatre and had never thought of trying to break into the world of celluloid. I discovered, however, that I enjoyed it – the studios fascinated me; everything, the way of life, was completely different. The make-up chair, with make-up men – I expected quite naturally that, as in the theatre, I should be in charge of that operation myself. Curtain up on the set at 8.30 a.m., instead of 8.30 p.m., and in place of the excitement and stimulation of an audience, a sudden deathly hush after a loud voice shouting 'Quiet please, Scene Thirty-nine, Take One': a sharp crack, a thin cloud of white chalk-dust as the clapper-boy snaps the board together two inches from the nose, and you're on. I found that first take in the studio almost as nerve-racking as a first night, but not quite: I knew if I blew it they would cut the camera and go for another take.

My first scene was a long, complicated and difficult shot. It started with a close-up of Midshipman Golightly, sweating profusely. (Studios in the early days were like Turkish baths; it was necessary, because of the slowness of the film stock, to use a battery of arc-lamps.) As I started the dialogue, the camera was slowly tracked back to a full shot, disclosing me at the piano surrounded by sailors and Jessie Matthews. The scene didn't end until I'd sung a verse and chorus – not the easiest entry into the world of the silver screen.

'Cut. Print. Well done everybody. Next set up please' – the director's voice broke the silence. By a small miracle everybody got it right at the same time – the operator, the focus-puller, the camera-grip in charge of the tracking, and the actors.

Since that first day in the studio forty-six years ago 'Take One' has been written on my hat. I firmly believe that, if everything works, Take One is always the best take. There is a freshness, excitement and electricity in it that one finds at the first performance of a play in the theatre. There the cast have four weeks to get up to pitch; they are ready, or should be, for the gun to go off. Perhaps it's because I had a solid early training in the theatre that I prefer to rehearse until everyone is as confident as possible, and then go for Take One. Some actors, and indeed some good directors, don't agree with this system and shoot take after take, which really means rehearsing on film. As far as I'm concerned, when this happens, by Take Fifteen the scene has become repetitious, monotonous and lost all freshness and truth. This is only a personal opinion. There is one great director, whom I've known and admired for many years, who shoots many takes and then, with unerring instinct, picks the best one; but exceptions prove the rule – there is only one William Wyler.

Without planning it, I found myself launched on a career in the studios. When *The Midshipmaid* finished I went straight into *Britannia of Billingsgate* with that marvellous cockney actor the late Gordon Parker, following this with two small pictures, *Bill M.P.* and *The Ghost Camera*. The last little epic deserves more than a mention.

At that time the 'quota' law dictated that every cinema wanting to show an American film was obliged to show an English film in the same programme. This resulted in the British studios becoming a hive of activity. Small budget films were needed and needed fast. Twickenham Studios, consisting then of two small stages, had two films going at once, and owing to lack of space one was shot at night and one during the day. *The Ghost Camera* was on the day shift. The atmosphere when I walked on to the set at eight o'clock the first morning was almost indescribable: the night shift staggered out at 7.30 a.m., leaving in their wake an aroma – a delicate blend of cigarette butts, orange-peel, stale beer, make-up and several unmentionable gases. The schedule for a picture was eight days; they never went over. If at any time it looked as if they might, the producer solved the problem by tearing some pages out of the script.

The make-up men at the smaller studios all seemed to have been acrobats in a circus. On my arrival in the make-up room I was greeted by an elderly man in a grubby white coat. 'Good morning,' he said; a small hand-rolled cigarette containing evil-smelling shag glued to his bottom lip emitted clouds of smoke into my face. 'You playing the juve?'

I nodded. My new friend belched loudly.

'Better out than in. Put it there,' he said indicating the make-up chair. He then reached for a large jar of grease paint, scooped out a dollop, rubbed his palms together and plastered it over my face. Next he picked up a black liner and attacked my eyebrows, finally drawing two painful lines along my upper and lower eyelids. A large powder-puff was then produced and dumped into a saucer of white powder. 'Close your eyes, son.'

I gratefully did as ordered. They were by this time full of make-up and smarting badly. The puff hit my face with a bang. He then brushed the powder off with what felt like a rather hard shoe-brush. 'Right, son? You're ready. Next?'

I stood up and looked at myself in the mirror. Staring back at me was what I can only describe as a young, queer, Chinese George Robey. I saw a thick yellow mask, with large jet-black eyebrows and black circled eyes. I looked away hurriedly.

Rather unhappily I made my way to the set. I was met by Henry Kendall, the leading man, who was studying his script. 'Good God!' he exclaimed. 'What the hell are you playing? Dracula? Did Charlie get hold of you? He should never have left the circus. He thinks we're all clowns. Go and take it all off and put a light stage make-up on, and never go near him again. Use my room. It's the first down the passage.'

'Thanks awfully,' I said, and flew. I'd never met Henry Kendall before. He was quite a big star at the time, and I discovered that little episode was typical of him. He was one of the kindest and most generous actors I've ever worked with.

The film was directed by an up-and-coming young director named Bernard Vorhaus, a keen eager beaver hidden behind an enormous beard and moustache. I liked the script and thought my part was outstanding – dramatic scenes, accused of murder, wrongly of course – and felt I had a chance of really making a mark. By this time I was fascinated by the new medium and decided that, as I'd turned down the chance of becoming a Hollywood film star, nothing was going to stop me from becoming an English one. I just needed one break – this could be it.

Halfway through the film – four days' shooting – the sweet smell of success was in the air. The only people allowed to see the rushes were the producer, the director, the camera man and the star. Each day after the showing this little group arrived back on the set looking more and more pleased with themselves. Nothing much was said, but a lot of 'thumbs-up' signs were going on. I tackled Henry Kendall. 'I've made quite a few of these,' he said, 'but I really think this one is good. The stuff today looked great, and your scene in the prison cell is a knock-out.'

We now dissolve to six months later. The Empire Theatre, Leicester Square, with the premiere of a new MGM film starring Clark Gable and Spencer Tracy. The supporting English quota film was *The Ghost Camera*, starring Henry Kendall and, in smaller letters, but nevertheless above the title, John Mills.

Feeling fairly confident about the film after the flattering remarks addressed to me during the shooting, I had lashed out and bought expensive seats in the front section of the dress circle. For the first half-hour of the film the audience seemed quite attentive. I was, however, slightly concerned about the interminable amount of time people seemed to take to walk in and out of doors, down corridors and in and out of cars. The editor really seemed to be taking his time. Then came my big scene in the prison cell. I paced up and down, stopped, hung on to the bars with an anguished look. Cut to a close-up of Henry Kendall frantically dismantling a camera to find the vital piece of evidence that would save my life – cut back to anguished young hero pacing the cell, stopping, hanging on to the bars – cut back to Henry Kendall with camera – cut back to cell, longer anguished look – cut back to Henry Kendall. The penny dropped. I realized that our producer had probably torn out too many pages of the script and had discovered too late that he was short of film.

After four more cuts backwards and forwards the silence in the auditorium was broken by a loud voice from behind me in the circle: 'Oh dear. Oh dear. Oh *dear*!' That started it. Within seconds the epic that was going to make me the idol of millions was sent sky-high. There was a barrage of laughs, shouts of 'Take it off', jeers and cat-calls. The gentleman behind me who had started the demonstration began blowing the loudest raspberries in my ear that I've ever heard in my life. I sank down in my seat, praying I wouldn't be recognized, and then, remembering the old sayings 'If you can't beat them join them' and 'The best form of defence is attack', I allied myself with the audience and, together with the expert behind me, attempted to blow my performance off the screen.

The following notice appeared in the *Picturegoer*: 'Henry Kendall in *The Ghost Camera* is right in being slow and eccentric, but that is just the reason why everyone around him should have moved with speed. They all seemed to be dazed.'

The British film industry was obviously going to have to wait a little longer for their new super-star, the idol of millions.

The fact that for the first time in my life I had been able, because of the continuous work in the studios, to accumulate a small amount of capital helped to offset the disappointment that the films had not been very successful. I was also beginning to miss the theatre. I was delighted, therefore, when my agent rang me with the news that a Hungarian actor, Ernst Verebes, might have to leave the cast of the successful musical *Give Me a Ring*, which was playing at the London Hippodrome. The Ministry of Labour had intimated, rather late, that they might not find it possible to extend the work permit granted to Mr Verebes. This news was received on a Thursday evening. The fact had to be faced that it was possible the Hungarian actor might not be able to appear on the following Monday. It was a very important part: the leading man, playing opposite Evelyn Laye, at that time one of the most popular stars in the theatre.

I had an interview with George Black, who owned and ran the theatre. He said that if I would agree to rehearse all through the weekend, with only the possibility of playing the part – he was quite honest and stated that if the permit came through Mr Verebes would naturally remain in the show – he would be grateful. He arranged for me to see the play that night, Thursday, and I was to decide whether I thought I could make it in the time – three days. I had already decided to say 'yes' anyway. When I'd seen the show, however, I wondered if I would ever make it in the time. The part was long and contained two big plot scenes, plus three song and dance numbers, two with Evelyn Laye.

I started rehearsing at 8.30 on the Friday morning, and from then until Monday afternoon I don't think I had more than two hours' sleep. I worked during the days on the numbers and main scenes with the understudies, and at night crammed the dialogue into my head. At four o'clock on Monday afternoon, during a rehearsal on the stage with the principals, Mr Black told me that the permit had not been renewed and that, if I thought I was ready, I could play that night. I knew the dialogue, the lyrics, the music and the steps. 'When am I going to get a chance like this again?' I thought. 'It's a gamble, but I can't afford not to take it.' I rehearsed until the call-boy called the half-hour, and then went to make up.

The two hours from curtain-up to curtain-fall passed in a kind of dream. I was too physically and mentally exhausted to suffer from first-night nerves. It was a strange experience. I knew it all, but I had very little idea where it all came in the show, and less idea of entrances and exits. I'm certain that I should never have got through without the lovely Evelyn Laye. She never left me; she pushed me on for my entrances, and when she was not on the stage with me, was always waiting in the wings when I came off, ready to grab me and prepare me for my next entrance. I didn't dry up in the dialogue or the lyrics, remembered all the steps (not very complicated thank goodness, as Evelyn was not the greatest dancer – she hardly needed to be, with that glorious voice) and managed not to tread on anybody's laughs.

By a coincidence Bud Flanagan returned to the show that evening after an operation for appendicitis. Audiences loved Bud and at this particular performance, luckily for me, they were in a very receptive mood. At the final curtain he received an ovation, but instead of stepping forward from the line-up he winked at Evelyn Laye, who took my hand and led me forward. As I took a bow Bud kicked me smartly in the bottom. This was a prelude to one of the most unpredictable and happiest runs I have ever spent in the theatre.

The next evening I walked through Leicester Square, stopped outside the London Hippodrome and looked up, there it was – *in lights*: Evelyn Laye, Flanagan and Allen, Will Fyffe and John Mills in *Give Me a Ring*.

Playing a straight leading man in a show with Flanagan and Allen is an experience I shall never forget. Unlike some comics who are rather morose characters off-stage, Bud was always bubbling with fun and vitality, and was a mass of practical jokes. I've seen few people who enjoyed life more than he did – he always seemed to be laughing. Chesney Allen was the perfect foil for him – one of the best 'feeds' I've ever seen. Bud knew this and never talked of going solo.

The practical jokes were mostly played on me; I was the obvious target: the straight man with all the serious scenes to handle. George Black was very keen on these and expected them to be played with the utmost sincerity. During one performance, before my entrance to play the love scene with Evelyn Laye, Bud came up to me in the wings and began a serious lecture on my future: what was I aiming at? Was I going straight, or staying with musicals? I had talent. But in what direction was I going to point it? During this monologue he became quite heated, and underlined his points by prodding me with his forefinger on my stiff white shirt front. My cue came, I walked on to the stage.

During the scene I took Evelyn gently by the shoulders and said, 'Look at me, I love you. Do you love me?'

'Yes, I do,' she said, and dropped her head shyly. Her expression changed; I heard a suppressed snort of laughter. I looked down: on my white stiff shirt were glued five large grubby pieces of chewing-gum.

One of Bud's jokes, however, nearly resulted in my being given the sack. At the end of one dramatic scene which took place in an office I had to grab my hat, which was always pre-set on the manager's desk, and after declaiming a long speech which contained the plot of the play, storm off the stage. On the performance in question, I grabbed my hat, and out of it flew two eggs, which sailed through the air and landed with a plop in the footlights two inches from Debroy Summers, who was conducting the orchestra. I tried all the tricks I knew – I bit my tongue, dug my nails into the palms of my hands, but nothing I could do would stop the hysteria that set in. To make matters worse, Aubrey Dexter, who was playing the manager, was a notorious giggler. He always found it impossible to look me in the eye, but chose a spot in the centre of my forehead which he glared at during our exchanges. This I found extremely disconcerting at the best of times. On this occasion we were defeated, and after a minute of gurgles, grunts and whinnies, I left the stage, leaving the audience in total ignorance of the plot.

That evening George Black happened to be in front. Aubrey and I were ordered by the stage manager to attend a rehearsal at eleven the next morning, and he added that Mr Black wanted to see us before the rehearsal. Needless to say I spent an uneasy night. I had the same feeling as when I was told to report to the headmaster's study at Norwich after the Woolworth's escapade. The Hippodrome the next morning was as still and quiet as the grave. The curtain was up and Aubrey and I stood on the empty stage nervously staring into the dark auditorium.

A voice we recognized as Mr Black's broke the silence: 'The theatre last night was full of people who had paid good money to see the performance. They left at the end of the show, thanks to you both, totally ignorant of the plot. As you are both as of this moment still under contract, and er ... therefore, entitled to rehearse, would you please be good enough to play the scene for me that you omitted last night.'

Aubrey and I stared at each other and took our positions for the opening line, which to my misfortune, happened to be mine. I took a deep breath and started, 'Now, look here, sir.'

Aubrey was staring at my hairline, his face going purple. Suddenly it broke. We whinnied, snorted, gurgled, trying to suppress the hysterical laughter that finally overcame us. As it was happening I thought, 'This is the end. I'm laughing myself out of my first leading part in the West End.' But control had gone: nobody who has not gone through this ordeal in the theatre can quite appreciate it. It is the mere fact of knowing one mustn't laugh that triggers it off. We laughed helplessly for a minute or two that seemed like hours until finally, through exhaustion, we came to a panting silence. I waited for the blow to fall.

'Right,' said Mr Black. 'Do you think you've both finished?'

'Yes, sir,' we gasped.

'Well, that's fine then. You'll be all right tonight, so don't worry about it. I've seen this happen before. I'll have a word with Bud. But he won't take any notice of me, so you must be prepared for anything.'

George Black was a marvellous man of the theatre and proved it that morning. If he had employed any other method, threats of the sack or cuts in salary, I'm certain that Aubrey and I would never have been able to get through the egg scene again.

After two months that marvellous comedienne Binnie Hale took over from Evelyn Laye. I had watched her many times from the gallery when she was playing opposite Bobby Howes in *Mr Cinders*.

Give Me a Ring was a milestone for me: it marked a return to the London Hippodrome as a leading man, four years after I'd started in the back row of the chorus there in 1929. The show closed at the end of the year. I shall always remember it with affection. Pictures remain in my mind of Will Fyffe sitting in the prompt corner waiting for his cue with a large neat Scotch in one hand and a Worthington in the other – the 'chaser' was a ritual, and he timed it to perfection and of Bud and Chesney, with their endless gags and practical jokes, and their racing exploits – Bud often arrived for the evening performance straight from Kempton Park with hundreds of pound-notes bulging from his pockets.

I had lunch with Chesney not long ago: he was as bright as a button and fit as a fiddle. Bud alas is no longer with us, but those of us who were lucky enough to have known and worked with him will never forget his warmth, humour, infectious gaiety and zest for life.

There was one small incident while I was at the Hippodrome which, in view of later events, is interesting to recall. I left the theatre one afternoon after the matinee, and as I walked past Daly's Theatre (now the Warner Cinema) out of the stage door emerged a slim young girl with a beautiful figure and a mass of golden hair. We both stopped simultaneously. She smiled. 'Hallo,' she said.

I stared. I knew I'd seen her somewhere before, but where, when? I smiled back. By the time I'd said 'Hallo' she was gone. It was quite a while before I could get the picture of her out of my mind.

At this time all was going too well, and because of this continuous run of luck I was lulled into a false sense of security. Immediately *Give Me a Ring* finished I made two more films – a quickie called *The Lash*, and *Those Were The Days*, adapted from Pinero's play *The Magistrate*: this was the film that introduced to the public that superb comedian Will Hay. I had an amusing part in it, but the film's success was almost entirely due to Will's subtle and peculiar brand of comedy, which adapted itself happily to the screen.

Then something happened. I read a book by C.S. Forester, called *Brown on Resolution*. The part of Able Seaman Brown must have been written for me – it was exactly what I had been looking for. By coincidence a notice appeared the next day in a film magazine saying that the picture was being made and casting was in progress. Owing to the fact that I had achieved a certain amount of success in the theatre and was not unknown in the studios, doors that had previously been closed to me were now comparatively easy to open.

I discovered that Walter Ford was directing the picture with his wife Cully. She had been an editor; now they were a team and worked together on every film they made. I was interviewed by them at the Gaumont British Studios at Shepherd's Bush. They were charming; both of them said they'd seen my work, but unfortunately, and they hated to say this, they felt they couldn't cast me in the part as in their opinion I didn't look like a sailor. This shattered me: I was prepared to be too short, too small, too light-weight, but to be turned down and lose the one opportunity I'd waited years for because I didn't look like a sailor, this was too much, because I knew they were wrong.

In those early days I had a great deal more courage than I have now, and refused to accept defeat. The next day I hired an ordinary seaman's uniform from my old friend Monty Berman and, attired in it, made my way to the studios and managed to worm my way into the Fords' office. 'Excuse me, Mr Ford. Could I have a word with you?' I said, flattening out the vowels to sound like an ordinary seaman.

'Who let you in here? I'm busy. Who are you?'

'John Mills, Mr Ford. You saw me yesterday, and said I didn't look like a sailor.'

He stared at me, looked me up and down, and then said, 'Good God, Cully, look at that, the boy's right. Well I'm damned.' There was a pause while they looked at each other. 'Wait outside a minute, will you?'

I was back in the room almost immediately. 'OK, you've got the part. You deserve it, if only for your colossal nerve. We don't need a test. We've seen your work. Ring your agent, tell him to fix your deal. He should only take five per cent, he's done damn all for you. Then go and get yourself really fit, it's going to be rough. We start shooting in three weeks.'

For the record, I have, since that time, spent altogether seven years in naval uniform, popping up and down like a yo-yo in rank from Able Seaman to Admiral and back again with bewildering rapidity.

Brown on Resolution, I discovered to my satisfaction, was intended to be the largest and most expensive production ever tackled by a British studio. Location work had never before been attempted on such a scale. A small, rocky island was bought off Falmouth, and for the first time in history the Admiralty, having approved the script, gave their full co-operation. Warships and personnel were all put at the film company's disposal. The location scenes, which did indeed prove to be rough going, were directed by a young, enthusiastic and talented director who became one of our family's greatest friends, Anthony Asquith – a slight, almost frail person, he was quite fearless, and the enormous success of the film was very largely due to his efforts.

Our first day's shooting took place at Portsmouth. The grand old warship *The Iron Duke* had been put at our disposal: she was lying alongside with a full crew aboard. A notice was posted on the ship's notice-board, asking for volunteers as extras. About sixty were needed. The entire ship's company offered their services; they were all due for shore leave that day, but the chance to appear in the film was obviously too good to miss.

The first scene was a long shot of Able Seaman Brown walking down the gang-plank in the middle of a group of sailors. I had to pause on a mark halfway down, spot my mother (played by the famous Betty Balfour), wave, then continue on down and meet her on the quayside. I was nervous, very nervous. After several rehearsals we were ready to shoot. Scene One, Take One: the clapper-boys smacked the boards together and ducked out of sight. I started off down the gang-plank but I was so jostled by the over-anxious extras that I missed my mark.

'CUT' – Tony Asquith's voice boomed through the microphone. 'First positions, please. Let's try it again.'

During the next half-hour everything that could possibly go wrong did exactly that. On one take the sun went in. On another the camera jammed. Then the sound boom was in frame. We reached Take Ten without a possible print. I was sweating with anxiety by this time and feeling certain that if and when all the technical things worked, I personally would blow it.

While we were waiting for the cameras to be realigned for Take Eleven, a young sailor with red hair and enormous ears, who'd been directly behind me during every take, looked at me very hard and said, 'John, what do you do?' Taken aback, I said that I was an actor. 'I know that John, but what do you do?'

'Well, um ...' I said, searching frantically for an explanation. 'As I ... said ... I'm an actor, and I act in the ... theatre, and um ... if I'm lucky, in a film like this one.'

'I know that,' said Ginger, 'but what do you do for a bloody livin'?'

In those early days of filming I always insisted that whenever possible I should be allowed to do my own stunts. Fire I was not keen on, but with anything else I was always ready to have a go.

Puffin (as Asquith was known to his friends – he looked very like one) described a shot that he said would be very effective without the use of a double. During a lunch break he took me up to the top deck of the cruiser we were shooting on at sea and showed me the plan of action. The scene was to be shot at night. It entailed Able Seaman Brown's escaping from the German cruiser. The camera would pick me up creeping through a cabin door, rifle in hand, boots tied round my neck; then, when no crew were in sight, I was to cross the deck, climb the rail, drop overboard into the sea and start the swim to Resolution Island. The point was, Puffin explained, that as it would be one continuous shot with no cuts, the audience would know that no double had been used and it would therefore have much more reality.

The day was warm and sunny. I had a look over the rails. A long drop, I thought, but not too desperate. I was a strong swimmer and confident that I could make it. 'Right, Puffin,' I said. 'No problem. It's a great shot.'

The call was for 8.30 the following evening. I arrived at the ship in a whaler at 7.30, changed in the mess, and at eight o'clock made my way to the top deck. The weather was appalling, bitterly cold with a damp sea mist. Puffin was huddled up in a duffle coat. 'Hallo, Johnnie, it's a lousy night, but exactly what we want for the scene.'

The ship looked ghostly in the arc-lights. 'Let's just walk through it several times. It's a tricky shot for the focus-puller. We've plenty of time, and we have to get this in Take One – for your sake. Props, get Johnnie a duffle coat – it's freezing.'

I walked to the ship's rail and looked down. At what seemed like a hundred feet below a small collection of rowing boats manned by sailors were floating in a large circle in the sea. Each boat contained life-belts and coils of rope. The floodlights cast eerie shadows on the oily water. A voice beside me said, 'It looks worse at night, doesn't it? They've got the boats down there. If anything goes wrong they'll fish you out in a flash. But it will be great if, when you surface, you could manage to swim away from the ship until you're out of the lights.' Puffin paused and looked sideways at me. 'Sure you don't want a double for the jump? I could cut the shot when you get to the ship's rail, you know.' The temptation was enormous to chicken out, but it would have required more courage than the actual jump. 'No problem,' I said. 'Why lose one of the best shots in the picture?'

We walked it through several times and, as there was still fifteen minutes to go until zero hour, Puffin suggested that I waited in one of the cabins out of the wind. I was sitting staring out of the porthole wondering if I had renewed my life insurance policy when the door opened and a Petty Officer appeared. 'Scuse me, sir,' he said, 'but I hear you're going in the drink tonight, and as it's a bit on the nippy side, we thought you might like to pop into our mess and have a small tot to keep out the cold.'

'That is the happiest thought you've had for years,' I said. 'Lead me to it.'

The small tot turned out to be half a tumbler of that marvellous, oily, amber-coloured liquid called Navy Rum. In a few minutes I was a new man. That tot really hit the jackpot. The effect on an empty stomach was electric – courage spurted from every pore. Then the second assistant came to tell me that they would not be ready for another half an hour – camera problem. 'Time for the other half, sir?'

'Thank you, Petty Officer, why not? Best drink I've ever had in my life.'

Twenty minutes later, when they were ready to shoot, Able Seaman Albert Brown was happily smashed and willing, if asked, to jump off the Eiffel Tower with no safety net. I made my way with great care and precision to the deck, where the wardrobe department undid my boots, tied the laces together and hung them round my neck; a rifle was put into my hand.

Puffin arrived. 'We're all set,' he said. 'How're you feeling?'

'Terrific. Abs'lutely trific.' Puffin gave me a rather old-fashioned look and took half a step backwards. Navy Rum is lethal up to four feet. 'All right, Johnnie, let's shoot it. I'm using a wide-angled lens, so if you don't hit all the marks on the way to the rail it won't matter. Take your time there. Look right and left before you jump. I want to make certain the audience will know it's you and not a double.'

Action. I opened the cabin door and crept slowly, bent double, across the deck. If the scene had necessitated walking upright in a straight line I couldn't have made it. I reached the rail, climbed it, looked right and left as directed and then down at the water. By the light of the arc-lamps I could see the rescue boats bobbing about on the fringe of the circle. The drop looked horrific. Taking a deep breath and mentally crossing myself, I jumped. During the fall, which seemed endless, headlines flashed through my mind: 'Gallant young actor drowned', 'John Mills, rising young star, extinguished'. I hit the water, which felt like concrete, and disappeared into the icy depths. After a struggle I surfaced and, still grasping the rifle, struck out away from the ship. Once out of the floodlit area hands grabbed me and I was hauled on board one of the rowing boats. Take One was OK. Everything worked. It was a print. Puffin was delighted, and so was I. By this time I was sober, and in that condition nothing in the world could have persuaded me to give a repeat performance.

I've just unearthed a cutting from the *Dorset Daily Echo* of 8 September 1934, which stated that the ship we used that night was HMS *Curaçao*, and that 'Mr Mills was in the sea off Portland at midnight, and after the scenes had been filmed he was rushed to Weymouth for a hot bath'. I don't remember that – probably because, before I left the *Curaçao*, the Petty Officers insisted that the best place to restore the circulation before leaving the ship was their mess.

Brown on Resolution (or *Forever England* as it was, mistakenly in my opinion, retitled later) opened with a gala première on 12 May at the New Gallery cinema. The First Sea Lord headed a distinguished audience. These were the days before royal premières, but the film made such an impact that King George V and Queen Mary requested a private showing before the official opening, which enabled the company to advertise on their bills, 'As shown to Their Gracious Majesties, the King and Queen'.

The film received rave notices from every critic, and this time I sailed with the ship. Campbell Dixon, the most respected film critic of the time, wrote that 'the acting of John Mills as Brown lifts him at a stride into the ranks of the stars'. That sentence put me above the title, and with luck, blood, tears, toil and sweat I have managed to remain there ever since.

I have enjoyed nearly all the movies that I've made, but none more than those in which I have been privileged to work with the Navy. The weeks and months spent aboard submarines, destroyers, cruisers and battleships hold memories that I shall always treasure.

II

Takes and Mistakes

Flushed with the success of *Forever England*, Gaumont British offered me a two-year contract. I accepted it, thereby making the first major mistake of my career. I made a series of small-budget films, most of them instantly forgettable: *Doctor's Orders* with the north-country comedian, Leslie Fuller, ill-served by an appalling script; and *Car of Dreams*, a musical with the German star Greta Mosheim. We sang the theme number together close-hauled in a white open Rolls Royce. Miss Mosheim was a splendid actress with an excellent reputation and an advanced case of halitosis. I had the brilliant idea of dispensing extra strong white peppermints to the entire unit just before the take. With everyone sucking away manfully I offered one to my co-star who, with a charming smile, turned it down and consumed her fourth chocolate eclair. The white Rolls Royce stole the film.

The glory of *Forever England* was fading fast, and when I was offered the chance to get back into the theatre I jumped at it. The show was a musical – *Jill Darling*. The stars were Arthur Riscoe, Frances Day (my old dancing partner from the New Cross Empire), Louise Brown and myself. *Jill Darling* was a typical English musical comedy, and a good one. It contained the essentials: a first-class book with a good story-line, attractive music and lyrics, and two or three hit numbers. For the first time I discovered what it was like to dance with a really superb dancer. Louise Brown had begun her career in the ballet, and she brought to the musical comedy stage all the poise and grace that she had learned during her years of training. After a few weeks' rehearsals with her I found that my dancing had improved beyond all recognition.

We opened at the Saville Theatre in Shaftesbury Avenue on 19 December 1934. The show became an instantaneous success. The critics were unanimous in their praise, predicting a year's run. On this occasion the public were in complete agreement with the gentlemen from Fleet Street, and we entertained them at the Saville for the following twelve months.

It is hard for me to write honestly about the next period of my life. I hate making mistakes and find it difficult to accept criticism, however well-meant. I am far too self-critical to welcome criticism from others, and will go to any lengths to try to prove that I haven't made a mistake when I know that I have. I also hate having to admit that I've failed in anything. However, my life, like everyone else's, has been a mixture of success and failure, and it is the latter that I must, like it or not, deal with now.

Professionally, everything in the garden was blooming. Fan-mail was pouring into the dressing-room at the rate of a thousand letters a month, and I was earning £150 a week in the theatre – in those days a large sum of money. I was also receiving a salary from Gaumont British. Financially, I had nothing to worry about. I should, on the face of it, have been contented and happy. I was neither. I had finally come to the reluctant conclusion that the gloomy forecast made in Calcutta by Jimmy Anderson was proving to be only too true.

During the past five years, my marriage to Aileen had slowly but surely started to disintegrate. We'd married when we were young, and had developed in different ways. Thinking back, the only way I developed was professionally. I remained the same dedicated, self-centred actor with no interest whatsoever outside my work except games. During the run of *Cavalcade* I bought a set of hickory-shafted golf clubs from the lost property office for £2, and very soon became golf bore number one. When I wasn't swinging a golf club, I was wielding a tennis racket. When I could, I skied in the winter. This was definitely not Aileen's scene: she was serious, well-read and found sport a bore. I think if she had found success as an actress her life would have been different. As it was, she looked for other interests, took up flying and moved into a completely different and new circle of friends.

It was during this time that I lost the one person I really adored and to whom I could always turn in trouble. My darling mother died suddenly in hospital in London after a short illness. I needed her desperately. I felt completely lost. It has been, and always will be, a great sadness to me that she did not live long enough to see some of the things that I have managed to achieve and that happened to me later on in my career. She was watching *Jill Darling* from a seat in the stage box. I slipped round to see her in the interval. I don't think I had ever seen such happiness and pride on any face before or since. She smiled at me. There were tears in her eyes. 'Oh Johnnie,' she said, and that was all she could manage. She squeezed my hand and kissed me.

'The next act is the best act, darling. Must dash, I'm on first. See you in my dressing-room after the show.'

I didn't see her there. I never saw her in my dressing-room again. Halfway through the last act she collapsed and was rushed to hospital. An hour later I was at her bedside, still in my make-up, white tie and tails. She was very weak but managed to smile at me. I held her hand, a terrible feeling of despair welling up inside me.

'Darling, I'm so sorry,' she whispered. 'It was so lovely, and so were you. I shall never forget it.'

She died in the early hours of the morning. I still miss her dreadfully.

I flung myself into a plethora of work which, luckily, was available. While I was playing eight shows a week at the Saville I made a musical film called *Charing Cross Road* at Beaconsfield Studios, playing opposite an enchanting American star called June Clyde. The hours were killing. I could never get to bed before 1 a.m., then up at 6 a.m., film till 7 p.m., car to the theatre, curtain up at 8 p.m.; and *Jill Darling* was a heavy show for me, with five big dance numbers at each performance. *Charing Cross Road* did not exactly take the town by storm; it was in fact rather a pathetic little picture. In one number I was dressed as a Bengal Lancer. My clothing was several sizes too large and during the last chorus, which I sang in front of a large Union Jack, my turban slipped slowly down over my left eye. The tight budget didn't warrant any re-takes, and that shot finally emerged in the picture.

In the 1930s, one of the highlights of the social season each June was the theatrical garden party, organized to raise funds for the Actors' Orphanage founded in 1896 with Sir Henry Irving as its president. I regret the passing of those garden parties; the profession enjoyed them and so did the public. This particular garden party was one of the most successful. The attractions were many and varied. The public could visit 'Mr Noël Coward at home' in a marquee, where they would be entertained by the Master and Gertrude Lawrence at the piano, later joined by Robert Montgomery, the American film star. They could then have a drink in the 'Yes Madam' bar with Bobby Howes and Binnie Hale, buy an ice-cream from Maurice Chevalier, or visit the Biergarten and enjoy a pint drawn by Sir Cedric Hardwicke.

There was usually one mammoth production: this year it was provided by the Theatre Royal repertory players who appeared in a play entitled *Alfred the Great*. The cast included Fay Compton, Bruce Carfax, Leslie Henson, Leslie Banks and Hayley Bell. I was in charge, with Arthur Riscoe, of *Jill Darling*'s galloping horses. While I was collecting the money for the next drive a girl came up to me and asked me for my autograph. I said I would be delighted to oblige but she would have to give me something for it, because the rule was no free signatures – every penny was needed for the orphanage.

'Of course,' she said. As she was searching for a coin I stared at her. She seemed strangely familiar. We must have met, but where? She looked up at me and smiled. 'You don't remember me, do you?'

'Yes, of course I do.'

'Where did we meet?' I racked my brains. 'China, Tientsin,' she said. 'You came to our house and we played tennis together.'

'Good God, you're the girl on the wire.' She looked blank. 'I'm sorry. I do remember now. I thought you looked like Peter Pan.'

She laughed and handed me a sixpence. Just as I was about to sign her programme Arthur Riscoe shouted, 'Put that bird down, Johnnie, you'll be off.'

I grabbed a horse as it came past and jumped on the merry-go-round. I looked back, and saw her small figure disappearing into the crowd, and felt a sudden urge to jump off and follow her. Instead I shouted, 'What's your name?'

'Mary.'

'Mary what?' I yelled.

'Mary Hayley Bell.'

By this time the noise from the hurdy-gurdy was deafening. I screamed above it, 'Marvellous name. I won't forget it.'

When the horses completed their first circle I searched the crowd for her, but she was gone.

When *Jill Darling* finished I went straight into two more films for Gaumont British. From the first, *Bad Blood*, where we shot the locations in and around Marseilles and Paris, three things spring to my mind: meeting Lilli Palmer, an enchanting young actress from Vienna who was making her debut in English pictures and who has remained a close friend ever since; preparing to dive into a swimming pool on the outskirts of Paris and spotting the dead body of a man floating face up in the shallow end; and driving a Chrysler car (with a platform built out from the back of it to hold the camera man and focus puller) round the Arc de Triomphe for three hours during the morning rush-hour traffic – a hazardous exercise under normal conditions, but on this occasion positively death-defying. The gallant French drivers drove straight at me and scored several direct hits. When the car was examined after the morning's work the chassis was found to be four inches out of alignment.

The second film, *Tudor Rose*, starring Nova Pilbeam and Cedric Hardwicke, like *Bad Blood* did nothing to further my career. I played the young Earl of Dudley and was beheaded in the third reel – not, in my opinion, a moment too soon.

At this period, as my film career was dwindling, another actor's was flourishing. He had made an enormous success in three pictures – *The Count of Monte Cristo*, *The Ghost Goes West* and *The Thirty-Nine Steps* (the Hitchcock version, and the first). Hollywood studios were wooing him. They were so keen to sign him that he could almost have written his own contract. Robert Donat's first love, however, was the theatre. He turned his back on the dollars, became an actor-manager and chose for his first venture a play by James Lonsdale Hodson called *Red Night*. I was offered the part of Syd Summers – a beautifully drawn cockney character who, because the author had given him most of the comedy in a tragic situation, I felt might prove too effective and upset the balance of the play. The cast was a strong one: it included an excellent young actor, Bernard Lee, who was starting to make a name for himself, George Carney, the Yorkshire comedian, and a very young actress, Meriel Forbes (now Lady Richardson).

We opened at Blackpool. The play was well received. Bob Donat gave a marvellous performance, but my prediction was proved right: it was obvious when the curtain fell that it had been Syd Summers's evening. As the play was intended to be a vehicle for Robert, who was the big star that most of the audience had paid to see, this wasn't from his point of view exactly the best thing to happen. The notices the following morning underlined the situation. They were good for the play, good for Robert but too good for me. For the first time good personal notices worried me. The West End was waiting eagerly for Robert's arrival as an actor-manager, and he naturally had hoped to have a big personal triumph.

We moved to Bournemouth – the same thing happened there. Rumours started to circulate that the management were even considering taking the play off and having it re-written, cutting some of the comedy and building up the dramatic scenes. I was naturally worried. I felt that if I played Syd Summers in the West End the odds were that I should have the success in a straight play that I badly wanted, but at the same time I could fully understand the position as far as Robert was concerned.

At Oxford, the last date before the suggested West End opening, Robert invited me to supper and told me that his backers and another director of his company had advised him, in his own interest, not to take *Red Night* into town. They had pointed out, he said, what to the company was fairly obvious: that his part really wasn't strong enough, and for his first venture they felt it essential that he should enjoy a big personal success. My heart dropped with a thud; although I was half-expecting it, it was still a bitter pill to swallow. 'Do you understand the position, Johnnie?'

'Of course I do,' I said.

'I know how bitterly disappointed you will be not to be able to play Syd Summers in London, especially as you're giving one of the best comedy performances I've seen on the stage for years.'

'Well,' I said, 'I shan't feel exactly like celebrating, but I'll get over it.'

'You won't have to,' was the reply. 'There is a tide in the affairs of men etc. You are going to give that performance in London and I hope you get the notices you deserve. It would be a crime not to let you have this chance. I've thanked my advisers for their well-meant suggestion and politely told them to stuff it. I'm taking the play in.'

We opened at the Queen's Theatre on 4 March 1936. The critic in the *New Statesman* wrote: 'Mr Robert Donat shows great courage and self-denial in producing this play as his first essay in management, for his own part is easily the least effective and worst written of the many characters in the story, and unlike most actor-manager parts he's very seldom in the limelight.' This is the notice out of all the others that I cherish. I cannot imagine a kinder or more generous gesture by an actor. It was more than gratifying, therefore, to find that one critic at least had the perception to realize how unselfish Robert Donat had been. It was entirely through him that I was able to establish myself in a great part in the legitimate theatre. But *Red Night* was only a medium success. The memory of *Journey's End* was still too strong, and the new play suffered in comparison.

Not surprisingly, my contract with Gaumont British was not renewed. I was thankful. I had not been provided with a really good part or picture since *Forever England*. Apart from missing the temporary financial security the contract provided, I was relieved. I was even more relieved, however, when I was offered, only a few days after *Red Night* closed, a leading part in a farce by Vernon Silvaine entitled *Aren't Men Beasts?* The whole project was exciting: I would be working with two of the greatest exponents of farce acting – Robertson Hare and Alfred Drayton. They made a superb combination – Bunny Hare, small, diffident, shy, continually embarrassed, and Alfred Drayton, large, belligerent and dominating. The play was to be directed by that superb little comedian with the hoarse, rasping voice and the face of a surprised frog, Leslie Henson. At the first rehearsal he told us that as it was a hilarious farce containing some very funny lines his advice to us was 'to face the front and bark them into the abyss'.

After a successful tour *Aren't Men Beasts?* opened at the Strand Theatre in May 1936 and began a long and happy run. Bunny and Alfie were a joy to work with and we became firm friends on and off the stage. Part of Alfred Drayton's enormous success as a farce actor was his discipline – he played everything straight down the line. The more sincerely and straight farce is played the funnier it becomes – mugging and over-acting detract from the comedy. Alfie and Bunny were shining examples of their craft. 'In' jokes on the stage were out. Nothing irritates an audience more than watching actors giggling at private jokes. Alfie in particular detested this – his bald head positively glowed with disapproval.

On two occasions, however, things happened that strained control to breaking point. During one scene with the three of us on stage Bunny Hare had to say, 'Indubitably' (a word he made famous), and then in excitement jump up in the air. On one momentous occasion at a matinee, after I can only suppose a large helping of baked beans for lunch, 'Indubitably' Bunny jumped as usual into the air and a foot from the stage produced one of the loudest and most spectacular farts it has ever been my pleasure to hear. There was no question this time of it being an 'in' joke – the audience heard it. There was no need to go through the agony of suppressing the laughter; the house went up in smoke and we went up with it.

The next happening, however, was much more difficult to cope with. At one point Alfred had to shout at the top of his considerable voice, 'Shut up.' During one performance we were all in a line facing front, obeying Leslie's instructions and barking it into the abyss. As Alfie shouted the words the top plate of his false teeth flew out of his mouth making a bee-line for the stalls. With a miraculously quick reaction he shot out his right hand and caught them in mid-flight. The whole thing was so fast that the audience didn't see it, but unfortunately Bunny and I did. The rest of the scene was torture for us. Alfie turned up-stage and returned his high-flying choppers to their rightful home, while we struggled with the agony of suppressing the laughter that threatened to overwhelm us. Somehow we managed to get through it. But Alfie himself was livid. We were in disgrace. The audience didn't pay to see that sort of behaviour. It was two days before he forgave us.

Bunny Hare and Alfred Drayton were a lovely couple – talented, dedicated actors; a pleasure to be with in and outside the theatre. One of the penalties of my age is that so many of my friends have decided that they have done enough entertaining down here and have taken off and are, I hope, playing to packed houses upstairs. Noël Coward once said to a friend, who was complaining about the fact that so many of his contemporaries were passing on, 'I do know what you mean, dear boy. When I have lunch with anyone these days I consider myself fortunate if he lasts till the coffee.'

The run of luck that I had enjoyed for so long seemed finally to be running out. I walked head-first into a series of flops. For the next two years everything that I touched seemed doomed.

I was reunited with Frances Day in a revue called *Floodlight* written by Beverley Nichols. It was, we thought, a delightful show, but the critics were less than kind, and we closed after a short run. It was memorable, however, for the emancipation of Frances Day. Frances had blossomed – there is no other word for it – into something quite special. She'd developedintooneofthemostfascinatingcharactersinthemusicaltheatre. Men adored her, but women disliked her – she became a permanent threat to their happy marriages from the moment the curtain went up. She had the most colossal nerve and powers of persuasion that were impossible to resist. When the show closed she decided to blow away dull care and sail to Deauville for a few days' holiday. She invited myself, Anthony Pélissier and an up-and-coming young solicitor, Isador Kerman, to accompany her on the trip.

The arrangements were typical of Frances's technique. She rang Captain Watts in Albemarle Street and informed him that she was thinking of purchasing a large, comfortable sailing-boat. If he had anything that might suit her, perhaps the captain would put it at her disposal for a few days' trial. I arrived at Folkestone Harbour on the Sunday morning after we closed to find Isador sitting on a case of champagne, staring up at one of the biggest yachts I've ever seen. The *Kestrel* was a double-masted schooner and quite beautiful. The crew were on board, making preparations for sailing. We stared at each other. Could this be it? At that moment a large chauffeur-driven Rolls Royce arrived, and from it emerged our hostess resplendent in white slacks, blue reefer jacket with gold buttons, and a sailor's hat perched at just the right angle on her platinum blonde hair.

The first hour was pure bliss: the sea was calm with a slight breeze. We sat on deck drinking champagne, watching Folkestone recede into the distance. But the English Channel, as all sailors know, is an unpredictable stretch of water; within an hour the *Kestrel* was tossing, twisting and rolling in a Force Eight gale. The rest of the crossing was a nightmare for everyone, except Frances. She didn't turn a single platinum hair, but the three of us turned a delicate shade of green and spent the crossing flat on our backs on the deck praying for deliverance. Our hostess came to tell us that lunch was ready. The ship's cook was apparently rather under the weather, and she had taken over in the galley and finished the menu. The roast pork, she said, looked delicious. We were not amused.

The rest of the short holiday was so marvellous that the few hours of torture were soon forgotten. We swam, sunbathed and gambled. The voyage home too was perfect. The Channel behaved itself; I fell in love with boats and the sea, and have remained in that state ever since.

Frances rang Captain Watts on our return and said that although she liked the boat she wasn't absolutely sure it was the right one. The owner's quarters were a bit cramped. Perhaps she should think in terms of something a little larger – that would need a crew of six, perhaps. One didn't want to make a mistake, did one? Captain Watts completely understood and would, he said, be only too happy to be of any assistance in the future. Who else, I thought, would have been able to lay on a trip like that for absolutely nothing? No one, except Frances Day.

Firth Shepherd, one of London's leading impresarios, decided to launch a new type of entertainment that was intended to relax the tired business-man and his wife after a good dinner. *Choose Your Time*, which opened and closed not long after at the Piccadilly Theatre, offered to an amazed public in the first half a newsreel, a Donald Duck cartoon and two variety turns – Nelson Keys and Florence Desmond. The second half consisted of a comedy played without an interval called *Talk of the Devil*, written by Anthony Pélissier.

Alas, this mixture just didn't work. Donald Duck on the fifteen-foot screen dwarfed the two brilliant artists, Bunch Keys and Flo Desmond, who were unfortunately for them next on the bill. The interval gave the tired businessmen and their wives the opportunity to knock back two or three quick ones in the bar and then leave for supper at the Trocadero. I was more concerned for Ant than myself. He had produced to order a well-written comedy that worked. It was well-acted by a cast that in-cluded Gertrude Musgrove, Naunton Wayne, that enchanting come-dienne Yvonne Arnaud and myself. The play received good reviews, but the evening on the whole was a disaster. It did, however, prove one thing to me: Anthony Pélissier could write.

During this gloomy period in the theatre the British film industry, after a promising start, was struggling for survival. Jympson Harman, the *Evening News* film correspondent, wrote in June 1938 an article which painted a depressing picture. His headline was '500,000 Pounds Worth of British Stars Who Ought To Be Busy'. He went on to ask, 'What has become of our favourite filmstars – Jessie Matthews, Clive Brook, Vivien Leigh, Lilli Palmer, John Mills and Cicely Courtneidge?' I could have told him – we were all out of work. He pointed out that over £4 million went down the drain in 1937. Unless things took a large turn for the better in the future I could see myself following it.

The prospect looked so bleak that Ant and I decided to drown our troubles in the spring snow at Saenenmoser, a delightful village in the Swiss Alps. Skiing was marvellous, the weather was perfect, the glühwein was heady, but I was uneasy. I can't remember ever really enjoying a holiday unless I had a job to come back to. One evening in the bar we were discussing the theatre as usual, and the Pélissier Follies came up in the conversation. After the second bottle of heavy Swiss red wine had been consumed we decided that London was ready and waiting with bated breath for a revival of the famous Follies. Ant had the rights of several of his father's famous numbers – 'Moon, Moon Serenely Shining' and so on – and he could put together rapidly and with little or no problem a superb show.

Fired with enthusiasm, heightened by the vino, we returned to London. Ant contacted a friend of his, Robert Nesbitt, who liked the idea, and together they devised the show. An excellent cast was assembled including my old friend Doris Hare, Gene Gerrard and an enchanting young musical comedy actress, Roma Beaumont. The Saville Theatre was again chosen as the battleground: I hoped it might prove to be third time lucky.

Initially things looked fairly promising. An enthusiastic reception on the first night, and a mixed bag of notices, some good, some fair; but unfortunately for us James Agate, the one critic who at the time was powerful enough to make or break the show, wrote a long, brilliantly written piece in the *Sunday Times* which I feel sounded the show's death-knell. Agate made the point that '... Pélissier's acting went on up to his death when all genius in his kind was not eclipsed but extinguished as far as we can see forever. The co-optivists who followed in 1921 were a pale echo of the follies and the Pélissier Follies of 1938 are a still paler echo of the co-optivists.' James Agate was right: Harry Pélissier *was* the follies. The shows that followed with his name on the bills, but without his presence on the stage, were pale, ghostly creations that never materialized.

A determined optimist by nature, I found it depressing and difficult to admit to myself that my career during the past two years had been disappointing. After a truthful stock-taking I came to the conclusion that I had been dissipating my chances of any real achievement by not channelling my energy in one direction. I had jumped from films to musicals and straight plays without staying long enough in any one of them to make real progress. Finance had, of course, a great deal to do with it. I had never been secure enough to turn down offers.

After nine years in the profession I knew what I wanted and what, come hell or high water, I had to achieve. Musicals had been fun: I had enjoyed them, but I needed and longed for the chance to play some of the great classical roles, and I knew this would only be possible if I got back into the straight theatre and stayed there. This I was determined to do, even if it meant turning down offers of musicals which would most probably come along.

I reckoned that as the year happened to be 1938, which added up to the golden number twenty-one, the prospect looked bright. Events, however, proved that piece of reckoning to be totally wrong. 1938 will go down as the most disastrous twelve months in my private history. During January and February my phone went dead – nothing, no offers of any kind. As an act of bravado Anthony Pélissier and I took off for a skiing holiday at Scheidegg, a small village at the foot of the mighty Jungfrau in the Swiss Alps. At that time we were still at the novice stage but keen to try some rather more difficult runs than resorts like Kandersteg could offer. The Cambridge team were in training at Scheidegg and suggested one evening in the bar that we should try the Devil's Punch Bowl with them the following day.

On a clear, crisp Swiss morning we took the small mountain railway that pulled us up the Jungfrau to the station from which skiers disembarked for the downhill runs in the Devil's Punch Bowl. Putting on our skis we walked with some of the Cambridge team up to the starting point, the edge of the Bowl. I looked down and blanched – the slope was more like the side of a skyscraper: it seemed to be practically vertical. Dotted here and there were fir trees and large menacing black boulders. At the bottom of the Bowl figures moving about looked like minute clockwork toys. The Cambridge team took off, disappearing like birds; they seemed to float down at incredible speed, their effortless christies sending up showers of powder snow. We looked at each other. 'We could, I suppose, wait around a bit, have a glühwein and take the next train down.'

'Yes, we could,' said Ant. 'But we can't, can we?'

'No, we can't,' I said. 'Let's toss up for who gets killed first.'

Ant lost the toss, checked his ski bindings, straightened up, solemnly shook hands and said, 'Au revoir! Tell them I was smiling when I left. *Vive la France!*'

He put his skis together, crouched, and took off. Having not mastered the full christy turn – the only hope in the Punch Bowl – Ant had obviously decided the only way to make the descent would be by a death-defying schuss. I watched him travel at speed in a straight line to the bottom. One of the large black boulders unfortunately happened to be directly in his path. He was about halfway down. To avoid certain death I saw him suddenly attempt to twist himself into a right-handed turn. The points of his skis locked, and he became airborne, turning at least two somersaults before he hit the snow. He then proceeded to bump and roll his way to the bottom. I watched, transfixed. After a moment or two a tiny figure struggled to its feet. I could only think of the little round Michelin tyre man in the advertisement. As I looked it raised two tiny little arms above its head and a voice rang and echoed round the Devil's Punch Bowl: 'GOD! ARE YOU LISTENING? YOU DON'T EXIST!'

Fifty falls later I joined my friend at the bottom. By some miracle neither of us was hurt in any way – not even a twisted ankle. Later that evening in the hotel bar the Cambridge team asked us what we thought of the run. 'Quite fun,' said Ant, 'but do you think you could suggest something tomorrow where we could be absolutely certain to break our necks ...?'

The daffodils were out and so was I. April, and still no sign of any work. A few weeks later an offer arrived: a small part – two days' work – in *Goodbye Mr Chips*, starring Robert Donat. MGM were making the film in England. My agent at that time was an American, Harry Ham, in the famous Myron Selznick office. He advised me to accept the part. An MGM film with Donat would be certain of an American release and, he added, with a wealth of meaning, 'You need the exposure, Johnnie.' He was right. I accepted the offer, and spent two enjoyable days with my old friend Bob Donat, who was giving the performance of his career, for which he was eventually awarded an Oscar.

Another gap – a long one. It always amazes me how quickly bank balances seem to deflate during out-of-work periods. Mine, at this time, was getting perilously near the danger mark. Then came the moment of truth: an offer arrived for a new musical at a salary of £150 per week. I sweated it out for a couple of days, gritted my teeth and turned it down. Things remained menacingly quiet on the straight theatre front and I began to think I had made an idiotic mistake in turning down all that lovely money. I asked my agent if he was worried. He said he wasn't; there was no point in both of us worrying.

I was saved from complete penury by a small budget picture which I made at Denham Studios called *Four Dark Hours*, with Rene Ray and Robert Newton. It was directed by a charming American, William K. Howard, who, although no one suspected it at the time, was happily hitting the bottle. I discovered this quite by accident. During the mid-morning break I noticed that the property man always brought a pot of tea and two cups to our director on the set. It was his habit during this fifteen minutes to discuss the previous day's work with his editor, whom he had brought with him from the States. On one occasion the editor was absent. I had missed the tea trolley and asked Bill Howard if I could have a cup of his tea. He hesitated for a second and then said, 'Sure, Johnnie, black or with milk?' 'Milk, please,' I said, and took a large gulp. It was neat whisky. Bill smiled at me as I choked. 'Heart-starter time,' he said. 'We don't have tea-breaks in the studios back home. Great idea.' Bill Howard had made some excellent movies in America, but by the time we caught up with him he was, I'm afraid, slightly over the hill. It was fortunate that at this time Bob Newton had not started the heart-starter technique: if he had *Four Dark Hours* might never have seen daylight.

After another three months of idleness I found myself in what my little Aunt Betty would have called 'a state'. I was at my lowest ebb, my optimism deserted me, and I began to doubt my ability; I had been just too lucky – a flash in the pan. I had built up such a massive inferiority complex that I often had to walk out of a play or a film before the end of the performance because I felt that if I ever did get another chance I would probably never succeed. Just when I was considering ringing up my old firm the Sanitas Company and re-applying for a job as a commercial traveller a minor miracle occurred.

During this period I spent a great deal of time with Larry and Vivien Olivier. They were wonderful chums and very conscious of what I was going through. In their company I found I could cope with the feeling of being at the bottom of the basket. On form they were the funniest couple it would be possible to meet – wonderful foils for each other, both great raconteurs, and their sense of humour was infectious.

On one momentous evening I was with them at Durham Cottage, their London home in Knightsbridge. Vivien was curled up on the sofa. I remember thinking she was one of the most exquisite creatures I'd ever seen. Larry was mixing the drinks. It was a celebration. Vivien had just plucked from under the noses of all the top Hollywood stars the prize plum they all wanted – Scarlett O'Hara in *Gone With the Wind*.

A tall, very tall young man arrived: he must have been at least six feet four, because he had to stoop as he made his entrance. His name was Tyrone Guthrie, one of the most exciting and successful directors of that time. I'd seen many of his productions and longed to work with him, but I had never even met him. Whether or not that evening had been arranged by Larry I shall never know. He strongly denies it, but it was too coincidental for me quite to believe it, coming as it did at the make-or-break point in my life. Tony Guthrie was discussing with the enthusiasm he showed for everything his forthcoming season at the Old Vic. I was sitting in a corner quaffing my third Olivier fire-ball, feeling totally out of it all: an out-of-work actor surrounded by success, three people with glittering prospects ahead of them and the world at their feet. I heard Larry say, 'What are you starting off the season at the Old Vic with, Tony?'

'I'm only doing two productions this time – *The Dream*, and *She Stoops to Conquer*.' He then launched into the marvellous new ideas he had for *A Midsummer Night's Dream*. It had been done to death, he said. It had to be different. For instance, he had persuaded Robert Helpmann, the famous Australian ballet dancer, to play Oberon, and he wanted the same sort of unusual off-beat casting for Puck. He had looked everywhere, but so far had drawn a blank.

'Well, you needn't look any further, Tony dear, the actor you want is sitting right there.' Larry pointed in my direction with his glass. There was a long pause. I gulped. Guthrie stared at me. 'Good God,' he said. Another even longer pause. 'It's right. Absolutely right. For me anyway – but I mean you'd never consider it, would you?'

'Why not?' I managed, faintly.

'Well, it's the financial angle. I know what you must be getting in musicals. Your salary at the Vic would amount to the magnificent sum of £15 per week. You couldn't possibly accept that, could you?'

Larry broke in: 'Tony, stop waffling. If you think it's a good idea, make him an offer.'

Tony Guthrie stood up suddenly and bumped his head hard on the ceiling. 'Johnnie, will you play Puck for me at the Vic for £15 a week?'

I stared at him. After the months of frustration, disappointment and despair I found it difficult to believe any of this was happening. 'I'll play Puck for you at the Vic or anywhere else you want me to for 15s. a week if necessary. There is nothing in this world at the moment I can think of that I would rather do.'

Hours later I weaved my way into the early morning air with the knowledge that I was to start rehearsals at the Old Vic in two weeks' time, to play Puck in *A Midsummer Night's Dream* and Young Marlowe in *She Stoops to Conquer*. I was convinced that, in spite of Ant's *cri de cœur* from the Devil's Punch Bowl, God really did exist.

12

Going Straight

The Old Vic Theatre in the Waterloo Road was dirty, smelly, in a poor state of repair, and glorious. It had an atmosphere all of its own, and I have never met a single actor or actress who didn't love it passionately. I was no exception, and remember the three months I spent there as one of the happiest and most stimulating periods in my career. The rehearsals were a joy. Guthrie had assembled an excellent cast – Ursula Jeans, Edward Chapman, Pamela Browne, George Benson, Margaret Yarde, Anthony Nicholls, Dorothy Hyson and Robert Helpmann. We were always at the theatre early in case we should miss a second of the whirl-wind that would arrive in the shape of that tall, gangly Irishman Tyrone Guthrie. He was usually accompanied by his wife Judy, who was nearly as tall as he was and looked exactly like him; in fact at first I took her to be his sister.

He worked at a furious pace, dashing backwards and forwards from the stage to the stalls. An excellent actor, he found it hard to resist show-ing us what he was trying to get at. Most of us found this somewhat intimidating as his performance (because he knew exactly what he wanted) was usually, or so we felt, infinitely superior to anything we thought we might manage to achieve.

The season, thanks to the maestro, was a triumph. Both productions, *The Dream* and *She Stoops*, were vintage Guthrie. The critics were unani-mous in their praise. The *Guardian* notice summed up the general re-action: 'This is in short an occasion for suspending the rigours of criticism and the Old Vic audience was left at the end in a state of just and John-sonian exhilaration.' Modesty forbids me to quote my personal notices, but given the chance I couldn't have written better ones myself. I do feel perhaps that I improved a little on the scintillating performance that I gave as Puck at Beccles at the age of nine.

My costume for Puck was a skin-tight, one-piece arrangement made of a sort of stocking material, painted all over with mystical signs. After a few weeks of concentrated physical effort – Guthrie had invented a highly gymnastic Puck – I discovered that the paint had melted or worn off in the area of my crutch. I was sharing a dressing room with Robert Helpmann, and after one matinee I showed him the damage. 'Not worth bothering the wardrobe for. I'll fix that. Stand up with one foot on each of those chairs.'

I did as I was ordered. A minute later the door opened and two of my old acquaintances from Felixstowe were greeted by the sight of Puck standing legs astride on two chairs facing them with a slightly strange look on his face, and Oberon, with his back to them, kneeling underneath delicately tracing yellow and pink lines on my crutch with two sticks of make-up. It's not difficult to imagine what my friends thought we were up to.

Another awkward moment came on stage. Tony Guthrie had arranged a superb entrance for Titania; she appeared from the wings up-stage, looking breathtakingly beautiful. Spotting Oberon waiting down-stage with Puck at his feet she tiptoed daintily through a guard of honour of her fairies who were formed up into a lane, each one of them holding a little star which they lit up by switching on the torches to which they were attached. Arriving at the footlights she dropped a graceful curtsey at Oberon's feet. It made an enchanting spectacle, and always brought audible 'Oohs' and 'Aahs' from the children at every matinee.

At one unforgettable performance the action was slightly different. Titania, halfway through the lane of fairies, caught her foot in her dress, tripped and landed with a thud on her bottom at Oberon's feet, exposing to a rapt audience a dainty pair of pink frilly knickers. Her crown, slipping over her left eye at a rakish angle, completed the picture. The audience, of course, were more than in the joke. Even so, it took Bobby Helpmann nearly ten minutes to get through 'I know a bank whereon the wild thyme grows . . .' It didn't help him to have Puck helpless with laughter hanging on to his knees staring up at him.

That season at the Vic more than fulfilled my wildest dreams. Tony Guthrie and I became close friends. He convinced me that I was ready to take on some of 'the big ones', and it was arranged that I should join him at the Vic next season and tackle *Hamlet*, *Richard III*, and *Henry V*. He advised me that whatever else I happened to be engaged in I should find time to do a great deal of homework on the three very different and daunting roles. Just to add the cherry to the icing on the cake I signed a contract to start rehearsals almost immediately for a new play by Keith Winter called *We At the Crossroads*.

No one, however brilliant and experienced they may be, can ever forecast the result of a play before it has been performed in front of an audience. Films and plays that the management, the cast, the backers and the director have considered to have every chance of success have flopped disastrously. *We At the Crossroads* is a shining if unhappy example. Everyone concerned with the production thought it had to be a winner. Well-written, with an excellent cast, including Robert Harris, Hugh Williams, Adrienne Allen, Ena Burrill, Ronald Ward, Jill Esmond and Harry Andrews, the direction was in the capable hands of Murray Mac-Donald, who already had several big hits to his credit. The Globe Theatre on Shaftesbury Avenue was perfect for the play. All the signs were favourable.

We opened and closed within three weeks. But the lucky streak that had deserted me for so long returned with a vengeance. Before I left the Globe Norman Marshall, the director, asked me if I would be interested in doing a play at the minute Gate Theatre behind Victoria Station. 'Well, as it's "art for art's sake"' – the salaries were even smaller than the theatre – 'it rather depends on the play. What is it?'

'*Of Mice and Men* by Steinbeck,' came the reply.

It took a while to sink in. George, in *Of Mice and Men*, was the one part I would have chosen to play. Wallace Ford, who had been a friend since we filmed *O.H.M.S.* in 1936, had played it in New York. It had run for two years and he had made a sensational success. A few weeks before Norman Marshall talked to me, Wally had sent me a copy of the play and suggested that if a management could be persuaded to produce it in England, come hell or high water, I had to play George.

Of Mice and Men is a great play – the story from which it is taken was probably the best thing that Steinbeck ever wrote. It is difficult in these enlightened (if that's the right word) days to believe that the Censor refused permission for the play to be performed in the commercial theatre because he considered the language was too strong and might offend the public. The words that he objected to were 'Oh Jesus', uttered by George in a moment of great stress, and 'several God-damned idiots'. At the Gate, however, since it was a club theatre, these disgusting and degrading slips of dialogue were allowed.

The Gate Theatre was unique. Unhappily, like so many others, it has disappeared. Theatres like the Gate where one could experiment and try out new plays in the centre of London are sadly missed. There were two small dressing-rooms – one for actors and one for actresses – and one loo, which made first nights more of a hazard than ever; the stage was about the size of a large tea-tray. There was no orchestra pit, which put the occupants of the front row well within arm's reach.

Niall MacGinnis was cast as Lennie, the huge, powerful simpleton who travels round from ranch to ranch with George, bucking grain bags. Clare Luce, who had played in the New York production, came over to repeat her performance as the blonde *femme fatale*. After two years' run in New York, she was still enthralled with the play and jumped at the chance to play it in London. I personally was glad she did; Norman Marshall, a fine director with a good record, was I felt slightly out of his depth with *Of Mice and Men*. Clare Luce was an enormous asset, and Niall and I often worked on far into the night when the general rehearsals were finished.

A picture of Jimmy Cagney's was playing at that time in the West End – *Angels With Dirty Faces*. During the rehearsal period I must have seen it at least twelve times; I had never played an American, I needed the accent, and incidentally a lot of Jimmy Cagney himself. He would have been terrific as George and I built the character with that wonderful little American actor firmly in mind.

I shall always feel indebted to the critics who saw the first night at the Gate Theatre. They all raved about the play; but what to us was more important, they quite savagely attacked the Censor for refusing a licence for the commercial theatre. During the four weeks' run at the Gate, they kept up the attack. They paid second visits to the play and lambasted the Lord Chamberlain in their columns the following morning. The suspense became unbearable. We were all naturally dying to transfer to the West End because this time we knew without any doubt that we would be basking in a smash hit. It wasn't until the last Saturday matinee that we heard the news. The gentlemen from Fleet Street had won the day. A licence was granted and we were free to invade Shaftesbury Avenue. The Censor made two stipulations – instead of 'Jesus', I had to say 'Jeeze', and 'God-damned' had to become 'God-darned'. He had protected the public – unbelievable but true.

We opened at the Apollo Theatre on 24 May. The atmosphere that evening was electric. First-night audiences can sometimes be cool and difficult to get hold of, but on this occasion they were totally with the play from the moment the curtain rose. We were all very keyed up, but the four weeks behind us at the Gate Theatre enabled us to keep the first-night jitters under control, and the performance on that evening was the best the company had given.

The last scene always had a profound effect on our audiences at the Gate. It was emotionally exhausting to play and must have been harrowing to watch. To save Lennie from certain lynching George is forced to shoot him in the back of the head as he stares out across the Salinas River, while he tells him of their dream for the future – their own piece of land with chickens, cows and rabbits. Lennie has insisted during the play on having this comforting story repeated to him again and again. Finally, George fires. Lennie crumples. After the shot the voices of the men are heard in the distance as the curtain slowly falls.

At the Gate Theatre Norman Marshall had arranged that the stage manager should hold the curtain down for about fifteen seconds and then slowly raise it, and instead of a normal 'call' Niall and I would hold the same positions until the curtain was lowered. Then the full company calls would go into operation.

On the first night at the Apollo the curtain fell, and Niall and I held our positions. Dead silence. Not even a smattering of applause for the full fifteen seconds. Blinking through the tears I whispered to Niall, lying on his face in the bullrushes, 'They've all gone home'. The stage manager pressed a button and raised the curtain. Although it was not possible to see very clearly into the auditorium, I was aware that they were all still there, but sitting immobile. The curtain was lowered again. Then it happened. In all my experience in the theatre I can't remember hearing such a thunderclap of spontaneous applause.

All the critics were present at the first night at the Apollo, and all of them wrote again fully of the play and the performances. Having mentioned how much I gained by watching a small (only in stature) American actor, I must quote a few words from one critic's pen that gave me considerable pleasure. The notice appeared in the *Sunday Graphic* on 28 May: 'Superbly acted by all, particularly by John Mills in a Cagney role that would make James touch his cap and say, if the word was in his vocabulary, "maestro".' The play was the hit of the season. The advance bookings were phenomenal. A year's run looked a bookie's cert.

One sure sign of success is when all the people you hope will come and see the play pour in within the first few weeks. The Oliviers arrived shortly after we opened. The word got round that they were out front, and as usual on these occasions when VIPs from their own profession are in the audience the cast were as keen to give of their best as they were on the first night. I was particularly on edge. The closer the friend, the more nervous I become.

There was one small but carefully thought-out gesture that I was proud of and felt to be moving and effective. After the murder of Curley's wife in the barn, realizing that Lennie has been the cause of it, George walks very slowly across the stage and exits through the door of the barn. My touch of genius was to leave my left hand on the door-post for a second or two when I was out of sight of the audience, then let it fall lifelessly and disappear from view. I was inordinately proud of this and looked forward to that magical moment at every performance. Larry and Vivien arrived in my dressing-room and raved about the play and my performance. Vivien was still in tears; she had found the last scene almost unbearably sad.

Later on at supper in the Moulin d'Or I said to Larry: 'Right. Now let's have it. I know you meant what you said in the dressing-room, and

I'm thrilled, but you also know we've always sworn to be as honest as we can with each other. Now was there anything in my performance that you didn't really like?'

'Well, there was one thing – it's only small.' He paused.

'Right! Tell me! Anything, please.'

'It was your exit after the murder – that lingering hand on the door-post. Just a shade too much. I honestly think you should cut it.' It was out at the next performance.

Now everything in the garden should have been more than lovely. The doldrums were over. I had achieved what I had longed for. I was back in the legitimate theatre playing a great part in a great play; and best of all there was a season at the Old Vic to look forward to.

By this time, however, my marriage had practically ceased to exist. Success I find can only really be enjoyed through someone who is very close to you; it is their reactions to it that are important. But I seemed to have no one.

I was very close to Ant at this time, and he, I felt, was concerned. I was always the last to leave any party after the show, and spent much more time dealing with the liquid rather than the solid refreshment. Hangovers are no help to a performance; and because at least I had the sense to deny myself the 'hair of the dog' before the show, occasionally the matinees became a refined form of torture. The situation wasn't made any easier by the fact that Niall MacGinnis, a lovely man, was as his name implies no slouch where the bottle was concerned. We became George and Lennie off-stage as well as on. Niall, with the best part of a bottle of Paddy Irish Whiskey inside him, was more than a handful. One evening he arrived in my dressing-room before the show: 'Hallo, Johnnie, me darling. Shake hands. Shake the hand of your old friend.'

I took it. A mistake. He leaned backwards, braced himself and the next second I found myself flying over his head and landing in the washbasin. On that occasion Niall had obviously decided to cure his hangover. The performance that night was memorable. During one scene the character called Curley, who hates Lennie, insults him and then finally hits him. George has drilled it into Lennie that on no account is he to retaliate because, with his great strength, he could and would kill or seriously maim any assailant. But George, seeing his friend hit several times in the face by Curley, suddenly says: 'OK Lennie, get him.' Lennie then grabs one of Curley's hands and squeezes it, breaking the bones. In every other performance Niall had of course 'acted' this, but that evening the several belts of Paddy took over. Niall *became* Lennie. He was enormously strong, and we realized that Curley's screaming had a frighteningly different note. It was for real. Niall had gone berserk. Before we could pull him off, Curley's hand looked as if it had been caught in a mangle. Niall was not alone in being affected by the play. It had a strong effect on all the cast, and after the curtain dropped it took some time to return completely to normal.

13

Mary

In June Ant gave a lunch party in his mother's (Fay Compton's) flat in Dolphin Square to celebrate his engagement to Penelope Dudley Ward. When I explained that I couldn't make it as I was playing in a golf match at Moore Park, Ant said, 'Ditch it. It's important. You must come. I've got a present for you.'

'A present for me? I should be giving you one. You're the one that's getting married. Anyway, can't you give it to me tonight at the theatre?'

'No,' said Ant.

'Right,' I said, 'but that present had better be something special.'

The party was fun. Noël was there with his great friend Joyce Carey, Fay Compton and several other actors and actresses from shows playing in the West End.

'Well, where is it? I'm enjoying the party, but I'm only really here because you mentioned the word present.'

Ant looked, I thought, slightly disconcerted. 'Actually, I can't give it to you yet, because it's ... well, it's not here.'

'Not here? You mean it's not been delivered?'

'Delivered's not exactly the word, but, well it's not here yet. But I'm sure it will turn up. Give it another fifteen minutes.'

At four o'clock I said, 'Thanks awfully for the present. You shouldn't have spent the money. I'm sure when I see it I'll love it. But now I'm off. See you later.'

He looked disappointed. 'I'm awfully sorry, Johnnie. Something's gone wrong.'

I pressed the bell for the lift. It arrived. The lift door opened, and there she stood – the girl with the golden hair and lovely sea-green eyes. She smiled at me. 'You owe me sixpence.'

'I know. I'm awfully sorry, I remember. You never got my autograph, did you?' This time, it all fell into place. Tientsin, Colonel Hayley Bell's house, Peter Pan on a wire, my tennis partner, the theatrical garden party.

'What's my name?' she smiled again.

The actor with the worst memory for names in the business for once came through. 'Mary,' I said triumphantly. 'Mary Hayley Bell. I told you at the garden party it was a marvellous name, and I wouldn't forget it.' There was a pause. We stared at each other. 'Are you coming to this party?'

'Yes, I am. I can't stay long though. I've got a dress rehearsal at five o'clock. But Anthony insisted that I turned up, if only for a few minutes. He said it was important. He said he had a present for me.'

'That's funny. He said exactly the same thing to me. But mine hasn't turned up. I'll come with you. Yours is probably there.' I took her hand and walked back across the passage to the flat. I felt I never wanted to let go of it, ever again.

Ant was perched on the window-sill with a glass of champagne in his hand. He looked up as we entered. I noticed a look of pleasure and relief come over his face. 'Hallo Hayley, I'm so glad. I thought you weren't going to make it. How did the rehearsal go? She's opening tonight in Diana Churchill's part with Lilian Braithwaite in *Tony Draws a Horse* at the Comedy Theatre.'

'Hayley,' a voice called from the other side of the room. It was Fay Compton. 'Come and tell me all about the rehearsal.'

Ant looked at me. 'What do you think of her?'

'Think of who?' I said.

'You know damn well who. The girl you were holding hands with when you came in the room. Hayley Bell.'

I looked across the room to where she was standing, talking animatedly to Ant's mother. She was dressed in a simple little frock with shoulder straps with a white silk blouse underneath it. She wore no jewellery. She didn't need it. She seemed to me the most radiantly exciting and utterly adorable little character I had ever met. 'Her name is Mary,' I said.

'I know that,' said Ant. 'That's her first name. But everybody calls her Hayley.'

'Well I don't. I call her Mary.'

'You haven't wasted much time old man, have you?' Ant said.

'Yes, too much. Much too damn much. And I'm not going to waste any more.'

'Well,' said Ant thoughtfully, 'it's always nice when a present is appreciated, and you seem intrigued, I might even say, delighted with yours.'

'But you said it hadn't turned up.'

'It has now. In fact you came in holding its hand. It's over there now talking to my mother.'

We spent about an hour together before she had to leave for her dress rehearsal. I can't remember much of the conversation, but I can remember being completely captivated. I had never met anyone so natural, unaffected, and totally entrancing in my whole life.

Later, I tackled Ant. He had, he said, been concerned about me. I was, as he put it, a 'carpet slipper' man at heart, and the gay Lothario sort of performance I had been giving for the last few years really didn't suit me; he had decided that I needed somebody to pull me together. Just anyone wouldn't do. It had to be the right person, and after months of thinking and looking around it had suddenly all fallen into place, or so he fondly hoped.

Fay Compton, his mother, had returned from an Australian tour with a young actress whom she had taken under her wing. Her name was Hayley Bell. She had fallen in love with an actor in the company and they had planned to get married a few weeks after coming back to England. Without any warning the gentleman in question suddenly took off to a registry office and married the girl he'd left behind him. Not a very elevating or original story, but it had naturally a shattering effect on Fay Compton's young protégée. Ant had suddenly found himself in a position of knowing and liking two people who were both, for very different reasons, going through emotionally distressing times; he had engineered the whole thing, telling us both separately that he had presents for us, to make sure that we would turn up at the party.

When one day in what I hope is the very distant future Ant faces St Peter at the golden gate, he will be able to say in all honesty, 'Well, St Peter, whatever else I may have done, or not done, I was responsible for getting John Mills and Mary Hayley Bell together.'

The next few months will remain in my memory for ever. We seemed to have known each other all our lives. Because of our separate situations and the complications that we knew must arise from the fact that I was still married, we both approached our relationship with a certain wariness and caution. Because of this, we fell deeply in love with each other without the assistance of the first available bed. Marriages that are arranged on this exciting piece of furniture too early on never, to my mind, have the same chance of success.

We were blissfully happy. Both our plays – *Of Mice and Men* and *Tony Draws a Horse* – were playing to capacity houses. *Of Mice and Men* was chosen by the critics as the best play of the year, and as a plus I picked up the Best Actor award. I was tempted to send it to Jimmy Cagney, who really deserved it, but conceit took a hand and it remained on my mantelpiece. I did, however, write to him and apologize for what, if he saw it, he would recognize as a flagrant copy of most of the mannerisms he had made his own. I received a charming letter back, wishing me luck and reminding me that imitation is the sincerest form of flattery.

Mary and I spent the long summer days wandering through Hyde Park, driving out into the country for lunch at some of our favourite pubs, returning just in time for our shows in the evening. There were suppers after the theatre at the Moulin d'Or with Larry and Vivien Olivier who, to my delight, were obviously from the first meeting enchanted with this divine little character with whom it was blatantly obvious I was besotted.

We decided that I must be introduced to her family. She adored them all, especially her father, and, as we were taking no pains to hide the fact that we were madly in love with each other, she didn't want to risk his hearing through rumours what the situation was. I approached this meeting with some trepidation. Colonel Hayley Bell was a great man, a soldier-poet with a brilliant record from World War I, but like many of his generation he adhered to strict principles of moral behaviour, and he was going to be faced with the fact that his favourite daughter was in love with a man who was not only an actor but, at the time of going to press, still married. Something else worried me too: 75 Walcot Square, Lambeth SE11 is a far cry from the Commissioner's house in Tientsin, and I wondered whether it would be possible to bridge that to me awe-inspiring gap.

The Colonel was, luckily for me, an avid theatre fan, and had even admitted at one time to his beloved daughter that he had nourished secret dreams of becoming an actor. The course was obvious. I arranged for Mary to bring her father to a matinee of *Of Mice and Men*. I pointed out that two seats in the stalls plus strawberries and cream in my dressing-room after the performance was part of the perks of being on fairly intimate terms with the leading actor. At that first meeting in my dressing-room her father and I established the beginning of a firm friendship founded on mutual respect; the fact that we came from completely different walks of life made no difference. *Of Mice and Men* undoubtedly helped.

Soon after this I was introduced to the rest of the Hayley Bell clan – Dennis, Mary's brother, a pilot in the regular Air Force, Winifred and Elizabeth, her younger sisters, and her mother, Agnes Hayley Bell. Instinct told me that the Colonel's wife might be the one to present a slight problem. I turned on the charm full blast, but I was never quite confident that the performance was succeeding. They were a marvellous family with a great capacity for laughter, and after the anxiety of the first meeting was over I always enjoyed their company.

Since the Munich crisis in 1937 the rumours of war slowly but steadily increased. During August 1939 the possibility of another conflict became a distinct probability. The thought was in most people's minds, and found its way into their conversation. The ghastly prospect refused to be dismissed. I, however, buried my head in the sand and refused to believe it could happen.

On one glorious English day, a Sunday late in the month, Mary and I drove out into the country in my pride and joy, a new Lancia car with a bonnet that seemed to go on for ever. After a blissful day we ended up in the early evening at a small country pub in a little village called Abinger Hammer in Sussex. We sat together by a small lake, drinking draught beer and watching the swans drifting slowly over the still water. A herd of Friesian cows was munching contentedly in the field beyond, their black and white coats gleaming in the evening sunlight. Mary was sitting with her chin cupped in her hand staring out across the water. Neither of us spoke. Words were not a necessary part of our relationship; we did not need to make conversation. She looked so touchingly young and beautiful at that moment that I suddenly knew, in spite of all the obstacles and problems that lay ahead, I had to make certain that we should belong to each other, today, tonight, tomorrow and for ever.

We drove slowly away from the enchanted lake. Dusk was falling as we headed back towards London. I couldn't bear the thought of leaving her. I looked at the petrol gauge – it was three-quarters full. 'Darling, we're getting short of petrol,' I said, pointing to the oil pressure gauge. 'We'll never make town unless I fill her up.'

This was the start of a nefarious plan that was formulating in my fevered mind. The next small country garage with one dilapidated pump was, to my delight, closed. 'This is dodgy,' I said. 'I don't think we're going to make it. It's Sunday and all the garages are sure to be closed.' I took a long, deep breath. 'Don't you think it might be a good idea if we stayed the night somewhere?' I was staring straight ahead through the windscreen with what I hoped was an honest, concerned look on my face. I was glad I was driving because it meant she was getting a view of my left profile which I've always considered to be the best side of my face.

'Stop the car, Johnnie, and pull over to the side.'

Rather surprised I did as I was ordered. She looked at me; her eyes were smiling. 'That's the oil pressure gauge, and *that* one is the petrol gauge, and it's three-quarters full.'

'Good God, so it is,' I said. 'It's a new car, but how could I have made that stupid mistake?'

She looked at me. I suddenly felt like a small boy caught stealing apples in an orchard. 'Darling Johnnie, I don't want to go back to town, I want to be with you tonight. I love you. I love you very, very much, and although there may be no future in it I'm willing to take that chance.'

'Oh my darling love.' I leaned across to take her in my arms. My right trouser-leg caught the gear lever, dragged it into first, and within two seconds the Lancia was in the ditch.

About a mile up the lane we came upon a pretty little pub on the side of the road surrounded by trees with a steep hill sloping up to the skies behind it. A board announced 'Bed and Breakfast'. We stood hand in hand looking at the sign, both feeling terribly nervous. 'Look,' I said, pulling off my signet ring, 'put this on your fourth finger, if it'll fit, and turn it round so the crest won't show. We'll have to pretend we're married.'

Mine host and his wife were a charming couple. We explained our predicament. Yes, they would be glad to accommodate us for the night. They only had one room which, luckily, was unoccupied. The price would be £1 including a cooked breakfast of bacon and eggs. The inn was called the Boy and Donkey; our room was tiny, with only just enough space to accommodate the enormous Victorian double bed with brass rails and knobs at each end of it, a minute dressing-table, a kitchen chair and a small table holding a china wash-basin, jug and soap-dish. We held hands tightly. 'Lucky we didn't bring our cabin trunks,' I whispered.

'We've got no dining-room, my dears, but my husband and I would be very pleased if you'd join us for a bit of supper in the kitchen.'

I hesitated. 'We'd love to,' said Mary. 'How very sweet of you. We're starving, aren't we darling?'

'Famished. Totally famished,' I said. 'Thanks awfully.'

'See you in a few minutes then.'

When the landlord and his wife discovered that we were actors, actually playing in the West End, they were completely bowled over. Before the advent of television, actors were much more secret people. It was, therefore, exciting and intriguing actually to see them in the flesh. Since that box has taken its place in nearly every living-room in the land actors have become rather more common property. They can play to more people in one night than they could in a whole lifetime in the theatre.

Our host was a great raconteur, and at the end of one particularly amusing anecdote my companion, the distinguished young actress whom I had introduced as my wife, threw back her head and laughed. At the same moment she raised her hands to the heavens disclosing the large crest on my signet ring concealed till then on the inside of her finger. I knew they had spotted it. There was a pregnant pause. 'How long have you two been married then?'

'Well ... hardly any time at all. Actually we're still on our honeymoon.' Oh lord, I thought, that really sounds feeble. They're never going to believe it.

'Ah, I see,' said mine host, 'that accounts for it. When that's over you'll be able to buy her a wedding ring, won't you?'

'I will,' I said looking at my love. 'You're damn right I will, the best I can get.'

We both knew then that fate and luck had joined hands with us. In those un-permissive days many people would, in similar circumstances, have politely or impolitely requested us to leave their establishment forthwith. On this very special occasion we were blessed by chance with the right people in the right place at the right time.

I have already in this book described several first nights. There is one, however, that will be a guarded, treasured and secret memory between two people for ever. Perhaps I may, because of its importance, with pride, humility and a deep sense of gratitude and appreciation, state for the record that on one heavenly night during the month of August 1939 at the Boy and Donkey a production was started that is still happily running forty years later.

Sitting on the slope of the hill behind the pub the next morning we discussed the future which, however optimistically we viewed it, seemed to present obstacles of all kinds. I knew, however, without any shadow of doubt, that I had found the one person in the whole world with whom I needed to spend the rest of my life.

14

Sapper Mills on Parade

During the last week of August the tension increased: war seemed pretty inevitable. The balloon, I felt, could go up at any moment. On the Saturday morning before the matinee of *Of Mice and Men* Anthony Pélissier and I toured London in the Lancia offering our services to King and country. We had decided that if we volunteered before the actual declaration we would stand a much better chance of (a) choosing our unit, and (b) getting a commission after a relatively short time in the ranks. To their astonishment and dismay the two gallant young men flushed with patriotism found that the particular services they had chosen to grace with their courage, ability and talents were not terribly interested. A naval recruiting officer informed me that there was 'really no panic'; they were not at the moment looking for volunteers, and anyway, if I would forgive him saying so, I was slightly over the age they might be enlisting. That shook me. 'Good God,' I said. 'Do you know how old I am?'

'Well sir,' came the reply, 'you must be over thirty. I've followed your career for years. I saw you last week in *Of Mice and Men*. If you don't mind me saying so sir, I think you would do much better at the moment staying in the play. It's terrific. Why don't you blow in and see us again in a few months' time?'

'That's very nice of you, but my intention is to join up now, and join up I bloody well will. The Navy's loss will be the Army's gain. At thirty-one, I shall most certainly be the youngest serving soldier ever to hold a field-marshal's baton.'

The Rifle Brigade was next on our list. They were gracious, thanked us for calling, and informed us that they had a waiting list. Ant and I took off at speed in the Lancia. It was mid-day, and my curtain went up at 2.30 p.m. Then, there it was on an Edgware hoarding – 'Recruits Wanted for the Royal Engineers. Join Up Now'. Our patriotic flushes had paled slightly by this time, but we were still determined to go through with our plan. I was not going to be deterred by the fact that I didn't know a carburettor from a magneto.

The sergeant in charge was a round, fat, jolly cockney with a large moustache, waxed to a point at both ends. 'Morning, gentlemen. Am I to take it we are to have the pleasure of your company?'

'Yes, Sergeant. If you're still looking for volunteers, you've got two more.'

'Very good, gentlemen. Please be good enough to fill in these forms. When you've completed them you take your medical in the next office.'

The whole thing seemed rather amateur and casual. In less than an hour we were sworn in. 'Right,' said the sergeant. No 'gentlemen' this time, we noticed. He was still smiling, but his tone had changed. It was now more than tinged with authority. 'Sapper J. Mills, Number 2100808, you will report to 346 Company headquarters at Royston, Herts at 17.00 hours. You will be in charge of the party.' (There were two of us!)

'Excuse me, Sergeant,' I said, 'but I'm afraid that's not possible. We've got two shows of *Of Mice and Men* today at the Apollo Theatre.'

'Well I'll be buggered,' said the sergeant.

I jumped in quickly, trying to sound as much like a young Guards officer as possible: 'Sergeant, unless you can help us, we are the ones who will be, as you politely put it, buggered. We' – for obvious reasons I added Ant to the cast – 'shall be disappointing our large and expectant audience, and on top of that we shall be sued by the management. May I therefore, Sergeant, ask you to use your undoubted authority and allow us to report to HQ at Royston at 14.30 hours on Sunday 3 September.'

The sergeant looked confused, and nervously twirled the ends of his moustache. 'Well, it's ... it's very irregular. You're in. You've joined. But under the somewhat un-bloody-usual circumstances I'll take a chance. Right. 14.30 hours. HQ. 3 September. And if you're one minute late you'll all be on a charge.'

On the way back to the Apollo Ant suddenly put into words what we were thinking. 'Supposing nothing happens this weekend? What do we do?'

'Well, in that case I wouldn't be able to leave the show. The management have only agreed to release me if war is declared.'

There was a pause. And then Ant said, 'I see. Well in that case you'll probably make history. You'll be charged as a deserter before you've even tried on the uniform.'

'Well, that's that,' I said. 'It looks as if we've just got to have a bloody war.'

After the evening performance I drove to the Comedy Theatre. I had arranged to have a farewell party with Ant and Janet Johnstone, a close friend of Mary's, at the flat they were sharing on the top floor of a house in Basil Street. She was sitting at her dressing-table taking off her make-up, looking, I thought, more adorable than ever. We found ourselves for the first time making conversation. We discussed the evening perform-ances, the audiences; both of us I knew were avoiding mentioning the bleak and lonely prospect that we would more than likely have to face. For the last three months we had been inseparable, but now our fate was in the lap of the gods. If war became a reality, there was no way of know-ing when and where we should see each other again. We were the last to leave the theatre. Panton Street was quiet and deserted. Outside the stage door of the Comedy Theatre there was an old-fashioned street-lamp. She stopped beside it, took my hands and looked up at me.

'Darling Johnnie, I am going to say goodbye to you here outside the theatre, because I know how much it means to you – it's your life, and because of that, it's mine. If it happens, and you have to leave tomorrow morning, I want you to know that I shall love you for ever. I've been looking for you all my life and now it seems I may have found you too late.'

I looked at this lovely girl who, with no apparent effort, had in a short space of time completely transformed my life. I took her in my arms. She was smiling at me, with tears pouring down her face. 'Now listen, my love, during the last months with you I've grown up. I am now a sensible, mature, wise, ravishingly attractive adult, and also a pig-headedly determined one, and I swear with my hand on my heart, which now belongs entirely to you, that nothing, not even that little bastard Hitler, is going to separate us. At this moment I know with absolute cer-tainty that we are going to spend the rest of our lives together in this world and hopefully in the next. Come on, my darling, let's get along to Janet's before our benefactor, Alcoholic Ant, has knocked back all the champagne.'

She sat very close to me in the car on the way to Basil Street. 'Johnnie, that was a marvellous speech. Did you really mean it?'

'You're damn right I did. And you'd better believe it too.'

'I'll try,' she said. 'I'll really try.'

Ant was in terrific form. We laughed and drank champagne as if tomor-row was just going to be another ordinary Sunday in our lives. In the early hours of the morning we waved goodbye to two small figures lean-ing out of the windows of the top flat. London that night looked beautiful – quiet, deserted streets bathed in moonlight – and it was almost imposs-ible to imagine that it might soon be shuddering under the impact of a rain of bombs from that clear, calm, peaceful sky.

On Sunday 3 September 1939 I was alone in the flat. Aileen was away. I had seen very little of her during the past month, and she was, I think, happy with a quite different circle of friends. At 9 a.m. precisely the doleful voice of Neville Chamberlain on the radio informed us that 'England was now at war with Germany'. I rang Ant.

'Well, that's it then, isn't it?' he said. 'Can you pick me up? I'll phone Stephen.' (Stephen Watts, at that time a brilliant young journalist in charge of the film page in the *Sunday Express* and a great friend of ours, had by some miraculous chance joined the same unit.)

The West End of London on that Sunday morning was quiet and deserted. The streets were empty. It seemed as if the city was holding its breath waiting for something to happen. I headed the Lancia north. Just as we were passing through Swiss Cottage the first air-raid siren went off. It was one of the most frightening, blood-curdling wails I had ever heard. 'God Almighty!' said Ant, 'it's started. Let's get away from the buildings and out into the country fast.'

I put my foot hard down on the accelerator. After a minute or two the screaming banshee gradually died away. Silence. We waited for the first bomb to explode. Absolutely nothing happened. After a few minutes we heard the 'all-clear' siren. It was a false alarm, a test-run; but at that time I'm sure every Londoner thought he was about to experience the first of Hitler's devastating air-raids. As we were slowing down approaching St Alban's, a very small man suddenly appeared from behind a hedge. He was wearing a gas mask and waving a large rattle. As we drew nearer he jumped up and down and pointed to the sky. I pulled up. He was shouting something, but because of the gas mask we heard nothing but unintelligible squeaks. 'It's over,' I shouted. 'It's over. The all-clear went half an hour ago.' He took no notice – just went on waving his rattle, pointing it to the sky and squeaking at us.

'He's round the bend. First casualty of World War II,' Stephen said. 'Let's find a pub. I need a drink.' I drove on. In the driving mirror I could see the strange little troglodyte receding in the distance, still performing his war dance in the middle of the road.

We arrived at Royston with two hours to spare and found a charming old pub called Banyer's Hotel. The condemned men ate a hearty lunch: roast beef and two veg. washed down by three bottles of château-bottled claret at 10s. per bottle. Fortified by this sumptuous repast we enquired where the HQ was situated. Our host informed us that if we had travelled from London we had passed it on the way to his hotel; it was in a field half a mile from the town.

346 Company HQ was a shock: a sad little collection of huts and tents surrounded by a hastily erected barbed-wire fence, huddled together for comfort two hundred yards or so from the main road in the enormous field. 346 Company, a keen territorial unit, was totally unprepared for an intake of gallant young men determined to serve King and country. They seemed to be, if anything, slightly more bewildered than we were.

The Quartermaster explained that there was a shortage of everything at the moment, and that he was expecting his store to be replenished daily. We were issued with one forage cap, one greatcoat, one pair of work overalls, three gas masks, utensils for eating, tin plates, knives and forks and three canvas palliasses. I would pay a great deal of money for a picture of the three of us on our first inspection parade. Standing to attention, facing front, Ant wore the forage cap (which really did nothing for him), a sports jacket and trousers; Stephen wore the greatcoat over a smart, lightweight grey suit, and I wore the overalls with no hat. We wore these hilarious outfits for nearly two weeks before our uniforms arrived. These turned out to be three battledresses, which would have hung loosely on the three largest men in the regiment.

HQ consisted of one marquee (the mess hall), two large huts (the company offices), and about two dozen small huts to accommodate the men. The latrine was a large hut fitted with a long bench containing twelve holes underneath which were twelve buckets. The three of us were allotted sleeping quarters in one of the huts which contained nine other young men from the Southall district; they were all friends, having been together in the territorial unit for several months. Relationships at first were tricky. They recognized me, and I think the fact that we were all suddenly on exactly the same footing living closely together made them wary and embarrassed, but as soon as they discovered that we were anxious to belong to the group and had no intention of 'pulling rank' or being in any way 'toffee-nosed' they were helpful and friendly.

The first night in camp was quite unforgettable. We were instructed to fill the three palliasses with straw. When we had completed the operation mine resembled a barrage balloon, Stephen's looked like a large lumpy rice pudding, but Ant's for some reason was perfect. We placed them side by side in one corner of the hut. After lights-out I lay perched on the top of my barrage balloon staring into the darkness, watching the cigarette butts glowing like fire-flies in the other parts of the hut. I thought of my dressing-room at the Apollo Theatre – empty, the walls stripped of the first-night telegrams, the theatre dark. I saw Mary standing under the lamplight outside the Comedy Theatre and saying, 'I want you to know that I shall love you for ever. I've been looking for you all my life, and now it seems I may have found you too late.' I remembered how young and agonizingly beautiful she looked. Oh God, I thought, it may be too late. She may be right. At that moment, with two friends beside me and a hut full of men, I felt lonelier than I'd ever been in my life.

346 Company was a searchlight battery. During the day we marched, drilled, dug trenches, filled sandbags, camouflaged huts. Hours were spent on aircraft recognition. We were trained in teams to work the searchlights and taught to dismantle and assemble the Lewis guns with

which we were expected to bring down any low-flying enemy bombers that became trapped in our beam. We soon settled down into the routine, and I began to believe that no other life had ever existed. The course lasted four weeks. After a full day's slog we were usually up half the night manning the searchlights and practising aircraft recognition with the co-operation of the RAF.

During the second week I was on painting duty, perched on the top of a hut, camouflaging the roof in the middle of the camp. I was vaguely conscious of some laughing and wolf-whistles going on in the distance. I looked down, and there, staring up at me, was Mary. She had a funny habit when excited or thrilled of jumping up and kicking her bottom with her heels. This she proceeded to do to the delight of most of the personnel of 346 Company HQ, who by this time had formed themselves into an admiring circle. I spotted the two MPs who were on duty at the entrance gates making a bee-line in our direction. They arrived on the scene as I scrambled down the ladder.

'Could I ask you how you got in here, Miss?'

'Certainly, Captain' – he was a Lance Corporal – 'I crawled under the wire. I've come to visit Sapper Mills.'

'Are you his wife then?'

'Not yet, but I hope to be,' said Mary.

This brought a round of applause from the audience. The MPs were not amused. 'Right. You can both come along and explain this to the Duty Officer. There's a war on, you know.'

At this moment, with a court-martial staring me in the face, a saviour appeared on the scene in the form of one Sergeant White, a super character who by this time had become quite a chum. We had shared many a pint at the local together. 'All right, Corporal. I'll take charge of this. No need to bother the Duty Officer.'

We followed him to his tent. 'Well, Miss, what's your story?'

Within a few minutes Sergeant White was completely under her spell. 'Well, Sergeant, you see, it was an emergency. I must tell you I'm terribly in love with Sapper Mills. I haven't seen him since he joined up. I couldn't bear it any longer, so I borrowed the ambulance that I drive in London at night and drove down here. I didn't like the look of the two gentlemen on the gate so I crawled under the wire.'

Sergeant White looked hard at both of us. 'I've got to take a very serious view of the situation. Sapper Mills, is this the young lady whose virtues you were extolling to me for two hours in the pub the other evening?'

'Yes, Sergeant, it is. This is Miss Mary Hayley Bell.'

'Right,' said Sergeant White. 'Miss Bell, I suggest you get back into your borrowed vehicle and drive to Banyer's Hotel. You, Sapper Mills, will go to the stores, apply for some turpentine, clean the paint off your face and hands, wash, change into your new uniform and report back to me. You will then be issued with a pass which will give you freedom until 18.00 hours precisely.'

'Sergeant, you're a . . .'

'I know I am. I always have been. Nip off, look sharp about it. Don't want to waste time, do you?'

Since that afternoon in September 1939 Mary and I have stayed in luxurious hotels all over the world – London, Paris, New York, Rome, Madrid, Beverly Hills – but none will hold quite the same place in our hearts as a small hotel in Royston, Hertfordshire, England.

One morning Ant, Stephen and I were lined up with the rest of our group outside our hut, standing stiffly to attention while the CO passed slowly along the lines, inspecting gas masks, badges, webbing belts, boots and hair-cuts. As he paused in front of me a voice, which to my horror I realized was mine, trilled in a high, clear, embarrassing tenor, 'I'm on a see-saw, you throw me up and you throw me down. I don't know whether I'm here or there.' It was the recording of a number I had sung in *Jill Darling*; someone had left the radio on in our hut. The CO's reaction is almost impossible to describe. At first he seemed to think I'd gone mad and was actually singing to him. I twisted my face into a sickly smile and tried to indicate where the voice was coming from. Our group was by this time on the verge of hysteria, emitting suppressed snorts and gurgles. Sergeant White nipped into the hut and switched off the radio. The CO, who was not blessed with the greatest sense of humour, passed on to the next group with a look of blank, dazed astonishment on his face. Needless to say, 'I'm On A See-Saw' became my signature tune. It had been a hit in the show, but at 346 Company at Royston it was a smash.

Towards the end of October we finished the training course, and the three of us were posted to different sites: mine was undoubtedly the worst of the bunch, it was situated in the middle of a vast stretch of open country between Royston and Cambridge; the nearest village, too small to boast of a pub, was six and a half miles away. The cold war was on, and as far as I was concerned the description could not have been more apt. We stood to from dusk till dawn beside the searchlight and the Lewis gun and nearly froze to death. Towards the end of November a heavy snowfall completely cut us off from civilization and we were without rations for three days. During this period I livened things up by catching a splendid dose of flu, which pushed my temperature up to the 104 mark. One of the crew, a Scot called Jock who in private life had been a shoe salesman in Dolcis in Oxford Street, refused to let me out of the hut in the Arctic conditions to pee, and insisted that I should use one of his gumboots; this unusually generous gesture was the basis of a firm friendship which we enjoyed until I left the camp.

The only enemy at this time was boredom: on duty all night, we slept till noon, did maintenance for two hours and went on duty again at dusk. I really think that without the flow of wonderful love-letters from Mary, I might have been tempted to desert. I've kept all the letters – they were warm, loving and funny; but apart from that I realized that they were beautifully written. I could not know however that her pen would one day provide me with two of the best plays I have ever acted in.

During the last two weeks of November a dispatch rider arrived at the site from Battalion HQ in Cambridge with a memo from the CO asking if I would be willing to form a concert party. The battalion's morale was apparently at rather a low ebb; they had been stuck out in the wilds with no entertainment whatsoever, and were becoming 'site happy' or, in other words, 'climbing up their own beams'. I hadn't joined the Army with the idea of entertaining the troops, but the temptation to get away from the site was too great. I accepted the CO's offer. Within twenty-four hours I was installed in comparative luxury in a large house in Herschel Road, Cambridge, which was being used as Battalion HQ. I wallowed in my first hot bath for months, and that night actually slept in a bed.

Colonel Gandar Dower was a charming man who was really concerned about, as he put it, 'the absolutely stinking winter my chaps are having'. He suggested a small mobile concert party that could travel round the sites on a lorry, giving one performance at each location. I reminded the CO that Stephen Watts, Anthony Pélissier and I had written to him from Royston applying for a commission and asking to be sent to an OCTU (Officer Cadet Training Unit) as soon as possible; I hoped that this job would not affect my chances in any way. He assured me it would not and that my name was down with the others in the request book.

After a few auditions I found there was quite a lot of talent available, and quickly slung together a one-hour show of music, sketches and monologue. I took a chance one night and slipped in the Crispian speech from *Henry V*. To my surprise it went down better than anything else. After the show I asked the boys what they had liked best. 'That Shakespeare sketch,' was the reply. From then on it was in. I closed the show with it to the accompaniment of 'Land of Hope and Glory' played softly on a gramophone in the wings.

In the last week of November the first bombshell of World War II arrived – not from that nasty little ex-painter with the black toothbrush moustache, but from the pen of Mary Hayley Bell. The situation was this: *Tony Draws a Horse* was due for a New York production in January and Mary had been offered the leading part in it. She'd made a big success in the London production, and the feeling was that she would more than probably repeat that success in New York. What did I think she should do? She was quite incapable, she said, of making the decision; so would I please make it for her. If the play succeeded she would be away in America for nine months. She simply couldn't bear the thought of it – could I?

I have, during the past fifty years, had to make some difficult decisions but this one still tops the bill. I wrote down all the pros and cons, but I had already decided. I knew that, whatever my feelings were, I had to tell her to go. I rang Mary that evening. Before I could speak, she said: 'Darling, it's no good your saying anything. I've already decided it's mad to go. I'm just not going to leave you here in the blackout eating that filthy army food while I'm on Broadway in a blaze of light devouring five-pound sirloin steaks. I love you and I'm not leaving you and that's that.'

'Listen, my darling,' I said, 'I'm madly in love with you. You know that, don't you? And that's why I've got to make you go.'

'But Johnnie ...'

'No, please listen, darling, we must be sensible, and I've got to look at the situation from your point of view. First of all, the war can't go on for ever; you are a really good actress with a future; you love the theatre as much as I do; so you just can't turn this chance down. It could lead to anything, and I'm sure it will. And look at the picture as far as I'm concerned. I'm still married, and although I've set the wheels in motion I'm not free. I can't say to you, "Darling, OK, you're right. Don't go. Let's get married on my next twenty-four hours' leave." I'm sure it'll be all right one day, and we shall be together for ever, but at the moment all I can offer is my devoted love, and that, in this case, is unhappily not enough.'

'Darling, I'm not going. I can't bear the thought of leaving you. How do you think I'm going to feel if you're posted abroad? I should be with you every moment I can, with this bloody war on.'

Everything in me, at that moment, wanted to say, Oh God, you're right. Anything could happen. How much more time have we got anyway? But I knew quite definitely that she had to go. I then had a small inspiration: 'Wait a minute, darling, there's another angle, an important angle. You could be doing it for both of us. The war has to finish sooner or later and then we'll get married, live in that cottage by the stream and have all those children we talked about. Now this is where the American deal becomes frightfully important. My bank balance, as you know, is almost nil. Wouldn't it be great if, through this American job, you are able to earn some money while I can't? Then when the golden moment arrives I could borrow enough from you to set up home for us ...' I paused for breath.

There was an even longer pause from the other end of the line. Finally, a rather faint voice said, 'Do you really mean all that, my darling? Do you honestly think it's right?'

'Yes, my love, I do. You've got to go, I'm sure of it.'

Tony Draws a Horse closed in London and Mary was free for two weeks. She was due to sail on the ss *Britannic* at the end of November. We stood together on a platform at Cambridge station on a cold, bleak, Sunday afternoon, waiting for the train which would take her back to London. I'd been granted twenty-four-hour pass and we'd spent the night at the Blue Boar, a warm, comfortable, sixteenth-century inn in the centre of the town. Mary was wearing a white lambswool fur coat and looking more adorable than ever. We had talked until the early hours, and there was nothing left to say. I knew what we were both thinking. 'When, if ever, would we see each other again?' The train arrived, we were enveloped in a cloud of white steam. I looked at her. 'Well at any rate, darling, the special effects are OK. We shan't need another take.' Heavens, what a feeble joke, I thought.

She tried to smile at me, but turned away quickly and stepped up into the carriage. We had agreed the night before that we would not allow the scene to become a sentimental over-emotional wartime farewell. She opened the window and looked down at me. 'Darling Johnnie, the play is going to be an enormous flop, and I shall be back; and did I remember to tell you I love you?'

The train started to move off. The other passengers were then treated to the interesting spectacle of a sapper in the Royal Engineers running along the platform with tears pouring down his face, shouting, 'I love you. I love you. I love you,' at the top of his voice.

A weekend pass plus three stripes on my arm helped to stop me thinking about the ss *Britannic* ploughing her way across the dark Atlantic surrounded by a pack of U-boats waiting to pounce. Two days after she sailed the CO asked me if I would produce a show at the Arts Theatre in Cambridge, the nucleus being the battalion concert party, with the added attraction of some stars from the West End stage. I would need, he said, some time in London to arrange things, and in his opinion a sergeant would have more authority. It would, of course, be an 'acting unpaid' appointment.

With the dignity of my new and totally unearned rank on my sleeve I took off for the bright lights accompanied by Anthony Pélissier and Jock. We spent a hilarious weekend floating round a strange blacked-out West End, and visited all the old haunts; but by the end of it we had, somehow or other, remained sober enough to have gathered together a quite remarkable cast: Naunton Wayne, Basil Radford, Arthur Young,

Aubrey Mather, Roma Beaumont, Annette Mills, Frances Day, Henry Kendall, Stefan Grapelli, Fay Compton and Sydney Lipton and his band from the Grosvenor House Hotel all appeared in the show. The Arts Theatre was sold out at £1 per seat, the front stalls were ablaze with brigadiers and red tabs; the show was a riot, and a considerable sum of money went into the regimental kitty. I hoped that this alone would prove that I was officer material and that my request to be sent to an OCTU would be granted.

On 23 December I received a cable from New York. It read as follows: PLAY GLORIOUS FLOP STOP PERSONAL SUCCESS STOP HOME SOON LOVE YOU MADLY STOP MARY. This was followed by a deluge of letters written on different dates all of which arrived on the same day. They had been opened by the Censor, who must have enjoyed them immensely. Mary was not exactly what one would call an introvert with the pen, and I'm sure provided him with some of the most enjoyable reading that he had ever been offered to blue-pencil.

After the play opened to mixed notices Mary had been offered a part in *Pride and Prejudice* in Hollywood by MGM, but she could only accept it if she signed a three-year deal. She wrote, 'I went to St Patrick's cathedral on Fifth Avenue and thought about it. God, I said, if you will let me go home safely to Johnnie I'll give all this up and just look after him and have a whole troupe of kids, and bring them up properly. Maybe one of them will do what I once set out to do, but now I know what's more important to me.'

Another letter contained a poem written at sea on 29 November. (This is printed under protest from the author.)

JOHNNIE
Could I come to Cambridge
If I died?
And find you on the same bridge
Just beside
Our moonlit water – hear the pennies drop
And your delighted laughter at the plop
That both our wishes made
Near the ducks, in the jade
Green water?
Could we walk there together
And not grow old
And kick the laughing leaves still turning gold?
And hold our arms
About the Blue Boar's neck
And chase away alarms
That haunt us, of a wreck
In grey sad waters?

Oh moonlight, gently kiss the square
And powder frost, faint, everywhere
These lovers danced,
That sunlit day –
Before Death passed their way ...

Three months later I was in the bar at the Blue Boar after a concert on one of the sites. We'd travelled for two hours on our open lorry in a below-zero temperature. Sergeant White looked at me. 'You feeling all right? You look a bit dickie. I'm going to get the MO to have a look at you.'

Ten minutes later I was in bed. I had a very high temperature and the MO said he wouldn't take the risk of returning me to HQ that night. It looked like pneumonia. He would clear it with the CO and visit me in the morning.

Fitful sleep, jumbled dreams, concert parties mixed up with ships at sea, submarines, searchlight beams wandering across the sky. Through the mist of sleep I seemed to hear a faint knock on the door. I opened my eyes. She was standing in the doorway in that white lambswool coat smiling at me. 'Hallo, my darling, what have you been up to? I'm never going to leave you again.'

15

Out of Commission

In March my request to be transferred back to a detachment on site was granted. Stephen Watts had left for an OCTU and Anthony Pélissier had applied for a transfer into the Merchant Navy; he was, as he put it, at least going to learn navigation at the Government's expense. They had their revenge: he ended up in a tramp steamer taking coal to Newcastle! I wondered if I was being black-balled by some high-up, anti-actor wallah in the War Office. I seemed to be no nearer that one pip on the shoulder that would open the door to the Officers' Mess than I was when I joined the ranks.

The summer months consisted of boredom, laced with anxiety. The blitzkrieg was on; Hitler's day bombing raids started during May. Mary was on tour with Fay Compton in *Fumed Oak*. With the telephone system in a chaotic state (it still is) it was impossible to make contact. The fact that I was stuck out in a field near Royston guarding a goat didn't make it any easier.

Towards the end of August we were standing to, just as dawn was breaking; London had been taking a pasting; we could see by the sky that the raid was over. The bombers – what was left of them – would be streaking for home. Suddenly an aircraft emerged from a cloud making a bee-line for the coast. Although I reckoned it might be just too high to be in range I ordered the crew to open fire. There was tremendous excitement – the first shot fired in anger. The telephone rang a few minutes later. 'HQ here. The CO wants a word with you.'

'Sergeant Mills. Did you open fire on an aircraft this morning at 06.00 hours?'

'Yes sir,' I said. 'But I'm afraid we didn't hit it.'

'Congratulations, Sergeant, the aircraft was a Wellington. Report to me at 09.00 hours.' The phone was slammed down. Oh well, bang goes that commission for good, I thought. I'll be in the ranks for the duration.

Two weeks later, however, a greatly needed piece of luck arrived in the form of the Brigadier, who was doing an off-the-record inspection of the sites in the battalion. Mine was luckily in great shape. I've always rather enjoyed spit and polish. The grass was cut, the post freshly painted and all the equipment in mint condition. 'Morning, Sergeant. A very good show. A very good show indeed.' He looked at me closely. 'Wait a minute, didn't you produce that show for us at Cambridge?'

'Yes sir, I did.'

'Good Lord. Damn good show it was too. What's your name, Sergeant?'

'Sergeant Mills, sir.'

'Good Lord. What are you still doing in the ranks? Haven't you put your name down for an OCTU?'

'Yes sir. I put it down the first week I joined the Battalion.'

'Mmm...' said the Brigadier. 'Well. It was a damn good show. Damn good. I'll look into it, Sergeant.' A week later I was posted to the OCTU at Shrivenham and reported to E Battery Watson Unit on 6 September.

The OCTU reminded me of school without the bullying. We did, however, live in a state of anxiety caused by the presence of the letters 'RTU' which were placed in prominent positions in every room in the building. These reminded us that if we were not good little boys and didn't work hard and obey all the rules we would be immediately 'Returned To Unit', which would also mean that we would never be given another chance to become officers and gentlemen.

The drilling and field exercises I enjoyed – the drilling particularly because, being an actor, I was rather good at it, and it gave me a chance to show off like mad on the parade ground. The mathematics which were necessary for the gunnery course I dreaded; and if it hadn't been for an ex-Member of Parliament who coached me at night I should never have got through the exam. I was commissioned on 31 October and posted to the 1st Rifle Battalion, Monmouthshire Regiment, whose HQ was in Trowbridge, Wiltshire.

Mary's tour had finished, and after the passing-out parade she picked me up in her car, a small green open Ford she had bought for £50; we drove to Bath and spent the weekend together. We had a lot to celebrate: my rise from the ranks, and the fact that the decree nisi had just come through. We would, DV, be able to get married in six months' time. The forty-eight hours disappeared in a flash; it was the best time we'd ever spent together. We laughed, drank champagne, talked of the future and made glorious plans of what we were going to do together when the war was over. Only one small worry niggled at my mind. For the last three months I'd been suffering from pains in the duodenum and, in spite of dosing myself with endless powders and pills, they were becoming steadily worse. I had been afraid to report to the MO at Shrivenham in case he diagnosed something that would interfere with my commission.

I hoped that improved conditions and the food in the Officers' Mess might help; I'd been living on a diet of fry-ups for the past nine months.

After reporting to HQ in Trowbridge I was given command of a dozen sites scattered over a wide area. The only means of transport available for me was an old four-and-a-quarter h.p. belt-driven Triumph. On this I made a tour of inspection. To my dismay I discovered that most of the men on detachments were still under canvas. There was hardly a hut in sight. My HQ was situated in a field at Nibley; my sergeant showed me to my sleeping quarters, which turned out to be a bell tent with duck-boards through which the mud squelched as I walked across them – not, I thought, exactly what the doctor would have ordered. After a few weeks of trying to cope with increasing pain I was persuaded by my sergeant, a marvellous Welshman who from the start had been an enormous help, to report to the MO, who packed me off to the Forbes Fraser Hospital in Bath for an examination. He was afraid, he said, that I was the possessor of a strong and remarkably healthy duodenal ulcer.

After a week of tests, which involved swallowing lengths of rubber tubing, they informed me that the MO had been right. Ulcer confirmed. I was to start treatment in hospital, and on 19 December a board would decide my fate. This all took some time to sink in properly. After a year in the ranks and a hairy course at Shrivenham I realized that after only a few weeks of playing the part I had been looking forward to all that time I stood a chance of being bowler-hatted.

The next three weeks seemed like years. The ulcer diet of those days was the most boring, depressing diet in the world – rice pudding, tapioca pudding, boiled eggs, milk, boiled fish. On 19 December the Board found me permanently unfit for active service. I was given extended leave to await War Office orders. Mary picked me up at the hospital. I had run through the gamut of emotions during the past weeks and was in a zombie-like state of acceptance. One thought, however, came through clear and strong; whatever else happened it looked as if, at last, we were going to be allowed to be together – for a while at least.

We were married on 16 January 1941, the only date I never forget: it's engraved on the back of my watch. Both our families were there, and quite a few close friends: Larry and Vivien Olivier, Noël Coward, Fay Compton, Roger Livesey, Ursula Jeans, Stephen Watts on leave from his unit, and Anthony Pélissier and Penelope Dudley Ward, whom he had married during one of his brief leaves from taking coals to Newcastle. It was exactly twelve years to the day that I had met the enchanting girl with the long golden hair at the Commissioner's house in Tientsin.

We were lucky with our first home; Diana Churchill rented us her attractive mews flat in Old Barrack Yard behind St George's Hospital at Hyde Park Corner. It was expensive – 27s. 6d. per week fully furnished. We had only two problems: one was my wretched duodenal ulcer which, in spite of being bombarded with the boring diet, showed little sign of disappearing; the other was our financial position: sooner or later something had to be dropped into the kitty, and with myself on sick leave and Mary out of work the prospects didn't look bright.

A few weeks later my old friend Anthony (Puffin) Asquith, with whom I had made *Brown on Resolution* in 1934, came to the rescue with an offer of the part of a German spy in a picture called *Cottage to Let* that he was due to make at Gaumont British Studios with Alistair Sim, Michael Wilding and a young twelve-year-old boy actor, George Cole. My final discharge from active service came through, and at 6.30 on a cold, bleak February morning ex-Second Lieutenant J. Mills mounted a bicycle and rode through the blacked-out streets of Knightsbridge to the Gaumont British Studios at Shepherd's Bush. I was back in front of the cameras again. It was a strange but wonderful feeling. The film for me, however, was a struggle; the diet of concentrated mush was having a bad effect on my brain and I found to my horror that for the first time in my life I was 'drying up'; the lines refused to stay in my head. Puffin was marvellous. It was a nightmare, but somehow or other I got through it without completely upsetting the budget.

After the last day's shooting Mary and I decided to celebrate the fact that I had managed to finish the epic. I booked a table at the Café de Paris, where there was always a good cabaret and Snakehips Johnson was in permanent residence with his band. I was changing in the bedroom, and Mary was in the living-room shaking a cocktail for me – egg and milk, laced for the first time, as a special treat, with a thimbleful of brandy. For no apparent reason I suddenly felt that the last thing I wanted to do was to go to the Café de Paris that evening. Although I couldn't explain this change of mind, Mary agreed to cancel it. We never really cared where we were as long as we were not separated. After supper in the flat we took Hamlet, the golden cocker spaniel I had bought for her on one of my leaves, for a walk in Hyde Park. The air-raid warning went off and within minutes London was rocking under a rain of bombs. We sat under a tree with Hamlet by the Serpentine and watched the mammoth firework display. We both had a horror of shelters and felt safer in the open.

The next morning we turned on the BBC news and heard that during one of the worst raids London had suffered so far the Café de Paris had received a direct hit. The bomb exploded in the middle of the dance hall: the casualties were appalling, Snakehips Johnson and his band were blown to pieces, dozens of officers and their wives or girl-friends were killed or seriously injured; very few escaped with their lives. We looked at each other. Neither of us spoke. There was really nothing to say. I knew, however, without any shadow of doubt, that last night God had decided that neither of us was quite ready to leave the stage.

When Fay Compton invited us for a weekend to her beautiful house, Hazel Hall, in Kent, we jumped at the chance to get out of London. The raids were increasing and Old Barrack Yard was not exactly the safest place in which to live.

Walking through a Kentish lane on that Sunday morning we came across a small, attractive, converted oast-house. 'You know, darling,' I said, 'it's pretty stupid really. Why live in London when we don't have to? We're not doing any good there, and next time we might not be so lucky.'

At that moment a large man with a red beard appeared at the gate.

'Excuse me,' I said, 'I suppose you don't know of any small place to let in this district, do you?'

'Yes I do – this one,' was the answer.

We both fell madly in love with the house and in half an hour had agreed to rent it for the duration at the exorbitant price of 25s. a week, furnished. It was primitive; cooking was by courtesy of primus stoves (temperamental horrors, as we discovered), and very partial central heating was supplied by a boiler that looked as if it had come out of the Ark. But what charm the place had! Set in three acres on the side of a valley, surrounded by cobnut bushes, roses and shaded by a giant walnut tree.

We drove back to London on the Monday morning to pack up our few possessions. We passed through the archway of Old Barrack Yard. 'Oh my God,' said Mary. We stared at our flat. The wooden stairs were smashed. We clambered up them. Every pane of glass was broken. The little living-room was a shambles – dirt and dust covered everything. We walked into the bedroom: there was a large hole in the roof, and underneath it our bed was a wreck. I looked at Mary. There were tears in her eyes.

'Well, that's that,' I said. 'It could be third time unlucky. Thank God for the oast. Let's get the hell out of here.'

16

In Which We Serve

After several months of sticking grimly to the ulcer diet the MO had advised, I seemed to be making no improvement whatsoever. I still suffered from the pain in my duodenum, but what was worse my brain seemed to be about as alert as one of the boiled eggs which I consumed by the dozen.

It was my sister Annie I had to thank for suggesting the cure (which, at first hearing, sounded drastic, and confounded all the conservative doctors' theories and treatments for ulcers), and Mary for helping me to carry it out. I have beside me, as I write, a book of some three hundred pages called *Health via Food*. It was published in America in 1934, and written by a famous doctor called William Howard Hay MD. In it, he explains quite simply all the reasons why the Hay diet is the only correct and sensible way for human beings to eat. Unfortunately the book is out of print, so I cannot advise you to buy it; but I can explain the method quite simply.

We have, Dr Hay explains, two digestive juices, one released to digest the starchy foods, and another to digest the proteins. If we cram the stomach at the same time with a mixture of high starch and high protein the result is indigestion which develops into acidity. Once the system becomes acid instead of alkaline any of the illnesses we are prone to find a breeding ground to grow in. All one does, therefore, is to separate the starches from the proteins at each meal. The result, in my case, was quite fantastic: after one week the acute ulcer pain had disappeared, and in six weeks I was x-rayed by our doctor, William Buky, who found that the ulcer had completely healed; only a slight scarring remained as evidence.

The Hay diet takes off weight if needed and puts it on if necessary. It has made all the difference to my life. Also, it's not a bore. Your hostess need never be offended because you can eat practically everything she provides, except the sweet course; but if you've behaved yourself for six days out of seven that one slip will have no ill effect whatsoever. I found, however, that after a few months on the diet I preferred to skip the sweet and press on to the cheese – with apple, not bread – and a further bottle of claret!

The Hay diet makes sense. I wish you could read the book, but it is the one volume that is never allowed to leave the house. The fly-leaf is inscribed in Mary's handwriting, 'John Mills's Bible – DON'T TAKE AWAY'. My daughter Hayley, years later, tried practically every diet in existence before she accepted the fact that Papa was right. Several years ago, when she was trying to lose her puppy fat, she embarked on yet another weird sample. At ten o'clock one morning I found her flushed and giggling at nothing in particular. 'What's going on, Hayl? Can I share the joke?'

'Well it's not a joke. It's the new diet, darling. I feel marvellous.'

'Oh, why?'

'Well, you see, it's three meals a day – breakfast, lunch and dinner, and they're all the same.' She giggled again. 'I mean, it's fabulous, and so easy. Just two hard-boiled eggs and a large glass of dry white wine – that's all there is to it. It's super!' She hiccuped her way up the stairs. A week later my offspring decided that it was a choice between Alcoholics Anonymous or father's Hay diet. The Hay diet won.

Those three months in the oast-house with Mary and Dr Hay's miracle message I look back on as one of the happiest times of my life. I had earned just enough money in *Cottage to Let* to relieve us of financial stress. We were able to relax and revel in being alive and together. I worked from dusk till dawn in the vegetable garden and managed to grow everything we needed. We were overrun with rabbits, which, with the help of an old and trusted 4·10 shotgun, provided us with enough protein for the delicious casseroles that Mary cooked up on the primus stoves when they could be persuaded to work.

Our home was open house at weekends – any chums who were on leave usually found their way down to our valley in Kent: the Oliviers (Larry by this time was commissioned in the Fleet Air Arm), Rex and Lilli Harrison, Carol Reed, the Pélissiers, Roger Livesey and Ursula Jeans and friends from my old unit in Royston.

By the spring I was fit enough to work and was asked to make three film documentaries for the Government at Ealing Studios – *Big Blockade*, *All Hands* and *Careless Talk*. Hitler's spy system was working too well and secrets were being leaked, mostly, MI5 felt, by people talking in pubs and public places about troop movements and convoy dates. The U-boats were having a field day; losses at sea were reaching an alarming figure. The documentaries were a reminder that the only safe subjects to discuss in public were football and mothers-in-law.

I was also re-united with Robert Donat in *The Young Mr Pitt*. The actor playing Wilberforce had died at the last rehearsal and I took over after an SOS from Carol at four hours' notice. We spent a hilarious hour in the wardrobe at Gaumont British. I finally appeared in the House of Commons wearing a velvet coat which must have been made for Wee Georgie Wood. The hairdressing department had supplied me with a wig which looked like a deserted crow's nest. I was hardly a match for Donat in his prime.

I made two more small-budget comedies, *The Black Sheep of Whitehall* with my old friend Will Hay at Ealing Studios, and *Old Bill and Son* (Bruce Bairn's father's famous character) at Denham studios.

We hadn't planned to start a family quite so quickly. The war made the future unpredictable, and we also felt that having wasted far too much of our lives apart we should allow ourselves time to enjoy life together without any other responsibilities. When, however, it was confirmed that the first of the bunch was due to arrive during November, after the initial shock (he or she must be a very determined character, we thought, to break through such a barrier of precautions) we were delighted, if somewhat apprehensive.

The air-raids were increasing in number. London was hardly the safest place in the world in which to produce a first-born. But I was anxious to have Dr Cedric Lane Roberts, one of the top gynaecologists, to take care of everything, and as he practised in London that helped us to make our decision.

On 21 November we were lunching at the Ivy with Noël Coward and Leslie Henson. Mary was looking radiant, but couldn't get nearer than two feet from the table. 'When is my godson or goddaughter arriving?' asked Noël.

Mary's eyes widened. She clutched at the table. 'I think', she said between clenched teeth, 'it's arriving now.'

A minute later we were in a taxi en route for the Royal Northern Hospital in the Holloway Road. Lane Roberts was the resident consultant. He was out on a call, and one of his assistants assured me that there was no problem, no panic, no hurry. So why didn't I leave them all in peace, stop worrying, go back to the West End and have some tea or a drink with some chums, if they could stand me, and ring the hospital at 8.30 p.m. There was no chance of the baby arriving before ten or eleven at the earliest. White-faced and trembling, the expectant father was persuaded to leave; the matron's parting words were, 'Now don't worry, Mr Mills, go and have a sip of brandy. You don't look at all well, but I'm sure you'll pull through!'

From Durham Cottage, Larry and Vivien's London home, I rang the hospital every half hour. I must have driven them mad. At 8.30 a voice said, 'All right, Mr Mills, there's no hurry but we think you could make your way here now.'

As I put the phone down all hell broke loose. London shuddered under one of the worst raids of the war. The only vehicles in the streets were ambulances. There was no way I could get to the Royal Northern Hospital. The next few hours were slow torture. I was frantic with worry, convinced that the Royal Northern Hospital would be a ruin when I finally if ever got there. At eleven o'clock the 'all clear' sounded. I found a cab with a marvellous cockney driver. When I explained the position he agreed to drive me to Holloway Road. That drive was something to remember – the streets were filled with rubble, smoke and dust, buildings were on fire, fire-engines and ambulances were tearing through the streets in all directions. I sat in the cab dreading what I might find. We turned into the Holloway Road. We passed two bombed-out houses still burning. There ahead of me was the hospital; in the light of the fires I could see it was unscathed – not even a window had been broken.

Mary was propped up in bed looking wonderful, relaxed and happy. 'Hallo, my darling', she said. 'You look awful. Are you all right?'

'No,' I said, 'I'm not. I'll never be the same again. I think this family business is very overrated. I don't think I want another baby. I'm too old. Oh God, darling, you look lovely. I can't believe it. Where is it?'

'The Bunch? It's in a ward with six other new arrivals. Go and have a look at it. I think you'll like it.'

There were six cots with six newly-born babies in them. I made a tour of inspection. I pointed. 'That's ours,' I said to the nurse. 'I'm sure it is. And it's a girl.' I was right. It was Juliet. She didn't look all red and wrinkled like some of the others. She looked as if she'd just come back from a holiday in the South of France – with a light golden tan, blonde hair and large blue eyes, she was, I thought, quite a dish. She still is.

Next morning at the hospital we drank the Bunch's health in champagne. The room was full of flowers. Telegrams started to pour in. They were a collection to be treasured: ' "Ah Juliet, if the measure of thy joy be heaped like mine and that thy skill be more to blazen it, then sweeten with thy breath this neighbour air and let rich music's tongue unfold the imagined happiness that both receive in either by this dear encounter." Dearest love to you and your superb Mama, Aunt Puss and Uncle Sub-Lieutenant Olivier.'

The next one we opened read: 'Hurrah! When do I start religious instruction? – Noël.' And then: 'Dear Juliet, go easy on the milk shakes, Robert Donat.' Almost our favourite was: 'I know your father – Carol Reed.'

I drove my family in the small green Ford down to the oast-house for

Christmas. It was bitterly cold, the primus packed up when the turkey was half-cooked, the boiler expired in the middle of the night; Mary – upstairs with Bunch – heard the sounds of battle coming from the kitchen on Christmas morning. A cry of rage echoed up the stairs. 'Oh you purple pisser!' After that the boiler was never referred to by any other name. The whole thing was a total shambles, and glorious. We both voted it the best Christmas we had ever spent in our lives.

During the first week of 1942 I received a fantastic New Year's present – the script of the film *In Which We Serve*. Noël had told me the previous September that he was going to make a film about the exploits of HMS *Kelly*, Lord Louis Mountbatten's famous destroyer. He was, he said, going to stick his neck right out and play the great man himself, write the script and the musical score and co-direct it with a young man called David Lean, who at that time had never directed, but who was considered a genius in the cutting room – an editor who, by sheer technical knowledge and a built-in sense of timing, could turn a mediocre rough-cut into a more than acceptable film.

In Which We Serve was one of the best scripts I'd ever had in my hands, and by a strange coincidence Noël, having been responsible for launching me on my career, twelve years later was providing me with a golden opportunity to re-start it with a part that he had written especially for me. Able Seaman Shorty Blake was a superbly drawn character; really good parts present no problem to an actor, and Shorty Blake was just that.

An entry in my diary for 5 February 1941 reads, 'First day's work on *In Which We Serve* with Noël Coward. This is the only way to make pictures – efficiency, drive, enthusiasm and a perfect script. Actors also word-perfect.' The Master had blown into the studios like a whirlwind, bringing with him all his dedication and excitement from the theatre. With a play everyone feels totally involved: he managed to achieve this state of affairs in the studio. Three weeks before the film went on the floor he insisted on every member of the unit being sent a script, not only the actors but the chippies, electricians, the sound and camera crews. Consequently, they were all interested and became personally involved in making the film. A letter was dispatched to each actor requesting them to turn up on the first day's shooting word-perfect – not only on the first day's scenes (the usual proceeding) but on the entire film.

On the first morning of shooting we assembled on Stage Five of Denham Studios at 8.30. One actor, playing quite an important part, who for obvious reasons must remain nameless, was late. We rehearsed the scene, the Christmas party, without him with a young second assistant director, Michael Anderson, reading his lines. At nine o'clock Noël said in a very clipped, controlled voice: 'I would like to make something crystal clear to all of you. I expect to find the same discipline in this studio as I enjoy in the theatre. I have never yet in my career known an actor to be late for the first day's rehearsal. I wouldn't stand for it there, and I am not standing for it here. Michael . . .'

Young Michael Anderson leapt to his feet. 'Yes, Mr Coward?'

'You are about to embark on a career as an actor. You are now playing the part. Nip along to the make-up department. Tell Tony Forzini to stick a moustache on you, part your hair in the middle and be back on the set in five minutes. I shall start shooting the scene at 9.30 sharp.'

The unfortunate actor turned up at 9.35 and was informed that his part had been re-cast and that his services were no longer required. Needless to say, none of the cast was even one second late during the entire shooting of the picture.

Noël's god-daughter, Miss Juliet Mills, made her acting debut in the film at the advanced age of eleven weeks. She played Shorty Blake's baby, a sensible piece of casting as her father was playing Shorty.

Mary had brought Juliet to the studios that morning from Mopes Farm Cottage in Denham, which we had rented for the duration of the film. The cottage was thirteenth-century, beautiful and extremely damp. Any coat hanging in the hall had to be wrung out the next morning. The scene that my daughter's services were required for took place in Mrs Shorty Blake's living-room – Kay Walsh, playing Mrs Blake, receives a telegram informing her that her husband is one of the survivors of the *Kelly* and expected home on leave. The scene was very moving at rehearsal – Kay, opening the telegram, calling: 'Mum, Mum, it's Shorty. He's all right, he's all right', and then dissolving into tears. Because of the danger of the arc-lamps Miss Mills did not take part in the rehearsals. When Noël was satisfied that they were ready and keyed up for a take, Mary placed our first-born in the cot. She seemed very happy, contented and quite at home.

'Ready everybody? Quiet please.' The usual deadly hush descended on Studio Five. Noël's voice said, 'Action.' That was the cue for Miss Juliet Mills to let fly a report from the cot which would have done credit to one of HMS *Kelly*'s four-inch guns. It reverberated round Studio Five. Strong men clapped their hands over their ears and the unit dissolved into hysterics. When the storm subsided Noël, looking at Mary, who was standing wide-eyed beside David Lean behind the camera, said with just enough projection to reach the 'sparks' on the top gantry: 'Mmm . . . Hereditary, I see.'

Noël was determined not to let his great friend Dickie Mountbatten or the Navy down. A few weeks into the shooting I was sure that we needed to have no anxiety on that account. I've had that feeling about a few of the films I've made, that smell of success, while still in production: *In Which We Serve* was one of them. No expense was spared. The largest stage at Denham Studios was entirely taken up with an enormous working model of the *Kelly*. It was a magnificent piece of engineering; the decks could be rocked by hydraulic lifts to angles of forty-five degrees.

A hundred extras were engaged. After one morning's shooting in 'rough seas' they suffered violent seasickness, and very few reported for duty after lunch. Lord Louis, who was taking a personal interest in the film, came to the rescue. He informed Noël that when he needed another bunch of extras he would see to it that the Navy supplied the necessary crew for the day.

The most uncomfortable part of the proceedings were the days we spent in the huge tank built on one of the other large stages, swimming to the Carley floats and hanging on to them after the *Kelly* had been sunk. The water was indescribable: gallons of diesel oil had been pumped into it. Other evil-smelling substances had been added to the brew and after a few days' shooting it stank to high heaven.

Swimming to one of the Carley floats I, as Shorty Blake, was supposed to be shot in the arm by a machine-gun bullet from a German aircraft that was strafing the survivors. The special effects man was suddenly at a loss. How could this be done? How could it give the impression of complete reality without too much risk? They tried everything. Nothing worked. Then the head man had an inspiration. A runner was dispatched to the nearest chemist and returned with several packets containing dozens of contraceptives – of the male variety. These were then fastened at intervals of twelve inches to a length of hollow tubing drilled with the necessary holes. The whole contraption was then wired electrically and lowered into the tank. Noël and David Lean were assured that this time it would not only work, but look terrific.

On action, I dropped into the muck and struck out for the Carley float. At the planned moment I heard the sound of sharp, staccato explosions in the water coming rapidly one after another. Special effects had blown compressed air into the tube and detonated the contraceptives. I felt a sharp crack on my right arm, grabbed it, shouted, and was hauled aboard the Carley float by Noël playing 'Captain D' and Bernard Miles, the Petty Officer. I am reasonably certain I can claim to be the only actor in history who has been shot in the arm by a French letter.

We spent two weeks in that unforgettable tank. It was filthy dirty work but we were very well taken care of. Dressing-rooms were erected on the set in which we were rubbed down and thawed out while we waited for the next immersion. On the final day of the tank sequence King George VI and Queen Elizabeth visited the set with their two young and very attractive daughters, Princess Elizabeth, who was sixteen years old at the time, and Princess Margaret who was four years younger. Also in the party was that beautiful lady, Princess Marina. I was sitting next to the Princess at the tank-side waiting for the next shot when my dresser, a marvellous character called Smasher, arrived with a mug of tea. 'There you are, John. Get this down you.' He looked at Princess Marina, sitting beside me. 'What about your girl-friend, would she like one?'

'Well, thank you, if you can spare it,' was the reply.

'Well of course I can, ducks. Here you take this one. I'll get John another.' And with that he handed the mug, covered in smears of diesel oil and with a large chip out of the rim, to HRH who smiled at him, and with her usual devastating charm said, 'How very kind of you. It looks a lovely cup of tea.' It was Smasher's special brew, so strong you could stand a spoon up in it, and laced with at least four lumps of sugar. I watched rather anxiously. She took a sip. 'Delicious, Smasher,' she said, 'absolutely delicious.'

Later on I informed Smasher who my 'girl-friend' was. 'Cor stone the bleedin' crows,' said Smasher, 'I'll shove a royal warrant over the dressing-room.'

In Which We Serve was a landmark in several people's lives. It started David Lean off on a brilliant career. With Ronald Neame, the cameraman, who did an excellent job on the photography, and Anthony Havelock Allen, he formed a company called CineGuild and made a string of successes which included two more of Noël's works: *This Happy Breed* and *Blithe Spirit*. Carol Reed was then already starting to make a name for himself as a director, and several years later, when David Lean had just notched up his third big hit, Carol said to me: 'You know Johnnie, when Noël asked me who I could think of as a co-director to work with him on *In Which We Serve*, and I suggested David Lean, that was about the silliest bloody suggestion I ever made in my life!'

The picture also introduced to the public a young actor, Richard Attenborough, who gave an outstanding performance as the stoker who loses his nerve during the ship's action. Since that debut, through total dedication, hard work and a sometimes quite brilliant choice of subject, he has become the most successful actor-producer-director in the country. I have been lucky to work closely with him on several ventures, and through the years Dickie and his wife, Sheila, have remained our closest friends.

As far as I was concerned, one of the greatest benefits that the picture provided was the honour and privilege of getting to know one of the great men of our time, Lord Louis Mountbatten. I've never met anyone quite like him, and I'm sure I never will again, and I'm grateful to have had the opportunity over the past thirty-seven years of working with him on many occasions for various charities, particularly the Variety Club, the children's charity to which he gave endless time and help. He always seemed to be more than equal to any emergency. I remember one particular occasion when Jimmy Carreras, now Sir James, one of the stalwarts of the Variety Club, invited Cary Grant and myself to the annual convention to be held in Puerto Rico. Lord Louis had agreed to be the guest of honour. Jimmy Carreras had engaged a team of experts to arrange a commentary on Lord Louis's life to be spoken by Cary and myself after the dinner in the hotel. The dress rehearsal in the afternoon was total chaos. We tried to rehearse at two separate microphones while the catering staff were arranging the tables. The mikes failed every two seconds, the spotlights couldn't be persuaded to work on cue, and I have a picture in my mind of Jimmy Carreras in the midst of it all clutching his head and muttering, 'And the trouble is, I hate bloody kids!'

At the performance, however, the mikes worked, the spotlights came on, and Cary and I were doing our act. I was giving thumbnail impressions of Winston Churchill, Field Marshal Montgomery, Admiral of the Fleet Lord Fraser and several other notable personalities who had played major parts in the great man's career. Cary Grant was tackling President Roosevelt and the American contingent. We started with Lord Louis's life as a cadet at Dartmouth and worked right through to the present day. When the performance was finished Lord Louis made a splendid speech. He was his usual charming and witty self. In the middle of it one of the guards of honour in the Marines, standing to attention just behind him, suddenly fainted dead away and collapsed with a thud across the table two feet from where Lord Louis was standing. Without even pausing, or looking down, he said, 'You will notice that one of the admirable qualities that the Marines possess is to be able to faint at attention.' He then continued to delight his audience. It is typical, however, of the great man that immediately the dinner finished he sought out the unfortunate marine to make sure that he was all right.

In Which We Serve opened in August 1942. This time the critics were unanimous. The *Sunday Express* headline read: 'Coward's Navy Epic will Thrill The World'. The *Graphic*'s lead was, 'Noël Coward Makes War's Greatest Film'. There was not one carping voice. The picture was acclaimed as a classic and time has proved that claim to be right. It has been shown at least twice a year at the British Film Academy since its première thirty-seven years ago. The good notices were splendid, because they meant the film would be assured of a box-office success; but what pleased us even more was the fact that Dickie Mountbatten, Captain of the *Kelly*, and the survivors of her gallant crew felt that we had done their beloved ship justice.

A few years later, when I had made several more films with the Navy, Lord Louis informed me that although I had been what was known as

Fred Berger and me as Lew Messenger in *Men in Shadow* (Mary's first play),
Vaudeville Theatre, 1942

Godparents Larry and Vivien Olivier, and proud parents of Juliet Mills
at her christening in November 1941

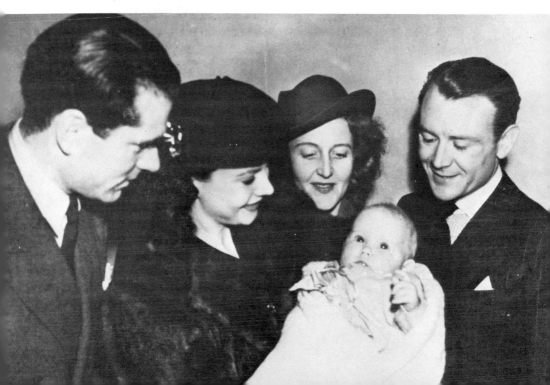

As happy as we looked, with 'Bunch' (Juliet) at the Oast House, Kent, 1942

Noël Coward (*right*) as Captain D and me just behind him as Shorty Blake in *In Which We Serve*, 1942

Joyce Carey, me, Mary and Noël relaxing at his home

'To London and a very happy future': Alec Guinness as Herbert Pocket and me as Pip in *Great Expectations*, 1945 – it was Alec's first film

A scene from *Scott of the Antarctic*, 1947

RIGHT 'Now listen, Juliet.' On the set of *Mr Polly*

Anthony Pélissier (*left*), J. Arthur Rank and myself on the set of *The History of Mr Polly*

LEFT With Dickie
Attenborough in
Morning Departure, 1950

BELOW LEFT Dickie and
I aboard HMS
Birmingham during a
break in filming *The
Baby and the Battleship*

ABOVE RIGHT As Willy
Mossop with Brenda de
Banzi in *Hobson's
Choice*, 1953

RIGHT Swiss Family
Mills: Jonathan, Hayley,
Juliet, Mary and me in St
Moritz, 1955

The 'daring' love scene with Sylvia Sims cut by the censor from
Ice Cold in Alex, 1957

a 'brown job' during the war, he felt that it was time I belonged to the Senior Service. At one of their annual reunion dinners he presented me with the *Kelly* tie and a plaque on which is inscribed the ship's motto: 'Keep On'. I am enormously proud to know that I am the only civilian member of that gallant ship's company.

I was wearing the tie recently at Lord Romsey's wedding at Broadlands. Prince Charles, whom I've never yet known to miss even half a trick, said, 'Hallo, Sir John, I'm glad to see you're wearing the right tie.' We talked about the great man to whom he had been very close and who had had such an influence on his life. HRH then told me something that I didn't know. In fact I don't think it has ever been mentioned in all the press reports about the unspeakable horror that took place on that summer's morning in Ireland. Earl Mountbatten of Burma, one of the last of the great heroes, was killed at sea wearing a T-shirt with the name of the ship he loved, HMS *Kelly*, blazoned across the front of it.

During the last week's shooting of the picture Mary and I were having supper in our 'damp delight', Mope's Farm Cottage; by chance the radio happened to be on and we heard Sir Stafford Cripps's famous broadcast to the V Army (the underground movement in occupied France). It was impressive and highly dramatic – so much so that we were both simultaneously struck by the same idea. 'It could be terrific, couldn't it?' I said. By this stage in our relationship we found that both of us seemed to know at a split second exactly what the other one was thinking.

'Yes,' said Mary. 'It could be.'

For the past months, after discovering some half-written plays of my child bride's, I had been trying to persuade her to put pen to paper. I thought her writing showed enormous potential, and as she had steadfastly stuck with her decision to give up acting I felt that it would be a wonderful compensation if she could still remain in the theatre by writing for it, without having to give up her life's work of looking after me. We kicked the subject backwards and forwards until the early hours of the morning.

Two weeks later to the day she had completed a full-length two-act play based on the underground movement in France, entitled *To Stall the Grey Rat*. I was not inexperienced by this time, and even after making allowances for a very natural bias on my part the play, I thought, was amazingly good. I simply couldn't believe it was a first play. The construction was good, with truthful, well-drawn characters, and dialogue that slipped easily off the tongue. Because of the aforementioned bias I was anxious to get another opinion, and so I gave the work to Bernard Miles to read. Bernard, who played the Petty Officer in the picture, had become a close friend. After twelve weeks' tough schedule, three of which we had spent clinging round each other's necks in a tank full of filthy water, you either hate someone or love them. Mary and I loved Bernard. A tremendous enthusiast who lived for the theatre, he was a stimulating companion. I always felt that Bernard, who was from humble beginnings, the son of a market gardener in Uxbridge, was one day going to make his mark. If at that time, however, I had thought that he was going to build the Mermaid Theatre almost with his own hands on a derelict bomb-site in the City of London, collect a CBE, then a knighthood, and finally end up as a peer in the House of Lords, I would have considered that was going perhaps a bit too far.

He was as keen on Mary's play as I was, and he agreed that after the film was finished, if I could get a management to accept the play, he would co-direct it with me. By this time the theatre was almost back to normal. In spite of Hitler's onslaught from the air, when an air-raid alert sounded the stage manager would make an announcement from the stage; the audience had two choices: stay in the theatre where the play would continue, or leave for one of the air-raid shelters. I never saw one person during any performance take advantage of the second choice.

I took the play to Binkie Beaumont, the brilliant young head of the most successful management at the time, H. M. Tennent Ltd. A few days later the phone rang: yes, he was thrilled, he loved the play and would present it in April. We could hardly believe it, it seemed just too good to be true. I was to act in a play written by my wife, co-direct with Bernard Miles, and the best management in London was going to present it.

Noël read it and was equally enthusiastic, but he said in his usual direct manner that he thought the title didn't live up to the play – in fact he considered it to be 'piss poor'. Next day the phone rang: 'I've got it,' said the Master, '*Men in Shadow*.' *Men in Shadow* it was.

We were in the middle of casting when the blow fell. Binkie rang to say that the Censor had passed the play to MI5 who had not only refused permission for it to be produced but wished, he said, to interview the author. To say that we were shattered is the understatement of the year. 'Miss Hayley Bell, may I ask why you picked the caves at San Sebastian as the point at the end of the escape route? Who gave you the information that the top button of a pilot's uniform contains a small compass? Where did you get the names André, Pierre, Philippe? And, by the way, Miss Bell, am I not right in supposing that you have a brother who is a fighter pilot in the Air Force?'

By an extraordinary chance Mary had hit on the exact escape route that was being used, plus several of the code names. She assured MI5 that this was pure coincidence, but they were unconvinced, and Squadron Leader Hayley Bell DFC was also sent for and questioned. Dennis, who was hardly ever out of his cockpit at this time, hadn't the faintest idea what they were talking about. He hadn't even heard that the play was being written. The Censor, however, refused to budge. That seemed to be the end of it.

When Mary had recovered from the initial shock I persuaded her to re-write the play, taking out most of the escapes, the route, the code names, and making sabotage the more important element. In three weeks the re-write was completed, and Bernard and I both felt the play had really not suffered by the operation. To our joy the new version passed the Censor with flying colours. Binkie Beaumont, however, by this time had lost enthusiasm. I think he was still concerned over the MI5 incident. During the early summer I hawked *Men in Shadow* round the managements with no success. It finally ended up with Bill Linnet, one of the partners of the production company Linnet and Dunfee. By this time our tails were very much between our legs. We both decided that it was unlikely that the last management on the list would be interested, and the best thing to do would be to lick our wounds and forget all about it.

17

Joint Operations

Almost immediately after *In Which We Serve* I started to make another film with the Navy called *We Dive at Dawn*, a story about the submarine service, again directed by my old friend Puffin Asquith. I had never worked with submarines before, and found it fascinating and exhilarating. Submarine crews were always made up of volunteers, and although the conditions were indescribably uncomfortable and the dangers intense, I never met one sailor who would have swapped places for a job in a surface vessel. I was allowed to go on patrol in one of the submarines from the mother ship up in the Clyde. I was determined to know what it felt like when a submarine crash-dived. Without actually experiencing it I didn't feel that I would be able to do those brave characters justice on the screen.

The skipper was an old sea-dog, twenty-two years of age; his Number One was still, he told me, in his prime – he had just celebrated his nineteenth birthday. 'I'm going to let Number One take her down,' the skipper said to me. 'He's not done a crash-dive before and he's got to start some time.'

I hoped I wasn't looking as nervous as I felt. A warning bell clanged in my ears – 'Action Stations, Dive Dive Dive.' The ship then seemed to stand on her nose and I felt her speeding like an arrow towards the sea bed; charts and crockery went flying in all directions; I hung on to a rail near the periscope trying to look heroic and totally unconcerned; the only thing that worred me was the fact that I was sure my face had turned a pale shade of pea-green. The skipper's voice broke in calmly and quietly, 'Just a trifle too steep, Number One. Level her out a bit, but gently does it.'

The angle of descent became less abrupt, and in a few seconds we were levelling out and proceeding on our course. For the next hour the skipper gave me instructions on the use of the periscope. I shall never forget the thrill of seeing for the first time a vessel emerge through the spray and click into focus. The crew of a submarine is like a large family who are totally dependent on one man – their skipper. He is the only member of the crew who sees anything of the action. They are all in his hands and have to trust him completely. This makes a very close relationship with the ship's company essential. In every submarine I worked in, and there were many, there was always a marvellous atmosphere of companionship that I'm sure was unique to the service. I was fortunate enough to make three films with the submariners; I got to know them well, and to admire them enormously. It would be impossible to meet a finer body of men in a day's sail.

Out of the blue, during the first week of June, the phone rang in the house in Fairholt Street that we'd rented after finishing the picture. It was Bill Linnet. He apologized for keeping us up in the air so long, but he said there had been differences of opinion in the firm about the play, but now they had definitely decided that they wanted to present it, and was I free?

We could hardly believe it. It was difficult to accept the fact that our first joint production, after Juliet, was going to see the light of day. I rang Bernard Miles, who was also free and rearing to go. By the end of the month we had assembled an excellent cast – all ex-service men who had been discharged on medical grounds as unfit for active service: Ralph Michael, ex-RAF, Derek Elphinstone, ex-RNVR, Rob Wilton, Hubert Gregg and John Rae, all ex-Army, and Paul Bonnifas, a French actor from the Comédie Française who had escaped from the Germans in 1940. Our set designer was also French, a young man called Frank Bauer, who had also worked at the Comédie Française, joined the underground movement, been captured by the SS and escaped to England. Alice Gachet (Mary's old French tutor at RADA) played Chérie, the only woman's part in the play. Rehearsals began on 20 July with Bernard co-directing.

After a short successful provincial tour we opened at the Vaudeville Theatre in the Strand on 3 September, three years to the day after war was declared. The author and I were sick with nerves and anxiety before the curtain went up. The word nepotism kept raising its ugly head. We were asking for it. The critics would be bound to have a go at us. It was just a bit too much: playing the leading part in a play written by my wife, and then having the nerve to co-direct it. Endeavouring to keep our first-night nerves under as much control as possible (the cast was as keyed up as we were) we dress-rehearsed until the half-hour was called. I sat in my small dressing-room sweating profusely. Mary was staring at a pile of telegrams which somehow or other she couldn't bring herself to open. She turned round to find me looking at her: 'Look darling,' I said, 'for the first time since we've been together I need to be alone.'

'Of course, my love, I was just going. I can't stand it in here another moment, but just remember, whatever happens to my silly play I'm lucky to have the best actor in London to act in it.' She kissed me and flew.

There is no doubt that the first performance of *Men in Shadow* had a profound effect on the audience. The underground movement was at that time very much on people's minds. During the last scene I, as Lew Messenger, was trying desperately to lift and push Ralph Michael, playing Mordan, an RAF pilot with broken legs in splints, through a trap door in the roof of the mill while the German troops are trying to break their way into the loft by smashing down the door with their rifle butts. The stage manager looking through the peephole could see the audience in the stalls rising a few inches from their seats and then lowering themselves every time I lifted and pushed.

At the final curtain the play received a standing ovation, and after countless curtain calls and shouts of 'Author, author' Mary, cowering in the wings, appeared on stage with a rush, propelled from the back by our stage manager. The applause died away to audible mutterings and gasps of astonishment. The author of the tough and at times quite brutal play they had just witnessed was not at all what they expected: a young woman looking not a day over twenty, a slight boyish figure in a blue frock, her golden hair falling all over the place, stood on the stage, thanked the audience and the cast and then kissed the leading man. There are a few rare moments when life just seems too good to be true – that was one of them.

My dressing-room was jammed with chums – Noël, Larry and Vivien, Michael and Rachel Redgrave, Rex Harrison and Lilli Palmer, Robertson Hare and my sister Annie. We all trooped across the road to the Savoy Grill where Noël gave a party for us. It continued into the early hours until the morning papers arrived. Everybody snatched at them. 'Well, Mary darling,' said the Master, 'it looks as if you will be able to keep that dreadful little husband of yours in a manner which he doesn't deserve. How do you like this one in the *Telegraph*? "An Exciting Play. Young Authoress's Success."' Noël looked at Mary. 'It's W.A. Darlington's notice, and he really knows what he's talking about. "If somebody had happened to walk into the Vaudeville Theatre at the end of last night's play and had seen a beautiful blonde young lady bowing her acknowledgement to the cheers of the audience, he would naturally have concluded that she was the leading actress in Mary Hayley Bell's *Men in Shadow*, and he would have been wrong. She was Miss Bell herself, who looked to me in her early twenties – something quite unusually youthful in the way of an authoress. It seems likely that her play will run for it is an exciting and adventurous piece of work."'

We really couldn't have asked for more. All the notices were in the same vein. The unanimous vote in the Grill that night was that we had a success on our hands. Events proved us right; Mary's first play enjoyed a long and successful run at the Vaudeville Theatre. At the same time it being played in two other cities – New York and Moscow, where it was the first British play to be presented during the war.

While the play was running we lived at Fairholt Street during the week as the cast were all on a fire-watching rota on the roof of the theatre. On Saturday nights after the show we drove down to the oast-house. It was there at three o'clock one Sunday morning we received a phone call from a hospital in Epping informing us that my sister had been severely injured in a car crash while being driven from an RAF concert she had been giving.

We arrived at the hospital to be told by the surgeon in charge that he thought she would survive, but her injuries were so serious that he considered it doubtful that she would ever walk again. Practically every bone in her body was broken. My sister on the other hand, when she regained consciousness, had absolutely no doubts whatsoever. She intended, she said, not only to walk again, but to be performing her act at the piano before a year had passed. To achieve this miracle she was going to need a great deal of support. I contacted the finest orthopaedic surgeon of the time, Reginald Watson-Jones, and put the case to him; we practically hi-jacked my sister from the hospital and moved her by ambulance to Oswestry, where the great surgeon performed a series of miraculous operations. With his encouragement and her amazing determination and courage, she made it. She was back at the piano in just over eighteen months' time. She only needed the help of one stick and her playing, with two completely reconditioned hands, was almost as good as ever.

The tragic part of the story was that the driver of the car on that evening was Wing Commander Hancock, a close friend of my sister's, who only received a slight cut on the ankle. Although no blame could be attached to him – in the black-out a lorry had parked without its lights on by the side of the road; he swerved, but my sister in the passenger seat received the full impact – he never really recovered from the shock. A few months after the accident he took off in a Spitfire from a fighter station on a test flight and was never seen again.

On 30 November Wing Commander Dennis Hayley Bell DFC was married to an attractive girl named Jane King, and I was his best man – with a difference ... I had mumps. I left the play, Bernard Miles took over at a day's notice (we had no understudies) and got through the performance by reading most of the dialogue from pages of the script which he plastered up at strategic points all over the stage. The trick was, said

Bernard, to manage to get to the right place at the right time for the right line.

I was off for three weeks. When I returned to the play at the end of January the raids were getting worse: sirens wailed at every performance. In the second act I had to say, 'They're a bit earlier tonight than I expected.' The second before I spoke, right on cue, the siren went off. It brought the house down. The daylight raids were on too. There are two notes in my diary – 20 January, 'Gerries killed children in playground at Peckham', 21 January, 'Bad night raid, hardly affecting business. Amazing what guts people have to leave their homes and come and sit in a theatre, but glad they do.'

In February we found it – the dream cottage we had talked about on the hill behind the Boy and Donkey before we were married. It was sitting beside a small bridge, a long low Elizabethan building leaning at all angles, a mass of beams with windows of different sizes, with its roof perched on its head at a jaunty angle. There, too, was the stream we had imagined, running along beside it and disappearing into the small garden flanked with willows at the rear of the house. A small board announced that Misbourne Cottage was for sale. It was sheer luck. I had been at a meeting at Denham Studios discussing the next film I was going to make, CineGuilds' first production for the Rank Organization – Noël Coward's *This Happy Breed*. We had driven into Denham village to have a beer at the Swan before returning to London. We bought the cottage for the exorbitant sum of £900 freehold (the asking price last year was £85,000).

It was our first home. Everything up to then had been rented; this one belonged to us. We spent weeks bashing walls through, leaving exposed the marvellous beams, painting and decorating it. We furnished it with a few things I had in store and old furniture that Mary had picked up for next to nothing in the antique shops she had haunted when we were touring with *Men in Shadow*. We worked like beavers and were able to move in complete with Nanny Evans – a tiny, mouselike creature, who was never seen without what appeared to be a thick woollen stocking on her head pulled down to her eyebrows – Juliet, and Hamlet, our cocker spaniel. Misbourne Cottage before long was as attractive inside as out. We fell in love with it, and the village, and hoped we could stay there for ever.

During this period I had put Michael Wilding, an old friend of Mary's who'd been on tour with her in Australia, into *Men in Shadow*. It would have been impossible for me to stay in the play and make the film at the same time because of the two matinees per week. *This Happy Breed* was to be produced by Noël Coward, directed by David Lean and photographed by Ronald Neame, the same team that made *In Which We Serve*. The cast included Celia Johnson, Stanley Holloway, Kay Walsh, and my old friend Robert Newton who, although he had the reputation of being an exciting actor, was known for his devotion to any form of liquid refreshment, and regarded somewhat warily by producers and directors. Noël and David both wanted him for the part. He was obviously ideal for it; but David, who frowns at anyone even having a light ale at lunchtime during shooting, was uneasy. Robert was finally offered the part, with a proviso written into his contract that if he even had one drink before the picture was completed he would forfeit his entire salary and the producers would be at liberty, if they so wished, to re-cast. Robert, seeing the way the wind was blowing, accepted the deal. Everything went smoothly. The film was up to schedule. Robert was behaving impeccably. The production company relaxed.

One evening during the last week's shooting I was mowing the small lawn in front of the cottage; a figure appeared in the distance, and weaving from one side of the road to the other approached the village. Mary was standing at the door, a watering-can in one hand and Bunch in the other. 'Look at that character,' I said, 'he's plastered, and the pubs aren't open yet.'

Nearer now, the character waved his arms and shouted, 'Hallo there, my hearties, my darlings, I've come to visit you.'

'My God,' I said, 'it's Robert.'

David Lean was living with Kay Walsh, his wife at the time, in a small Georgian house not more than fifty yards up the village. From his front windows he had an uninterrupted view straight down to our cottage and beyond. I grabbed Robert and hustled him as quickly as possible into the cottage; not an easy procedure as he had both arms round our necks, hugging and kissing us and informing the village in a loud, clear voice, what darling people we were and how much he loved us. We poured gallons of strong black coffee into him. At one period of the treatment he escaped into the garden, and we found him standing in the middle of the stream with his fascinated audience (Juliet, who was two and a half at the time) watching him wide-eyed from the bank. Our hero suddenly plunged his hands into his pockets, produced handfuls of silver and notes and flung them in all directions over the garden, shouting, 'Treasure trove, Juliet, treasure trove,' at the top of his voice.

Juliet had watched him act several times on the set during the picture, but I could see she considered this to be by far his most exciting performance. Several hours later, after feeding him scrambled eggs, we considered him sober enough to leave. I drove him home in the car. He fell asleep on the sofa in the middle of a sentence. He was safe that night; but had he been spotted, and what would tomorrow bring forth? We were both due on the set at 8.30 a.m. for a very important scene. At 7.45 I was in the make-up chair. A minute later Robert walked in looking pretty rough, but stone-cold sober. He lowered himself into the chair next to me and said, 'Morning darling boy, I hear you had a bit of a party last night. How do you feel?'

'Fine, Bob,' I said. 'How about you?'

'Never felt worse old darling, but I'll survive.' He gave me a broad wink and then slept soundly until Tony Forzini had finished his make-up. That evening, a case of champagne arrived at Misbourne Cottage with a note which read, 'Darling chums, A friend in need etc. Love Robert.' The Company never discovered that he'd broken his contract, and he finished the picture, as far as they were concerned, without touching a drop.

Round about this period, 1943 and onwards, Denham Studios became a hive of activity, and because of transport problems many people made their homes in the area – the Oliviers, David Lean, Ronny Neame, Robert Helpmann, Constance Cummings, Robert Donat and David Niven. Misbourne Cottage, three minutes from the studio across the fields, was open house to all the friends. Larry was making *Henry V* at this time, and one Sunday morning he invited Vivien and Bobby Helpmann, Niven, Mary and me, and Angela Baddeley to ride the horses he was using in the picture. They were magnificent-looking beasts and we eyed them with some apprehension. With Larry in the lead we left the studios. All went well until we reached the open fields, when our mounts, with no warning, stood straight up on their hind legs and jumped up and down like pogo sticks. In seconds four out of the seven saddles were empty. The animals had been taught to rear up for the film, and by this time an open stretch of country to them meant 'Action'. Larry naturally stayed aboard, and so did Niven and Mary, both excellent riders. The rest of us bit the dust. Thereafter, Larry, Vivien, Mary and I rode nearly every Sunday together until *Henry V* was completed. I became bitten by the horse bug and during that time, with tuition from Mary, I learned to ride and jump with a certain degree of confidence.

Before the end of the year I made a picture called *Waterloo Road* with Stewart Granger. Jimmy Granger had been invalided out of the Gordons and was married at that time to a very beautiful young actress called Elspeth March (Mary's oldest friend – they were at Sherbourne School together). Jimmy looked like everybody's idea of a film star, which by hook or crook he intended to become, and eventually did. He was tall, dark, handsome and a good actor, having had years of experience in rep before the war. He played the 'heavy' in *Waterloo Road* and gave an excellent performance. I've always felt that if he'd been satisfied to stay on that side of the fence instead of playing heroes his career would have been even more successful and prolonged that it has been.

Waterloo Road is still remembered for the fight scenes. Jimmy and I had both done a lot of boxing and with the help of Dave Crowley, an old friend of mine and ex-lightweight champion of Great Britain, we rehearsed the fight for a week before we shot it. We only used a double for one take, which entailed my upper-cutting Jimmy at the top of a long flight of stairs; he then was supposed to fall backwards and, halfway down, crash through the banisters to the left of the stairs and land on cardboard boxes and mattresses out of camera range. Jimmy offered to have a go at it, but Sydney Gilliatt, who was directing, flatly refused. It was, he insisted, much too dangerous, and needed an experienced double. The young man they had engaged looked remarkably like Jimmy. The action was explained to him; the banisters had been half sawn through so that they would snap easily when his weight hit them.

He stood facing me at the top of the stairs with his back to the cameras, which were shooting upwards. I explained that I would hit him in the solar plexus with my left, pulling the punch of course, and then as he leaned forward from the impact, upper-cut him with my right. (With the camera behind the victim, if the fist travels upwards and fairly fast just missing the chin it gives the impression of complete reality.) As I started the punch to the stomach, out of the corner of my eye I noticed the young man had his fingers crossed. Strange, I thought, but the punch was already on its way. He fell backwards, but instead of falling to the left through the banisters he continued on down the flight of stairs with a series of bumps and crashes, landing with a sickening thud on the studio floor, missing Camera Number One by inches. He was out cold. We carried him into my dressing-room. The first aid arrived. After a minute or two he came to. He looked pretty ghastly. 'Are you all right? What the hell happened?' I said. 'Why didn't you do the fall as arranged? You must have done hundreds of stunts like that.'

'Well, I haven't actually,' was the reply. 'I haven't done any. I'm a sailor on leave from the Merchant Navy.'

Sydney Gilliat made a success of his first job as a director. The film was well received and made money at the box office.

In the spring of 1944, I received an SOS from Admiral of the Fleet Bruce Fraser. Bernard Miles and I quickly put together a small show which included Josephine Wilson, Bernard's wife, and Mary. We took off for Scapa Flow. The next six weeks were hectic and unforgettable. We played all the small RAF and Army stations stuck out in the wilds of the Orkneys and Shetlands. We travelled in small planes in gale force winds and on drifters through rough seas. The hospitality was more difficult to handle than the travel and work; the men were so grateful for the sight of a new face that we were seldom able to escape from any mess party until dawn.

Practically the entire Fleet was lying at anchor in Scapa Flow. There was a feeling of big things in the air. Shore leave had been cancelled and it was the C-in-C's idea for us to give our show aboard as many ships as possible. I've lost count of the names; but among them were HMS *Kent, Belfast, Sheffield, Jamaica* and the flagship HMS *The Duke of York*.

During the last week of the tour Bruce Fraser told us that someone interesting was arriving for a flying visit, and would we join him for drinks aboard the flagship at 7 p.m. The interesting character turned out to be none other than Field Marshal Montgomery; to Mary's delight, she found herself sitting next to him at dinner in the boardroom. There was no doubt in our minds then that the invasion of Europe was imminent. D-day could not possibly be far off. The next morning we were smuggled into the projection box of the enormous cinema at Flotta, and listened to Monty make a speech to the Navy. Monty was a great showman, and on this occasion he was at his best.

Another visitor made a surprise hush-hush visit. His Majesty the King arrived to inspect the Fleet. We gave a 'command' performance for him aboard *The Duke of York*. The girls were green with envy, but for security reasons it had to be men only this time. We had a marvellous evening; Bruce Fraser was one of the best hosts I have ever met in my life. Judging by the remarks we heard during our six-week tour he appeared to be the most popular and admired sailor in the entire Navy.

One of the most wonderful sights I have ever seen in my life was a 'musical sunset'. The Fleet lay at anchor, the ships dressed from stem to stern and the ships' companies lined up on deck. The weather that evening was perfect; the sea was calm and still, the giant ships standing out against the skyline. The massed bands of the Marines on the quarter-deck played the national anthem, during which a flag was slowly hoist to the top mast; as the last note died away over the water and the flag reached the top, a single shot was fired from a musket. The C-in-C raised his cap and called for three cheers for the King. His Majesty then walked to the rail, took out a white handkerchief and waved to all his ships. It was an unforgettable moment.

Our last show of the tour was given to a battery on Shaplin Island: twenty grateful soldiers who had seen nothing but seagulls for six months. We had time to visit the Bay of Scail – a beautiful, weird place with a strange atmosphere. Mary, with her Celtic imagination, was convinced it was haunted by the ghosts of Lord Kitchener and the men who were wrecked there during World War I. Even I had to admit that there was something odd about it. Perhaps it had to do with the little stone-age village Scara Brae, built around 3000 BC, at the other end of the bay. It was in a remarkable state of preservation – bedrooms, bathrooms, kitchens, all still there. We spent hours wandering about. Mary, who on these excursions hardly ever drew breath, on this occasion was peculiarly quiet. Something was brewing, I thought. I was right. Twenty-four hours later she started writing her second play, set in the Orkneys.

During that summer, while she was writing, I was working on a film written by Terence Rattigan, called *The Way to the Stars*, an RAF subject with Puffin Asquith again directing. Michael Redgrave, Rosamund John, Bonar Colleano and an American actor, Douglas Montgomery, were in the cast.

The day before I left for location work at the RAF station at Catterick, I was sitting on the lawn at the back of Misbourne Cottage studying the script; Juliet was beside me. I heard a strange, rather different noise. Looking up I saw appearing out of the clouds about three hundred feet up, a strange, cigar-like object. I recognized it from the drawings I had seen in the paper that morning. It was Hitler's new toy – a pilotless plane, a flying bomb. The engine suddenly cut out. I knew what that meant. It started to lose height coming straight for the cottage. There was no time to do anything. I put my arms round Juliet and stared up at it. Not more than 200 feet from us it banked, swerved to the left, and disappeared over the roof. A few seconds later there was an almighty explosion. One of the first doodle-bugs, as they were later nicknamed, had dived into the ground on one of the lots behind Denham Studios, just missing Gabriel Pascale, who was directing a scene from the top of the twenty-five-foot rostrum. The bomb did no damage whatsoever, but Gabby Pascale was not amused.

The Way to the Stars will probably be remembered as Asquith's best film – it had a wonderful score by William Walton and poems by John Pudney. There is another reason why the film will stay in my mind. I returned home one evening after the day's shooting and told Mary that I had just played a short scene with a young actor who impressed me very much; and I remember saying that, with any luck at all, I was certain that he must become a star. His name was Trevor Howard.

1944 was the year of the great Old Vic season at the New Theatre. Laurence Olivier and Ralph Richardson were making theatrical history.

Mary and I were at home getting ready to leave for the first night of *Richard III* when the phone rang. It was Larry: 'Johnnie, you're coming tonight, aren't you?'

'Yes of course. You know we are. We can't wait. Good luck, Larry boy. See you after the show.'

'Come and see me before the show in my dressing-room.'

'But surely you don't want ...'

'I do want. It's important. See you in half an hour.'

I looked at Mary: 'What the hell's going on? In his dressing-room before the show? Before *that* part?'

We arrived at the New Theatre just as they had called the half-hour. As we walked into the dressing-room, Larry was pacing up and down, fully made-up and dressed. The beaked nose, the long black hair, the hump, the lot. He pointed a long, black-gloved finger at us. 'Sit down darlings and listen to me. I just want you to know that you are going to see a bloody awful performance. The dress rehearsal was chaotic. I dried up at least a dozen times. It's a dreadful production, and I was an idiot to let them persuade me to play the bloody part. If this evening is anything like this afternoon's débâcle, you are in for four hours of boredom. Anyway, I just wanted *you* to know that *I* know. Also I don't give a damn. I'm past it.'

After trying to say all the right things and make all the right noises we left hurriedly for the pub outside the stage door and braced ourselves with two large drinks for the ordeal ahead.

There was an air of excitement and expectancy in the theatre. An Olivier first night had become an occasion. We sat in the stalls with our fingers crossed; that scene in the dressing-room had been too real to disregard. The curtain rose, the hum of the audience died away into silence. Laurence Olivier made his entrance, limped slowly to the centre of the stage, glared around the house and then proceeded to give the most majestic, and inspired performance I have ever seen. Fiendish hatred was cunningly concealed behind a smile that froze the blood. I am sure no audience has been so shocked and frightened since Kean gave his first performance of the part at Drury Lane all those years ago. The mood that Larry was in before the show had obviously worked for him; he was reckless and didn't give a damn. We learnt later that he did things that night that he had never done at rehearsals. This gave an added edge of anxiety to the rest of the cast, which also helped to give the drama a feeling of spontaneous vitality. I have never been sure to this day whether Larry played that scene to us in his dressing-room to get himself into the right mood, or whether he really meant it. But what I am sure of is that his performance at the New Theatre was pure magic, and anyone who was fortunate enough to be present on that occasion will never forget it.

The other occasion we shall always remember took place during a performance of *Henry IV*. We were again sitting in the stalls of the New Theatre, and Larry was playing Hotspur. We had seen him look fairly staggering in other characters but we were not prepared for this vision of beauty that confronted us. He has always been a master of make-up, but this time he had excelled himself. Everything was right – his constume was gorgeous – but the crowning glory was his hair, which was a glowing golden red. He looked sensational. The curtain went up on the next scene to disclose him standing in one single spotlight, which lit up the best wig that Nathan's had ever made. The effect was stunning. Before he started the first line of the soliloquy – obviously giving us a second or two to drink in the beauty of it all – the man sitting next to me said in a loud clear voice, 'Oh here's old Ginger again!'

We have sent our dear friend dozens of first-night telegrams since that evening in the New Theatre. They've always contained exactly the same message: 'Oh here's old Ginger again. Love Johnnie and Mary.'

Early in the new year Mary completed the play which had been conceived in the Orkneys. It was a strange and, to me, fascinating piece of work. I couldn't believe that it wouldn't make a riveting evening in the theatre. Briefly, the play was concerned with a brilliant surgeon performing an operation that had never before been attempted. He sutures on to his patient, who has lost his hands in an accident, hands from a man who has just died. The discovery that the hands are the hands of a murderer provided a highly dramatic last scene.

I sent the play to Binkie Beaumont, who promptly turned it down. He thought the idea too far-fetched for the audience to accept. We were naturally disappointed, and I suggested we got another opinion. Garson Kanin, the brilliant American writer-director, was in England during most of the war working for American Intelligence – slumming it, as he put it, in the mud and blood of Claridges Hotel. I can still see a picture of that little bald-headed gnome of a man curled up in a large armchair in the cottage reading the script. We were in the garden watching anxiously through the window. He finally put the play down, and said: 'Cut the god-damn prologue – it's unnecessary – and in my well-known conceited opinion you'll have a smash hit.'

Thus encouraged, I again became a commercial traveller. Something, however, made me decide not to try all the established managements for straight plays (they had all turned down *Men in Shadow*). Instead I called Jack Hilton, the ex-bandleader who was mostly concerned with putting on musicals and variety bills. I'd known and liked Jack for years in my musical comedy days. Within a week, he rang and said he would be delighted to present the play and give me a free hand with the production.

Mary and I decided that if our old friend Anthony Pélissier was keen on the play, we would offer him the job of co-directing it with me. A few days later he rang to say that, as he was only going to co-direct the play (which he thought was marvellous), he would have to insist on designing the set. The fact that he had done neither of these jobs before didn't worry him in the slightest. We gathered together an excellent cast: Elwyn Brooke-Jones, an almost unknown actor we found in Worthing rep, Mary Morris, Elspeth March and Merle Tottenham. Being married to the author again enabled me to grab the leading part.

Duet For Two Hands opened at Blackpool. Walking along the front after the first night, Ant suddenly tore off his hat, flung it into the sea, and shouted: 'I don't believe it, but I think we've got a hit.'

We opened at the Lyric Theatre on 27 June 1945. Ant's sudden premonition at Blackpool looked as if it was going to prove correct. It was obvious from the first-night audience that we were in for our second success. We had taken a suite, rather recklessly, at the Savoy Hotel. The following morning the reviews were all we could have hoped for. The phone rang at mid-day; it was Larry Olivier. He and Vivien had just seen the press. They were thrilled, and could I get them two seats for the matinee? They couldn't wait to see it. I rang the box office at the Lyric – number engaged. It took me half an hour to get through. 'What's been going on?' I said. 'Are you out of order?'

'No,' came the reply. 'Just busy. Congratulations. What can I do for you?'

'I want two stalls for the matinee this afternoon,' I said.

'I'm sorry, Mr Mills. You can't have them.'

'What do you mean? I'm not asking for complimentaries. I'm going to pay for them. They are for Laurence Olivier.'

'Well I'm sorry, he's out of luck. We're sold out.'

I took Mary to the window. 'Look,' I said, 'there's the Thames, shining in the morning sun; we're staying in a suite at the Savoy Hotel; your second play opened at the Lyric Theatre last night; today's matinee is sold out; we have some money in the bank; we are married and I'm still in love with you. How's that for starters?'

Duet For Two Hands settled down to a long and happy run, the high spot of which was, naturally enough, the ending of World War II. The lights went up again in the West End, and after years of groping about like moles in the black-out, London at night seemed like a giant fairground.

When we discovered that another member of the clan was due to arrive in the spring of 1946 we reluctantly decided that Misbourne Cottage would be bursting at the beams, sold it, and bought Rex and Lilli Harrison's house facing the sixth green on Denham golf course. It was a modern house, but attractive, light, airy, and large enough to accommodate us all. We moved in in November and spent a real old-fashioned Christmas there: thick snow, clear blue skies and hard frosts. I tobogganed with Juliet on the golf course and taught Mary to skate on the pond near the house.

18

Scott of the Antarctic

I had always felt that Charles Dickens's novel *Great Expectations* would, if properly handled, make a magnificent film. I was therefore more than delighted when David Lean rang me with the news that he had chosen it for his next picture; and, he added, he couldn't see any other actor playing Pip (incidentally, neither could I!). He warned me that Pip was a 'coat-hanger' for all the fantastic characters that Dickens had woven around him, and the part would need everything I could give it to prevent our hero from being swamped. I was more than ready to take a chance.

We started shooting in January. Three months later David had completed what was arguably one of the best films ever turned out from a British studio. The casting was perfect, and there were some memorable performances, particularly from an actor who was making his first appearance on the screen – Alec Guinness, whose Herbert Pocket was a delight; Francis L. Sullivan as Mr Jaggers, Bernard Miles as Joe Gargery, Valerie Hobson as Estella and Martita Hunt as Miss Haversham were all excellent. Estella as a child was played by an enchanting young actress, Jean Simmons.

I look back on the mid and late 1940s as a very rewarding and exciting period of my life. On 18 April 1946 there is an entry in my diary: '11.40 p.m. Hayley Catherine Rose Vivien Mills arrived, very fat, very sweet, told Mary not to put her back, the boy will have to wait.'

1946 was a full year. I made two more films at Denham Studios, *So Well Remembered* with Martha Scott, directed by Eddie Dymitrik, and *The October Man* with Joan Greenwood and Kay Walsh, directed by Roy Baker.

The first Royal Film Performance took place in November. The picture chosen was *A Matter of Life and Death*. The police on this occasion completely underestimated the drawing power of a host of top-ranking English and American stars, plus the King and Queen with the two

Princesses. Hours before the royal party's arrival Leicester Square was jammed with about 50,000 fans. When the royal car appeared the crowd broke through the police cordon; the last fifty yards to the Empire Cinema took roughly twenty minutes, mostly on two wheels. We watched from the foyer, where we were waiting with Juliet, who was detailed to present the bouquet to Princess Margaret.

The police finally managed to get the royal party into the cinema safe and intact. The King, however, was visibly shaken by the experience. The front pages of all the papers the next morning told the story of how serious the situation had been. First-aid men treated a hundred cases on the spot, several people were taken to hospital with broken legs; a police inspector said: 'It was the nearest shave we have ever had. We got the Royal Family in with a shoe horn. It was touch and go. They nearly got mobbed in the scrimmage like the others.' Film stars were marooned in the vast crowds; people swarmed on to the roofs of taxis and private cars; fireworks were thrown and two rockets whizzed into the air as calls for police reinforcements went out all over London. Shoeless, their evening dresses tattered and torn, women came limping into the foyer, while outside the roaring fans tore their stockings, grazed their knees and ruined their shoes in the stampede. Altogether an evening to remember.

During the early part of 1947, after weeks of discussion, I signed a deal with the Rank Organization. It was, or appeared to be at the time, a wonderful opportunity, a straight, no-option deal to act, produce and direct for seven years. It meant financial security and a chance to choose any subject I wanted. We celebrated by immediately buying a lovely Regency house called Fernacres at Fulmer, set in eight and a half acres, with a paddock and a small lake. This, we said, was it. We shall never move again. It's perfect for us. It has everything. Famous last words. Since that pronouncement we have moved twelve times into houses we have actually bought – not taking into account the rented ones we have lived in on various locations all over the world. This restless hopping from one nest to another has probably something to do with the fact that when we were young we never stopped travelling; even now, after six months or so, we still feel the wanderlust creeping over us.

To stop us becoming conceited, fate then decided to deliver a sharp and salutary lesson. Mary, after months of research and study, had written a new play called *Angel*, based on the famous trial of Constance Kent, which took place in the late 1880s. As the drama needed many scenes in which to unfold, she had planned a production which could be performed without scenery. Small, easily moved pieces of furniture were all that would be needed. All the effects would be obtained by lighting different areas of the stage, dimming and blacking out to denote the passage of time. It was ingenious and would, I thought, make it possible to move the play along rather like a film with no hold-ups for scene-changes. Binkie Beaumont read it and was immediately enthusiastic, but he insisted that we were wrong about the presentation: the play, he said, needed sets – solid, impressive sets, to make it believable. He persuaded us that he was right.

Mary and I had decided that this time I should direct the play and not act in it. We felt it was chancing our arm to hog it to such an extent for a third time. Also I had been offered the chance by Sir Michael Balcon to play a part I had always hoped to tackle – Captain Scott in *Scott of the Antarctic*, an ambitious production he was mounting at Ealing Studios with locations in Switzerland and Norway. I was due to start this immediately after the London opening of *Angel*.

During the dress rehearsal at Liverpool I knew we'd made a mistake: the cast were magnificent, Joyce Redmond as Constance Kent giving an electrifying performance, backed up by that marvellous actor Alan Webb as her QC. The rest, however, was not silence, but pandemonium. The enormous, cumbersome sets, jurors' platform, judge's chair and bench, all on wheels, sounded during the long changes like several train-crashes in Waterloo Station; the changes prolonged the play by at least fifteen minutes. Alan Webb, playing a scene in the front cloth during the back-stage nightmares, even with his magnificent voice, was practically drowned out.

We opened on 6 June at the Strand Theatre in London, and closed on Saturday 14 June. Joyce Redmond received rave reviews, but the play and particularly its director took it on the chin. I felt miserable and re-sponsible. The play just didn't stand a chance; the waits between changes, I'm sure, killed it. Mary was marvellous about it but, like me, bitterly disappointed. An entry in my diary the day after the opening is short and to the point. 'Stinking press; don't think we can survive it; well, can't have success all the time: probably very good for us darling.' Two days later I had to fly to Switzerland for location shots on the Jungfrau for *Scott of the Antarctic*, and was forced to leave Mary literally holding several babies – Juliet, Hayley, and an ailing third offspring, limping along to an early demise at the Strand Theatre.

Because of weather conditions the schedule of *Scott* was split into two parts. We filmed for ten days on the Jungfraujoch doing all the ice-climbing and some of the glacier sequences, all of which needed fair weather with blinding sun; then shooting stopped until October, when the unit left for Norway for the blizzards and the final shots at the Pole.

Charles Friend, who was directing, had, with Sir Michael, taken enor-mous trouble to cast the film, with the result that all the principal charac-ters bore a quite striking resemblance to the team that Scott had led on the expedition. The photograph of Harold Warrender as Dr Wilson, James Robertson Justice as Taff Evans, Derek Bond as Titus Oates, Reginald Beckwith as Birdie Bowers and myself as Scott, taken at the Pole, bears an uncanny resemblance to the famous original picture.

The great difficulty in shooting the exteriors in the snowfields and glaciers arose from the fact that it was not possible to rehearse with the sledge, because the vast stretches of virgin snow had to remain virgin. Footsteps and marks in sand can be obliterated with helicopter propellers, blasting the surfaces smooth, but this does not work with snow. All Charlie Friend could do was to point out to me marks ahead – a boulder, or a discolouration, which would give me a line on which to proceed. On one particular occasion he pointed to an ice-covered rock about fifty yards ahead and said, 'Johnnie, you lead off with your team' – at this time there were still eight men and two sledges on the expedition – 'and just before you reach that rock, stop, look into the distance, turn round and shout the line over your shoulder to the second team, who will be waiting behind you.' (The line was, 'All right chaps, follow me – this seems to be a good way up.') 'Then, if you have enough puff left, carry on hauling till I shout "Cut".' I hoped I would have enough puff. We'd only arrived from England that morning, and here we were hauling sledges up the Jungfrau at a height of about 11,000 feet, and although we had all gone into strict training for weeks, we were already blowing like grampuses.

Action: I started hauling; reached the approximate spot; and after gazing into the distance, took a deep breath, turned as directed, and shouted over my shoulder, 'All right chaps, follow me – this seems to be a good way up.' I then took one step forward and completely disappeared from view. If my harness hadn't been securely fastened to the sledge and my three gallant companions hadn't dug their heels in, in all probability I should not be here at this moment. I had fallen through a snow bridge, which was not more than a few inches thick, into a crevasse, and as I hung swinging like a pendulum from side to side I looked down: beneath me the drop must have been at least 200 feet. It took them some time to haul me to safety, because of the risk of a possible collapse of snow at the edge of the crater. Needless to say, for the rest of the location the word 'snow bridge' was written on our hats.

It was an unforgettable experience. The beauty of the Jungfrau in the late evening sun after the day's shooting, skiing down through the glacier with Willi Steuri, a famous Swiss guide, on powder snow to Grindelwald, hot, steaming glühwein, then the mountain railway up to Scheidegg, our base camp. After twelve days we arrived back in Zurich, and I felt that strange let-down and depression that I always experience after leaving the mountains. I had never spent so long at that height before, and the feeling persisted until I saw Mary waiting for me at Heathrow. The news was good – the new Nanny was adorable, the children loved her, and we could, Mary said, sail as planned for America in four days' time.

This trip was a present from Mr Arthur Rank who, after I had signed the contract with the Organization, suggested that I should take Mary on a tour of the United States and do a public relations job with *Great Expectations*, which was playing in all the major cities and had received rave reviews from the American critics. We sailed on 25 June in the *Queen Elizabeth* with Jimmy McHugh, our American agent, who had fixed the deal with Rank. I couldn't believe it. The suite was luxurious – a double bedroom, a sitting-room and a large bathroom. In my mind's eye I had seen two bunks and a shower. The vast size of the ship amazed me. The voyage was over all too soon – perfect weather and a flat, calm sea. We steamed up the Hudson to find the famous Manhattan skyline and the Statue of Liberty invisible in a thick, pea-soup London fog.

We discovered very rapidly what 'American pressure' was all about. We were driven to the Sherry Netherland hotel where we were allowed half an hour to pack overnight cases (I managed to grab a few seconds to stare out of the window at the breathtaking view across Central Park). The usual limousine, lunch at the Starlight Roof with press, tour of Manhattan, tea, press conference, Plaza Hotel. Dinner at the famous Twenty-One Club, then Ethel Merman in *Annie Get Your Gun*. At midnight we found ourselves on the express to Pittsburgh, where, just to keep us in trim, a large press reception had been arranged at nine the next morning at the Hotel Penn. By midday, we had done four radio interviews, the temperature was well over 100 degrees and I was on my third shirt. We took off for one of the large stores. I approached the salesman behind the counter and said, 'Could I have a plain white shirt, size fifteen collar?'

His eyes opened in surprise. 'Say that again, sir, please.'

I did so. He looked even more surprised, and beckoned over his shoulder to another assistant: 'Hey, come here a minute,' he said. He was joined by his friend. 'Could I ask you to repeat that once more, please sir?' I obliged. He turned to his friend, and with a look of total amazement on his face, said, 'D'you hear that, Joe? I can understand every God-darned word he said.' Every American seemed to be under the impression that all Englishmen spoke in such a clipped way (without moving their lips) as to be totally incomprehensible.

After lunch, more interviews, and at 9 p.m. we were flying back to New York in a rather small aircraft which behaved in a hair-raising way when an electric storm hit us just before we landed. We were steadying our nerves with brandy and coffee when the plane suddenly seemed to drop like a stone. Mary's coffee went straight up in the air and then descended all over her. As she was dressed from head to foot in a white ensemble, the result was quite startling.

From then on, for another week, the same frenetic routine continued in New York, Washington and Toronto. We were allowed one short weekend off, and spent it at Westport, Connecticut, with Jack Wilson (Noël's then business manager). The two days were stimulating rather than restful, because Tallulah Bankhead was also staying in the house. We had never met the legend before, and she didn't let us down. Our first sight of her was when she emerged from the pool house, waved to the guests on the patio, walked to the springboard and executed a perfect swallow dive. The only unusual thing about this otherwise ordinary performance was the fact that Miss Bankhead was stark naked. No one took the slightest notice; Jack continued to discuss the production of *Private Lives* that he was putting on at the Little Barn Theatre in Westwood for the summer season with our topless and bottomless lady playing Gertie Lawrence's part.

We all attended the dress rehearsal that night. Jack Wilson had invited an audience of students who, that evening, received an education that their colleges could have in no way provided. Tallulah was as high as a kite. After her swim she had obviously made a hearty lunch of a very large dry martini, and during the performance spent a great deal of time tearing the management, the designer and the director into very small pieces. She then addressed the students, and informed them, in language that would have made a serjeant-major blush, that if they ever considered getting into the god-damned theatre they were even more f——g stupid than they looked.

I rang Jack from New York to thank him for the weekend. He told me that on the first night Tallulah had given one of the best performances, apart from Gertie's, that he had ever seen in the play. But I'm still glad we saw that dress rehearsal. It was an evening in the theatre neither of us will ever forget.

Back to New York, Washington, a reception at the Embassy, more interviews, press conferences, until finally we found ourselves slightly punch-drunk on board the Super Chief, the fantastic train that was to take us to Los Angeles, where we had been promised two weeks' holiday. All we had to cope with was one press conference. That train journey across America was one of the most wonderful trips we have ever had. In those days before the coast-to-coast air service everybody travelled by train. It was the height of comfort; there was a double drawing-room, and the food was superb. We sat in the observation car and sipped mint juleps as we travelled through some of the most beautiful scenery in the world: the Rockies, the Grand Canyon, the Deep South – an unforgettable experience. I miss trains and boats. Flying to me is merely a way of getting from one place to another in the shortest possible time; and as we both dread it, although we have flown many thousands of miles, we pour down Bloody Marys before take-off and continue with nerve-deadeners during most of the flight.

We were lucky to see Hollywood while it was still in its heyday. All the big studios were working full blast and all the famous names we had known for years were still living there. We stayed with Rex and Lilli Harrison at their house in Mandeville Canyon. The two weeks seemed to disappear in a flash; Americans are generous hosts and we were nearly killed by hospitality. Parties were given for us and we dined with nearly all the people we had admired through the years: Gary Cooper (I spent an hour inspecting his enormous collection of guns), Tyrone Power, Spencer Tracy, John Garfield, Edward G. Robinson, Joan Fontaine, Bob Mitchum, Zachary Scott, Ida Lupino, John Huston, Ethel Barrymore, Olivia de Havilland, Ronnie Coleman and Benita Hume, Sir Aubrey Smith, my old friends Melville Cooper, David Niven and the Fairbankses. We did it all: Hollywood races, the Hollywood Bowl, sailing, deep-sea fishing off Catalina Island, golf at Bel Air. I also made a round of the studios, trying to find a subject that I could make in England under my new Rank contract. I found one, and it was available: the best script I'd read for years, with a marvellous part for me, and another equally good for Bette Davis, who was keen to do it with me. To my dismay, the deal finally fell through. I couldn't persuade the Rank Organization to put up the extra $100,000 needed to reach the asking price.

If I'd been able to make that picture I would in all probability have become a successful producer-director. For the first time in my life I felt confident that the script would make an enormously popular picture. I was eventually proved right. The film was called *The African Queen*: Katie Hepburn and Humphrey Bogart played the parts and it made a fortune at the box office. I have, I am grateful to say, few regrets in my life – *The African Queen* is one of them.

After a farewell party at Rex and Lilli's – Hoagy Carmichael, one of my heroes, played the piano until 5 a.m. – we caught, only just (Rex had of course forgotten the tickets), the Super Chief for New York.

The journey out had been divine. The return trip was very different. A dam had burst and we were held up in the middle of the Arizona Desert for ten hours from nine in the evening until five next morning. The air-conditioning failed, the heat was stifling. Where there is a minus, however, there is sometimes a plus. The plus in this case was the fact that on the same train there was someone I really wanted to meet and whom I'd not seen in Hollywood. We were sitting in our compartment sipping iced water when a slight, dark young man appeared in the doorway with a bottle of Jack Daniels in one hand and a glass in the other. 'Johnnie and Mary Mills? I missed you in town. I was in Vegas. Frank Sinatra. Can I come in?'

By the time the line had been cleared in the early hours of the morning we had become old friends. Many stories, some good, some bad, have been written about Sinatra since then, but I personally will never hear a word against him. I wouldn't like him for an enemy, but from my own personal experience, as a friend he's hard to beat.

We sailed for England on the *Queen Elizabeth* on Sunday, 17 August. America had been a marvellous experience. I loved the country, and we'd been shown nothing but kindness and hospitality. Life in Beverly Hills was luxurious, the climate was glorious. I hoped we would soon have a chance to go back to work there. But I knew with absolute certainty that there was only one place I ever wanted to live permanently, and that was home.

We spent a blissful summer at Fernacres with the children. There were ponies in the paddock and a small boat on the lake. I bought Mary a Romany caravan and fitted it up as a study for her to write in, far from the madding crowd in a clump of rhododendrons by the water.

On 1 October I sailed with the rest of *Scott*'s expedition from Newcastle in a small Norwegian ship that did everything but capsize in a gale force eight storm on the crossing to Stavanger. Captain Scott and his gallant men were, without exception, violently sick. We went from Stavanger to Bergen, then by train to Finse, a small resort in the mountains with one hotel which was to be our home for weeks. Finse had been chosen for the appalling weather conditions we needed on the glacier and plateaux. It didn't let us down. Every morning we left the hotel at six and climbed for one and a half hours up the glacier to the plateau. The cold was so intense it froze our packed lunches which we wore around our waists under several sweaters and anoraks. Before we could put on our skis it was necessary to light fires to thaw out the leather bindings which were frozen stiff. The conditions were quite unbelievable. Two of our cameramen were sent home with frost-bite; the moment they took their gloves off the skin of their fingers stuck to the instrument. On the day we were supposed to shoot the ponies one of the explorers, Quintin Riley, who had been to the Pole and was acting as an adviser on the film, was heard to remark that 'On a day like this no self-respecting explorer would have been seen outside his tent.'

We had to learn to work with the huskies. These dogs, when they fought, became serious about it. No snapping and scuffling: they fought. Ears were bitten off, and in no time at all the snow was covered in blood. One of the reasons why Scott died in his gallant attempt was because he couldn't bear the sight of blood and the vicious kicking that was necessary to separate the dogs who were fighting.

While the production was being prepared (Mary worked on the script with Charles Friend and wrote some of the additional dialogue), I did a great deal of research on Scott. He was a fascinatingly complex character – a born leader, with tremendous physical stamina and courage. He had a quick temper, which he often found difficult to control. This I was never allowed to show, because of the possibility of upsetting relations still living. The picture had, I think, more influence on me than any I made before or since. Because of our beards, which had to grow progressively longer, we shot the film in continuity, which meant that I started as Scott did with a full complement of men for the expedition and five months later ended up in a tent, as he did, with only two of them left: Birdie Bowers and Wilson. It had a strange, chilling effect on me. No one knows how long Scott lived in that tent after Bowers and Wilson died. Several months later, when the rescue party found the tent buried under a mountain of snow and dug their way through and opened the flap, they were faced with the heartrending picture of Scott sitting upright with his eyes open and two large tears frozen on his cheeks. He had opened his anorak and his arms were round the shoulders of his two companions.

Mary joined us for the last two weeks' shooting. When the final shot was in the can we were told we could shave off our beards. A bunch of tough, weather-beaten, dirty, bearded he-men disappeared upstairs to their various bathrooms. An hour later we appeared in the bar looking like a group of very young French poofs, with baby-pink cheeks and scarlet lips. Our Norwegian guides, who had worked with us for weeks and been a tower of strength, roared with laughter, rushed at us and kissed us. The party went on, Norwegian-style, drinking under the table (I've never understood why) until dawn.

We returned to England and finished the remaining interior shots at Ealing Studios. A young actor whom I'd never seen before played Lieutenant Evans. It was not a large part – in fact if my memory serves me correctly he only had about one close-up, but he made such an impression in that short space of time I was sure that one day he must become a highly successful actor. His name was Kenneth More. I was also lucky to get to know a charming and fascinating man who paints and draws the wild birds that Scott saw on his trip to the Antarctic – Peter Scott, now Sir Peter, was extremely helpful to me at the time of making the picture, and although he was too young to have known his father, the cuttings and letters he put at my disposal were invaluable.

Scott of the Antarctic was chosen for the Royal Film Performance in 1949. It was a good film, well-made and well-acted under appalling conditions. But I feel that if we'd been allowed to delve more deeply into the characters of the men themselves, it could have been a great one.

Noël Coward once said to me, 'If someone after a first night says, "The play will have a great artistic success", it is only a polite way of saying it will have a walloping great commercial failure. I've yet to see an artistic success take any money at the box office.'

My first two productions under my new contract for the Rank Organization to my great disappointment proved that statement to be correct. Looking back I realize the major mistake lay in my choice of subjects, neither of which were in any way safe bets. Anthony Pélissier came along with a screen play he'd written of H.G. Wells's *The History of Mr Polly*, a book I'd always liked, and I persuaded the Rank Organization to let him direct it with myself producing and playing Mr Polly. We took enormous trouble casting the picture and all the parts, even the minor characters, were beautifully played. The principals were Finlay Curry, Betty Ann Davis, Megs Jenkins and a very young Sally Ann Howes as the schoolgirl. Miss Juliet Mills, aged seven, begged me to engage her to play the part of Little Polly. She gave an excellent performance, and as she insisted on talking to my agent I had to pay her for it! At this moment in my first-born's life I got the message: she was, I discovered, despite anything I might say to dissuade her, determined to become an actress.

We searched England for the location needed – an attractive pub on a river, next to a church, and a churchyard – with no success, and finally built the whole set on the river behind Denham Studios. We had several problems to contend with. There was a strike during the shooting; I was locked out of the meeting as an actor but allowed in as a producer, and consequently was never sure which hat to be wearing at any given moment. The day we began shooting scenes on the river a thick fog descended and no work was possible before four in the afternoon for two weeks. *Polly* was a labour of love; we worked all hours for months, cutting, editing, polishing, and by the time we saw a fine cut we were too close to it to know what we had got up there on the screen.

As an actor I had always hated and avoided, whenever I could, attending press shows of any pictures that I had appeared in. During the inevitable after-showing drink with the critics I was never sure which face to put on: the 'I don't give a damn what you think or write' face, or the 'charming, ingratiating, humble, I do hope you like it' face. You've made the bloody film, you've sweated and slaved for months, and it's too late to do anything anyway. I was, however, persuaded in this case that it was my duty as the producer, not the actor, to attend the press show of *Polly*.

I've always considered that press shows are dreadful events. Comedy in particular never really gets a chance. The overworked critics are often asked to see, or were, in those boom days, two films per day. What chance has a comedy got at 10.30 in the morning in a practically empty theatre, with no ordinary members of the public, for whom the film was made, to react to it? No theatre management would dream of inviting the critics to a rehearsal in an empty theatre. They see the play on a first night, and even if they personally don't approve of the work, the honest ones will always state in their notices the next day, 'but I was in a minority – the audience enjoyed it and laughed their heads off'. This at least gives the play a chance.

With *Polly*, however, we needn't have worried. The critics were fulsome in their praise. I was warmly congratulated on my first effort as a producer and Anthony Pélissier on his first job as a director. They praised the film as a splendid artistic piece of work. We thought we were off to the races. I visualized a future where I could sit back in a large office with an enormous Corona-Corona and decide which fantastic part I would care to play next in my own production. We lived in this fool's paradise until the picture went on general release. To our amazement, the returns were disappointing: Mr and Mrs Public did not approve. I began to receive letters from irate fans. They apparently didn't want to see me playing, for the first half of the film at least, a rather angry, petulant, hen-pecked husband with a quiff and an untidy moustache. I was stuck with the hero image and hadn't realized it.

It has always disappointed me that *Polly* didn't succeed at the box office. I've seen it several times since at the British Film Academy: looking at it objectively, it was nothing to be ashamed of. In fact it was a professional and extremely well-made and well-acted film. The sad fact of the matter is that at that time the public were not ready for it, disliked me in the character and did not besiege the cinemas to see it. *Polly* didn't lose money – it made a profit; but compared to any of the 'Carry On' epics it was a commercial flop. Strangely enough, out of 102 films I've made (in several of which I've picked up some very flattering awards) *The History of Mr Polly* is the one I'm most proud of.

Mary and I buried our disappointment in the snows of St Moritz where, with Juliet and Hayley, we spent a glorious Christmas. Three fascinating and very different people, none of whom we'd ever met before, were staying in the same hotel: Montgomery Clift, that superb and tragic young actor, Thornton Wilder, the famous playwright, and Errol Flynn. We spent our evenings in the *gaststübel* of the hotel, drinking and talking, or, to be more exact, listening to Thornton, who was a brilliant conversationalist on any level, on any subject. After his first very dry martini he would lean forward, fix us with his eager, professional eye, and say, in his clipped voice, 'Now, what shall we talk about this evening?' One prompt was enough to set him off. An hour later we were still listening, riveted, while his brilliant mind hopped, jumped and slipped from one topic to another – politics, religion, the arts. He illuminated everything with a wicked sense of humour. He was, in fact, the greatest story-teller that we had ever met.

In January 1949 Anthony Pélissier suggested D.H. Lawrence's *The Rocking Horse Winner* as my next production. Although I considered it to be a difficult subject to tackle, flushed with what I thought at the time was the box-office success of *Polly*, I decided to take a chance. *The Rocking Horse Winner* finally emerged as another artistic triumph and a box-office disappointment. It was again well-directed, well-acted, by that superb actor, Ronald Squire, Valerie Hobson and a young child actor, John Howard Davis. Looking back I realize I made one stupid mistake – I played a small part in the picture. This, at a time when I was a big draw at the box office, and able to carry a picture on my name alone above the title, was asking for trouble. I got it, and deserved it. I was deluged with mail from my fans, who said they didn't expect to pay good money only to see me on the screen for about ten minutes.

As I have said before I am, like most actors, superstitious, and I had a premonition that the two set-backs I'd suffered were not going to be the end of a run of bad luck. Two box-office failures one after the other would not have the money-boys begging me to make another film. I was not, however, prepared for the next set-back, which had nothing to do with my career.

Writers, especially the playwrights I have met, are highly intelligent, highly emotional people, subject to highs and lows of exhilaration and despair. Mary Hayley Bell is no exception: she has always been deeply concerned about everything, even the smallest problems that I have always determinedly brushed aside and refused to worry about. In the spring of 1949, however, a problem arose that not only disturbed me, but worried me to death. Mary was pregnant again; a further addition to the family was expected in December. She was convinced that I desperately wanted a son, and that it would be an enormous disappointment for me if she produced another girl. Nothing could have been further from the truth. I tried in every way I could to persuade her that I honestly didn't care a damn if she produced a chimpanzee, as long as it was normal and healthy and we could occasionally get it down out of the tree. But no jokes, nothing, absolutely nothing helped. She was going to fail me, and what had been an idyllic marriage would probably founder, because she was not going to be able to produce a son and heir.

Within a few weeks she developed chronic asthma, and became for the first time really ill. I was distraught. Our doctor suggested a sea voyage. I chartered an old, converted MTB, and with Anthony as skipper we took her across the Channel from Ramsgate to Calais and spent three weeks exploring the Dutch waterways to Amsterdam. The asthma showed signs of improvement; getting away from the home environment helped. We laughed a great deal and drank Dutch beer at the little inns by the locks, and I began to think we were out of the wood. On our return to Fernacres, however, the asthma came back with a vengeance, and she needed injections in the arm during the night to enable her to breathe. Then something happened which had a disastrous effect on Mary's illness and our whole way of life.

We had been in London at a charity dinner where I'd been making an appeal for funds. Getting back to Fernacres at 1.30 in the morning we discovered the house surrounded by police cars all lights blazing. At the entrance to the drive an inspector said, 'I'm sorry, sir. We've got some rather bad news for you.' I felt myself go white. 'Oh my God,' I said. 'The children?'

'Oh no, sir, they're fine. And so are the staff, but I'm afraid you've been done, sir. They went up the wistaria into the bedrooms and took the lot.'

The relief was so great we couldn't have cared less. The burglars had obviously been brilliant professionals. Having made an entrance through our bedroom window they locked all the bedroom doors, quietly took a fur coat and the jewellery, and departed the way they had come, without waking Nanny or the children. The after-effect on Mary, however, was shattering. She became seriously ill. Fernacres was no longer a haven of refuge for her; she had constant nightmares of the burglars appearing at the open window, and woke up unable to breathe. The doctor warned me that if I didn't sell the house and move her to completely different surroundings where she felt safe, she would probably have a serious nervous breakdown. That was enough for me. Fernacres was put on the market. In two weeks it was sold. Looking back over my shoulder as the car drove out of the gates I remember thinking, I shall never care in the future about leaving any other house again. I love this one so much. But what was a house compared to the woman sitting beside me? I would live anywhere, in any old shack, as long as she was happy and regained her health. We moved back to London, to 98 Cheyne Walk, a tall house on the Chelsea Embankment.

The move didn't help. She became steadily worse. In desperation I called in another doctor: I was advised that the pregnancy should be terminated. I agreed immediately. Mary was naturally my only concern. By chance Elspeth March, Mary's best friend, rang up and implored us to see a brilliant gynaecologist, Roy Saunders, who was at the top of his profession and famous for his handling of very complicated cases. To cut a long and nerve-racking story short, after an examination and a long talk to both of us, he convinced us that the asthma was caused by nothing but anxiety and fear of not producing a boy.

He told us that he was willing to take full responsibility; he wouldn't, he said, put his professional reputation on the line unless he was convinced that all would be well. Praying that I was doing the right thing I agreed. The baby was born on 3 December 1949. Roy Saunders rang me at the Garrick Club where I had been dispatched: I was, he had said, undermining the morale of the entire staff in the London Clinic, who, if I stayed a moment longer, would without doubt all develop asthma and severe nervous breakdowns. 'Johnnie, it's Roy. You've got a son. What will please you even more, the asthma has completely disappeared. She's asleep now, so don't disturb her. See you at the Clinic in the morning.'

There is a strict rule at the Garrick Club that members do not tip the staff. I plunged my hand into my pocket and pulled out all the money I had – some twenty pounds or so – forced it into the head steward's hand, kissed him on both cheeks and, with the words, 'The asthma's gone and I've got a son' I departed into the night. For the first time in my life I was too high with emotion even to think of having a drink.

19

The Bewildered Carrot

I approached the 1950s somewhat warily. Until the last two dis-
appointments everything had been smelling of roses. In 1947 I picked up
the Best Actor Award for Pip in *Great Expectations* and was voted Top
Actor of the Year in the National Film Awards for 1948 and 1949. I was
therefore terribly anxious not to make a mistake with the next job I under-
took. In February an offer came along that sounded almost too good to
be true. It came from the one man I really wanted to work with, and
never had. He was already acclaimed as the best actor in England, but
also, after *Henry v* and *Hamlet*, as a brilliant film director and producer. Laurence Olivier had taken the St James' Theatre and was embark-
ing on yet another phase of his career, as actor-manager.

The play he chose was *The Damascus Blade* by Bridget Boland. He
offered me the leading part and to my delight said that he had decided
to direct it. The set-up seemed to me to look like a bookmaker's cert.
The cast was first class: Peter Finch (who became one of my closest
friends), Beatrix Lehmann, Austin Trevor, Barry Jones and Mary
McKenzie. The rehearsals were exciting and interesting, and for me, to
start with, slightly worrying. I had never worked before with a director
who had meticulously worked out every single move and every single
piece of business on each line. His prompt script looked, with its red and
blue arrows and diagrams, like a blue-print for D-day. Because, however,
he had made his plans work for him, I soon found that with determination and application I could make them work for me too. I still, however,
prefer more freedom of movement at the early rehearsals.

We opened at Newcastle on 14 March. Larry, who was playing in
Venus Observed, was able to be at the opening, as there was no performance of *Venus* on Monday nights. The house was packed – standing room
only. The fact that I had a picture playing in town no doubt helped. The
reaction was polite, but the audience left us in no doubt as to their reaction
to the play: they just didn't like it. I could feel from the stage that they

were not coming along with me as the play progressed. Larry, Mary, Roger Furse, who designed the sets, and I had supper after the show. We all knew that something was wrong with the play, but what? 'I just don't feel they had any sympathy with me, Larry. They just don't seem to give a damn.'

We thrashed it over, backwards and forwards, and decided to make a few cuts in the dialogue. The notice in the Newcastle paper the next morning was, frankly, a bad one. The critic hated the play, and said so in no uncertain terms. He was kind to the actors, praised Sir Laurence's direction, but pulled the piece to shreds. Larry looked at us across the breakfast table. 'Well darlings, that's not the greatest notice we've ever had, is it? It's just not his cup of tea. Don't worry about it. He's probably on loan from the sports page. I'm sure it will be better in Edinburgh next week.'

It wasn't. It was, if anything, worse. Brighton and Glasgow were no better. The telephone rang in my dressing-room after the last show on the Saturday night there. 'Johnnie, it's Larry. How did it go tonight?'

'Oh well . . . just about the same, Larry boy. They didn't exactly tear the place down.'

There was a very long pause. 'Listen Johnnie . . . you are my dearest friend. The last thing I want to do is to bring you into town and have you find yourself with a flop on your hands. Would you be very upset if we accepted defeat and called it off?'

'No, Larry boy, I should be relieved. We've tried. We can't make the bloody thing work. And I don't think we ever will.'

'All right, boy, I know it's right. Come down to Notley Abbey with Mary next weekend and we'll drown our sorrows in the cellar and dream up something else together.'

We managed the first half of the proposition, but sadly never the second. I have not had the pleasure of acting on the stage with my chum (one can hardly count 'Top Hat, White Tie And Tails', the Fred Astaire number, or Noël Coward's 'Three Juvenile Delinquents' which, with Vivien Leigh and Danny Kaye, we performed at Drury Lane at the Night of the Hundred Stars shows in aid of theatrical charities), and now sadly I never will.

I had suffered two major set-backs in the theatre. It was no help whatsoever to a career to have a play fold on the road, and I needed at this time to get back on to the silver screen in a successful picture, playing the leading part. Suddenly, out of the blue, it arrived: a film called *Morning Departure*. Jay Lewis, who was producing, sent me the script, which gripped me from the first page to the last. Another plus, as far as I was concerned, was the fact that my co-star was going to be my friend Dickie Attenborough, whose career since *In Which We Serve* had been progress-

ing by leaps and bounds. The story of *Morning Departure* concerned
a submarine on peace-time manoeuvres. The ship hits a mine and sinks
to the sea bed. The rest of the story is about the efforts to rescue the
crew; in the end three are left to die with the skipper. By a ghastly coincidence, not long after the shooting finished on this picture a submarine
called the *Truculent* suffered the same fate on a dark night in the Thames
estuary, and sixty-four men lost their lives. The headline of an article
in the *Daily Mail* which appeared, oddly enough, on 22 February, my
forty-second birthday, was 'Film so real it was nearly not shown. *Truculent* story over again':

Mr J. Lewis, the producer, went to the Odeon, Leicester Square, yesterday,
for a preview of the film he wished he had never made. But he came away
proud to have made it, *Morning Departure*, starring John Mills and Richard
Attenborough. It was completed before the loss of the submarine *Truculent*.
The film opens next Monday at the Gaumont, Haymarket, but its story and
the facts of the *Truculent* tragedy are so similar that for a time it was doubtful
whether it would ever reach the screen . . . Producers, financiers and distributors
got together to decide its fate. Some wanted it shelved indefinitely. Others,
the Admiralty included, thought it should take its chance on its merits as a
sincere naval story and not be allowed to suffer for having inadvertently fore-
told a real tragedy. The censor said, 'Had we found a false note in it we might
have hesitated to pass it on at such a time, but we think it deserves to be seen.'
They therefore gave an Adult certificate, subject to this foreword. 'This film
was completed before the loss of HMS *Truculent*. Careful consideration has
been given to the desirability of showing it so soon after this grievous disaster.
The producers feel, however, that the film will be accepted in the spirit in which
it was intended, as a sincere tribute to brave men and as an expression of pride
in the Royal Navy.' Was it a wise decision? From all the congratulations after
yesterday's preview the producers are satisfied that it was. Normally, *Morning
Departure* would have been highly publicized. Instead, in deference to the relatives of the *Truculent* victims, it is going out without fanfares. But as a film
it is outstanding – as a tribute to the officers and men of the submarines, it
is beyond reproach.

Morning Departure is one of the films I am proud to have been associated
with. The decision to show it proved to be right. It received many letters
from relatives of the men who lost their lives; they all said, in so many
words, that they were glad they had seen the film: it had made their loss
more bearable to see the gallant and courageous way in which men in
the same situation as their loved ones faced almost certain death.

1950 began to look bright. Mary was well; the asthma hadn't returned.
We had completed the decoration of 98 Cheyne Walk, all five floors of
it. It cost a fortune, and looked like it. One morning I was standing on
the small balcony painting a picture of the river with Battersea Power

Station in the distance shrouded in mist. The traffic noise was deafening, and although I had only been painting for an hour and a half I was black with London grime. Mary appeared. She looked at the picture. 'Not bad, darling. In fact, it's good. It's very good. Do you miss the country?'

I looked at her with surprise. We'd been at Number 98 for nine months. It was the first time she'd mentioned it. Of course I knew why. It was Fernacres. I thought hard for a moment: 'Yes, I do, darling. Like mad. Do you?'

'Yes I do, like mad.'

I went on painting.

'The house looks lovely now we've finished it, doesn't it?' I nodded. She went on: 'Do you like it?'

Something told me this was the point of no return. I took the plunge. 'Frankly, my darling, if you want the truth, I hate it. And I hate living in London, and so do you.'

She looked at me and burst into tears. 'Oh Johnnie, why oh why did I drag you away from Fernacres? You loved it and so did I, and I've landed you in this bloody lighthouse. Oh darling, we're trapped.'

I took her in my arms; the people on the barges moored alongside were enjoying the scene, but I couldn't care less. 'Now listen, Angel, that's all I wanted to know. I'll handle it.' (Oh my goodness, how? I thought.) 'We'll sell the lighthouse and get back to the country.'

I hoped I sounded confident. I wasn't. It was at that moment definitely not a seller's market. I gave the house to three of the top London house agents, and after a month not an offer had arrived of any description. Then quite suddenly a miracle happened. I was on my way out of the house one morning, en route to yet another house agent, when I saw a letter lying on the mat. It had been delivered by hand. After reading it I sat down on the hall chair and read it again:

Dear Mr Mills,

I do hope you will forgive this great impertinence, but I wonder if I might enquire if there is any remote possibility of your wishing to sell 98 Cheyne Walk. I own the house next to you and my great desire is to restore the building to its original façade. Our two separate dwelling places were originally called Lindsay House. I have the original drawings, done in 1778, and it would give me enormous satisfaction to achieve this idea. I would, of course, be prepared to pay the correct price for 98 should you wish to dispose of it. Again I ask your indulgence. I am sure you will wish to stay in your lovely house.

Yours sincerely,
Peter Kroyer

Three weeks later the deal was completed, and we had sold 98 Cheyne Walk and made quite a respectable profit. The door was now open. We discussed in what area we should look for another house. It had to be near London because of the theatre, but where to start? Before we'd even commenced the search, the second miracle took place.

During the past two years Mary and I had become great friends of the Grieg family. Sir Louis and Lady Grieg, lived with their two children in the Thatched House in Richmond Park (which for the last few years has been the home of HRH Princess Alexandra and her husband the Hon Angus Ogilvy). Sir Louis was an all-round sportsman: he captained Scotland at rugby for several years and played an excellent game of tennis. He was a very close friend of the late King, who himself was no mean performer at the game: they were in fact good enough to play in the men's doubles one year at Wimbledon.

We were often invited to lunch and tennis at the Thatched House. The weekend after we'd sold 98 we poured out our problem to Sir Louis. 'By an extraordinary coincidence I think I know exactly the house you're looking for. It's not on the market yet, but I know it will be soon, because Colonel Stirling is a friend of mine and he's moving back to Scotland. I'll ring him up.'

That afternoon we saw The Wick on the top of Richmond Hill for the first time. It seemed almost too good to be true. One of the most beautiful houses we'd ever seen, Georgian – built by Robert Mylne in 1775 – with a breathtaking view from every window down the stretches of the Thames. The garden was on three levels, with a gazebo at the bottom, behind which was a stable yard, two garages and a gardener's cottage. We fell madly in love with it at first sight and without referring to an agent or our bank manager we agreed a deal; and when we left, after a celebratory drink in the study, The Wick was ours.

A few weeks later we moved in. There was a wonderful atmosphere about the place and we spent some of the happiest years of our lives in that divine house on the top of the hill.

While I was on tour with The Damascus Blade Mary had seen a play at the Citizens' Theatre, Glasgow, called Top of the Ladder, written by our old friend, that brilliant director I had worked with at the Old Vic, Tyrone Guthrie. She thought it was one of the best plays she'd ever seen in her life, and when I read it I too was fascinated by it. I could see that the leading part could be vastly exciting to try and play. The character had to switch from a five-year-old in the nursery to a man of sixty in a split second with no time for any change of make-up. The performance had to do it all.

Larry read the play, liked it and agreed to present it at the St James's Theatre, under his management, with Tyrone Guthrie directing. The cast included Rachel Kempson, Mary Kerridge, Alison Leggatt, Toke Townley and Miles Malleson. The part of Bertie was a terrific challenge

– incredibly difficult and longer than Hamlet. I was never off the stage.
I even changed clothes on stage behind a screen, continuing the dialogue
with another character in view of the audience.

Larry unfortunately had to leave for an Australian tour with the Old
Vic before rehearsals started. I have always felt that, had he been there,
the story would have been different. I had an uneasy feeling during
rehearsals that the play was over-length; the strange and brilliant idea
that Guthrie had conceived was, I felt, being dissipated by some unnecessarily long dialogue scenes. Guthrie didn't agree, and was backed up by
Miles Malleson; both of them were used to plays running for three hours
at the Old Vic. If we had opened out of town, and played a few dates before
coming into the West End I feel fairly sure the tightening-up that was
needed would have been done. Tony, with his eagle eye, would have
sensed the places where the play sagged and lost the audience's interest.
However, because the St James's was free and the sets were expensive
and cumbersome to tour, it was decided that we should open cold.

The first night was at the St James's Theatre on 11 October. Many
of our chums were in front: Lord and Lady Vansittart, Sir Louis and Lady
Grieg, Noël Coward, Clemence Dane, Sir Charles and Lady Cochran,
James Bridie and the Douglas Fairbankses. I was too numb with shock
thinking of what was ahead of me to care if even God was in front.
In fact I hoped he wasn't. I prayed he was back-stage with me.

Halfway through the second act I knew with a dreadful sinking feeling
that I had been right. It was too long. I could sense the critics easing
themselves in their seats from one cheek to another. When the curtain
fell I knew that I'd given the best performance I was capable of, but I
also knew that it wasn't enough. The applause was warm, but it was
for the actors, and not the play.

The notices were, by and large, a disaster. Harold Hobson's headline
in the *Sunday Times* stated in bold, black type: 'Notable failure'.
Another critic called it 'a feverish over-length dream'. Ironically enough,
my own notices, which didn't help the play one iota, were the best I had
ever been given in my life. The critics probably felt that as they had blasted
the play the least they could do was to over-praise me – 'Magnificent',
'the best thing that has happened to the theatre since Olivier', 'it is a tragedy that Sir Laurence wasn't there to protect Mr Mills by cutting away
some of the boredom surrounding him'.

In my dressing-room after the show my chums, I noticed, although
being fulsome in their praise of my performance, seemed reluctant to discuss the play. The door opened. Noël's head appeared round it: 'You
were ... absolutely marvellous, Johnnie dear, one of the best things I've
ever seen you do. But the play, my pet, is a mother-f---er.' The door
closed.

A council of war was called at the theatre next morning. Tony admitted that he had obviously indulged himself. We took twenty minutes out of the play and the improvement was enormous. The glossy magazines' reviews were very good indeed. It was, however, too late – the damage had been done. We didn't survive at the St James's Theatre for more than a few months. It was an enormous disappointment to all of us, particularly to Mary, whose enthusiasm had stimulated the whole project. She genuinely loved the play and found its failure very difficult to accept. She would, she said, always feel responsible for it. In December, when I was given an award for Outstanding Achievement in the Theatre in 1950, I pointed out that she was entirely responsible for that too. The names of the other recipients on that occasion are worth recording: Alec Guinness, whose career on the screen since *Great Expectations* had taken wings, received the film award, Evelyn Waugh, the award for literature, Jimmy Edwards for radio, and that master of the new medium, the late Richard Dimbleby, for television.

During the last three years the film industry had been going into a steady decline – costs had mounted alarmingly, and box-office receipts had fallen to a worrying level. The future looked grim. A meeting was arranged at Wyndham's Theatre for actors, studio workers, trade unionists and MPs. A ten-point plan was put up for getting the film industry back on its feet. Sir Laurence Olivier was in the chair, and the committee consisted of David Lean, Dame Edith Evans, Vivien Leigh and myself. Larry who, the moment he sets foot on any stage, whether he is speaking at a meeting or playing Hamlet, sniffs the air, takes command and gives a stirring performance, on this occasion made an impassioned appeal for a change in the system. He pointed out that the main problem was that out of every million pounds made at the box office the government took £400,000 in tax, the exhibitor £400,000 and the picture was left with £200,000 to pay production expenses. It was agreed that a delegation should present the problem to Harold Wilson, who was at the time Minister of the Board of Trade (and in my opinion the best Minister we ever had in that position). He was very keen on the film business and saw its potential in the world market; but despite his and everybody else's efforts however, the situation failed to improve. Studios began to cut down on production and many people felt the draught. I came to an amicable arrangement with the Rank Organization. A settlement was made, my contract was cancelled, and I found myself once more on the open market.

During the next two years I made three pictures, *Mr Denning Drives North*, *The Gentle Gunman* (in Ireland – if a re-make was considered now the title would unfortunately need changing) and *The Long*

Memory. When the offers came along I accepted them; when an actor stops acting the money stops coming in. No actor, at any rate in England, can afford to be out of work for long. The three pictures just mentioned were rent and tax jobs. I never expected them to blaze a trail across the silver screen, but they were honest pieces of work and nothing to be ashamed of.

Another reason why actors and comedians like to be busy was demonstrated by Bob Hope, who is working harder than ever these days in spite of being even older than I am. A short time ago Bob was ordered by his doctor to take it easy for a while and he suggested a month's sea cruise. After a week the comedian was back in Los Angeles. His doctor, surprised, asked the reason for the quick return. 'Fish don't applaud,' said Bob.

The Long Memory, produced by Hugh Stewart and directed by Bob Hamer, was actually an extremely good thriller, which would have been even better if our director could have stayed off the juice. Bob Hamer had done some brilliant work at Ealing for Sir Michael Balcon, but by the time *The Long Memory* arrived his great talent had been blunted. Twice, during night-shooting on a barge in the Thames, he fell in the river walking backwards with a viewfinder glued to his eye.

I did, however, in 1951 manage to break my run of bad luck in the theatre. I flew over to Paris with Mary and saw a play called *Bobosse* by André Roussin. Arthur Macrae, who was with me in *Cavalcade* and had since become a successful writer, did an excellent adaptation. We opened after a provincial tour fraught with the usual difficulties. Peter Ashmore, a good director with the right play, was definitely not right for *Figure of Fun*, the English title. I sent an SOS to Binkie Beaumont from Manchester, and within twenty-four hours he had arranged for a young director called Peter Brook to take over. After working night and day for a week, plus the eight performances, young Mr Brook achieved a minor miracle. We opened in London with a superb production. The play was a hit and played to excellent business during its long run. The cast included Brenda Bruce, Joyce Heron, Natasha Parry, Peter Bull and Arthur Macrae, who had very sensibly written in an excellent part for himself.

The play opened with the main character, which I was playing, standing on his head in the middle of the stage. This feat luckily happened to be one of my accomplishments, but we found it almost impossible to find an understudy who could do it. The gag was repeated several times during the performance. Standing on one's head bang on cue, and continuing the dialogue, wasn't exactly easy.

Mary brought Hayley and Jonathan, aged seven and three years respectively, to a matinee. Because of my son's age we decided the royal box would be the best place to accommodate him. I held his interest for the first ten minutes and performed the rest of the play to the accompaniment of the sound of running flushes from the royal loo. One other thing happened that made that particular matinee unforgettable. Peter Bull, who always insisted he couldn't act at all, but on the contrary could act very well and, incidentally, cooked the greatest scrambled eggs I've ever tasted, at the end of a scene with me in the first act was required to lose his temper and storm out of my studio apartment, which was on the top floor of a block of flats in Paris. The attractive set had one door through which to exit and enter from. Through long studio windows the audience could see the rooftops of Paris stretching into the distance. Purple with simulated rage, Peter shouted, 'I've had enough of those insults, I'm leaving. Good day.' He strode upstage, grabbed the door-handle and pulled, but he made no exit. The door-handle had parted company with the door. Peter Bull's expression was a study. He gazed at it in his hand as if he'd never seen a door-handle before, then looked at me, which was of course fatal. I couldn't resist it, and said: 'I thought you just informed me you were leaving.' His lips quivered, 'I am,' he said, 'I am.' He then attacked the door with his fingernails. Nothing. Then he kicked it. Nothing. The stage hands must have all been at tea-break. No one gave it a helping shove from the off-stage side. Peter fell apart at the seams. 'I'm leaving,' he shouted, 'I'm leaving.' 'I know, you've said so several times,' I said, 'why don't you?' He seemed to be on the point of a serious apoplectic fit. Then with great dignity he walked to the large studio window, stepped through it and made a spectacular exit, stepping over the chimney pots of Paris. The sound of the running flush from the royal box was this time drowned by the roar of laughter from a delighted audience.

Ever since our success together with *Men in Shadow* and *Duet For Two Hands* Mary and I had been hoping one day to pull off the treble. While I was shooting *The Long Memory* she read a report in the press about a young man who had been illegally committed to a mental home and who spent fifteen years in it before being released. She discussed the idea with me and we both decided that it could be the basis for a strong dramatic play, with an entirely different role for me to tackle. Early in 1953 the play was finished, sent to Henry Sherek, a friend and an impresario with a list of West End successes to his credit. He read it, liked it and bought it in the space of thirty-six hours. That to us seemed a more than promising start.

Henry engaged a successful young director, John Fernald, to direct it, and the cast was a strong one: Joan Greenwood, who gave such an engaging performance opposite me in *The October Man*, Cathleen Nesbitt, Lyndon Brook and Clive Morton. The set by Hutchinson Scott was beautiful, inspired by our drawing-room at The Wick.

The saga of *The Uninvited Guest* can, I think, be told more economically and succinctly if I merely quote entries from my diary:

16 Jan 1953 – First rehearsal, *Uninvited Guest*.

19 Jan – Concerned about J.F. who doesn't seem happy or v. keen on play. Suggest new end.

23 Jan – Rehearsed new end Mary has written. Not sure about it, but accepted it.

16 Feb – Opened King's Theatre, Southsea. Wonderful reception. They love your play my darling. Ten curtains and a speech.

17 Tuesday – We are full. No seats available.

19 Thursday – Matinee sold out. Manager says unusual.

20 Friday – Photo-call 10.30 a.m. John Prebble from whose report in paper Mary got idea for play, very enthusiastic.

22 Sunday – My birthday. God help me, I'm middle-aged. Don't look it, or feel it. If Southsea is anything to go by, my love, we have a success. We've brought off the treble. Sold out for week.

23 Monday – Theatre Royal, Nottingham. Big reception.

1 March – Sold out all week. Left in new Bentley with all the cast. Only five – lucky. For Blackpool.

2 March – Good opening. Sold out for week.

8 March – Golf at Royal Lytham and St Anne's, round in 79. Shall obviously win Open next year. What publicity!

9 Monday – Opera House, Manchester. Best audience yet.

10 Tuesday – Terrific house, but snooty notice in *Manchester Guardian*, typical, never liked the boring paper anyway.

14 Saturday – Broke the Opera House record by £3.

15 Sunday – Drove with Mary to Glasgow in Bentley. Grand Central Hotel. Usual deadly Sunday night in Scotland.

16 March – King's Theatre, Glasgow. Opened to sold-out house for Jewish charity. Usual dreary charity audience. They pay too much to enjoy it. Cathleen seems uneasy. Not up to form.

17 March – Called rehearsal, had a go at Cathleen who took it beautifully. She really is a divine woman.

21 Saturday – Sold out for week. Mary back to nursery. Nanny problem. Oh Gawd!

22 Sunday – Jolly [my chauffeur-dresser] drove Joan and me to Gleneagles. Perfect weather. Cancelling my entry for Open next year. Played King's course. Started badly and got steadily worse. Round in 96. Ridiculous game. Mary's father quite right when he said, 'Golf's a good walk spoilt.' Tea at Crown Hotel in village, run by Patterson, a Scot, famous goal-keeper, played for Arsenal. Wouldn't let me pay for tea. God, what wonderful perks I get. Edinburgh 6 p.m. talked to H. Sherek, long into night. Want original end back, new one doesn't grip. *Manchester Guardian* critic was right.

23 March – Lyceum, Edinburgh, rehearsal put back original end with few alterations.

24 March – Good reception, feel original end right. J.F. doesn't agree. We decided amicably that he should hand over the reins. Cold sweat department. Need another outside brain.

25 March – Queen Mary died. Awful matinee. Not surprising. Everyone loved her. Reminded me of day at Wimbledon final last year. Louis Grieg asked me if I could get a parasol for Queen Mary to borrow. She always stayed in her seat until the final ball was played, weather scorching. He was afraid of sun-stroke. Told Monty Berman. He lent me beautiful antique ivory parasol. I presented it to HM in the Royal Box before the final, suggesting she might like to use it for the afternoon. At the end of the day she thanked me in her most charming and gracious way and departed with the parasol under her arm. Phoned Monty next morning. 'Well I'll be damned,' he said, 'that cost a bloody fortune. Still, she's worth it, isn't she?'

28 March – Business up again. Nearly full week.

30 March – Alexandra Theatre, Birmingham.

4 April Saturday – Capacity all week.

6 April – Theatre Royal, Brighton, big success. Bunch [Juliet] home from Elmhurst School, staying in hotel.

7 April – Wonderful notice from local critic. Dreaded Derek Grainger. Original end must be right.

14 April – Broke theatre record. Obviously we'll never keep Bunch out of theatre. She took over from Jolly as my dresser and never left my side for a whole week. Knows most of play by heart.

13 April – Hippodrome, Bristol. Poorish Monday night by comparison.

15 April – Heard we had St James's Theatre. Dear God, hope we're luckier there this time.

18 April – Young, v. clever director, Frank Hauser, taken over direction. Good. Like his work.

20 April – Cardiff. Rehearsed all week with Frank. Put in yet another and I hope better end to the play.

27 April – Newcastle, rehearsing all and every day with Frank, tightening and polishing.

4 May – Wimbledon, good week, great business.

11 May – Liverpool.

17 May – Great week's business, played Royal Birkdale, won on the 17th, decided will enter for Open after all.

18 May – Leeds. Grand Theatre. Good opening. £70 up on *Figure of Fun*.

23 May – End of provincial tour, good notice Birmingham paper. Back to Wick, Mary and the kids. Thank God.

The next entry in my diary is on 27 May. It simply states 'Open *Uninvited Guest* St James's Theatre'. From then on until 26 September the book is completely blank. I have always been a regular recorder of day-to-day events. I can only suppose that the shock I received on the morning after we opened prevented me from putting a single word of my feelings down on paper. The first night had gone, we thought, well. The applause had not been vociferous, but quite solid. We'd taken six or seven curtain calls. We were therefore totally unprepared for the assault from the critics which hit us when we opened the morning papers at The Wick the next day. The first one we read was in the *Daily Express*. The thick black headline was 'MR MILLS DESERVES BETTER, MRS MILLS'. The critic then proceeded in about twenty lines to decimate the play. His pay-off line was 'Author of this nonsense is John Mills's wife. She should know that good actors deserve better than this.' They were all dreadful notices. The critics, this time, were united, and the ghastly thing as far as I was concerned was that all the attack was directed at the play and the author. The cast was treated sympathetically.

The last notice we read dismissed the play in a few lines, but it contained one sentence which at that moment in our lives helped more than the gentleman who wrote it could have thought possible. I read it aloud: 'And John Mills wanders about the stage in a red wig looking like a bewildered carrot.' We looked at each other and roared with laughter. Up to that moment, for the first time in our lives neither of us could find the right words to say. I was already suffering from a feeling of guilt; I had been so desperately anxious for Mary to have another success with me that I knew in my heart I had allowed my critical faculties to become blunted. I had never really had the same enthusiasm for *The Uninvited Guest* as I had had for *Duet* or *Men in Shadow*. The fact that she was putting up such a front and taking it so well made it all the more difficult for me to cope with my own feelings on the disaster.

Marriages, they say, are made in heaven; in my opinion, based on years of experience, marriages are made or broken on earth. On that particular morning one thoughtless word from either of us could easily have done a great deal of damage to our relationship. Marriages have to be worked at. It is dangerous to sit back and assume that they are going to continue being successful. They need constant care and attention to prevent them slipping unobtrusively into a partnership of convenience. There will always be problems and situations to cope with; I am sure most people, if they were honest, would admit that some of these have been serious enough to rock the boat dangerously. Looking back, our only real problem has been to do with the professional part of our lives. My one deep regret is that since our first two big successes in the theatre I have failed in my efforts to help her produce the third; and always having in my mind the fact that she gave up a very promising career as an actress, I have felt inadequate, blamed myself, and at times been close to despair.

We both knew, after talking to the box office, that we had to be prepared for a short stay at the St James's Theatre. All day we talked ourselves into the right 'Don't give a damn mood': 'You can't win them all – that's what the theatre's all about, we've already had a great deal of luck and success', etc. Every time our morale looked like flagging I made some crack about the bewildered carrot and laughter boosted it up again.

At 7.30 p.m. I found myself sitting in my dressing-room at the theatre, my make-up completed – pale face, slightly hollow-cheeked, eyes shaded with dark blue to give that haunted look. I reached out, lifted the red wig off the wig block, placed it carefully in position on my head, brushed a small amount of spirit gum on to the lace, and pressed it into position with a damp towel. A knock on the door. 'Overture and beginners please, Mr Mills.' I looked at myself in the mirror and suddenly, with no warning, the bewildered carrot burst into floods of tears.

On 15 June 1953, Cecil Wilson's column in the *Daily Mail* was headed 'JOHN MILLS'S PLAY IS OFF AND SO IS HIS RED WIG':

John Mills yesterday put away the red wig he has been wearing nightly in *The Uninvited Guest* at the St James's Theatre, and went into the country with his wife, Mary Hayley Bell, to forget the first failure of their actor/dramatist partnership. The play came off after a two-and-a-half week run. Not even the box office value of Mr Mills's name could enable it to compete with the rival attraction of the Coronation and its aftermath of sightseeing. The play toured triumphantly for fourteen weeks, and broke the house records everywhere it played.

All work and no play, etc. – I decided that we both needed to play. We'd worked hard and often, and we both needed a break away from it all. We had a few pennies in the bank – we would take the whole summer off.

I had always had a hankering to own a farm, and after searching for a few weeks we found exactly what we had been hoping to find – a lovely Elizabethan farmhouse standing in 175 acres at Cowden in Sussex. We bought it, lock, stock and barrel, and had a marvellous summer there. The kids adored it and we could think of no more perfect place to bring them all up.

In July we accepted an invitation to spend a week with Rex and Lilli Harrison at the new villa they had built in Portofino. After a few days of swimming, water-skiing, over-eating and drinking a cable arrived from David Lean. It read: 'Dear Johnnie, this is an S O S. Can you drop everything and return home immediately. Bob Donat ill. You can't turn down Willy Mossop in *Hobson's Choice* can you?' We were on the train four hours later.

I was in the make-up chair at Shepperton the following afternoon looking tanned, fit and ravishingly handsome. One hour later I looked in the mirror and saw a white-faced young boot-maker with shaved eyebrows and a ghastly pudding-basin hair-cut. But it was Willy Mossop. I only got this chance because poor Bob Donat had, after a week's rehearsal, succumbed to the most ghastly attack of asthma and was forced to withdraw from the film. David frankly admitted to me that he saw Willy at first as a largish, awkward, shambling sort of man, and he thought Bob was much better casting than I was. I was excited at the idea of acting with Charles Laughton, whom I had always considered an extraordinarily brilliant actor. David, who had never worked with an international star before, was, I felt, slightly in awe of him. Laughton was a strange but likeable man, who had a habit of expressing himself in a very odd way. For instance, when we were discussing the big comedy scene in the kitchen, Charles informed David and myself that he thought the scene when played should appear to be like 'star shells and rockets'. David looked thoughtful and chewed hard on his cigarette holder. 'Yes, Mr Laughton,' he said, after a pause, 'that was exactly what I had in mind.' And he knew that I knew neither of us had the slightest idea what the great man was talking about.

Hobson's Choice was 'a David Lean production' directed by David Lean; this time my chum had decided to carry the whole load, and carry it he did. *Hobson's Choice* will probably go down in history as one of his best pieces of work. His direction was superb, and his actors served him well. Brenda de Banzie gave the best performance of Maggie I have ever seen and Charles Laughton was Charles Laughton on top form.

I shall always be grateful to Willy Mossop. I think I enjoyed him as much as any part I have ever played, and I needed him badly. I had not been in a really successful picture with a great part since *Morning Departure*, three years before. And that state of affairs, if an actor is in first position over the title, is not in any way desirable.

During the first year at The Wick I had become a polo fanatic. We bought two ponies, and Mary and I schooled them every morning in Richmond Park with Billy Walsh, who owned the riding stables at Ham and ran the polo club. After a few months Billy decided I was good enough to play for the club in a match at Cirencester. I was definitely under-rehearsed. I galloped madly about for four chukkas and only managed to hit the ball once. It was an extremely good shot, but unfortunately it went straight through our own goal.

The polo revival after the war was fun, and within reach of many people's pockets. Our ponies only cost about £100 each. We had a wonderful time; Mary played for the ladies' team and we spent weekends playing in county games round the country. Polo was Lord Louis Mountbatten's favourite game. One of my treasured possessions is his book on it; he gave me a signed copy after one of the HMS *Kelly* reunion dinners.

During that summer Jimmy Edwards, who was also a polo maniac, arranged a charity fête at his farm in Fletchling. The main event of the day was a race called 'The Thespian Stakes' over a mile course. The riders were Jerry Desmond, Terry-Thomas, Mary Hayley Bell, Jimmy Edwards and myself. We were all riding the ponies we played polo on so I knew the form. My pony, Victory Song, was a flier, and I was certain she would walk it unless I fell off at one of the hairpin bends. Victory Song finished six lengths ahead of the field. I couldn't find anyone to place a bet for me so I missed the only cast-iron racing cert I shall ever have.

In the late autumn Binkie Beaumont asked me to play a part I had first played in London in 1930 – the Aunt in *Charley's Aunt*. It was to be a prestigious production – no expense spared – with costumes by Cecil Beaton and Sir John Gielgud as director. I knew but had never worked with Johnny G., as he is affectionately called, and I looked forward enormously to the experience. I can't remember a dull moment. He has a wonderful sense of humour, and is famous for dropping the most marvellous clangers. My favourite moment was during the dress rehearsal at the Haymarket Theatre. Some plays are absolutely hellish to rehearse. *Charley's Aunt* is one of them: without an audience it seems to be just about the un-funniest piece ever written. I finished the first act pouring with sweat after tearing round the stage in the heavy black frock, wig and bonnet. Johnny G. was out front in the stalls. There was dead silence. I walked to the footlights and, shading my eyes from the glare, peered out into the auditorium. 'Johnny,' I said, 'are you there?'

'Yes, I am.'

'Well ... what did you think of it?'

'Interminable, my dear fellow, absolutely interminable.'

He was right, of course; the cast collapsed. But it wasn't exactly the shot in the arm we needed. The revival, however, was a success – so much so that we ran on into the warm weather and by the time the play finished I had lost nearly a stone in weight.

For the rest of the 1950s I concentrated entirely on films. The reason for this was largely a financial one. I had become very caught up with farming, and my ambition, which I eventually achieved, was to restore Sussex House Farm to its former glory. I gradually bought back the land that had originally belonged to it, and finally finished up triumphantly with a large farm of nearly 500 acres, and an even larger overdraft. I was caught in the treadmill and couldn't really afford to go back into the theatre, even if I wanted to.

Over the next six years I made seventeen films, and I obviously only have space to mention the ones that I hope may be of some interest. *The Colditz Story*, for instance, I shall remember not only because it was a fascinating film to work on, but because during it I made several friendships that have survived the years: Lionel Jeffries (*Colditz* was his first film; and since then he has had a very successful career as a first-class character actor and later as a fine film director. He wrote and directed that enchanting picture *The Railway Children*); Eric Portman, who I hadn't acted with since *We Dive at Dawn*; Ivan Foxwell, who produced the picture; Guy Hamilton, now a very successful James Bond director; and a young actor/writer Bryan Forbes, who has had success in nearly every branch of the industry, and with whom I have worked several times since.

The Baby and the Battleship, a comedy about the Navy, I shall always remember with affection. Dickie Attenborough was with me again, and Lionel Jeffries with Bryan Forbes, who re-wrote the script incorporating an idea I had for the main character. It worked; *The Baby and the Battleship* turned out to be a very funny film. It will stay in my mind, however, chiefly because of something that happened while we were filming on location in Italy.

For over thirty years I've always had the same stand-in-cum-stunt-man, Freddie Clarke; a few years my junior, Freddie has been a close friend of the family since I first met him. The children adored him; we have travelled the globe together and there are few locations that haven't been enlivened by his presence. Freddie is a cockney to his fingertips. He started his career at the Old Ring in Blackfriars earning £1 a fight. He has done a bit of everything; he has been a tic-tac man on a race course, has owned and run greyhounds, and is a first-class bricklayer. During the war he built factories and shelters.

We had been filming at Naples, and I'd promised Freddie that on our first free day I would take him to see Pompeii. He looked blank. He'd vaguely heard about it, but I could see that no bells were ringing in his head. The great day arrived. Mary, Dickie, Freddie and I took off for Pompeii. I gave him the full Cook's tour, describing everything in detail – the grooves made by the chariot wheels, the Roman builders' original central heating, the baths, the forum, the lot. After an hour I paused for breath. Freddie had been silent. He'd followed us round gazing at everything. I could see he was terribly impressed. Looking out over the vast ruins from the top of one of the walls, I turned to him. 'Well, Freddie, what do you think of it?'

He continued gazing round for quite some seconds, and then said, in a voice full of concern, 'Well. They'll never do anything with it.'

The glory of the remark was that he really meant it. He was shattered. All his bricklaying instincts came to the surface. As far as Freddie was concerned, it was a typical Italian mess. We laughed all the way back to Naples. I laugh now every time I think of that look on his face.

Before we left Naples we were invited by Gracie Fields to spend a day with her and her husband Boris at her lovely villa on Capri. She was in tremendous form, but I remember thinking how strange it seemed to find that the lass from Rochdale had settled for life on that island – beautiful and restful though it was.

As well as comedy in the 1950s there was tragedy. My darling sister Annie died quite suddenly of a brain tumour. She was at the height of success in her second career with Muffin the Mule, and was adored by all the children in the country. Her memorial service at St Martin's in the Fields was unbelievably moving. Thousands of children who couldn't get into the church waited on the steps and in the streets outside. On the altar was a replica of Muffin in red and white flowers, and St Martin's was overflowing with wreaths with messages on them: 'To darling Muffin and his lovely Auntie Annette.'

I had always adored her and been amused at the apparently happy-go-lucky way she had managed her affairs. After her death we found that everything had been meticulously taken care of to the last detail. She had bequeathed her body to the Royal College of Surgeons and had actually arranged this in 1944 with Sir Reginald Watson-Jones, the surgeon who carried out some of her many operations. She left us with dignity, surrounded by flowers and the children who loved her.

20

Juliet and Hayley up in Lights

In 1956 I made what I thought was one of my cleverest moves which, several years later, proved to be not only not clever but totally stupid. I sold The Wick. It seemed at the time ridiculous to own a farm of 500 acres as well as a house with a large garden which needed a full-time gardener. Mary was not keen on the idea, but I pressed ahead with the plans. I then added a large, beautiful drawing-room to the farmhouse and bought a small but attractive Regency house in St Leonard's Terrace to live in and work from during the week when I was filming at the studios.

September brought me a chance to work with that great director Willie Wyler. We flew on the Monarch night flight to New York and the next day started rehearsals for *The Letter* by Somerset Maugham. Willie, having conquered the medium of film, had decided to try something new – live television. I'd been so anxious to work with the great man that although I was scared to death at the prospect, after an hour's conversation on the transatlantic telephone, I had allowed myself to be talked into it. 'Hell,' Willie had said, 'we've got to try everything once. Come on in with me.' And here I was 'in it'.

The first set-back happened a few days before we started rehearsal. Paul Scofield, who was cast to play the other leading part, had to back out. The film he was making was running over schedule, and Willie, in trouble, engaged Michael Rennie, who had never tackled anything quite as difficult in his life. The leading lady was that lovely Irish actress, Siobhan McKenna, who was so keen to be directed by Willie that she agreed to take on the long and difficult part in spite of the fact that she was giving eight performances a week of *St Joan* on Broadway.

Rehearsals were as far as I was concerned a nightmare. Willie had blinkers on: he could only see Michael Rennie, who had his entire attention. Siobhan and I were left to work out our own salvation. My nerves by this time were in such a state that I was certain I was being ignored because my performance was beyond salvation. Mary had a bad time with me. I couldn't eat, I couldn't sleep, and for the first time in my life the lines refused to stay in my head. On the last day before we moved from the rehearsal rooms to the NBC studios, I said to Willie: 'Well, I'm sorry. You've made a mistake, haven't you? I'm ghastly in the part, and there's nothing you can do about it. I just don't think I'll get through the show, that's all.'

He looked at me. 'What the hell are you talking about? You're terrific. So's Siobhan. I didn't have to bother with you two. You didn't need me. Michael's the one that needed help.' I was, however, too far gone by this time to believe him.

NBC had suggested to Willie that as he had never directed a live television play before he should have an experienced young TV director to help him block the show (i.e., arrange the camera positions and movement from the control room). At the first technical rehearsal all went fairly smoothly until Willie, who was up in the control box and suddenly confronted with his actors on the monitor screens, began to alter some positions. Our young director pointed out deferentially that they had to be locked in with what they had; there simply wasn't time to make any major alterations. Willie, however, insisted, and several camera angles and positions were changed.

A few hours later, Mary found me in my dressing-room in a complete state of panic, gabbling lines from the script that I knew but that refused to come out on cue. What had really finished me was the moment when the stage manager had come on to the floor at the end of the rehearsal and said, 'Well everybody, don't forget there'll be forty million people watching you tonight; but don't worry, you're all great. Good luck.'

'Darling, I'm not going to make it. I can't remember the bloody lines. What am I going to do?'

'I know exactly what you're going to do. I have talked to the ASM. You're coming with me.'

A few minutes later we were in a doctor's consulting room. 'Mr John Mills? Yes, I know all about it.' The doctor then filled an enormous syringe with a pale liquid and injected it into my arm. 'Now Mrs Mills, take him back to his dressing-room, give him these two pills, put a blanket over him, put out the light and don't let anyone disturb him until fifteen minutes before he goes on.'

What the injection was, or what the pills contained, I have no idea. What I do know, however, is that when Mary woke me, my brain was clear and my nerves were under control. It was just as well. If they hadn't been the events of the next two hours would have undoubtedly been the cause of a severe nervous breakdown.

The countdown started. We were on the air. In the first scene of the play Siobhan, during a violent row on the verandah, picks up a revolver and shoots a man dead. I was standing off-stage waiting for my entrance, feeling calm, cool, collected and obviously as high as a kite on the doctor's wonder-drug. I saw her aim the revolver and pull the trigger. There was a faint click; the blank cartridge was a dud. Siobhan looked at the revolver then back at the man, 'You swine,' she said, and pulled the trigger once more. Another faint click. In desperation, but with the adaptability of a true professional, Siobhan reached for a large paper-knife that happened to be within reach.

'You swine,' she shouted, approached her victim, and raised the knife to stab him. At that split second the property man fired a shot off-stage. The actor playing with her, who throughout this unrehearsed piece of drama had been staring at Siobhan with a strange 'I can't believe it's happening' look on his face, came to slowly, and after the count of three, gasped, clutched his heart, and collapsed in a heap on the stage. Not one of those forty million viewers would, I was sure, be switching over to another channel. They *had* to be hooked.

After this hilarious opening things proceeded smoothly, but were comparatively dull until my big scene with Michael Rennie which took place in a replica of the Conservative Club. I was blackmailing him. The tense moment arrived when he looked me in the eye and said, 'How much do you want?'

'Sixty-four thousand dollars. That's what I want.'

At that moment two cameras, whose positions had been changed at the last minute, collided with a crash a few feet from us and a large painting of King George V behind us on the wall fell with a thud to the floor. *The Letter* was my first and last live play on TV.

Amazing though it seemed to me, the evening was a big success for Willie and for everybody concerned with the production. I was stopped every few minutes the next morning on Fifth Avenue. The public had loved it, and to my astonishment nobody mentioned the gun or King George V.

We sailed on the *Queen Mary* for England two days later, and had a farewell party aboard with Willie, the cast, and Douglas and Mary Lee Fairbanks. My diary entry states, '17 October 1956: sailed on the Queen, 11.30 p.m. Survived it all. Decided after much thought to stay in the profession.'

In 1957 I made four more films – *Dunkirk*, again with Dickie Attenborough, and that excellent actor, Bernard Lee; and *Ice Cold in Alex* which was directed by J. Lee Thompson, who was, although I didn't know it at the time, to have a great influence on all our lives. In the cast there were two actors I greatly admired and had never worked with –

Anthony Quayle and Harry Andrews. We spent six weeks in the desert together, outside Tripoli, and have remained firm friends ever since. The leading lady in the film was a young and talented actress, Sylvia Sims.

I had never in the past, in films at any rate, had the chance to play a full-blooded love scene. I made up for this omission in *Ice Cold in Alex*. Sylvia and I rolled around in the sands of the desert in the moonlight with no holds barred. Lee Thompson was very happy with the scene and I personally enjoyed every minute of it. I found it a refreshing change from 'Up periscope'. Nine months after we had finished this purple, passionate passage, among the notices, which I'm glad to say were excellent, appeared a piece in the *Daily Express* by Tom Lambert, with a large picture of myself and Sylvia in a tight clinch in the moonlight. The heading was, 'Yes, this is John Mills, and his hottest scene yet hits censor trouble':

John Mills, usually the most unswervingly upright of British screen heroes, has come up against censor trouble. His love scenes with Sylvia Sims in *Ice Cold in Alex* are said to be too scorching. Mills is unrepentant; says he, 'It's a sheer relief to play a real love scene with a girl for a change, after so many years of giving them polite pecks on the cheeks between battles.' But he is riled at the censorship: 'Love scenes in British films are often condemned as cold,' he says. 'But often it's because the actors are not given the chance to warm up. The Censor's scissors get clipping too quickly.' Why? 'Because he thinks that love scenes are all right so long as they are imported. Look at what the Americans get away with. Some of their current epics are just two hour smooching sessions with dialogue. As soon as a British actor takes a girl in his arms the scene has to fade out.'

When I saw the film the scene had totally disappeared. Lee fought for it but it ended up at the Censor's request on the cutting room floor. Of course it *was* very daring. Sylvia had two, not one, of the buttons of her khaki blouse undone! This explicit sex-scene took place only twenty-two years ago. How times have changed.

Ice Cold did one marvellous thing for me – it destroyed for ever that ridiculous stiff upper lip image I had been stuck with. Captain Anson was a man driven by nervous exhaustion to drink. During the trip across the desert he and the other characters discuss the ice-cold lager they will drink if they ever reach Alex. We shot the famous scene at the bar in the studio on our return to Elstree. The property master mixed everything he could think of to look like lager. Nothing worked. Lee decided I would have to drink the real thing. At 8.30 one morning on the set I took a deep breath and downed, without pausing, a pint of continental lager. Six takes and six pints later I was completely plastered; shooting was postponed until after lunch to give the gallant captain time to sober up. I still reckon that to be the happiest and most enjoyable morning I have ever spent in any film studio.

In the same column in the *Daily Express* there was another heading, 'Problem for Miss Mills':

Meanwhile, John's sixteen-year-old daughter Juliet had been facing an awkward dilemma. She had just won a place at the Royal Academy of Dramatic Art, hard to get these days if you're a girl. Then 'just for fun' she went to an audition called by Sir John Gielgud in search of a very young girl for the new play *Five Finger Exercise* by Peter Schaffer. Embarrassing result. She got the part.

Her problem was, should she accept, or should she learn some more about acting? She plumped for the part. Mary and I went to the first night; Juliet had made the right decision. We were highly nervous, but a few minutes after her first entrance we relaxed. She gave a brilliant, completely professional performance, and seemed thoroughly at home on the stage. We both felt very proud. The first filly out of the stable looked remarkably like a winner.

In August 1958 during a lunch party at Sussex House Farm something happened that was to change our way of life completely. Lee Thompson had sent me a script called *Tiger Bay*; I liked it, and the part. Lee had come down to the farm to discuss it. Shooting was scheduled to start in six weeks' time. There was a part in the film for a small boy of twelve, and I could see straight away that if Lee managed to get the right little boy he could easily walk away with the picture. This didn't worry me. The script was the thing, and I was more than anxious after *Ice Cold* to work with Lee again, whom I thought brilliant.

Our friend seemed slightly distrait during lunch. He didn't really talk about the film. Most of his conversation seemed to be with Hayley, who was only too happy to regale him with the latest news of her pony, her white mice and the three new calves she had seen born that morning. After lunch Lee suggested a walk round the farm. There was something important he said he wanted to discuss. 'Listen, this may seem quite mad to you, but I've got a terrific hunch. I want to make a switch and change the little boy into a little girl. I know it's right. The whole story will be much more touching and moving in every way.'

'Well, I can see that's possible,' I said, 'but isn't it a bit late for a major change? It's a difficult part. A star part, really. The picture will stand or fall on that character, and it could take you weeks to find the right girl.'

'It won't, you know,' said Lee, 'I've already found her.' He stopped and looked at me. 'It's Hayley.'

I stared at him. 'Hayley? But listen, Lee, she's never been in front of a camera in her life. She might be ghastly. And then how do you think I should feel?'

'Johnnie, I told you I've got a terrific hunch. I think she'll be sensational. She's got the most divine personality. Anyway, I want her. Will you let her at least make a test?'

The moment of truth had arrived. Mary and I had long ago decided that we would never persuade any of the kids to join our frantic profession. In fact we were determined to put them off by pointing out what a rough, tough, heart-breaking job it can very often be. But if they insisted, if it was the only thing in the world they wanted to do, then we would give them our blessing, cross our fingers and hope for the best.

My daughter was exercising her pony in the long meadow. She was lovely to watch on a horse – she had good hands like her mother, and rarely bothered about stirrups or a saddle. I waved. She galloped over to us. 'Get off, darling. Lee has something to ask you.'

'Hayley,' said Lee. 'Have you ever done any acting?'

'Oh, nothing very much. Just a few lines in school plays at Elmhurst. Why?'

'Well, I was just wondering, would you like to act with your father in the next film I'm making?'

'Oh Lee, I'd absolutely love to. When?' She paused. A thought struck her. 'Will it be during term-time?'

'Now listen, Hayl,' I said, 'this is serious. It's a big part. It's about the best part in the film. You must think seriously about it. You're only twelve, and I can't let you do this unless you really, honestly want to.'

'I see, Daddy. Well, I'll think about it seriously.'

Lee broke in: 'Well, Hayley, it is important. When can you let me know?'

'Now,' said my daughter. 'I've thought about it seriously, and I want to do it. Lee, will you please excuse me, I've got to rub her down, she's sweating. See you at tea-time.'

That was typical of Hayley. We'd always found it difficult to get her to take anything seriously or to concentrate on anything for long. She lived in a very happy world of her own and seemed to enjoy every minute of it. Juliet had always been the dedicated one. She finished up at Elmhurst as head girl, and landed the first job she went after. She made things happen. Hayley, on the other hand, always seemed to sit back and let things happen to her.

After a long discussion with Mary we decided that we would at least give Lee the chance to make the tests. We would then take it from there. I rang him and told him of our decision. 'That's great Johnnie, but I don't want to test her. I don't want to make it look important.'

'But Lee,' I protested, 'you're taking an awful chance. Don't you even want to see how she photographs?'

'No, I don't. I could photograph her myself with a Number Two Brownie Kodak box camera with my eyes shut, and she'd still look good. Oh, and by the way, don't let her read the script, even if she asks you. I'll send the wardrobe department down to the farm, and they'll sort out a few old things for her to wear. Just keep her relaxed; that shouldn't be difficult.'

A few weeks later Hayley and I were in the car heading for the little studios at Beaconsfield. At Lee's suggestion we read the scene we had to do together a few times. I was surprised; my *enfant terrible* seemed to have a photographic memory. It was a long and difficult scene, for me at any rate. I was playing a detective investigating a murder, and therefore had all the questions, which of course made it slightly easier for her.

We started shooting the first take at 9 a.m. I simply couldn't believe what was happening. She looked as if she'd been born in front of a camera. All the other children I had suffered with in films had to be told continually not to look into the lens. Lee shot close-ups with the camera two feet away from her face. She looked left, right, over it, below it, but never at it. I am usually very secure on my lines, but that morning I was so astonished at what was going on that I dried up at least three times.

'All right. Let's break for lunch.'

'Lee. It's only twelve o'clock. We don't break till one,' I said.

'I know. I think we've done enough.' He called Hayley's dresser. 'Take my leading lady to the canteen, give her some lunch and then make her put her feet up for half an hour. I'm taking Mr Mills off. I want to talk to him.'

'Where are we going, Lee?'

'To the Bull at Beaconsfield. I want to get out of the studio for a bit.'

Not a word was spoken until we reached the bar at the Bull Hotel. 'One bottle of the best champagne you have in the cellar, please.' Lee stood fiddling with one of the paper darts he made daily from a copy of *The Times* throughout all his films. A bottle of Dom Pérignon was opened. He raised his glass. 'Well Johnnie,' he said, 'I've made a lot of films, but I'm going to drink to the most exciting and magical morning I've ever spent in any studio. That child is going to be a bloody sensation. Here's to her. Cheers!'

'Cheers!' I said. I knew without any shadow of doubt that J. Lee Thompson was right.

Tiger Bay was an experience. Hayley was extraordinary. She never seemed to be listening and hummed quietly to herself while Lee was explaining the scenes. I asked him if this was driving him mad. 'Good

God no,' said Lee, 'as long as she keeps humming we're OK.' He didn't allow her to see any of the rushes of the previous day's work until the time came when she had to re-enact for me, as the detective, the murder she had watched through the keyhole.

Hayley sat in the theatre enthralled. When the lights went up, she turned to Lee and said, 'Oh Lee, it's terribly exciting. Am I in this film?' 'Yes, Hayley, I believe you are. And now let's get back on the set and shoot the scene.'

It was Take One, Cut, Print. All Lee did was to ask the little monster to act the scene she had just watched. With no rehearsal she just did it. One second she was Horst Bucholz with a gun and the next second the girl. At the end of it, she did a grotesque fall ending up flat on her back. It was one of the best pieces of mime I've ever seen.

We finished the picture bang on schedule after some very tough, rather dangerous locations in Cardiff Docks and at sea in dreadful weather. Lee and I both felt that we had something very exciting in the can, but neither of us, I am sure, quite visualized the enormous impact that Hayley Mills was finally going to make not only in Britain but in the rest of the world.

In December I flew off to Australia to make *The Summer of the Seventeenth Doll* with Ernest Borgnine, Angela Lansbury and Anne Baxter. Leslie Norman was directing. Mary, Hayley and Jonathan, plus Nanny, arrived ten days later, when the school holidays started. Their flight took a week. Engine trouble started at Prestwick where they were grounded for thirty-six hours. Elvis Presley's picture *Jailhouse Rock* was playing at the local cinema. The kids were all Elvis fans; Mary was forced to sit through it six times. Luckily, she was a fan too.

We enjoyed our first visit to Australia and made many friends. We rented a house on Point Piper, which was always full of the cast, and the English cricket team, Peter May, Colin Cowdrey, Freddie Trueman and co, who were taking it on the chin in that particular Test, not only from the Aussie bowlers but from the English critics who were hammering them – quite unfairly, in my opinion. I was able to watch quite a lot of the cricket. Keith Miller invited us to the members' stand, and the first person I walked into was my old chum Trevor Howard who had flown out especially to see the Test.

I enjoyed making the picture, although we were the forgotten men. Hecht Hill and Lancaster had bought the subject after the play had become a smash hit in Australia and London, and intended to make an expensive epic with Burt Lancaster and myself playing the leading parts and Carol Reed directing. When the play opened in New York, it flopped. Burt pulled out of it and so did Carol, after hearing they intended cutting the budget to the minimum, which meant losing all the big exterior cane-cutting scenes. At this point I also wanted to withdraw, but Carol persuaded me to make the film. 'Parts like that don't grow on trees,' he said. 'You're an actor. Go ahead and play it.' I'm glad I took his advice.

I took enormous trouble to get the rather difficult Australian accent absolutely right. I worked with tapes for hours before I was satisfied. The dailies were sent back to Hollywood to be processed, which meant that we had to shoot blind for four weeks without having any idea how the stuff was coming out. Finally Leslie Norman received a cable from the production company. It read: 'Dailies good. Atmosphere excellent. Photography OK. Mills's accent entirely unintelligible. Regards.' Leslie looked at me. 'Well, what are we going to do about it, Johnnie?'

'Absolutely sweet f.a.,' I said. 'That's the first word we've heard from them. I'm damned if I'm going to muck up my performance. Ernie Borgnine can understand me, and if they can't, bad luck.' The accent stayed, and that was the last we heard of it.

We flew home via Singapore where we were guests of Sir Run Me Shaw, staying at his beautiful house on the ocean; then on to the wonders of Bangkok and finally home at the end of February.

Tiger Bay opened in March. The picture got great notices, but Hayley's were nothing short of sensational. She was acclaimed as the most exciting and brilliant child actress since Shirley Temple. An entry in my diary of 27 March reads: 'Hayley's press quite amazing. Never seen better for any young actor. Hayley unimpressed. Her only concern is for the new chicks just hatched out at farm.'

One or two of the critics said that she acted the entire cast including her father off the screen, and suggested that I might be perhaps a little jealous of her success. This seemed to me to be an idiotic assumption. If a filly that you've bred comes out of the stable and wins the Derby, how is it possible to be anything but very proud and delighted with the result? Juliet was the one who, at her tender age, found it difficult to cope with the sudden overwhelming success of her younger sister. I didn't know anything of Juliet's problem at the time. It wasn't until much later on that she confided in me that she couldn't help feeling jealous. She had had quite a big success in *Five Finger Exercise*, but because Hayley had clicked in a film the publicity was, of course enormous. She told me that she had made herself see *Tiger Bay* six times. That apparently did the trick. The feelings of jealousy were finally swamped by her enormous admiration. When she told me this, I remember feeling very proud of her. It showed, I thought, a strength of character far beyond her sixteen years.

Hayley was apparently also concerned. The weekend after the premiere I couldn't find the Sunday papers. It wasn't until nearly lunch-time that Mary found them hidden in a cupboard. Hayley had got up early, read the notices, decided that I would be upset by them saying that she had 'acted me off the screen' and that it would be better for my morale not to see them. I thought that was one of the nicest things anyone, especially at that age, could ever do. It took me some time to persuade her that I expected the result, wanted it, and was thrilled to death by it. 'But Daddy, it's not true. It's so stupid.'

I looked at my offspring, and said, 'All right, my darling, if you go on thinking like that, you'll never become big-headed and conceited.' She never has.

After the première life settled down to normal. Hayley went back to school at Elmhurst, Jonathan to Fonthill, and Juliet was playing in *Five Finger Exercise* which was still running in the West End.

It was, I'm afraid, typical of the British film industry that after *Tiger Bay* had laid that small golden egg none of the producers seemed to be aware of it. We were surprised and frankly relieved when no offers for any other film materialized. Mary and I took deep breaths and relaxed.

Not for long, however: Laurie Evans, our agent, rang to say that Walt Disney was in town; he'd seen the picture and was anxious to talk to us. We knew what it meant. Walt Disney, apart from being a genius, was one of the most charming, immediately likeable men I have ever met. His enthusiasm for anything he was concerned with was enormous. Hayley's performance in *Tiger Bay* had bowled him over. It would, he said, be a crime if we didn't give him the chance to build her into a big, international star. He had never seen a child like her. And how could we deprive the public of all that talent and pleasure? Walt Disney was genuinely fond of children. It didn't need Disneyland to prove that to us. Hayley adored him from the first meeting.

A few days later Laurie rang us with a firm offer – a contract for five years, a picture a year, three to be made in Hollywood, two in England. Financially the deal was fantastic; the contract was worth a fortune. It was, for us both, a hideously agonizing decision to make. I spent hours with Hayley trying to make her understand the importance of it and how much it would alter and influence her whole life and, incidentally, her parents'. I begged her to think hard before she made up her mind, because if she had any doubts at all we would turn it down in a flash. But Hayley, being Hayley, was I could see approaching it in much the same way she had approached *Tiger Bay*. 'Yes, Daddy darling, I would love to do it. I would really.'

'Are you sure, Hayl? I won't be in the pictures with you, you know.'
Her face fell a little. 'Oh I see. But you'll be there, won't you Daddy?'
'Well, when I can. Mummy of course would be there all the time.'

That was the part we dreaded most. After weeks of heart-searching and brain-bashing and with Hayley seeming very keen, we agreed. The deal was signed. Her first picture for Walt was to be *Polyanna* with shooting beginning in Hollywood in July. By a strange coincidence (later on, when I'd got to know Walt Disney well, I wondered if coincidence was exactly the right word), soon after Hayley's deal was completed, I was offered the part of the father in *Swiss Family Robinson* that Walt was making in Tobago in August.

For the past eighteen years Mary and I had never been separated for more than a week or so at one time. From now on we knew life was going to present a very different picture. But we were determined, even if it cost us a fortune in air fares (which it did), that we would make the gaps as short as possible, and keep the family together. We hoped that the education of travelling in foreign countries would, in a way, compensate for the disruption of school-life.

21

The Mills Family in Disneyland

In July we flew to California with Jonathan and Hayley. We had to leave Juliet behind, because she was still playing in *Five Finger Exercise*. Mary wasn't at all happy about this, but as Bunch was eighteen by this time we hoped that she would be all right until she flew out to join me in Tobago when the play finished.

Walt Disney was wonderful. Anything that he could think of was done to make us feel happy and at home. He'd put us into one of the luxurious bungalows at the Beverly Hills Hotel and we had two cars at our disposal. We spent a weekend with the great man and Lily, his wife, at Disneyland before Hayley started shooting. It was an experience we shall never forget. Disneyland was Walt's baby – he enjoyed every minute of it. He was a compulsive builder and new strange buildings, enchanted rivers and lakes always appeared shortly after each of his visits. He took us on everything – the jungle trip, Niagara Falls, the big dipper, the ghost train, the race track – no queueing. Walt beckoned an attendant and we were in, with one exception. At the Niagara Falls entrance the keen young college boy who was picking up a few extra bucks during his summer vacation by working in Disneyland said as Walt approached the gate at the top of the queue: 'Hey there, bud, just wait a minute. Who do you think you are? Walt Disney?'

'Yes,' said Walt. 'I ... think I am.'

Hayley's baptism of fire took place on location in the lovely Santa Rosa valley. I was worried; I could see that, for the first time, she was genuinely nervous. It had suddenly, to her, become a serious job. David Swift, who was directing, was worried too. At the lunch-break I had a talk with him. I told him how Lee Thompson got the result he wanted by keeping her totally relaxed, pretending the whole thing was terribly unimportant. *L'enfant terrible* would then stop humming, walk in front of the camera and deliver the more than acceptable goods. I then sought out my ex-co-star and gave her a short but stimulating pep-talk. It worked. Walt called us from the studios the next afternoon. The dailies were no surprise to him, he said. His new girl friend was sensational.

In August I had to leave them and fly to Tobago to start shooting *Swiss Family Robinson*. I hated going. Mary was in tears at the airport; Hollywood and Beverly Hills I knew were not really her scene. One Hollywood reporter had asked her what her impression was of Beverly Hills. 'Well,' said my wife, 'if you really want to know I think with all these white Christmas-cake houses it looks rather like Forest Lawn Cemetery – the only difference here is that people walk out of them.' She liked the Americans, but the freeways with their thousands of cars, travelling in lanes four abreast as if linked by invisible cuff-links, terrified her. She disliked hamburgers and Coca Cola was her unfavourite drink. But the main horror was the fact that we knew we shouldn't be seeing each other for eight weeks, and old-fashioned though it may seem, we hated the idea.

Freddie Clarke, my old chum and stand-in, met me at the small grass strip that passed for a runway in Tobago. I was more than glad to see him. Freddie was always good for a laugh. I asked him what Tobago was like. 'Not bad. Not bad at all. Quite pretty. Better than Italy. And at least they can speak our bloody language.'

Freddie was the original understatement-maker of the decade. I knew by his reaction that Tobago had to be the most beautiful island I have ever seen. I was right. Unlike a sugar island like Barbados it was lush; the scenery was varied and very beautiful. I was lucky to see it before it became popular, with the inevitable golf course and noisy water sports. It was simple and totally unspoilt: miles of empty golden beaches lapped by the sea which was full of exotic and highly-coloured fish that, as they were never shot, were so tame they poked their noses against our face-masks as we swam amongst them.

Walt Disney had decided to shoot the whole film on location. All the animals needed for the picture were flown in: elephants, lions, tigers, giraffes, zebras, ostriches, monkeys by the dozen, alligators and two enormous snakes – boa constrictors. An English director, Ken Annikin, an old friend of mine, was in charge of an epic that was going to cost over £2 million, in those days considered a very large budget. I was playing opposite that lovely American actress, Dorothy McGuire, and also in the cast were James MacArthur, Janet Monro and Tommy Kirk.

I had found the location work in *Scott* tough and rough, but compared to *Swiss Family Robinson*, it was a picnic. During the first week's shooting a hurricane hit the island. We were filming in a mangrove swamp at the time, an unhealthy oozing mess, with sucking quick-sands, spider-like trees and thousands of slow-moving crabs. We were caught in torrential rain and winds up to nearly 100 miles an hour.

Many people seem to think that film stars lead a very cushy, easy, sheltered life. I described a typical working day in Tobago in an interview I gave in the London *Evening News* of 11 October 1959: 'If a scorpion doesn't bite me during the night I get into the car, and if it doesn't skid off the edge of a cliff, I reach the mangrove swamp. I walk through; and if I'm not sucked in by a quick-sand, eaten alive by land crabs, or bitten by a snake, I reach the beach. I change on the beach, trying to avoid being devoured by insects, and walk into the sea. If there are no sharks or barracudas about, we get the shot – and then do the whole thing in reverse, providing, of course, we haven't died of sunstroke in the meantime.'

Freddie Clarke, when he wasn't standing in for me, volunteered for stunt work. I overheard the following dialogue when Ken Annikin was outlining what he hoped to get in the action during the next day's filming: 'On Thursday,' said our director, 'I'm going to shoot the big scene with the pirates. I want you to do a fall from the edge of those cliffs, missing the rocks below, and then hit the sea.'

Freddie looked at the eighty-foot drop, the sharp rocks, the shark-infested ocean. 'What do I do Friday?'

Ken looked suitably embarrassed. 'I hadn't planned anything for you on Friday.' He coughed slightly and walked away.

In October I left the Blue Haven Hotel and rented an attractive bungalow on the beach. Juliet's play finished in London and she arrived bursting with excitement, fell madly in love with Tobago and decided she wanted to live there for ever, providing, of course, that she could organize and run her own repertory company. A few days later Mary, Hayley and Jonathan arrived from Los Angeles. The family, after the first long and definitely unpopular separation, was once more complete.

Walt Disney was, Mary said, delighted with the picture, and with his new star. After her rather nervous start Hayley had settled down and had seemed to enjoy it all. Mary, on the other hand, had not; Hollywood without me, she said, was difficult to take. I thought of the next five years ahead of us when this pattern was bound to be repeated, and prayed that the family life we had known for so long would not be affected.

After two weeks' holiday, we packed Hayley and Jonathan off to the local school. They had both had lessons from a governess during the film at the Disney studios and, rather than fly them home to school in England, we thought that Bishops High School would be, for a short time, a stimulating and interesting experience. They were, of course, a minority group: two white faces amongst ninety-five black ones. They both settled down very quickly, and were accepted and happy. I asked Jonathan if they had played any games in the afternoon. 'Yes, football,' said my son.

'That's great,' I said. 'That's your favourite game, isn't it?'

'Not this afternoon it wasn't. When we got to the pitch they all took their boots off. So I did too,' said Jonathan, looking at a big toe that was giving a very good imitation of a small, overripe banana.

Actors dread working with children and animals, and in *Swiss Family* I had more than my share. One particularly nasty ostrich took an instant dislike to me, and while I was trying to hold him steady before the start of the famous race, he did his best to disembowel me from all angles with sudden vicious kicks, before finally breaking away and running straight through the wall of a stout wooden hut and out the other side. But I shall always remember the ostrich scene for quite another reason.

During the lunch-break a messenger arrived with a cable from my agent Laurence Evans. It read as follows: 'PHIL AND LIZ DECORATORS OFFER YOU THE PART OF CHARLIE BIRDSEED ESQUIRE OPENING PALACE FOLLIES JAN I STOP CABLE IMMEDIATELY IF YOU ACCEPT STOP LOVE LAURIE.' Whenever I've been on location, Laurie, who has a great sense of humour, had often in the past sent me amusing telegrams with gags or hidden jokes in them. But on this occasion I was stumped. I just didn't get it. Mary and I both read it several times before I finally gave up and threw it away.

Three weeks later Mary flew back to New York for Juliet's opening in *Five Finger Exercise*, leaving Hayley and Jonathan with me. The evening she arrived, Laurie phoned her from London. He sounded concerned. 'I've been trying for a week to get through to Tobago. But the phone's impossible. I never get further than Trinidad. What was his reaction to the cable? I've heard nothing, and it's urgent. What's happened?'

'Do you mean that gag about Charlie Birdseed Esquire? We couldn't make head or tail of it.'

'You mean he's done nothing about it? He hasn't accepted it?'

'Accepted what?' said Mary. 'He threw it away.'

'Threw it away?' Laurie's voice crackled across the Atlantic. 'Now listen, darling, I can't be too explicit over the telephone, listen: Liz and Phil, decorators. Don't you get it now?'

'No I don't,' said Mary.

'Listen, Liz and Phil . . . Elizabeth and Philip – decorators. Charlie Bird-seed Esquire. Got it? January 1st. Think of the first three letters.'

The penny dropped with a thud.

'Good God,' said my bride, 'you mean Johnnie's being asked if he will accept the . . . ?'

'Yes,' said Lol, 'but don't say it. It's all terribly hush-hush as you know. But for God's sake get him on the phone now, and tell him to cable *yes*. I only hope it's not too late.'

Luckily, for once the line was reasonably clear from New York and after a few minutes Mary was able, without actually spelling it out, to make me understand that two weeks ago I had thrown away a cable asking me if I would accept a CBE. I was stunned. Ever since I won a toast-rack for the Hundred Yards Under Twelves as a small boy, I had always loved prizes, and here I was, by ignoring the offer, probably about to lose one of the most marvellous prizes I could ever think of winning.

I tore into Tobago post office and rushed off a belated acceptance. Two weeks went by with no word from anyone. I thought miserably, well that's it. You've insulted Her Majesty the Queen, you'll never get anything now. You're obviously blackballed for ever.

Then one morning – very early, it was hardly light – I heard a scream from Hayley's bedroom in the bungalow. I dashed in to find my daughter sitting up wide-eyed in bed enveloped in the mosquito net which had collapsed over her head, staring at two very black police officers with guns in their holsters. One had a letter in his hand. 'I'm sorry, sir, to frighten the young lady, and to disturb you at this early hour, but this here letter arrived by special messenger from Trinidad. It's from the Governor, and marked "urgent". So we brought it right away.'

This time I didn't take long to get the message. His Excellency was coming over from Trinidad and requested the pleasure of my company for dinner at the Governor's residence in Tobago the following evening. My relief was intense.

I shall never forget that evening. It was straight out of a Somerset Maugham story. A dinner party of fourteen, the ladies in long dresses, the men in white dinner jackets. After a splendid repast, coffee and liqueurs were served on the verandah. The setting was perfect. A full moon, palm trees, fire-flies, a cool breeze off the sea. The conversation had been general. Not a word had been mentioned about the reason for my invitation. 'Mills,' said the Governor, 'let's take a stroll along to the other end of the verandah, the view from there is quite splendid.'

There was an interminable pause as we leaned over the rail. 'You enjoying the island?'

'Very much sir. I think Tobago is quite beautiful.'

Pause. 'What do you think of Peter May?'

This quick switch made me think.

'Well, um, in what way do you mean, sir?'

'Er, I mean, do you think he'll make a good skipper? He's a fine classic bat, but is he a leader?'

'I think he is, sir. I saw him in Australia when they were up against it. Yes, I think he is.'

'Glad to hear it. Glad to hear it. We've got to get those Ashes back, haven't we?'

'Yes sir, we have.'

'Yes. Of course. The Aussies always take a lot of beating.'

The Governor glanced at me. 'Very well deserved, Mills. Good show. Shall we rejoin the ladies?'

That was the full extent of the conversation. But it was enough for me. I drove home to the bungalow that night on a Caribbean cloud.

Two weeks later Mary arrived back from New York with good news: the play was a success, the New York critics had been kind, Juliet had made a very successful debut.

Swiss Family Robinson finally came to an end and we were able to fly to New York in time for a family Christmas. Then, when the school holidays were over, we had to return home to put Jonathan and Hayley back to their respective schools, leaving Juliet in New York. We hated the idea but there seemed to be no alternative. I had a film to make in January in England and neither of us felt like being separated again, not for a while at least. The new pattern of our lives was already established for the next few years. We flew thousands of miles trying to keep in contact with the family and, because of the circumstances, found it increasingly difficult to congregate in the same place at the same time. The title of this book could have been inspired by our lives in the 1960s: we spent a considerable time 'up in the clouds'. We made thirty round trips to California with Kenya, Nairobi and Australia thrown in for good measure.

Tyrone Power, Laurence Olivier, Vivien Leigh and me in
Night of a Hundred Stars at the London Palladium in 1958

With Hayley in her first film, *Tiger Bay*, 1958

Tunes of Glory: (*left to right*) Duncan Macrae, me, Richard Leach, Alec Guinness and Gordon Jackson

LEFT 'Three Juvenile Delinquents' at the London Palladium: (*right to left*) Laurence Olivier, Danny Kaye and me

With my old friend and stand-in Freddie Clarke (*right*) taking a break during the filming of *The Truth About Spring*, 1964

A trial of strength with Hywel Bennett in *The Family Way*. In the background are Marjorie Rhodes, Liz Fraser, Hayley and Wilfred Pickles

RIGHT David Lean directing me in *Ryan's Daughter*, 1969

On the back of this still from *Oh! What A Lovely War* Larry Olivier wrote: 'Johnnie, from the look on my face, you *might* think I was propositioning you – from the look on yours, there can be no doubt about it!'

LEFT It's nice work if
you can get it! My Oscar
for *Ryan's Daughter*

BELOW LEFT With John
Gielgud in *Veterans* at
the Royal Court Theatre,
1972

RIGHT We've always
laughed a lot – this was
Bermuda in 1973

BELOW RIGHT The Mills
clan at Beverly Hills,
1976: in the back row,
me, Mary (only just),
Juliet with Melissa,
Jonathan, Hayley and,
in the front row, Henry,
Sean, Ace and Crispian

Young At Heart, 1980

22

Silver Screen and Silver Wedding

If an outsider romps home at long odds its success is always sweeter. *Tunes of Glory* was a shining example. The script was turned down by every major company. An independent producer, Colin Leslie, sent it to me; I thought it was terrific but the budget was small. It meant black and white, and the subject screamed for colour. I would have turned it down if Mary hadn't threatened to divorce me if I didn't do something about it. To preserve the marriage I sent it to Alec Guinness. Sir Alec (an early knighthood well deserved) thought it was daring but liked it, and agreed to stick his chin out if mine was lined up beside it. 'Which part do you want to play?' Alec asked.

'I don't mind. They're both as good as each other. Let's toss up for it,' I said.

We finally decided that we would do some 'off-beat' casting: I would play the neurotic, nerve-wracked Colonel Barrow, and Alec would play the hard-drinking, tough Scots colonel up from the ranks. With Alec's acceptance the combination and the chemistry looked strong. Colin Leslie was able to raise the extra money, which meant the film could be made in colour. Ronnie Neame, who made his debut as a director in this film, did a marvellous job. He resisted the temptation to show what a brilliant technician he was; his direction was smooth and unobtrusive; the highly dramatic scenes that Alec and I had to handle were therefore much more effective.

Tunes of Glory caused quite a sensation in Britain and in America when it was released in December. Everybody came out of it smelling of roses. Alec and I were, in one critic's opinion, 'giants of the screen'; but what really pleased me was the fact that during the picture we became very close friends, so close in fact that Mary and I were within an inch of becoming Roman Catholics. Alec was a convert and took his faith very seriously, and we had long talks far into the night. I firmly believe that if a young Jesuit priest, straight from ten years in the Gobi desert, had not on one moonlit night on the promenade deck of a P & O liner in the Red Sea lost all control and flung himself at Mary (who was seventeen at the time) and bitten her lip, we would, with Alec's enthusiasm, have embraced the faith.

In June, with Mary and Hayley in California on the next Disney film, Juliet in New York with *Five Finger Exercise* and myself in Spain shooting *The Singer not the Song*, the inevitable happened. Juliet fell madly in love with an Adonis named Russell Alquist, who was leading a pleasant, well-ordered existence: he kept himself on ice in the winter as a skating attendant in Central Park, and thawed himself out in the summer months as a life-guard on the beach at Atlantic City.

After finishing *Singer not the Song* (I saw my first bullfight in Malaga and was so nauseated I struck a young Spaniard who was laughing at my reactions – if Freddie Clarke hadn't been with me I might not have left the bull-ring alive), I flew to LA and had my first meeting with my prospective son-in-law. Juliet, having finished the play, had flown him down on appro. She was serious, she told me in a letter; she had found the one man she ever wanted in her life. There was nothing one could possibly dislike about Russell – he was, apart from being extremely good-looking, charming, rather shy, with not an ounce of vice in him, and, like thousands of his fellow Americans, a thoroughly nice young man. 'Do you like him, Daddy?' It was quite obvious after a few days in their company that Juliet was besotted.

'I like him very much, darling. He's a very nice young man.'

'Oh Daddy, I'm so glad. I was sure you would. We want to get married. Are you pleased?'

I took a long, deep breath. 'Frankly, darling, I'm not.'

My daughter looked shattered. 'But why Daddy, why? I thought you liked him.'

'I do, darling, very much. Now listen. I've always been honest with you, and I have to be honest now. I can't see the marriage standing a chance. The boot will always be on the wrong foot. You will always be the most successful, and you will always be the money-earner; and in the end I'm afraid it will turn sour on you. He is at the moment leading a pleasantly happy, amiable sort of life which suits him, and if you drag him off the beach which he loves I believe one day you will regret it, because, given the chance, he will fly right back to it.'

In October 1961 Juliet married Russell. We gave her the white wedding she wanted at Cowden Church, across the fields from Sussex House Farm. There were two ceremonies: the vicar, on discovering that the bridegroom had never been christened, arranged to put that right first. The service was arranged on the day before the wedding. I excused myself. I explained to Bunch that when the vicar picked Russell up he would undoubtedly give himself a hernia and I should have a fit, so it would be safer for everyone if I stayed at the farm.

The day was beautiful. Juliet looked adorable; Russell looked handsome, if slightly bewildered. The reception was held in the big cowshed, which was a mass of flowers; they almost, but not quite, conquered the aroma of the Guernsey herd. The best man was Brian Bedford, Juliet's great friend.

The bride and bridegroom left for a honeymoon in Paris, a present from the bride's parents. Forty-eight hours later the phone rang. It was Juliet. Could I possibly send them some money; Russell had taken her to the races at Longchamps and they had lost the lot. Five years later they were divorced. Russell was back on the beach.

Mary and I were in Atlantic City last year on business. I talked to our ex-son-in-law on the telephone. He sounded contented and happy. It had, as I sensed at the beginning of it all, just not been his scene.

In the summer of 1961 I received an offer to play Ross in Terence Rattigan's play of the same name about Lawrence of Arabia, in New York the following December. The prospect frightened me to death. I hadn't been on the stage for eight years – far too long a gap. Also, I had never acted in New York. Mary was convinced that I should do it, but I shied away from it and couldn't make up my mind. It was Larry Olivier who finally persuaded me to take the plunge. We were spending a short holiday together at Cap Estelle in the South of France.

One morning, after the second bottle of ice-cold Blanc de Blancs, I was moaning on about the terror of opening cold in New York – David Merrick, the producer, considered the production too expensive to try out on the road. 'I'll never give any sort of performance on the first night. I'll be too paralysed by nerves. It's different for you, Larry, you're always at it, but I haven't set foot on a stage for eight years. I'm going to cable Merrick; life's too short; I'm going to turn it down.'

'You're not, you know,' said Larry. 'Now listen to me: if you don't do *Ross* you'll never do another play, and that would be a bloody awful waste of a damn fine actor; and you're wrong, it's not different for me at all, I still feel panic-stricken before a first night, but I've learned how to control it, and I'll tell you how to do it. Fifteen minutes before the curtain goes up, walk on to the stage and address the audience from behind the iron curtain: "Tonight I'm going to walk on to this stage and own it, and you are going to have the privilege and pleasure of watching a great actor at work. I've given some miraculous performances in the past, but tonight I shall excel them all. You'll be riveted by everything I do. You'll find it impossible to take your eyes off me from the moment I set foot on the stage until the final curtain."'

On Boxing Day, 26 December 1961, I found myself sitting in my dressing-room at the Eugene O'Neill Theater waiting for the curtain to rise on the first night of *Ross* in New York. I had never prepared myself more thoroughly for any part. I read everything Lawrence had written himself, including *The Seven Pillars of Wisdom*, and everything that had been written about him. The more I delved into his character the more intrigued and totally involved I became. Knowing that he neither smoked nor drank I gave up both these wicked vices for four months. The first was easy, the second, with the tensions building up, I found much more difficult. Glen Byam Shaw, who directed Alec Guiness in the play in London, was a joy to work with. He approached the play from a different angle, making it, by slightly cutting some of the rather over-long soliloquies, more physically exciting. He was an enormous help to me. He worked hard on my voice which, after years away from the theatre, needed tuning up.

The call-boy knocked on the door. 'Fifteen minutes, Mr Mills please.' I rose to my feet and looked in the mirror. A young man with blond hair dressed in airman's uniform stared back at me. 'Well, at least you look right,' I thought. I left the room, walked on to the empty stage, and delivered the Laurence Olivier build-up in a loud and clear voice to the iron curtain. Larry had been right. I suddenly felt calm, confident and ready for the greatest challenge of my theatrical career.

The feeling persisted, and I was still in that mood ten minutes later waiting in the wings for my first entrance. The cue came. I marched on to the stage feeling terrific. Then it happened: something that I had simply not taken into account. The American audience, who had never before seen me in person, decided to give me a warm welcome – a thunderous round of applause broke out and continued for at least fifteen seconds, during which time my carefully built-up façade of invincibility slowly disintegrated; my knees started to tremble under my service trousers, my mouth went dry and my throat closed up. Finally, when the applause died away, I opened my mouth and spoke my first line in a voice that sounded like a high-pitched, strangulated Mickey Mouse. After that first short scene I recovered, and what followed turned out to be one of the most exciting nights in the theatre I can ever remember. The American audience gave us a reception at the end of the play that I shall never forget. The cast all gave excellent performances, especially Geoffrey Keen, who had been in the London production, and a very good English actor, John Williams, who had made a successful career in America in the last ten years.

We celebrated at Sardi's after the show. Mary, Hayley and Jonathan had flown over for the opening and Christmas. (Jonathan will never forget that particular Christmas lunch: during a break in the dress rehearsal we were guests of Jack Dempsey at his restaurant on Broadway.) Also in the party was Terry Rattigan, Glen Byam Shaw, Helen Hayes and Laurie and Mary Evans. We all agreed there seemed to be no doubt about it – we had a smash hit on our hands. My diary tells the story of *Ross* more factually and concisely than I feel I could re-write it.

27 Dec – After twenty weeks on wagon, hung over. Worth it. Fantastic press. Best I've ever had. One exception – Kerr, *Tribune* (most important), rather critical of play, still gave it three columns. Before matinee (great after first night, *je ne pense pas*) Terry arrived distraught. Merrick, because of Kerr's notice, talking of closing Saturday. Unbelievable. He has to be out of his mind. He asked Terry to give up all royalties. Sent a message via Terry to me stating if I don't take cut in salary may close play. Told Terry to inform Merrick to get stuffed. Quite happy, dislike long runs anyway. Happy to sail home with family in *Elizabeth* on 14th.

28 Dec – Silence from D.M.

30 Dec – Show still on. Two very good houses indeed. Tremendous reception. No publicity of any kind for show. Not even quotes (and they were great) outside theatre.

31 Dec – Sunday press terrific. D.M. must be wrong.

1 Jan – Two shows. Business fair.

2 Jan – Business up.

3 Jan – Really good house.

4 Jan – D.M. finally advertises in press. New York may discover we're on.

6 Jan – Mat. and eve. shows both packed. Looks like we've won.

We settled down to a very happy run. The play was not the smash hit we'd hoped for, but it did well enough to survive a transfer from the Eugene O'Neill Theater which I loved to the Hudson Theater which I hated. Back-stage was a replica of Sing-Sing, with minute dressing-rooms in a row like cells. Mary flew home with the children on the fourteenth. I enjoyed that winter in New York; the climate was invigorating, rather like Switzerland: crisp, clear, cold days with blue skies. Americans are generous hosts, and as there were many friends in town parties were thrown for us every week. There was quite a big English contingent – Paul Scofield, Robert Shaw, Terry Rattigan, Donald Pleasance, Googie Withers and Michael Redgrave. Mary arrived back in February. We stayed at the Algonquin, the haunt of writers and actors for many years. We loved this hotel, possibly because it seemed very English, rather like the Connaught in London. The head waiter, Bob, was English and a keen Chelsea football fan.

During the last three years I had become increasingly worried on two counts. Although we loved the farm, I found it was slowly but surely starting to take over my life. Having increased to nearly five hundred acres, it had become an enormous responsibility, and I realized that I was actually turning down films if they entailed long foreign locations. All our capital was tied up in the project. There's an old saying in the country, 'Unless you're prepared to be a stick-and-dog farmer, keeping an eye on things, you'll never make money.' Farming needs a higher capital investment and shows a smaller return than any other business I know of.

The other thing that worried me was the fact that I could not, however hard I tried, get The Wick out of my mind. I missed it more and more every year and frequently dreamed that we were back living there. If I had to drive to Shepperton Studios, rather than pass The Wick I would make a detour that would add miles to the journey. The Bowmans, who had bought it from us, had invited us repeatedly to visit them, but I couldn't bear the thought of seeing the house again.

In the spring of 1963, yet another invitation from the Bowmans arrived. Mary said that not only was I being a bore about it all but that if I didn't have the courage to go back and lay the ghost I would never have any peace of mind. We accepted. Paul and Gaby Bowman were charming. We toured the house and garden. The ghost not only refused to be laid (if you know what I mean) but took me by the throat and nearly choked me. By the time we were having drinks in the study I was in the most ridiculous mood of depression and despair – this was *our* house; I had been a short-sighted, mean-minded idiot even to have thought of selling it. 'It really is a divine house, isn't it?' said Gaby.

I looked at Mary. She knew how I was suffering. 'Yes it is,' I said. 'It's the most beautiful house I've ever seen. You must love living in it.'

'We do,' said Gaby, 'but the awful thing is, we've got to sell it. We have to move back into London.' The situation was too amazing to be coincidental. They had only decided that morning to put the house on the market.

Three months later we moved back into The Wick. I was of course totally insane. It cost me four times the price I originally paid for it; I had not received a single offer for the farm or the flat in town; I had an overdraft of £50,000, and I couldn't have been happier. We faced financial ruin for a considerable time. Just before Christmas the ball dropped into the right number. We sold both properties, and by another stroke of luck, the whole family managed to be home for the holidays, so we spent a united Christmas in our beloved old house on the top of Richmond Hill.

During the next few years I worked solidly in films. This was a very happy period of our lives. It was an enormous relief to be living in one home again, and in such wonderful circumstances. We engaged a lovely Italian couple, Pio and Gina, who became part of the family and were with us for over twelve years. My work took me across the world again – to Tahiti, for *Tiara Tahiti* with James Mason, produced by my old friend Ivan Foxwell. It was the first time I had worked with Jimmy Mason. Apart from being a splendid actor, I found him a shy, charming but rather sad man, who I felt would have been happier if he had resisted the call of Hollywood, which he apparently didn't much like, and stayed in these shores. He lives in Switzerland, and I'm sure must be more than financially secure, but every time I meet him I feel more certain that before long he will come back home and live where he really belongs.

After Tahiti which, although it was beautiful, in my estimation couldn't compare with Tobago, it was back to Shepperton for *The Chalk Garden*, directed by Ronnie Neame with two talented actresses of slightly different ages – Dame Edith Evans and Hayley Mills. Then off to Hollywood for *King Rat* with George Segal and James Fox. *King Rat* was brilliantly directed by Bryan Forbes; I thought it one of the best things he'd ever done, and I shall never understand to this day why the picture didn't make a fortune at the box office. Bryan had the usual problems to cope with. The producers built a fantastic replica of Changi prison camp on a site twenty miles outside Hollywood. They forgot one small thing – the relentless Californian sun. After a few weeks' shooting, to their great concern they discovered the green countryside was being toasted a dark shade of brown. When we arrived on location one morning we found six helicopters spraying the whole vast area with green paint.

Before the end of 1964, Hayley and I had made *The Truth About Spring*, a comedy shot all on location at a beautiful little place called Sagaro in southern Spain, with our old chum Lionel Jeffries and James McArthur in the cast. If the picture had turned out to be half as good as the food, the wine, the time and the laughs we had on that location, it would have been a sensation – unfortunately it wasn't.

During the previous twelve months Mary had been writing a story called *Bats with Baby Faces*. We both felt that it would make an excellent film, with a marvellous part in it for Hayley. I took it to John Davis at the Rank Organization; he liked it, agreed to do it, and also, to my delight, entrusted me with the direction. I knew that I was sticking my neck out. The set-up on paper seemed to invite criticism: story by Mary Hayley Bell, starring Hayley Mills (plus Hamlet Mills, our cocker spaniel), directed by John Mills. I read the odds, but I was desperately anxious for Mary's sake to make another success for her after failing with our last two ventures in the theatre. If one plan hadn't gone wrong at the beginning of the exercise I think I might have made it.

The story concerned children; it was emotional and at times verged on the sentimental. For this reason I was determined to get a writer or writers on the script who were up-to-date, modern, down-to-earth and tough. Keith Waterhouse and Willis Hall, who had written such a great script from Mary's last marvellous story *Whistle Down the Wind*, would be perfect. They read it, liked it, but were too tied up on another script to take it on. With hindsight I realize I made a mistake: I allowed myself to get locked in to studio space on a specific date, which meant that I had a restricted time for preparation. I tried several other script-writers with no success. Time was running out. I finally engaged an excellent writer, John Prebble who, after he delivered the first draft, I knew was not right for the film. By this time the production ball was rolling too fast downhill to stop. The result was that I started shooting with a script that I was not entirely happy about, which anyone who has any knowledge of the film business will know to be a worrying and unsatisfactory state of affairs.

I had a wonderful team with me – Jack Hanbury, producer, Carmen Dillon, designer, Arthur Ibbetson, cameraman, and a hand-picked crew, every one of whom I had worked with many times over the past twenty years. We toured England and Wales searching for exactly the right village with all the necessary qualifications – church, churchyard, village green, pub and cottages clustered together that I could frame in one long shot. We finally found it – Badminton. It was perfect, except for one thing – the church had no tower. So we built one out of steel scaffolding and fibreglass.

The Duke of Beaufort was marvellous. He gave us the run of the place and took a personal interest in the making of the film. The cast included Annette Crosbie, Ian McShane and Laurence Naismith, all of whom gave excellent performances. Hayley was superb and a joy to direct. The only member of the cast I had any problem with at all was Hamlet. Our spaniel had the reputation of being the best pee-er in the business; no tree, lamp-post or gatepost in the Richmond area was left unchristened. As soon as he knew the camera was turning on him, however, he dried up. I needed a very important shot: Hamlet was supposed to show his disapproval of a preceding scene by peeing on the churchyard gate as he made his exit with Hayley. Just to make sure he would be in the right mood and well primed for his performance I kept him in my caravan for a couple of hours before the shot with a large bowl of water; and to make absolutely sure, we primed the gatepost as well. On action Hamlet, as ordered, trotted along beside Hayley through the churchyard; he approached the gatepost, glanced at it disdainfully, and passed it by. He then proceeded to pee on the camera legs, the sound truck, the catering wagon and the make-up table. I tried for an hour to get the shot, but Hamlet just wouldn't come through. A month later, back in the studios, I got the props to erect a gate in the studio grounds. Hamlet made it in Take One. In fact, if the gate hadn't been very firmly built, he would have flattened it.

Although *Sky West* didn't succeed in breaking any box-office records we shall never regret making it. The whole unit was terrific – no strikes, no problems, everybody mucked in. Union rules about who did what job and when were brushed under the table. Before the picture started I asked the production department to see that every member of the crew, including the sparks and the chippies, were given scripts. The result was they all felt they were part of it and became personally concerned with making the picture. At the end of shooting the crew presented me with a super movie-editing machine; the inscription on it read: '*Bats with Baby Faces* re-christened *Sky West and Crooked*: 1965. To Johnnie, with thanks for a very happy picture.'

After spending a considerable time on *Sky West* with no great financial reward I was grateful when Bryan Forbes offered me a part in *The Wrong Box*, a wild, farcical comedy he was about to adapt from the story by Robert Louis Stevenson, and I was particularly pleased to hear that all my scenes would be played with that remarkable and brilliant actor Sir Ralph Richardson. I had known and been a friend of the great man for years but had never had the chance of acting with him. I enjoyed every minute of it. I found Ralph to be one of the easiest and most generous actors I have ever worked with.

In January 1966 Mary and I celebrated our Silver Wedding. Looking back, however, over the past four years I was forced to admit that my career as an actor in films at least had not been nearly so successful. I had, I'm glad to say, for my sake and the Inland Revenue's, been working steadily, but the last really great part that had come my way was Colonel Barrow in *Tunes of Glory*, and I was hungry for something good to get my teeth into. Then out of the blue came a phone call which not only provided me with the part I was looking for but also had a profound effect on our lives.

The Boulting brothers, Roy and John, known in the business as 'the terrible twins', were a brilliant film-making team. I admired their work enormously. They were responsible for some of the finest films that had ever been turned out of British studios. Their satirical comedies based on serious subjects are now rightly considered as classics. I had never had the chance to work with either of them. When, therefore, Roy offered me the part of Ezra in *All in Good Time* (the title was later changed to

The Family Way, which incidentally I thought was rather cheap and not good enough for the picture), I jumped at it. I'd seen Bernard Miles play it at the Mermaid Theatre and I knew that it was right up my street. The other plus, as far as I was concerned, was the fact that the Boulting twins offered Hayley a part in the picture, which was exactly what she needed at that time to help her step out of the 'little girl' image.

During the first half-hour on the set of the first morning's shooting I knew that I was going to enjoy myself. Roy was not only a superb technician but, because he was pro- and not anti-actor, his direction was helpful and sensitive. We all felt perfectly safe in his hands, and I personally owe a great deal to him for the final success of Ezra and indeed the whole film. Hayley was excellent and so were the entire cast, from Hywel Bennett, Marjorie Rhodes, Avril Angers down to the smallest part. *The Family Way* emerged as one of the Boulting brothers' best films. The press were unanimous in their praise, including Bosley Crowther, the famous and sometimes dreaded critic of the *New York Times*.

During this period Jonathan left Millfield School. He had up to this time showed no inclination to join our profession; I was more than surprised, therefore, when he told me that he had obtained a job as a 'runner' – tea-boy and fourth assistant in a small-budget film at Pinewood Studios. I had booked him into a finishing school in Switzerland because I felt sure that with the jet age shrinking the world into a small ball, languages were going to be a passport to almost any interesting job that he might choose to embark on. My son was persistent and came up with an argument I found difficult to knock down. 'You, Dad,' he said, 'chucked up the job that your family had arranged for you, and started at the bottom in the chorus. Well I want to do the same, because, like you, I know what I want and I'm determined to do it. In a few years I'm going to be the best director in England, and by that time you will probably need a job, so you'd better keep in my good books and not waste all your money sending me to Switzerland where after two years I should be skiing like a bird and speaking lousy French and German.' I was finally persuaded, and cancelled the school in Switzerland – thereby making a very big mistake.

In the summer of 1967, just when the future was looking financially fairly secure, the blow fell. The Inland Revenue decided that the golden handshake I received when my Rank contract was cancelled was taxable at the full rate. On advice from my solicitor I fought the case, lost it, and was landed with an enormous amount of tax to pay, plus costs. I needed some money and I needed it quickly. An offer arrived which, under the circumstances, I was forced, after hours of agonizing indecision, to accept. The deal was to make a pilot film in Hollywood for *Film Ways*.

If the pilot was accepted, CBS guaranteed to put up the capital for a series of thirteen one-hour TV programmes. That alone would not have been too bad; the salary was large and would have got me out of trouble. The contract, however, contained a clause that scared us to death: they would make no deal unless I signed for five years in the event that CBS picked up the option. This could only mean one thing: with the fortune I would have earned we would be forced to do something we had all sworn we would never do, i.e., leave the country and be domiciled for at least five years in America.

We tried to talk ourselves into believing that it was not only the necessary but the right thing to do – I was fifty-nine years old; wasn't it about time I made sure of providing us with the wherewithal for a luxury retirement? Like all actors in successful, long-running TV shows I would buy an island, a yacht, a chalet in Klosters, and while I was working we would live in a fantastic house in Beverly Hills with 'his' and 'hers' convertible Rolls Royces to transport us to our retreat in Palm Springs. After the contract was finished I would graciously return home to England in triumph as an enormous, international, respected and much-loved super-star.

The press got hold of the story and exaggerated it slightly by assuming that the option would be picked up. They stated categorically that we were leaving the country, following the golden trail to them tha' hills that several other English actors had already taken. Mary was attacked by the local tradesmen in every shop she visited in Richmond. 'We can't believe it', 'We never thought *he* would want to go', 'What's the idea? Don't you like England any more?' We were surprised at their genuine concern. We were flattered, but shattered. I rang Alec McFarlane, our bank manager at Lloyds Bank, who had looked after our fluctuating finances since my army days. I put him in the picture. After a considerable pause a Scottish voice sang over the phone, 'We don't want to lose you, but we think you ought to go.' That did it. The die was cast.

One other thing made the decision even more harrowing. I had been working for weeks on a film script of *Oh! What a Lovely War* with Len Deighton. It was one of the most exciting projects I had ever been connected with. My intention was, if and when we could arrange the finance, to direct the picture, with Len and his partner Brian Duffy as producers. Accepting the series meant losing the chance of directing again, which I was longing to do.

Sitting in the study at The Wick one evening before we left for Hollywood I had a sudden brainwave. I remembered that Dickie Attenborough had once said to me that he'd enjoyed producing but was determined if he could find the right subject to try his luck as a director. Ten minutes later (he lived on Richmond Green, a stone's throw from The Wick) the script was in his hands. The phone rang at eight the next morning. It was Dickie: 'It's absolutely fantastic, Johnnie.' He sounded excited. 'I've got one or two ideas, but I really think it's terrific. What are you going to do about it?'

'Nothing,' I said. 'I can't. It's yours if you want it. I'm out, as I told you. I'm off to Horrorwood.'

Dickie made a sensational debut. His direction was nothing short of brilliant. He handled an incredibly difficult subject with a sure touch and impeccable taste. Having been associated with him as a producer I was not surprised at the marvellous way he treated the actors; even the ones playing the smallest parts were made to feel vitally important to the picture. He had, of course, because he is held in such high esteem by his profession, been able to assemble a fairly experienced and reasonably well-known little cast – Sir Laurence Olivier, Sir Ralph Richardson, Sir John Gielgud, Sir John Clements, Sir Michael Redgrave, Jack Hawkins, Kenneth More, Dirk Bogarde, Vanessa Redgrave, Maggie Smith and yours truly. No distributor could complain about that little collection on the front of a marquee.

The critics fell over themselves to praise the picture. Reading the notices again it is hard to find a superlative they didn't use. Dickie's personal press was incredible. One famous critic wrote: '*Oh! What a Lovely War* is worth a million peace demonstrations. It kicks the hell out of jingoism and makes Attenborough one of the great directors of cinema art.' Another critic, Alexander Walker, said, 'Attenborough has used his ear as well as his eye and made one of the most moving and memorable films I've ever seen.' They were all on the same lines. When one day, which I hope will be in the far-distant future, I shall reluctantly have to accept the fact that my acting days are over, I shall look back and remember with enormous pleasure the fact that I was instrumental in providing my great friend Dickie Attenborough with an opportunity that he so richly deserved.

23

Oh What a Lovely Oscar

I find that the older I get the faster time seems to fly. It is, I suppose, because I am happy and working as hard as ever – not that I could afford to stop even if I wanted to. The American saga seemed to be over in a flash. The pilot was a success, and CBS bought the series. On 17 May 1967 we sailed on the *Queen Elizabeth*, and commenced filming on location at Flagstaff, Arizona, having travelled through the Grand Canyon, Scotsdale, Tuscan; then on to the CBS studios for the interiors. The American crew were wonderful; I was treated like royalty. I happened to mention that I preferred tea instead of their eternal coffee in the afternoon, and at 4 p.m. in the middle of the Arizona Desert in a temperature of 108°F the property master arrived with a table napkin over his arm carrying a tea-tray on which was a silver tea-service, a plate of cucumber sandwiches, scones and honey. This routine continued until I'd finished the series.

After five of the one-hour films were completed the feeling was that the series was going to be a hit, and it was at this time that Mary and I decided that if it did succeed and CBS picked up the options, thereby forcing us to leave England, we would in all probability cut our throats. Then the unexpected happened: our brilliant writer-producer had a disagreement with CBS and walked off the series, with the result that the remaining eight episodes deteriorated slowly but surely into very inferior hours of entertainment. We finished shooting at the end of September. CBS were supposed to let my agent know if they intended to pick up the option within three weeks. We stayed on at Beverly Hills waiting for the result. CBS shut up like a clam; nobody at the studio would talk.

We decided to take off for Jamaica; we had been invited by Noël to use his guest-house. Two days after our arrival I had a cable from Laurie Evans in London, telling me that an article in the *Daily Mail* announced that CBS were not continuing the series *Dundee and the Culhane*. That was the first we heard of it – not perhaps the most courteous way for a major company to inform their star.

Our reaction to the news, I am sure, would have surprised them. When it finally sank in that we were free and could kiss goodbye to the island, the yacht, the chalet in Klosters, the luxurious house in Beverly Hills, the retreat in Palm Springs, the 'his' and 'hers' convertible Rolls Royces and return to our clapped out old Mini and antique Bentley sitting waiting for us at The Wick on Richmond Hill, we drove into Jamaica and celebrated with the most wonderful dinner we've ever had in our lives. The champagne was nectar, the fresh lobster was unbelievable. We drove home along the coast in a haze of delight; surely no failure had ever tasted so sweet. As we entered the house the phone rang, 'Mr Mills, Mr Sinatra on the phone for you.' We had dined with Frank and Mia Farrow several times in Beverly Hills. Frank had gone out of his way to make us feel at home, and we had become close friends. 'Johnnie, it's Frank. Just checking. Everything OK? Heard anything from CBS yet?'

'Yes I have, Frank. It's off. I just heard from my agent in London.'

There was a pause. 'You mean to tell me CBS didn't contact you before you left?'

'No Frank, but what the hell? I couldn't care less.'

'Well, I do.' His voice had a different note. 'I'm not going to let those s.o.b.s get away with it, treating you like this. You're a friend of mine – I'm going to take care of them.'

He said it quietly, and it scared the hell out of me. 'No Frank, honestly, I don't mind. We really are happy about it. I'm sure it was just an oversight.'

It took me ten minutes pleading with my chum to do nothing about it. Finally he agreed. 'OK Johnnie, but I still don't like it. Don't forget that if there's anything you want, call me.'

That little incident proves what I said earlier in this book about Sinatra. If he's a friend of yours, you're lucky, because he is a real one.

During the series I had frequent calls from Dickie Attenborough; he wanted to know if I would be free to play Haig in *Oh! What a Lovely War*. 'At least you've got to be in it,' he said. The last time he called, he'd said he daren't wait for more than another few weeks – he just had to cast it. Before we caught the plane for home the next morning, I called him: 'Dickie,' I said, 'this is Field Marshal Haig speaking from Jamaica. Is it too late to join your war?'

There was a gasp from the other end of the phone. 'Johnnie, good God yes. When can you get here?'

'In twelve hours' time, DV,' I said. 'We're getting on the plane now.'

Always hopeful that I would be able to play Haig, Dickie had sent pictures of the Field Marshal to me in Hollywood. I spent most of the flight home working out the make-up in my mind and decided that an addition to my nose was essential; mine was neither aristocratic nor important enough. It was in this thoughtful mood that I approached the barrier at London Airport with Mary to find Hayley waving excitedly at us. I looked at my watch – 7.15 a.m. My daughter, unless she was filming, did not as a rule compete with the birds in the early rising stakes. There must be a reason for this show of filial affection, I thought. We received the usual warm, loving welcome. 'Darlings, could we have some breakfast? I'm starving and I'm dying to talk to you,' she said.

The three of us sat perched like birds on high stools at the quick service counter. I was tucking into my scrambled eggs and bacon when Hayley suddenly said, 'Darlings, I've got some news for you. Look!' She pointed to a large and beautiful ring on her engagement finger.

Mary and I looked at each other. 'Well, it's lovely, darling,' I said, 'where did you get it?'

'From Roy – I'm in love with him.'

To give myself time to think I leaned forward to get a closer look at the ring. The stool tilted, my elbow nudged the plate and the next second I found myself flat on my back with egg all over my face – an unintentional but fortunate piece of comedy relief at exactly the right moment. The laugh broke the tension, and by the time they'd cleaned me up I was slightly prepared for the next piece of dialogue, which I had a feeling would not exactly trip off my tongue. 'Well Daddy, what do you think about it?'

I glanced at my daughter, who was looking radiantly happy, if somewhat anxious. 'Darling, it depends. I mean, are you very serious about it? Are you going to get married?'

'Well, not right away. But one day, I hope Daddy, yes.'

Shades of the conversation with Juliet passed through my mind. I took the plunge. 'All right, my darling, if you really want to know what I think, I'll tell you. If you're thinking in terms of a long, no-option contract I'm afraid I don't think it a good idea. I like Roy and admire him. He's erudite, educated, intelligent, and a brilliant director, but he's almost my age. The generation gap isn't important now, but later on it will be. When you are forty, a marvellous age for a woman, Roy will be seventy-three, and at that age any man, whoever he is, must be considered slightly over the hill. And another thing . . . all his friends will be his age, or thereabouts, and that's another minus. The great danger, however, as I see it, is that sooner or later there's a chance you may fall in love with a man more or less your own age, in which case you would find yourself landed with a ghastly situation which could only cause a great deal of distress and heartache for everyone concerned.'

I paused for breath, and looked at Hayley. She had tears in her eyes. I put my arms round her. 'Listen, my darling, I've always been honest with you, and this is only what I think. I could be totally and utterly wrong, and I hope I am. If, after thinking about what I've said, you're sure you're doing the right thing, go ahead and do it, and Mummy and I will accept it, go right along with it, and do everything we can to make Roy feel part of the family.'

'Thank you Daddy darling, but I know now what I want. I'm sure this time you're wrong, and everything's going to be wonderful.'

Hayley and Roy Boulting were married in the south of France – a secret wedding with the grocer and the local mayor as witnesses. We were not invited. Roy, who can never be accused of not being outspoken, told us that he would prefer it if there was no publicity. We were quite naturally hurt and upset. For the first time a thin, but slightly dangerous wedge had been driven into our very close and loving family.

Eventually my vision in the crystal ball at London Airport materialized: Hayley fell in love with a young, attractive, talented actor called Leigh Lawson when they were appearing together in a play in the West End, and after the heartache and distress that I had so gloomily forecast, Roy and Hayley were divorced.

I have perhaps too many times in this book mentioned how important a part luck plays in an actor's life. This fact was once again brought home to me by a chance meeting in Rome in 1968. I had been shooting a film there for several weeks, an all-Italian production. My co-star was that lovely Italian actress Luciana Paluzzi. She spoke fluent English, but the rest of the cast spoke a sort of gibberish, which was totally incomprehensible. I watched their lips and, when they stopped moving, I said my line. Somehow or other, and I don't know how, it worked.

My agent in Rome called me one evening to tell me that David Lean was in town working on a script for a new film with Robert Bolt. I hadn't seen David since he left England all those years ago, and now, after *Bridge on the River Kwai* and *Doctor Zhivago*, he had become one of the world's top directors. I rang him. He sounded just the same and seemed delighted I'd called.

We had dinner that evening. There were four of us – David and Sandy, his very attractive girl-friend, Mary and myself. It was a marvellous reunion. We talked of the old films we'd made together: *In Which We Serve*, *Great Expectations*, *Hobson's Choice* and *This Happy Breed*. Suddenly Mary, who never misses a chance (she's always been much quicker than I to sense an opportunity) said: 'David, you and Johnnie haven't worked together for years. Surely there must be something in the picture he can play?'

'I'd love to have Nob in the picture, Mary, but I can't think of anything that he would be right for, or want to play.'

'Oh well, never mind,' said my wife, 'it was just a thought.'

A few days later David rang and said, 'Nob, can you come over to the hotel? There's something I want to talk to you about.' I walked into a suite at the Hotel Principe. Through the thick cloud of smoke I could just discern David in earnest conversation with Robert Bolt. 'Hallo Nob, come in. Bob and I have been talking. Would you like to play Michael? He's a village idiot who is deformed and can't speak.'

'Yes,' I said. 'It's perfect casting. When do I start?'

Not many months later, on 5 March 1969, I found myself in front of the camera in southern Ireland about to shoot the first take of *Ryan's Daughter* with my old friend David Lean once again directing me. I looked right, and felt right, because it had taken me three months of study and work to prepare for that moment. I had watched hours of film showing patients with brain damage to the left side of their heads. From them I'd built up a composite picture – Michael. The walk, the posture, the angle of the head were all as real as I could make them.

I worked on the make-up for two months with a man who was a master of his craft, Charles Parker. Charlie was as thrilled as I was at the challenge. We wanted to get the maximum effect with a minimum amount of actual make-up. We worked by a process of elimination. We started with everything and ended up with practically nothing – a small, upturned tip on the end of my nose, horrific uneven teeth which he made to clamp on to my own, with a slight bulge in the top set to distort my face, and a small piece of plastic behind one ear to push it forward. He then gave me what was undoubtedly the worst hair-cut that has ever been seen. He shaved the back of my head and allowed long pieces of hair to fall over the bald patches. The whole make-up was so simple I was only in the make-up chair for fifteen minutes every morning, and the result, as I hope you will agree if you have seen the film, was staggering. I was totally unrecognizable. David was in on the final stages and announced himself delighted. I found out later that MGM had at first refused to accept me as Michael. They considered it ridiculous casting, but David, being David, insisted and won the day.

Ryan's Daughter took over a year to make; it was so full of incident and drama that I could write a whole book about it. The location was staggeringly beautiful. We were based in the little fishing village of Dingle in County Kerry on the west coast, with the Blasket Islands in the distance. Miles of glorious beaches could be reached within minutes in any direction. The Irish weather was as always unpredictable. This not only proved to be the biggest problem but also nearly cut me off in my prime during the first two weeks of the schedule.

We were shooting a scene in Coumeenoole Cove which had the reputation locally of being a highly dangerous area of water, known for its off-shore currents that flowed between the mainland and the great Blasket Islands. The action started with a long shot of myself as Michael and Trevor Howard as the village priest in a small rowing-boat called a cur-ragh (these have been used for generations by Irish fishermen; they are made of canvas, tarred, and stretched over wooden struts, and have no keel). A curragh is very light in weight and extremely difficult to handle, and although I am no slouch with the oars it took me two weeks of prac-tice before the film started to be able to handle the boat efficiently. David wanted me to start way out beyond the surf then catch a wave and come in on it up the beach.

The morning was fine and clear, but there was an ominous feeling of impending storm in the air. I took the curragh out and did a couple of dummy runs – no problem. I caught the waves at the right moment and fairly flew up the beach. 'Right,' said David, 'we're ready to go. Where's Trevor? Go and dig him out, and hurry, the wind's getting up.'

He was right, it was. And what's more it was getting up fast. I didn't like the look of it. By the time Trevor (who by some oversight hadn't been called) arrived on the beach the waves were quite high and the wind was increasing in velocity every minute. David was livid. 'All right, get in the bloody boat. We'll just make it.'

We had six men in frogmen's suits in the water with ropes round their waists. With Trevor in the stern and myself at the oars they swam, push-ing us out, until we were past the point where the waves were breaking. On an impulse of, I suppose, self-preservation I unhooked my ghastly teeth and put them in my jacket pocket. The camera, I thought, would be too far away for it to matter anyway.

David waved a flag for action; we couldn't have heard a shout even through a megaphone. I straightened the curragh up. A big swell came up behind us, I rowed like mad and caught the crest of the wave. For a second or two everything went splendidly; we were surfing as straight as an arrow for the beach. Suddenly, with no warning, the wind shifted. I caught sight of an enormous wave coming towards me on my left. I pulled hard on my right oar to try and face it, but it came at us too fast and hit us with a crash; the curragh went up in the air and turned over. I felt a sharp blow on the back of my neck and blacked out.

The rest of the story I got later from Freddie Clarke, who was watching the action from the beach. Luckily, the frogmen, being in the water, were able to reach us in a few seconds. They saw Trevor first and grabbed him. Then they spotted me floating face-downwards, being sucked rapidly out to sea by the undertow. As I was being carried up the beach still unconscious, Charlie Parker, who had been watching the drama through binoculars which he always carried, was heard to shout in a loud voice, 'Where are my bloody teeth?'

Mary was shopping in Dingle when the news of the drama reached the village. She rushed to the unit office where Jonathan was working as one of the two third assistants. 'Dad's been hurt,' she said. 'Get us out there. I don't care how fast you drive.' That was one of the most attractive orders my son had ever received. He put his foot down and my souped-up Mini took off. After having travelled halfway to the bay, mostly on two wheels, they saw a unit car approaching with a blanketed figure on the back seat.

The x-ray showed no damage. All I had was concussion, and after two days I was back at work, with Charlie's precious teeth once more clamped firmly into place.

I enjoyed making *Ryan's Daughter*, which we started in Ireland and finished in South Africa. Knowing David, I was prepared for a long film. We rented a cottage with a garden and an orchard, and from time to time the family, including the grandchildren, came over to see us. On our free days we fished and played golf. I had never met Robert Mitchum before and enjoyed acting with him. He has, in my opinion, always been a very underestimated actor; I didn't need to work with him to discover just how good he was. He was also one of the most unselfish actors; with the strange half-animal character I was playing, it was sometimes difficult to hit crucial marks, and on one particular occasion, during the wild scene outside the public house on Rose's wedding night, when Michael is being pushed and thrown round the circle of revellers, as I landed against Bob's shoulder I felt him unobtrusively turn me round until I was in exactly the right position for the camera to zoom in on a close-up.

Three times a week I went to the local cinema to see the rushes. One evening I was sitting next to David watching my scene with the lobster in the village street. During a pause, while they were changing reels, David suddenly said, 'Johnnie, have you ever won an Oscar?'

'No I haven't. Why?' I asked.

'Nothing . . . I just wondered.' The next reel came on and that was the end of the conversation. A year later I received a cable from the Academy of Motion Picture Arts and Sciences informing me that I had been nominated for an Oscar for my role in *Ryan's Daughter*.

On 15 April 1971, Mary and I were sitting up in bed in Juliet's house in Beverly Hills. Our daughter had just brought us a delicious breakfast of pamplemousse and lime, boiled eggs, her own home-made marmalade and coffee. She switched on the television. Every channel was devoting its entire day to the Academy Award ceremony, which was due to take place that evening. On the programme we were looking at, the chat show host was discussing the chances of all the nominees with one of the local Los Angeles film critics: 'Well Mac, there are some strong contenders this year for the Oscars, especially from England. Glenda Jackson, Mac. What do you reckon her chances are?'

'Great,' replied the critic. 'She's terrific. I think she should grab it. They don't come any better.'

'What about Johnnie Mills? He's nominated, as you know, Mac, for his performance as the village idiot in *Ryan's Daughter.*'

'Too much make-up and on too long,' the critic replied without a second's hesitation. My mouth was full of coffee at the time – I choked and did the nose trick. We laughed hysterically, but our friend Mac's remark was not exactly encouraging.

In February we had been guests at a small dinner party that Oliver Messel had given for Princess Margaret and Tony Snowdon at Oliver's beautiful house in Barbados. We dined in the garden by candlelight. It was a marvellous evening. The Princess was enchanting and Oliver was in top form. He was a brilliant raconteur and mimic, and his stories of the theatre were hilarious. Just before the party broke up Juliet rang from Hollywood with the news that I had been awarded the Golden Globe by the Foreign Press Association for *Ryan's Daughter.* That put the topper on a really super evening.

It is a well-known fact that the recipient of the Golden Globe award becomes a hot tip for the Oscar. Ever since I had heard that I was nominated I had done my best, because I wanted the damn thing so desperately, to persuade myself that I really didn't care, and that I had very little chance. After all, Michael was a relatively small part, without a single line of dialogue. Winning the Golden Globe therefore made the anxiety even more acute. All that day the phone rang continually; reporters, gossip-writers. 'How did I feel?' etc. Several of them told me that the rumours circulating round town made me favourite. The more of this stuff I listened to, the more convinced I was that I really didn't stand a chance.

The atmosphere in the theatre was electric. The one thing about the American Academy Awards that really builds the tension is the fact that no one, not even the President of the Academy, has the slightest idea who the eventual winners will be. I was sitting halfway back in the stalls with Mary on one side of me and Juliet on the other, endeavouring to look cool and totally relaxed; and totally failing. I wanted that well-known golden statue, knowing that at my age it was in all probability my last chance of winning one. After what seemed like an eternity the moment arrived: Maggie Smith, that lovely English actress, held in her hands the envelope that was going to decide my fate. She opened it and smiled broadly. I knew before she made the announcement I'd made it.

'And the award for the best performance by a supporting actor goes to John Mills.'

I should, of course, have remained in my seat looking dazed, amazed and delighted, before making a move. On the contrary, I was on my feet making a bee-line for the stage almost before Maggie had finished speaking. A more eager recipient had probably never been seen before at any Academy Awards.

The next half-hour is hazy. I had considered preparing an acceptance speech, but thought that would be tempting fate. I remember saying something about being speechless in front of the camera for a year in Ireland and being speechless tonight; and then found myself off-stage being ushered into the first of the press interview rooms. After half an hour of questions and holding up the Oscar, which weighs a ton, with my right hand (my left was in a sling – two weeks before I left home, a temporary doorman outside the White Elephant Club, looking over his shoulder for the next tip, slammed the door and chopped off the top of my fourth finger), I found I could hardly get the Oscar above the horizontal, and during the session in the next press room I had to sit down with it on the table beside me. The evening was memorable for several other reasons. Glenda Jackson won the Best Actress award, which Juliet accepted for her; my great friend Freddie Young, that brilliant English cameraman, won his third Oscar for his photography on *Ryan's Daughter*; and finally my old chum Frank Sinatra was presented with a special Oscar for 'humanitarian and charitable work'.

We all celebrated at the ball after the show, and when finally we said 'Good morning' at 4.30 a.m. we all felt that the evening had without doubt been one of the most exciting of our lives.

I could never have accused the 1960s of being dull, and the 1970s had got away to a flying start. August 1971 found me in Morocco playing Kitchener in *Young Winston*, again with Dickie Attenborough directing. It was an exciting location, but the food took its toll on the unit. Tummy trouble was rampant. I don't know how Dickie kept going. I shall always have a picture in my mind of him grimly striding across valleys and up and down mountains followed at a respectable distance by his bearer carrying an umbrella and an elsan.

It seems sensible to let my diary tell the following little drama:

Wednesday 20 Sep – Arrived at Wick. Dinner Hayley, feeling rotten. Jonathan arrives. Informed us getting married Friday. Also informed us he and bride both devotees of young, fat, and as far as I was concerned, totally phoney Guru Maraji – Oh Gawd!
Thursday 30 Sep – Temp. 102°. Mary frantic. No time for arrangements.

Friday 1 Oct – Jonathan and Chrissie Twaites married St Peter's Peter-sham. Both dressed head to foot in white, smothered in beads. Insisted on going. Temp. 104°. Couldn't stop groaning loudly throughout service. Nearly fainted twice. Back to Wick. Passed out. Put to bed. Doctor. Jumbo-sized injection. Vaguely remember saying goodbye to Jonathan who was off to Singapore with Chrissie. Mary ghastly palpitations. Doctor called for.
Saturday 2 Oct – Both ill in bed together. Best family show so far!

Jonathan escaped my, by this time, well-known lecture on his proposed marriage. A few years later in California he was granted a divorce with the custody of our grandson Henry, thereby bringing off a rather unfortunate treble.

Now that the children had left the fold we decided more than reluctantly that the beloved Wick was too expensive to maintain. We bought a large, pleasant flat in Green Street, and after a long search we also bought an attractive Mill House in Oxfordshire. We felt that this combination would prove to be an ideal way for the two of us to live. We couldn't have been more wrong. After a very short time we both simply hated it. After all the years we had spent in the country (Richmond with its park is almost country), London stifled us, and the weekends at the Mill were spent cooking and cleaning. Dailies were unobtainable. It was too remote. I was desperately worried about Mary, who had been seriously ill with double pneumonia, and whose spirits were at an extremely low ebb.

I was luckier. It isn't possible to dwell on one's domestic problems when the curtain goes up, and it went up for me, after nine years in the studios, at the Lyceum Theatre, Edinburgh in a play called *Veterans* written by Charles Wood. To my delight it gave me the opportunity to appear on the same stage with one of our greatest actors, John Gielgud. I'd known Johnny for years and been directed by him, but had never acted with him. The play was intended for the Royal Court but the management decided that we should play Edinburgh, Nottingham and Brighton before the London opening. Charles Wood had written the screenplay of *The Charge of the Light Brigade* starring John Gielgud and Trevor Howard; *Veterans* was concerned with the private lives of the actors and the goings-on off set during the shooting of the film on a foreign location. Johnny played Sir Geoffrey Kendall (obviously himself) and I played Laurence d'Orsay (obviously Trevor Howard). It was, I thought, a hilarious comedy, but full of 'in' jokes, and some scenes which contained language that was definitely not for the ears of Auntie Mabel or the grand-children. Edinburgh received the play in shocked, stony silence. John and I got letters informing us that we should be ashamed of appearing in a play that contained such disgusting language. One letter to me enclosed a ten-shilling note. The sender wrote, 'I enclose this more in sorrow than in anger, to my hero Scott of the Antarctic, who must be very hard up.' Nottingham reacted in more or less the same way. It was the time of the power cuts, and I remember being almost grateful at times when we were blacked out in the middle of the play. 'Hang on,' the management said. 'It's Brighton next week. They're much more sophisticated. Things will be very different there.' Truer words have never been spoken – things *were* different. Halfway through the first act a riot broke out in the theatre. There were shouts of 'Disgusting', 'How dare you?' etc. from all over the house. Johnny G. was on stage at the time, and I was waiting in the wings. His face was a study; he couldn't believe it was happening. I had received 'the bird' before, in cabaret, but for one of our leading, classical, actor-knights it was a first experience, and a hair-raising one.

Mary, who happened to be standing at the back row of the dress circle watching this incredible audience reaction, saw a very large man get up out of his seat, and, in a voice loud enough to drown the rest of the hub-bub, address his fellow customers in the circle: 'I have been coming to this theatre for years, and this is the last time. John Gielgud and John Mills should be ashamed of themselves. There are ladies in this audience, and I've never heard such disgusting, filthy language in all my life; and if you're not leaving, I am.' He then pushed his way through to the end of the row. As he passed Mary on the top of the stairs, purple with rage, she heard him mutter, 'And I paid good money to see them two fuckers.'

We opened at the Royal Court Theatre on 9 March. The evening produced another riot, but to our intense relief a riot of a very different kind. I have never known a comedy capture an audience so completely as *Veterans* did on that first night. At times the laughter became almost hysterical. Johnny G. gave a superb performance with no sign of nerves, and his timing was impeccable. All the cast rose to the occasion – Gordon Jackson, James Bolam, Bill Hoskins, Frank Grimes and Ann Bell were all superb. In a strange way the horrors of the tour seemed to work for us on that evening. Apart from being a sensationally successful first night, it was also for the cast a thanksgiving service of deliverance. Ronald Eyre, who had directed the play quite brilliantly, was seen at prayer during the first enormous laugh which echoed round the theatre soon after the rise of the curtain.

The Royal Court was totally sold out for the run of four weeks, and the management asked the two veterans if they would consider a transfer to the West End. During a very pleasant lunch together the two veterans decided that it would be tempting fate. They might, they thought, walk into the same reception as they had experienced at Brighton. We were having a ball at the Court. Every actor in town had been to see the play, which was absolutely right in the theatre for which it was written.

I spent the rest of that year making a picture in America call *Oklahoma Crude* with that great actor, George C. Scott, and an actress I had always admired, Faye Dunaway. The director was Stanley Kramer, who had made some of the best pictures of the decade. The script I thought excellent; all the signs pointed to a success. For some reason I shall never understand the public decided they didn't like it, and to my great disappointment it failed at the box office, therefore doing nothing to further my career on that side of the Atlantic.

In 1973 I made a series of four one-hour films called *Zoo Gang* from the novel by Paul Gallico. Lew Grade, that small dynamo of energy, sent me the first script, which I liked. At 7.30 a.m. in his office he acted the three remaining scripts for me. He played all the parts – Brian Keith's, Barry Morse's and mine; he was, I thought, particularly good considering that he was not perhaps quite right, physically, as Lilli Palmer who, I was delighted to learn, I would be acting with again.

We were based in Nice, and if the scripts had been half as good as the time we had, the series would have been nothing short of a sensation. Unfortunately the last three didn't come up to Lew's performance. They were in fact pretty dreadful. We did our best with them; we even pulled in Mary to re-write one completely unplayable scene; but even that didn't save the day. And we all felt, even before we'd finished shooting the last episode, that the 'Zoo Gang' had failed, although we had tried, some harder than others – Brian Keith, an excellent actor, seemed completely to lose heart halfway through, and strolled through the scenes looking bewildered and lost. It was at least a joy for me to work with Lilli again; the last close-up we shot together had also been in the south of France, thirty-eight years ago. She was, I thought, looking younger and more attractive than she did in 1935, and even then she was somewhat more than an eyeful. Several times during that early epic I remember wishing I'd been single.

The rest of the year I spent at the Savoy Theatre in a new comedy *The End of the Day* by William Douglas Home, with two old friends in the cast – Michael Denison and Dulcie Gray.

When Bernie Delfont, now Lord Delfont, who started like myself as a hoofer, offered me the part of Jess Oakroyd in a musical version of J.B. Priestley's *Good Companions*, I jumped at it. It was, unbelievably, forty years since I had worn my tap shoes, and I was longing for the chance to put them on again. André Previn wrote the music, Johnny Mercer the lyrics and Ronald Harwood the book. I shall always look back on those 250 performances we played at Her Majesty's Theatre as one of the happiest times I have ever spent in a show. There is a magic back-stage in musicals that one never feels in the legitimate theatre. The atmosphere is terrific, with the cast all opening up their pipes and limbering up; one never feels the tension that builds up before the curtain rises on a straight play. I had some marvellous numbers. After the vocal of 'Ta Luv' I went into four choruses of a complicated tap routine (it nearly killed me during rehearsals, but it was worth it). On the first night it stopped the show. The fact that most of the audience probably had no idea that I had spent eight years in musicals must have had something to do with the really wonderful reception I was given.

Miss Trant was played by a young actress whom I'd admired for years. Her performances in both comedy and drama had always been impeccable. She was that mighty atom, Judi Dench. Judi was as easy to act with as she was to watch, and during the course of the run we became close friends. I hope that one day, even if I have to play her great-great grandfather, I shall have the enormous pleasure of acting with her again. *The Good Companions*, which included Christopher Gable, Marti Webb and Ray C. Davis, was one of the happiest companies I have ever worked with, and we were all sad when after nine months the show closed. Mary gave me a *Good Companions* visitors' book for my birthday, and it is full of interesting signatures. Larry Olivier brought his family to a matinee. Tamsin, aged eight, wrote: 'Dear Uncle Johnny, this is the best show I've *ever* seen – love Tamsin.' Larry read it and said, 'I've obviously been wasting my time messing about with silly little parts like Hamlet and Richard III, haven't I darling boy?' He then wrote, 'And I agree. Love Larry.'

24

Enter Sir John

We had for the past six months been desperately searching for a house near London that we would be able to live in and work from. Our way of life, trying to run two establishments and spending hours in the car every weekend, was becoming too much of a strain. Just when we had almost given up hope, on the front page of the January issue of *Country Life* appeared a colour photograph of one of the most beautiful houses I have ever seen. There were more pictures inside of the back of the house and the garden, plus an orchard which was a mass of blossom and seemed to go on for ever. We looked at the display for a long time without speaking. Finally I said: 'We know that house, don't we? It's at the other end of the village we lived in when we were first married.'

'You're right. It is,' said Mary, 'and it's only half an hour's drive from London. Oh darling, it's divine, but we could never afford it. They're going to ask the earth. I mean, look, the house stands in nearly five acres. But oh wouldn't it be wonderful!'

I looked at my wife, who I knew had never really been happy since leaving her beloved house on the top of Richmond Hill. I thought, 'I'm going to get that house if it bloody kills me!' I rang the agents. They told me the asking price. After a short, but severe black-out I said, 'We would like to see the property.'

We fell madly in love with the house the moment we walked in through the front door. The earliest part was Elizabethan; the front of the house showed William and Mary influence – the roof was faced with the attractive arched curves of that period. It was quite perfect, exactly what we wanted, where we wanted it, and in immaculate condition throughout. We drove through the village, past our little cottage by the stream at the other end where we had lived so happily thirty-five years ago, and then on back to London.

'That is our house, darling,' I said, 'and we are going to live in it.' I rang the agent and made an offer. A few days later, on 7 January to be exact, the offer was accepted. The house we never dreamed we would ever find was ours. Fate was kind. I had taken a huge gamble buying without selling, but I was amazingly lucky. I sold the Mill and the flat in Green Street and was able to conclude the deal without robbing a bank, and we moved into our new home in March. It was full circle: we were back where we had started all those years ago in the village that we loved.

When I started writing this book I wondered how I was ever going to finish it. In my profession there is a line that stems from the old days of variety, which actors still frequently use: 'I wouldn't like to follow *that* act.' Thinking of this line, I knew with absolute certainty that I would, unless I wanted to risk an anti-climax, have to bring the curtain down on the year 1976, because I am sure that whatever is in store for me in the future, nothing could follow *that* act.

The year started off very happily. Duncan Weldon who, with Louis Michaels, runs Triumph Productions, offered me the chance of doing another musical. After the glorious time I had spent in *The Good Companions* I couldn't wait. Time marches on, and in this production of *Great Expectations* I played Joe Gargery, the blacksmith. I suggested to Duncan that perhaps on the stage, with make-up and a wig, I could still play Pip. Duncan agreed, but he suggested, very delicately, that he thought I might possibly still look a little bit . . . too old – not much, maybe . . . thirty-five years or so. (One of my great problems in life has been, I'm convinced, that I don't look a day older than thirty.)

The show was a sell-out on the road. Moira Lister played Miss Haversham and Duncan's wife Janet Mahoney played Biddy. Cyril Ornadel wrote some lovely numbers for me, which I still insist on doing at charity shows whether I'm asked to or not. The book and lyrics were written by Hal Shaffer; *Great Expectations* is a long, complicated story containing three or four plots, and Hal was never able to condense it satisfactorily.

After the provincial tour in England we took the show to Canada, ending up at the gigantic O'Keefe Theatre in Toronto. Cyril Ornadel took over the baton and conducted an orchestra of forty pieces. We played to excellent houses throughout the tour; but after long and earnest discussions Duncan, Cyril, Hal and I decided that the show was not quite up to West End standards. Toronto saw the last performance of *Great Expectations*. Louis Michaels, who had watched the show from the front many times at Guildford, Bath, Richmond and Toronto and had heard the genuine enthusiasm of the audiences, thought we were quite mad not to want to bring the show to town. He was certain we would have a hit, and the theatre is so unpredictable that he could easily have been right; for all we know *Great Expectations* might have turned out to be a triumph and run for years.

One morning in May I was following my usual routine. The Teasmaid, which was the only staff we had then, had made the tea and woken us at 7.30 a.m. Sorting through the morning's mail I noticed an envelope with 'Urgent Personal' typed in the left-hand corner. It was official paid, and the thick black print informed me that it had come from the House of Commons. There was obviously an enclosure: I could feel the paper-clip through the envelope. 'It's an invitation to lunch,' I said to Mary. 'We haven't been to the House for ages. It's probably from Tony Royle' (an old friend of ours from the Richmond days – he had been an MP for that constituency for some years). I opened the envelope and read:

IN CONFIDENCE
Dear Mr Mills,
   I should be grateful to know if you are agreeable for your name to be submitted to The Queen with a recommendation that Her Majesty may be graciously pleased to approve that the honour of knighthood be conferred upon you in the Resignation Honours List.
   If this proposal is acceptable to you, the enclosed form should be completed and sent, by return of post, to the Principal Private Secretary at 10 Downing Street in the envelope provided.
   This should of course be regarded as strictly confidential until publication of the List.
Yours sincerely,
HAROLD WILSON

Mary looked up from reading her mail: 'Bills as usual,' she said. I was sitting staring at her. 'Darling, what's the matter? You've gone as white as a sheet. It's not bad news, is it?'
   'No, it isn't,' I managed in a weak voice. 'Read it.' I gave her the letter.
   'Oh darling, how wonderful. I simply can't believe it.'
   'Neither can I,' I said. 'I am stunned.'
   We read the letter again together. 'Look darling, it says the form must be completed and sent by return of post. You know how long letters sometimes take to get to London – a mule train would be quicker. Get a pen, fill it in now. I'll call Bryan Archer at the garage and he can take it up by car.'
   My acceptance must have broken all speed records. It arrived at 10 Downing Street before the ink was dry on the paper.
   On 28 July 1976 Mary, Juliet and I left home at 8.30 a.m. en route for Buckingham Palace. The investiture was timed for 11.15. Hayley was the reason for our early start; my second daughter has never had the reputation of being punctual, and so on this unique occasion, to safeguard

ourselves, I told her that we would be picking her up at her house, which is only thirty minutes from us, at 9 a.m. This would give us three-quarters of an hour's leeway before leaving for the Palace. To our astonishment, for the first time in her life Hayley was ready and waiting on the doorstep. We arrived in London with over an hour to spare; so to fill in time we went to the Carlton Tower Hotel and consumed a large breakfast of grapefruit, coffee, bacon and eggs. Hayley was happily and hugely pregnant. The baby was due at any minute, and there seemed a distinct possibility that the latest member of the clan might decide to arrive during the investiture.

At 10.30 we joined the slow procession of cars in the Mall. The weather was glorious, but hot – one of the hottest July days on record. The convoy crept along at walking pace. With no air-conditioning in the car the heat was stifling. Juliet looked at Hayley. 'Hayl,' she said, 'either your waters have broken or my feet are sweating!'

Half an hour later found me in one of the large anterooms of the Palace. A tall, impressive major-domo told us that he was going to demonstrate the routine we were expected to follow. I was suddenly seized by an attack of first-night nerves. The major-domo had a very quiet delivery, and I, being a bit deaf, was craning to hear the instructions – 'Walk along, stop in front of Her Majesty, bow, kneel, with right knee on stool, incline your head, hold it steady, unless of course you want to lose an ear, don't hurry, take it easy, stand up, turn right and make your exit to the anteroom; and then join your family in the throne room.' I was repeating these quite simple directions to myself, feeling certain that the only actor in the cast would be the one to ruin the production, when I felt a hard thump on my shoulder, and a voice said, 'Hallo Johnnie, got it all taped?' It was my old chum Group Captain Douglas Bader CBE, DSO, DFC.

'I hope so, Dougie. Have you?'

'No point, old chum. D'you know what happened to me? My phone rang two weeks ago. I was in the bathroom. It was a chap from Buck House, and he said, "Could I ask you a rather personal question?" I didn't know what the hell was coming, but I said, "Sure, go ahead. Shoot." "Well," he said, "it's rather a delicate subject, but I must ask you, I mean, you see, it's . . . well it's a custom, as you know, for the recipient to kneel down on one knee on a stool to be knighted, and we thought we must ask you – I mean I hope you'll excuse this – if you think you can manage it? I do hope you don't mind me asking, but we have to know." "Course I don't mind," I said. "How high is the stool?" "About one and a half feet. And it has a handrail on one side of it." "OK. Hold on a minute, will you?" I said.' Dougie had left the bathroom, and after several minutes returned and picked up the phone: 'Hallo? Buck House? Are you still there? I've tried it – I'm afraid it's no good. I've just fallen on my arse.'

Half an hour later I witnessed a scene that I shall never forget. Dougie Bader of the RAF, one of the great heroes, who lost two legs in the last war and still insisted on flying, stood in front of the Queen; the sword rose high in the air before touching each shoulder. That knighthood will, I am sure, go down in history. Sir Douglas must be the only man not to have knelt before the monarch to receive the accolade.

I was next on the bill. What an act to follow! During the ceremony the Guards band had been playing; Mary had been concerned that their enthusiasm was rather drowning out the voice of the gentleman who was announcing the recipients' names just before they appeared to accept the honour. After Sir Douglas's exit the band stopped playing, and at the precise moment that I made my entrance the pianist on his own started a quiet rendering of 'Oh why was he born so beautiful, why was he born at all?' The timing, as far as my family was concerned, was perfect. I managed to conduct myself throughout the ceremony without letting down my profession. The Queen, after I had risen to my feet, smiled that devastating smile and said something to me which, owing to the fact that the band had decided to re-start their activities at that particular moment, I didn't, with my Dunkirk ear, quite understand. It was hardly the moment to lean forward and say, 'Ma'am, I'm awfully sorry, but I didn't quite catch that.' So I smiled, nodded and murmured, 'Thank you, ma'am,' hoping that her remark didn't call for a shake instead of a nod.

Apart from the pleasure the gong gave me, I was touched by the number of telegrams and letters that I received from friends, acquaintances and complete strangers. They cascaded through the letter-box for twelve hours non-stop. I remember two with particular pleasure; they arrived one after the other. The first one read: ONCE A KNIGHT IS ENOUGH. DEAREST LOVE. HAYLEY, and the second: CONGRATULATIONS SIR JOHN AND THANKS FOR THE EXTRA BUSINESS. THE POSTMASTER. SOUTHALL POST OFFICE.

Later that evening, Mary and I were sitting under the golden catalpa tree in our garden, which was looking particularly beautiful at that moment. I raised my glass of champagne —what else on such a day?

'To you, my darling,' I said, 'for all these wonderful years.'

Unlike Mr Polly, who had been a gallant failure, looking at my wife beside me I felt that I could say that my life up to this moment had, by and large, been a success. I look forward eagerly to the next fifty years, but I swear to you, dear reader, that I shall not, when I reach the age of 120, write another book. One book, for this actor at any rate, is quite enough.

List of Awards

1947   Best Actor for *Great Expectations*
1948   Nationwide Film Award: Best Actor
1949   Nationwide Film Award: Best Actor
1950   Nationwide Film Award: Best Actor
1950   *Sketch* Theatre Award: for Outstanding Achievement in the Theatre
1951   Nationwide Film Award: Best Actor
1956   Nationwide Film Award: Best Actor
1960   Best Actor Award: Venice Film Festival for *Tunes of Glory*
1961   *Films & Filming*: Best Actor
1961   Blue Ribbon Box Office Award (American)
1964   Blue Ribbon Box Office Award (American)
1965   Blue Ribbon Box Office Award (American)
1966   Blue Ribbon Box Office Award (American)
1967   The Film Daily *Filmdom's Famous Five* Poll (American): Best Actor for *The Family Way*
1968   Best Actor: San Sebastian Film Festival for *The Family Way*
1971   Best Supporting Actor: The Oscar from the American Academy of Motion Picture Arts & Sciences for *Ryan's Daughter*
1971   The Golden Globe from the Hollywood Foreign Press Reporters' Association for *Ryan's Daughter*
1971   The Golden Rose Bowl awarded by public vote in New York and Los Angeles for *Ryan's Daughter*
1976   Received from Her Majesty The Queen the Order of Knighthood, having received the CBE (Order of Commander of the British Empire) in 1960

List of Films

1933   *The Midshipmaid*
        Britannia of Billingsgate
        The Ghost Camera
        Bill M.P.
1934   *The Magistrate*
        The Lash
        Those Were the Days
        Brown on Resolution (*Forever England*)
        Doctor's Orders
1935   *Car of Dreams*
        Royal Cavalcade (Jubilee film)
        Charing Cross Road
        Bad Blood
1936   *Tudor Rose*
        O.H.M.S.
1937   *Goodbye Mr Chips*
1938   *Four Dark Hours*
1941   *Black Sheep of Whitehall*
        Cottage to Let
        Big Blockade, All Hands, Careless Talk (Government film documentaries)
        Old Bill and Son
        The Young Mr Pitt
1942   *In Which We Serve*
        We Dive at Dawn
1943   *Waterloo Road*
        This Happy Breed
1944   *The Way to the Stars*
1945   *Great Expectations*
1946   *Land of Promise*

1946 *So Well Remembered*
      The October Man
1947 *Scott of the Antarctic*
1948 *The History of Mr Polly* (Produced and played the title role)
1949 *The Rocking Horse Winner* (Produced and played in)
1950 *Morning Departure*
1951 *Mr Denning Drives North*
1952 *The Gentle Gunman*
      The Long Memory
1953 *Hobson's Choice*
1954 *The Colditz Story*
      Above Us The Waves
      The End of the Affair
1955 *Escapade*
      War and Peace
1956 *It's Great To Be Young*
      The Baby and The Battleship
      Town on Trial
      Round the World in 80 Days
1957 *My Friend Charles*
      Dunkirk
      Vicious Circle
      Ice Cold In Alex
1958 *Monty's Double*
      Summer of the Seventeenth Doll
      Tiger Bay
1959 *Swiss Family Robinson*
1960 *Tunes of Glory*
      The Singer not the Song
      The Valiant
1961 *Flame in the Streets*
      Tiara Tahiti
1963 *The Chalk Garden*
1964 *King Rat*
      The Truth About Spring
1965 *Sky West and Crooked* (Produced and Directed)
      Operation Crossbow
1966 *The Wrong Box*
1967 *The Family Way*
      Chuka
      Cowboy in Africa
1968 *Adam's Woman*
      Lady Hamilton

1968 *Oh! What A Lovely War*
1969 *Run Wild, Run Free*
 The Return of the Boomerang
 A Black Veil for Lisa
 Ryan's Daughter
1970 *Dulcima*
1971 *Young Winston*
1972 *Oklahoma Crude*
 Lady Caroline Lamb
1976 *Trial by Combat*
1979 *The Devil's Advocate*

List of Theatrical Productions

1929   *The Five O'Clock Girl* (debut)
1929/   With the Quaints in:
  30   *Journey's End*
        Young Woodley
        Hamlet
        Julius Caesar
        Mr Cinders
        When Knights Were Bold
        Funny Face
        The Girl Friend
1930   *Charley's Aunt*
1931   *London Wall*
        Cavalcade
1932   *Words and Music*
1933   *Give Me A Ring*
1934   *Jill Darling*
1936   *Red Night*
        Aren't Men Beasts?
1937   *Pélissier Follies*
1938   *Floodlight Revue*
        Talk of the Devil
1939   Old Vic Season including:
        A Midsummer Night's Dream
        She Stoops to Conquer
1939   *We at the Crossroads*
        Of Mice and Men
1942   *Men in Shadow*
1945   *Duet for Two Hands*
1947   *Angel*
1950   *The Damascus Blade*

1951   *Figure of Fun*
1952   *The Uninvited Guest*
1953   Revival of *Charley's Aunt*
1961   *Ross*
1963   *Powers of Persuasion*
1972   *Veterans*
1973   *The End of the Day*
1974   *Good Companions*
1976   *Great Expectations*
1977   *Separate Tables*

Index